AutoCAD Assignments

Paul Whelan

Stanley Thornes (Publishers) Ltd

© Paul Whelan, 1994

The right of Paul Whelan to be identified as author of this work has been asserted by him in accordance with the Copyright, Designs and Patents Act 1988.

All rights reserved. No part of this publication may be reproduced or transmitted in any form or by any means, electronic or mechanical, including photocopy, recording or any information storage and retrieval system, without permission in writing from the publisher or under licence from the Copyright Licensing Agency Limited. Further details of such licences (for reprographic reproduction) may be obtained from the Copyright Licensing Agency Limited, of 90 Tottenham Court Road, London W1P 9HE.

First published in 1994 by Gill & Macmillan Ltd, Ireland.

Published in Great Britain in 1994 by:
Stanley Thornes (Publishers) Ltd
Ellenborough House
Wellington Street
CHELTENHAM
GL50 1YD
United Kingdom

A catalogue record for this book is available from the British Library.

ISBN 0 7487 1784 6

Designed by Identikit Design Consultants, Dublin, Ireland
Print origination by Identikit Design Consultants, Dublin, Ireland
Printed in Ireland by ColourBooks Ltd, Dublin, Ireland

CONTENTS

Preface

1. Your Computer System and AutoCAD — 1
2. The Drawing Editor — 13
3. A Twenty-Minute Tour of AutoCAD — 21
4. Moving from Traditional Draughting to AutoCAD — 34
5. Beginning a New Drawing — 46
6. Relative and Absolute Co-ordinates — 64
7. Speeding Up the Drawing Process — 79
8. Major Drawing and Editing Commands — 103
9. Linetypes and Further Editing — 125
10. Viewports, Breaking and Extending — 146
11. Layers, Basic Dimensioning and Hatching Patterns — 168
12. Multiple Prototype Drawings, Text and Style — 189
13. Working with Blocks, Divide and Measure — 207
14. Attributes — 224
15. Detailed Dimensioning — 235
16. Isometric Drawing and Sketching, UCS — 261
17. Editing Polylines — 275
18. Plotting — 284
19. Installing and Configuring AutoCAD — 290
20. DOS for AutoCAD Users — 306

Appendix A: AutoCAD System Variables — 321
Appendix B: Character Mapping — 326
Appendix C: AutoCAD File Extensions — 327
Appendix D: Dimensioning System Variables — 330
Practical Assignments — 332
Multiple-Choice Questions — 339
Index — 345

For Yaqoub Bouaynaya—a member of the younger generation—and Fran

PREFACE

This book is an introduction to the use of the AutoCAD draughting program. The core of the book consists of a series of tutorials. Assignments at the end of chapters have been developed to give you the opportunity to practise the new commands covered in the preceding tutorials. With the exception of chapter 1, each chapter requires you to work directly at the computer.

The screen images used in the book were taken from a standard VGA screen of 640 × 480 pixels. If your display uses a higher or lower resolution there may be small differences from the images in the book.

How information is shown in this book

The primary method of interaction with AutoCAD is through the command prompt. The drop-down menus and screen menus are secondary methods of command input.

The command prompt is shown in the text in italic type, thus: *Command:* All AutoCAD commands issued at the command prompt are shown in bold capital letters; for example, the line command is shown as **LINE**. Data that the user must input is shown in the same way; for example, the co-ordinates for the centre of a circle are shown as **23,154**. Helpful comments on actions or procedures are shown to one side and start with an arrow.

The example below illustrates all these conventions.

Command: **LINE**
From point: **23,154**   ← Type in the value 23,154 and press **[enter]**
To point: **69,18**   ← Type in the value 69,18 and press **[enter]**
To point: ← Press **[enter]** to finish the command
Command:

A circumflex (^) indicates that the 'control' key is held down while entering a letter: thus **^C** means that you press **C** while holding down the ctrl key.

Versions of AutoCAD

The tutorials refer to release 12 of AutoCAD, Windows and DOS versions. The book may be used with releases 10 and 11 with a little previous knowledge of AutoCAD or with the help of a tutor. All AutoCAD's commands will work if they are typed at the command prompt. Remember, the text shown on a drop-down menu is not a command: it simply calls a command that could have been typed at the command prompt.

The assignments

The drawings in some of the assignments (particularly the earlier ones) may lack some standard drawing characteristics, such as centre lines or section hatching. These features have been abandoned until the procedure for drawing them has been covered in a tutorial.

Note to teachers and students trained in manual draughting

Drawing on a computer requires you to change your approach to the drawing process (see chapter 4). An AutoCAD drawing is made up of predefined entities such as lines, circles, arcs, etc. AutoCAD allows you to build up a drawing by assembling these entities. To make rapid progress it is essential that you do not try to draw on the computer in the same way that you drew on paper. An example of the type of change of approach that is required is seen in the use of scale: all drawings on the computer are input without a scale. Do not waste time and energy trying to scale a drawing; at a later stage the drawing can be scaled automatically by the computer to fit it on whatever size paper you select. Any drawing in AutoCAD can be plotted to paper at any imaginable scale.

In traditional drawing the calculation of line lengths, of angles and of points occupies a considerable amount of time and dictates a drawing sequence. AutoCAD will pick the centre points of line or circles with very little effort: it will calculate the size of angles and allow you to assign pen weights to lines (and change them at any stage). This will modify how you construct the drawing. Construction lines can be drawn rapidly and then removed or hidden without trace.

Acknowledgments

My thanks to my students at Dún Laoghaire Community College, who tested and contributed drawings; to Anthony Geoghegan and Gregori Meakin, for their close reading of the text and their many suggestions; to Frank Scallan, who continually reminded me to view the text from the beginner's point of view; to Mr John Howe, who commented critically on the drawing assignments; and to J. S. Bach and W. A. Mozart, who sustained my energy throughout.

chapter 1
Your Computer System and AutoCAD

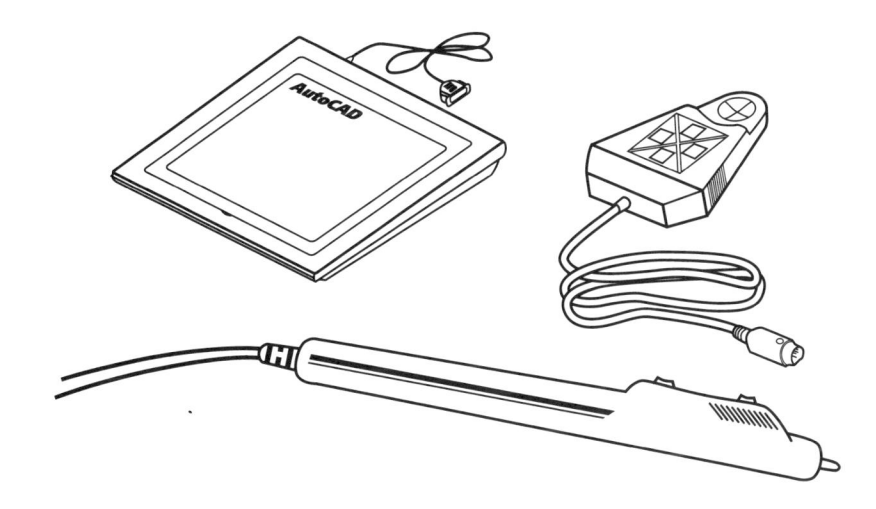

Tutorial objectives

By the end of this chapter you should be able to
- describe a computer's basic hardware
- say what the CPU is
- give the function of the maths co-processor
- describe the variety of graphics cards available
- name the connectors on the back of the computer
- state the function of the AutoCAD hardware lock device
- describe the types of diskette available and give the capacity of each
- list the computer's basic input devices
- list the computer's basic output devices
- give the function of a computer's operating system
- state the minimum hardware requirements for AutoCAD releases 11 and 12

INTRODUCTION

AutoCAD—a leading computer-aided design (CAD) program—is available for a wide range of microcomputers, including most IBM and IBM-compatible computers, some of the Apple Macintosh range, and 'work-stations' (high-powered microcomputers) using the Unix operating system. It is not possible in a book of this size to describe all the computer types that are capable of running the program. This chapter describes the basic components of a typical DOS computer system that is suitable for running AutoCAD.

The principal components of a microcomputer system can be categorised into (*a*) hardware and (*b*) software.

HARDWARE

The 'hardware' is essentially the electronic circuitry, integrated circuits ('microchips') etc. that form the system physically. The hardware elements are the *system unit*—which houses the *central processing unit* (CPU)—the *monitor,* and the *keyboard*. The *mouse* and *digitising tablet* are peripheral hardware devices.

Monitor types:
Super VGA
VGA
EGA

System unit with disk drives and fixed (hard) disk

Input devices:
Mouse and keyboard

Fig. 1.1. A typical microcomputer system used for running a CAD program.

The CPU

The central processing unit or CPU is the 'brain' of the computer, the microchip where most of the processing is carried out. There are several models available, called the 8086, 80286, 80386, 80486, and Pentium. These CPUs are available in a variety of speeds: 10 Mhz, 16 Mhz, 25 Mhz, 33 MHz, and so on. AutoCAD 11 was the last release that could run on an 80286 chip; release 12 and later releases require the 80386 chip as a minimum.

The Macintosh range of computers uses the 68000 series of chips manufactured by Motorola.

The maths co-processor

CAD programs carry out many mathematical calculations and consequently put more pressure on the CPU than many other programs. As the CPU has a multitude of other jobs to carry out in addition to processing calculations for AutoCAD, the presence of a special microchip called a *maths co-processor* is required. Many of the vector calculations that AutoCAD manipulates are sent to the co-processor; this reduces the workload on the CPU. The overall effect for the user is that AutoCAD runs faster.

The Intel maths or numeric co-processors are the 8087, 80287, and 80387, to match the 8086, 80286 and 80386 CPU, respectively. The 80486 and Pentium range of computers have a maths co-processor built in as part of the CPU and consequently do no require the purchase and installation of a separate processor.

Graphics cards

A variety of display types are available for IBM and IBM-compatible computers. The monitor or 'visual display unit' (VDU) needs a special printed circuit board or 'card' to control its display. These graphics cards are responsible for the resolution, quality and number of colours displayed on the screen. These characteristics are controlled by the number of dots or *pixels* the screen is divided into. Graphics cards are installed inside the system unit. The characteristics of some common graphics cards are described below.

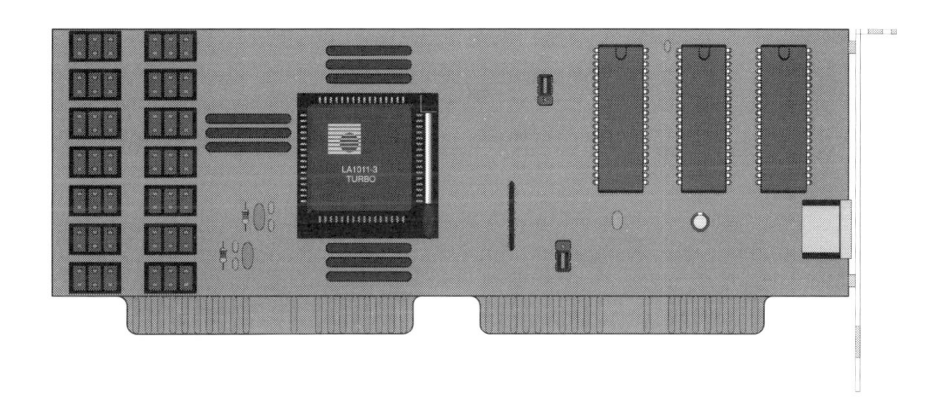

Fig. 1.2. A graphics card.

The **Hercules** graphics card produces monochrome text and graphics. The graphics have a resolution of 720×348 pixels. This is a very low resolution for graphics-based programs, in particular CAD applications.

The **CGA** (colour graphics adapter) has a lower resolution (320×200 pixels) than the Hercules card and is not suitable for CAD applications. It displays in four colours from a possible eight.

EGA (enhanced graphics adapter) cards produce a colour image with a resolution of 640×350 pixels. Sixteen colours are possible simultaneously.

VGA (video graphics adapter) cards produce a good colour image of sixteen colours at a resolution of 640×480 pixels.

The **PGA** (professional graphics adapter) can display 256 colours at 640×480 pixels.

Super-VGA or **SVGA** cards can produce resolutions of 640×480, 800×600 and $1,024 \times 724$ with suitable monitors. Up to 256 colours can be displayed.

Other specialised graphics cards are available for use with large high-resolution colour monitors. The specialised cards and monitors are frequently set to run in *dual mode*, with two monitors attached to a single computer. One screen will display the colour graphics while the other displays the text.

Fan   COM 1   COM 2   Video port

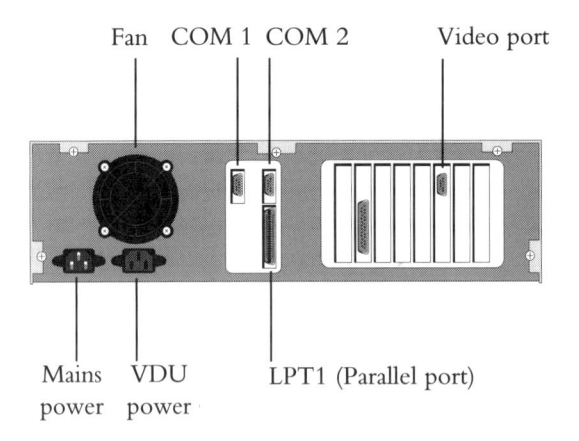

Mains   VDU   LPT1 (Parallel port)
power   power

Fig. 1.3. The system unit connectors.

The system unit connectors

The back of the system unit has several standard connectors for attaching peripheral devices. On IBM-type computers these include the following:

Power input connector: connects to the wall socket for the computer power supply.

Power output connector: usually supplies power to the monitor.

Keyboard connector: connects the keyboard to the system unit.

Display connector: connects the graphics card inside the system unit to the monitor.

Parallel printer port (LPT1): frequently used to connect the printer to the computer. There may be more than one printer port on the computer; a second printer port is labelled LPT2.

Serial port (COM1): this is the communications or 'comms' port. Most computers will have two serial ports (COM1 and COM2). Printers may be connected to a COM port, but more frequently it is the mouse or digitiser that uses it.

Hardware lock device

The hardware lock device or 'dongle' fits into the parallel port at the back of the computer. It allows the AutoCAD program to work. Without the use of the hardware lock device AutoCAD is disabled and will not run. Its function is to prevent AutoCAD from being copied by unlicensed users.

The hardware lock device is 'transparent', in that the port can be used for its normal functions without interference from the dongle. For example, the printer can be connected to the hardware lock device. To ensure transparency of the hardware lock device it is advisable to switch on the printer connected to the computer before the computer itself is switched on.

Note: Versions of AutoCAD earlier than release 10 used a hardware lock device that was connected to the serial port.

Memory

The system unit contains the computer's temporary storage or 'memory'. This memory (called random-access memory or RAM) is used to store programs when they are loaded into the computer. RAM is measured in *bytes* (one byte is roughly the equivalent of one character); 1,024 bytes are a *kilobyte* (1 Kb), and 1,024 kilobytes are a *megabyte* (1 Mb). A fairly standard desktop computer should have at least 640 kb.

RAM is volatile: its contents are lost when the computer is switched off or when a program is terminated. AutoCAD 11 requires about 4 Mb of memory to run efficiently; AutoCAD 11-286 will run on an 80286 computer with as little as 640 kb of RAM. The recommended RAM for release 12 is 8 Mb.

Drawings or any programs or data that are in RAM must be stored in a more permanent form of memory if they are to be retained for later use. Diskettes ('floppy disks') and fixed ('hard') disks are used as peripheral memory storage media. The transfer of a drawing in AutoCAD to a diskette is executed by the commands **SAVE**, **SAVEAS**, or **END**.

RAM holds the AutoCAD program and the current drawing.

The drawing must be transferred to a hard or floppy disk before the computer is switched off. The commands QSAVE, SAVE and END accomplish this.

Fig. 1.4. Saving data to a disk.

Disks

Diskettes are flexible, thin disks that are coated with a magnetisable material. They may be contained inside a stiff plastic cover. The 3.5 inch disk is available as
- a double-sided double-density (DD) disk, which can hold 720 kb of data, or
- a high-density (HD) disk, which can store 1.4 Mb of data.

The 5.25 inch disks are available as
- double-density double-sided 360 kb format and
- a high-density (HD) version, which holds 1.2 Mb of data.

All disks must be magnetically *formatted* before they can be used on a computer. The formatting process allows the computer to magnetically mark out the disk into areas for the storage of the data. (See chapter 20 on the DOS operating system.)

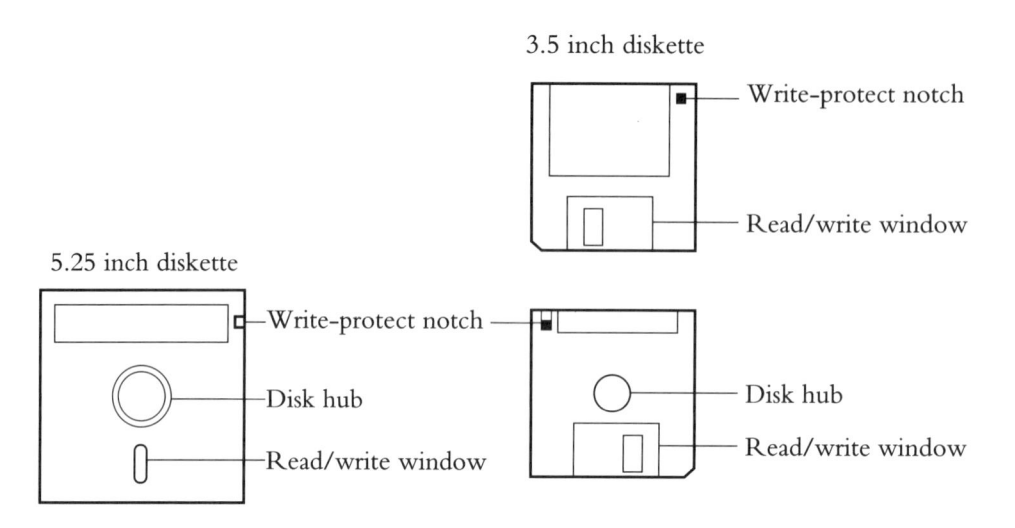

Fig. 1.5. Diskettes can be used to store drawings.

Fixed disks or 'hard disks' are sealed inside an airtight box that is normally held inside the system unit. Large programs such as AutoCAD need to be run from a hard disk. A hard disk typically has 30 to 42 Mb of storage space, although disks with a capacity of 200 Mb or more are required for serious CAD work.

RAM	Holds the computer programs and drawings, but volatile	Not permanent
DISKETTE	Permanently stores programs and drawings	Permanent but slow
FIXED (HARD) DISK	Permanently stores programs and drawings	Permanent and fast

Fig. 1.6. Permanent and volatile memory.

Input and output devices

Some computer hardware can be classified as devices that allow you to *input* data into the computer, and devices that allow you to *output* the processed data.

Input devices

Keyboard

The keyboard is the primary input device on today's computers. Users can type in data or issue commands to the computer on the keyboard. Apart from the alphabet, numerals, and some special characters, the keyboard also has a set of *function keys*, labelled *F1* to *F12*. The term 'function key' is applied to them because computer programmers often assign them a specific function. Within AutoCAD, for example, the F7 key will overlay a reference grid on top of the drawing.

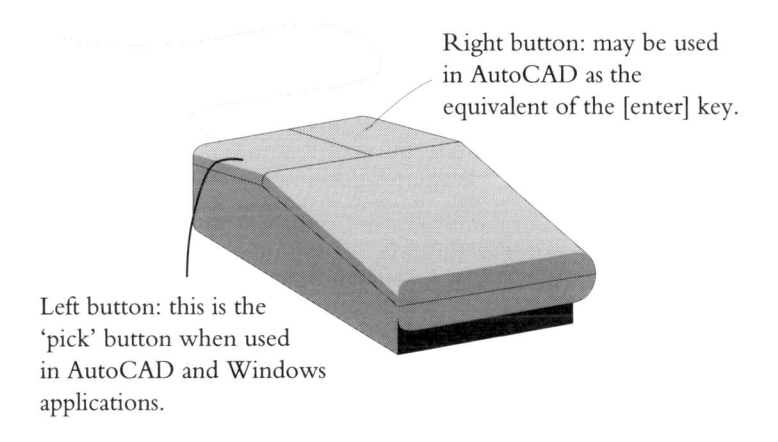

Right button: may be used in AutoCAD as the equivalent of the [enter] key.

Left button: this is the 'pick' button when used in AutoCAD and Windows applications.

Fig. 1.7. The mouse.

Mouse

This is a small box with one to three buttons. It is frequently attached to the computer by means of a wire or 'tail' to a COM port. It is moved around the desktop on a small ball. The buttons are used to input instructions to the computer by pressing on them ('clicking').

Movement of the mouse causes a small pointer (often an arrow tip) to move around the computer's display. The pointer may take on different shapes within a program: in AutoCAD the pointer changes from being an arrow to various types of cross-hairs. It is generally used to select commands and place entities such as lines and circles in position on the screen.

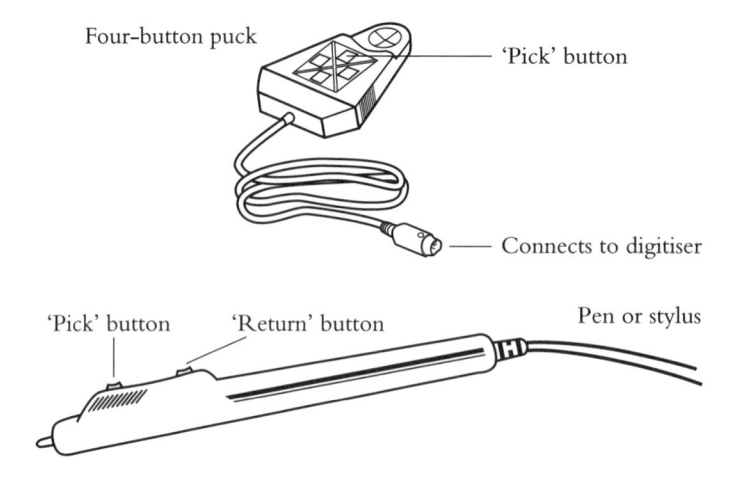

Fig. 1.8. Other AutoCAD pointer types.

Digitising tablet
This is a square or rectangular tablet that is electronically active. By moving a pointing device such as a pen or puck across its surface, a pointer will move across the computer display. Like the mouse, it is used to input commands and data to the computer. AutoCAD makes extensive use of a digitiser. A drawing may be digitised using the tablet (see chapter 19).

Note: Do not place a diskette on a digitiser that is switched on. The magnetic field around the digitiser will corrupt data on the disk.

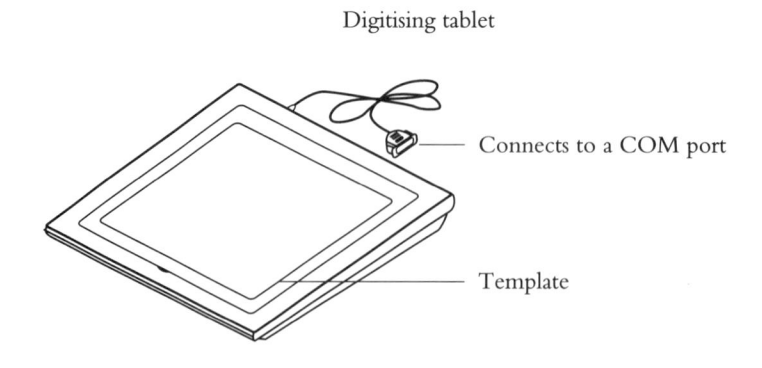

Fig. 1.9. The digitising tablet and puck.

Scanner
Scanners are traditionally used in computerised page make-up or 'desktop publishing' to scan images. The scanner is passed over the image (such as a photograph or drawing). The scanner then *digitises* the image—turns it into a series of digital values that the computer understands—so that it can be displayed on the screen and saved to the hard disk. Scanned images must be

turned into vector images before they can be used by AutoCAD. There are many programs available that can accomplish this. AutoCAD release 12 is capable of turning some scanned images into vector images itself.

Output devices

Display

The display is the primary output device.
(See above for a description of graphics cards.)

Printer

Printers are responsible for producing a print-out or 'hard copy' of your work. The technology behind printers is developing rapidly. At the moment the principal printer types are **dot-matrix**, **daisywheel**, **bubble-jet**, and **laser**. The ink that produces the print-out is 'thrown' onto the paper by various means: the dot-matrix and daisywheel printer hammer the ink onto the paper, while the lasers and bubble-jet printers shoot the ink. AutoCAD can output drawings to all printer types except the daisywheel: daisywheel printers can only produce text. Bubble-jet and laser printers produce the highest quality, at 300 dots per inch.

Plotter

Traditional plotters draw on the paper using a pen (some plotters can use pencils). The pen movement is controlled by vector plotting instructions sent from the computer to the plotter. Plotters can output to sheet sizes from A4 to A0.

SOFTWARE

The 'software' is any coded set of instructions that enables the hardware to function. All programs are software. The AutoCAD program is very sophisticated and demands a high level of hardware to run efficiently.

The operating system

The most important item of software for all computers is a set of programs called the **operating system**. Most IBM and IBM-compatible desktop computers use an operating system called DOS (Disk Operating System). Microsoft have also released a new operating system named Windows NT, which is capable of running on IBM and IBM-compatible microcomputers.

Some IBM-type computers use an operating system called OS/2. Apple Macintosh computers use their own operating system.

The operating system enables other software to run on the computer. It also controls the disks, printers, display, etc. It must be loaded into memory as soon as the computer is switched on; this is called 'booting up' (see chapter 20). Users of hard-disk machines will find that the operating system will automatically load once the computer is switched on.

IBM-type microcomputers

The DOS operating system was developed at the beginning of the 1980s; a licensed version distributed by IBM is known as PCDOS.

DOS is supplied on several diskettes. The first version to be released was version 1 (no surprise!). This was followed by versions 1.25, 2.0, 2.01, 2.11, 2.25, 3.0, 3.1, 3.2, 3.3, 4.0, 4.1, 5.0, and now version 6.2. A change in the first part of the number indicates that the system underwent a major revision; the numbers after the decimal point indicate a minor update. For example, there is only a small difference between versions 2.11 and 2.25; however, there is a major difference between versions 2.25 and 3.0.

Digital Research also produce an operating system resembling MSDOS, called DRDOS.

The AutoCAD program

Computer-aided design (CAD) has existed since 1964. However, it was restricted to mainframe computers and minicomputers until the early 1980s, at which time the desktop computer became more powerful. AutoCAD was released in December 1982 for use on computers that used the operating system DOS. Each release since then has made more demands on the computer as hardware development increased its power and efficiency. AutoCAD is now available for use on computers running the operating systems DOS, Unix, OS/2, and Windows NT.

With regard to the DOS versions of AutoCAD, AutoCAD 2.6 (the release before version 9) was the last one not to require the additional maths co-processor. Release 10 was the last to run on the complete range of 8086, 80286, 80386 and 80486 computers. The manufacturers have confirmed that release 11 of the DOS version was the last to run on an 80286 or lower computer; the 80386SX will now be the 'bottom of the range' computer that will be able to provide AutoCAD with the power it requires.

Hardware requirements for running AutoCAD

Minimum requirement for AutoCAD 11-286

- A computer with an 80286 central processing unit
- An 80287 maths co-processor
- 1 Mb of RAM
- A hard disk
- A single high-density disk drive
- DOS version 3.3 or later
- A digitising tablet or mouse
- A hardware lock device
- A parallel port

Minimum requirement for AutoCAD 11-386
- A computer with an 80386 or higher central processing unit
- An 80387 or higher maths co-processor
- 4 Mb of RAM
- A hard disk
- A single high-density disk drive
- DOS version 3.3 or later
- A digitising tablet or mouse
- A hardware lock device
- A parallel port

Minimum requirement for AutoCAD 12
- A computer with an 80386 or higher central processing unit
- An 80387 or higher maths co-processor
- 8 Mb of RAM
- A hard disk
- A single high-density disk drive
- DOS version 3.3 or later
- A digitising tablet or mouse
- A hardware lock device
- A parallel port

SUMMARY

The principal components of a computer system are the hardware and software. The fundamental hardware components are the system unit, keyboard, and monitor. The fundamental software component is the operating system. AutoCAD requires a maths co-processor to help carry out some of its calculations. Graphics cards are needed to drive the visual display unit.

The back of the system unit has connectors for the mouse, digitising tablet, keyboard, monitor, printer, plotter, and hardware lock device. The hardware lock device is a copy protection device that is required for the running of AutoCAD. It attaches to the parallel port and is transparent in use.

The principal peripheral storage devices are the diskettes and hard disks. AutoCAD requires a minimum of a single diskette drive and a hard disk. The operating systems DOS, Unix, OS/2 and the Macintosh system can be used to run the AutoCAD program. This book is concerned mainly with the DOS version of AutoCAD.

SELF-ASSESSMENT QUESTIONS

1. Using a simple diagram, describe the basic components of an AutoCAD work-station.

2. Write a short note describing the types of CPU chips. Why is a maths co-processor necessary for the operation of AutoCAD?

3. Which port on the system unit is the hardware lock device attached to? Name two peripherals that could be attached to the COM ports on the system unit.

4. What is the function of the hardware lock device? Why is it considered to be 'transparent'?

5. Explain the following terms: RAM, input device, digitiser, VGA.

6. Explain the statement 'RAM is volatile.' What commands in AutoCAD transfer a drawing from RAM to a more permanent form of storage? Write a short note describing the more permanent forms of storage.

7. State the minimum hardware requirement for the full and efficient use of AutoCAD releases 11 and 12.

chapter 2
The Drawing Editor

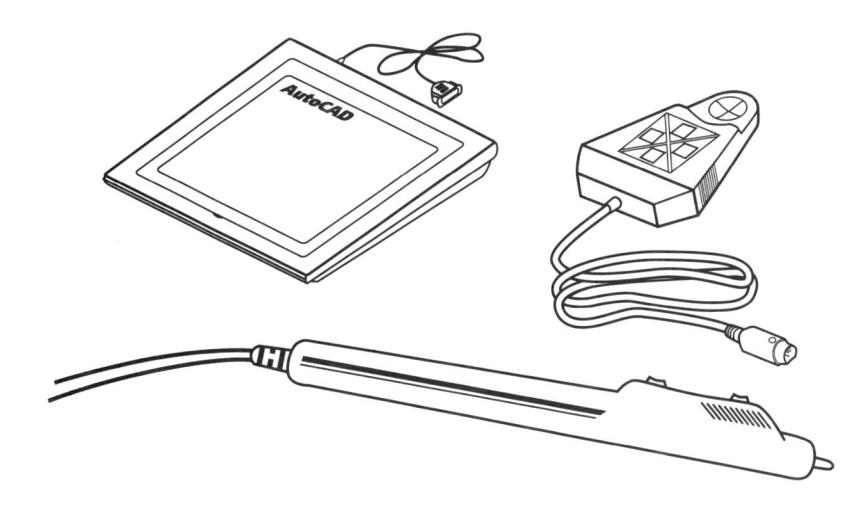

Tutorial objectives
By the end of this chapter you should be able to
- start the AutoCAD program
- describe the main areas of the drawing editor
- work with the command prompt
- use the F1 function key
- communicate with AutoCAD through the screen menu
- use the dialogue boxes to tell AutoCAD what you want
- understand the information on the status line
- use the commands GRAPHSCR and TEXTSCR as an alternative to the F1 key
- use the F9 function key
- call AutoCAD commands through the drop-down menus
- work with the commands LINE and QUIT
- try rubber-banding before you make up your mind

INTRODUCTION

This tutorial will introduce you to the AutoCAD drawing editor and briefly examine some of its features.

The AutoCAD program is supplied on a set of diskettes. The program has to be transferred to the computer's hard disk before it can be used. This process is called *installation*. After the installation procedure AutoCAD must be *configured* to recognise the peripherals attached to the computer. This installation and configuration should have been carried out by the AutoCAD dealer. (See chapter 19 on installing AutoCAD.)

Tutorial 2.1

Windows and DOS users of AutoCAD will start the program in different ways. Both methods lead to the drawing editor.

Starting AutoCAD 12—DOS users

After the installation of AutoCAD, a file called ACADR12.BAT should be installed on the hard disk. Type **ACADR12** to start the program. AutoCAD will be loaded into the computer's memory, and you will be placed directly into the drawing editor.

Starting AutoCAD 12—Windows users

Click on the AutoCAD *icon* in the Windows Program Manager. Press **[enter]** if required. You will be placed directly into the drawing editor.

THE DRAWING EDITOR

The graphics and text screens

The drawing editor is the area of the screen where you actually create and edit drawings. It is the AutoCAD graphics screen. You can switch to the AutoCAD text screen by pressing **[F1]** (DOS version). This function key will toggle you back to the graphics screen if you press it again.

Users of the Windows version of AutoCAD will need to use the F2 key to accomplish this.

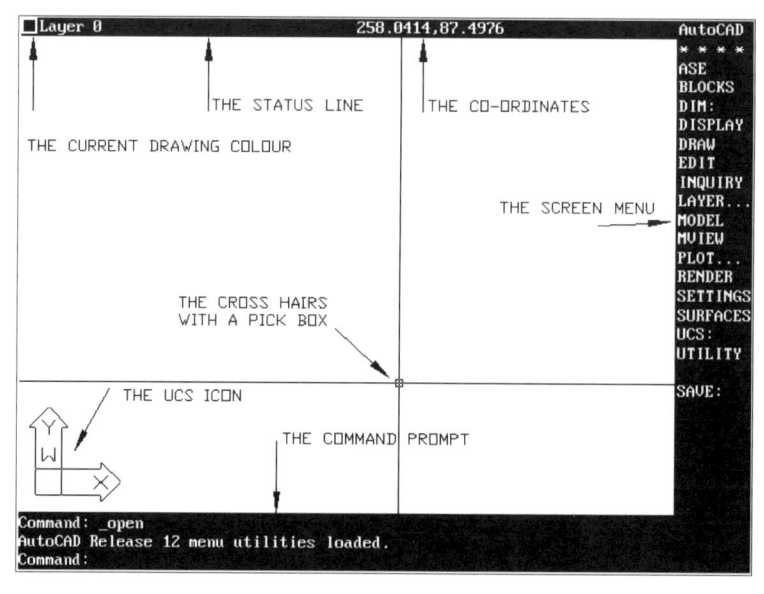

Fig. 2.1. The AutoCAD drawing editor.

The command prompt

At the bottom of the screen is the word *Command:*. This is known as the command prompt. Most of your interaction with AutoCAD takes place here. A command is given to AutoCAD by typing it on this line and pressing **[enter]** (sometimes called [return]) or the space bar.

There are other methods of inputting commands (see below). However, the command prompt is the primary method.

You can switch to the text screen by typing **TEXTSCR** at the command prompt and pressing **[enter]** or **[space]**. The command sequence for this is:
Command: **TEXTSCR**   ← Press **[enter]** or **[space]**
The text screen appears as though you had pressed **[F1]**.

The graphics screen can be called up by using the command **GRAPHSCR**. Try it now.
Command: **GRAPHSCR**   ← Press **[enter]** or **[space]**

The screen menu

To the right of the drawing editor is the 'screen' menu. Commands can be given to AutoCAD through this menu system. Some of the items on the menu have a colon (:) after them. These are AutoCAD commands. The other options on the menu (without the colon) will lead you into a list of commands associated with the selected menu item.

A selection is made from the screen menu by highlighting it with the cursor and clicking on the pick or left mouse button.

Try the following. Move the cross-hairs in over *Draw* on the screen menu and pick it. AutoCAD will list a 'page' of items or entities that you can use in constructing your drawing. Picking *next* will display another page of commands related to 'Draw'. To return to the 'root' of the screen menu pick the word *AutoCAD* at the top of the menu list. Clicking on *previous* will return you to the previous menu page.

The status line

The status line at the top of the screen displays information about your drawing. At the moment it probably has *Layer 0* at the left and some co-ordinates to the right of screen centre. The co-ordinates locate the centre of the cross-hairs.

AutoCAD allows you to use **layers** to build up a drawing. The layers can be thought of as transparent sheets placed directly on top of each other. Different elements of the drawing can be placed on the different layers (see chapter 11).

AutoCAD allows you to create and name the layers. The default layer name is 0. If **Snap** is present on the status line, your cross-hairs should jump in discrete units as you move the pointing device. Pressing **[F9]** toggles the snap mode off. The current colour being used is shown at the left end of the status line.

In addition to the above features, the status line in the Windows version of AutoCAD also displays a series of icon buttons. Picking the appropriate button will switch the snap on or off, etc.

The drop-down menus

When the cross-hairs are moved into the status line area they change into an arrow cursor, and a sequence of drop-down menu names becomes visible.

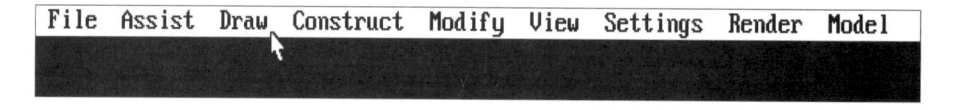

Fig. 2.2. The drop-down menu bar in the DOS version of AutoCAD.

These titles are highlighted as the arrow cursor is moved over them. To view the contents of a highlighted menu, click on the pick button. The drop-down menu will appear, displaying the available commands. Further selection of a command is made by highlighting and clicking the pick button.

The Windows version has the extra drop-down menus 'Edit' and 'File'.

Structure of a drop-down menu

Click on *Draw* on the drop-down menu. Some of the commands listed on this drop-down menu, such as **Rectangle** and **Points**, execute directly when selected, as though they were typed in at the command prompt. Other options on the menu have either an arrow (>) or omission points (...) after them. The arrow points the way to further options for that particular command (see fig. 2.3). The omission points call up a dialogue box (see below).

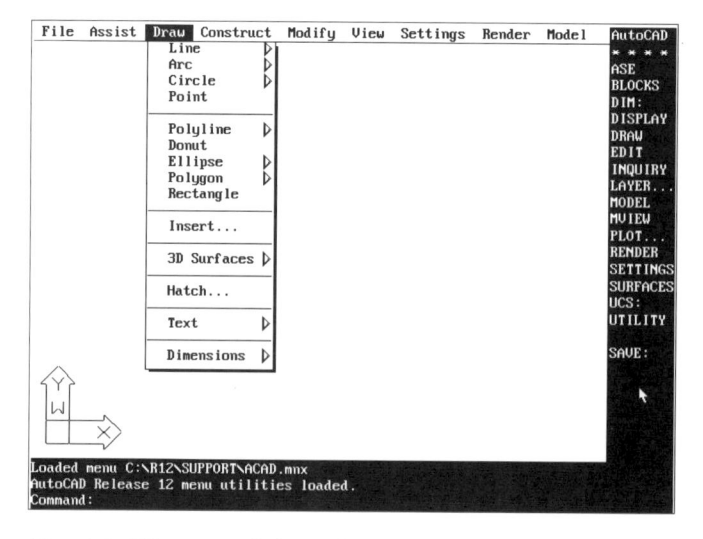

Fig. 2.3. The 'Draw' drop-down menu.

Drawing a line

The command **LINE** will draw line entities in the drawing editor. You cannot specify a thickness for the line.

How the command works

When the command is executed, AutoCAD will ask you to specify the starting and end points of the line. AutoCAD can draw a single line segment at a time, or allow you to draw numerous segments repeatedly. Some of these options are seen if you select 'Draw' on the drop-down menu. Select the first option, **Line**. A submenu will appear off this offering the various options for drawing a line (see fig. 2.4).

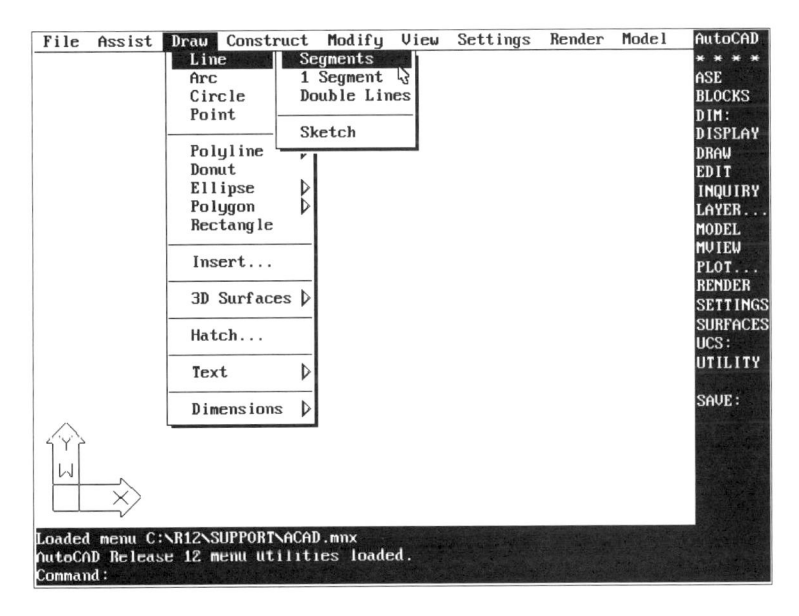

Fig. 2.4. The line submenu.

The first option, **Segments**, will allow you to continue drawing connected line segments for as long as you like. Pick this option now and note the following.

The command prompt area at the bottom of the screen will respond to the selection by asking _line From point:.

AutoCAD is asking you to select a point in the drawing editor that will mark the beginning of the first line segment. Pick any point on the screen. When the cursor is now moved, a line will extrude from the selected point (this effect is often called 'rubber-banding'), and AutoCAD will respond with *To point:*.

Pick a second point. Continue picking points to draw line segments. AutoCAD will continue offering you *To point:* until you decide to press **[enter]** or **[space]** to terminate the command. Fig. 2.5 shows five line segments drawn in this way. The ends of the segments are marked by 'blips' (small temporary x marks).

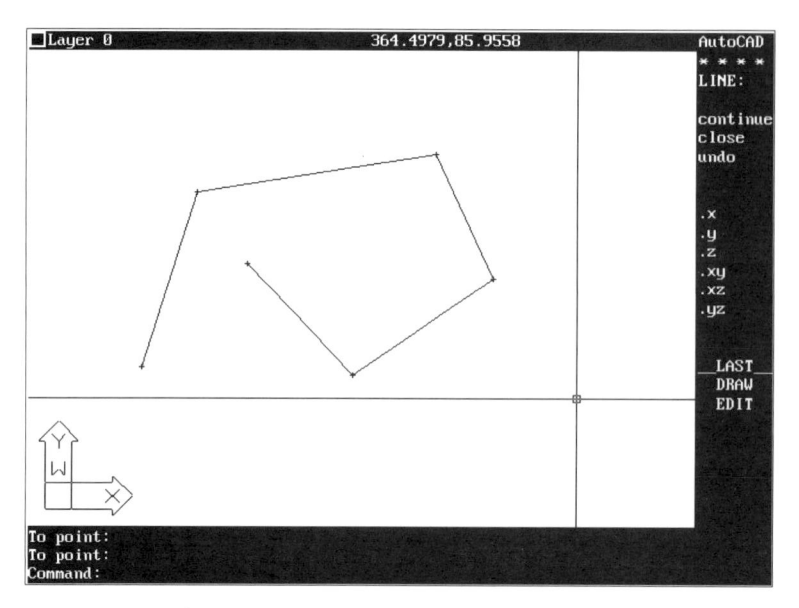

Fig. 2.5. Five line segments.

Drop-down options with omission points (…) after them lead to an AutoCAD *dialogue box*. For example, clicking on 'Settings' and then 'Drawing Aids …' will open up a dialogue box (see fig. 2.6 below) that will allow you to set up some of AutoCAD's tools to help you draw with greater ease. While the dialogue box is on the screen the cursor will have changed to an arrow pointer. Leave the dialogue box by selecting the 'Cancel' box.

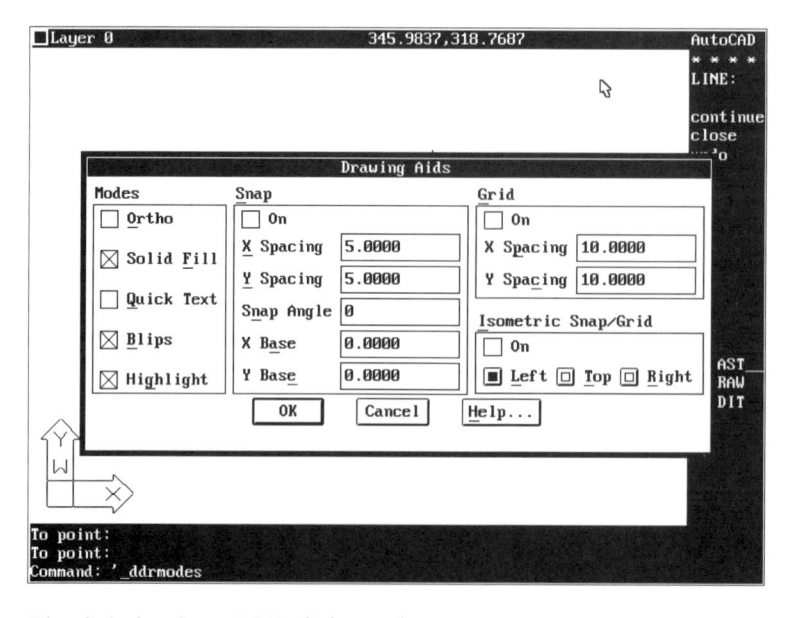

Fig. 2.6. An AutoCAD dialogue box.

The co-ordinate system icon

This icon is visible at the bottom left of the drawing editor. It shows the orientation of the X and Y axis. It is particularly useful in three-dimensional drawing. The icon will not appear on your drawing when it is printed. It can be turned off using the **UCSICON** command.

The grid

A grid can be placed on the screen as an aid to drawing. Press **[F7]** to toggle the grid on or off. The grid is not part of the drawing: it will not appear on a printed drawing. The distance between points on the grid can be changed.

Leaving AutoCAD and returning to DOS

Before you leave AutoCAD you must decide whether to keep the drawing or not. At this stage you should leave AutoCAD and discard the changes to the drawing. To do this type **QUIT**. A dialogue box appears. Click with the mouse in the box 'Discard Changes'. AutoCAD will close down.

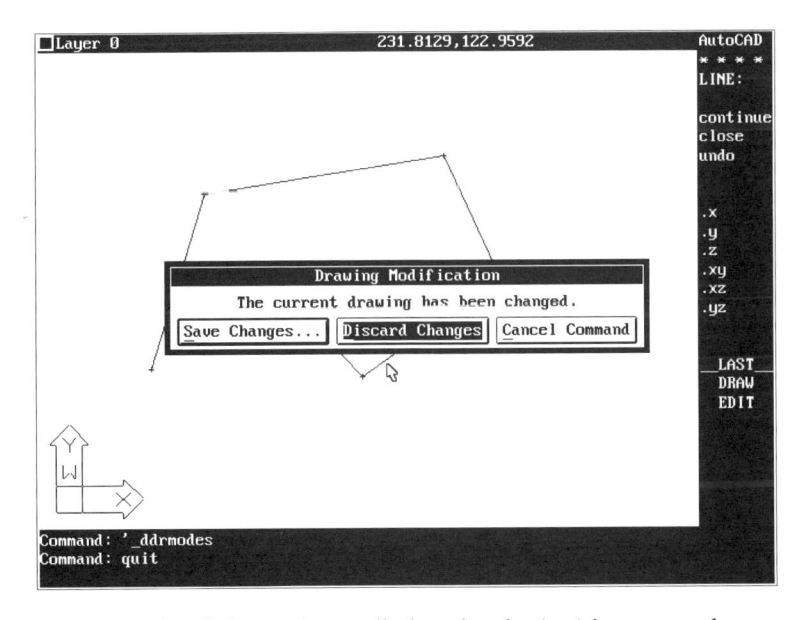

Fig. 2.7. The dialogue box called up by the 'quit' command.

SUMMARY

In this tutorial the following topics were demonstrated:
- How to start AutoCAD
- The main areas of the drawing editor
- The command prompt
- The F1 function key for toggling between the graphics and text screen
- The basic structure of the screen menu
- The areas of the status line.
- The F7 key to toggle the GRID mode
- Drop-down menu selection and structure
- The commands LINE and QUIT
- Rubber-banding
- The use of a dialogue box for giving AutoCAD information

SELF-ASSESSMENT QUESTIONS

1. List three methods of command input with AutoCAD. Write a brief note on each. With reference to the AutoCAD screen menu, what is understood by each of the following terms: (i) root menu, (ii) page, (iii) the colon, (iv) 'previous', (v) 'next'.

2. List three items of information that can be displayed on the status line. Explain the term 'rubber-banding'. State the function of the F1 (or F2) and F9 keys.

chapter 3

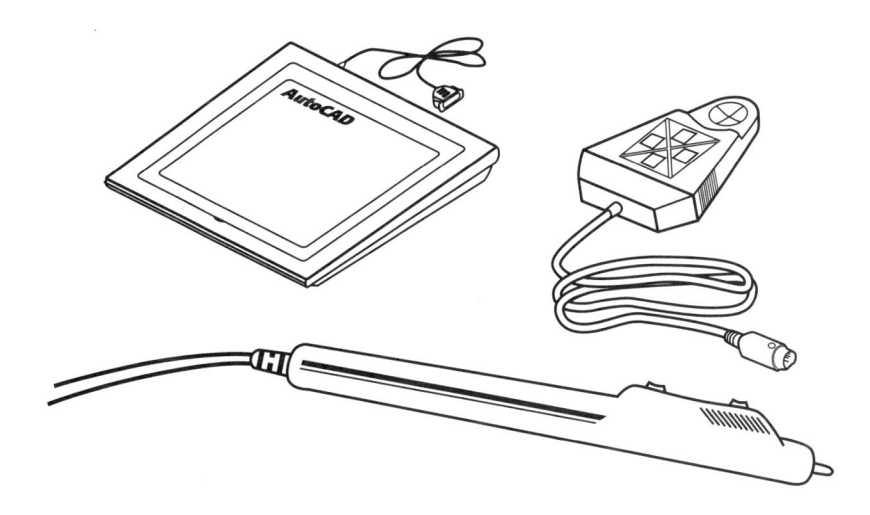

A Twenty-Minute Tour of AutoCAD

Tutorial objectives

This tour is for people with a little knowledge of AutoCAD. It is intended to refresh their memory and to introduce some of the power and techniques involved in working with AutoCAD release 12. Complete beginners should move directly to chapter 4.

INTRODUCTION

After your introduction to the AutoCAD drawing editor, it's time to take a small tour through AutoCAD's drawing and editing procedures.

Starting AutoCAD

Type **ACADR12** at the C prompt and press **[enter]** (or click on the appropriate icon if you are using Windows or an Apple Macintosh). You are presented with a blank drawing editor.

If at any time you make a mistake use **^C** to cancel the operation and start again.

Starting a new drawing

Select *New* from the *File* drop-down menu and give the drawing the name CLOCK. AutoCAD returns you to the drawing editor. In traditional drawing terms this is a blank sheet of paper.

Setting the limits

To set the paper size, use the **LIMITS** command. Type **LIMITS** at the command prompt and press **[enter]**. AutoCAD responds with
Reset Model space limits:
ON/OFF/<Lower left corner><0.00,0.00>:

The lower left corner of the drawing page is set as 0,0. AutoCAD is offering you the values in the angle brackets as the default. To select this default just press **[enter]**. If you have values here other than 0,0, type in **0,0** and press **[enter]**. You have now set the bottom left of the page as the bottom left of your screen.

AutoCAD will now present you with
Upper right corner <420.00,297.00>:

If your values differ from these, then type in **420,297** and press **[enter]**. This is the size of an A3 sheet of paper. The clock will be drawn at a scale of 1:1, that is in *Real World* size, and consequently will fit on the A3 sheet.

Setting the drawing tools

AutoCAD provides you with some tools to aid in the construction of the drawing. These tools can be set using the drop-down menu *Settings*. Highlight settings on the drop-down menu and click on *Drawing Aids...* A dialogue box will appear.

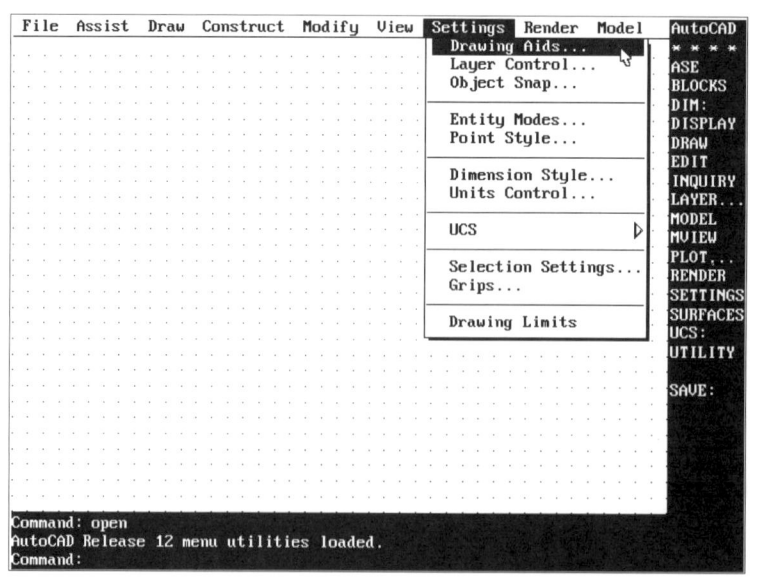

Fig. 3.1.

Some of the values in the dialogue box are toggled on and off, while others need specific values to be input. To change a value move the arrow cursor into the box and click with the mouse.

The toggle entries in the dialogue box either have an **X** or are blank. The **X** indicates that the mode is active.

Place an **X** in the boxes to switch on *Grid, Snap,* and *Blips*.

The edit boxes allow you to set values. Set the values to those in the dialogue box in fig. 3.2. You will see that when you set the X spacing for either the snap or grid values, AutoCAD will also place these values in as the Y spacing.

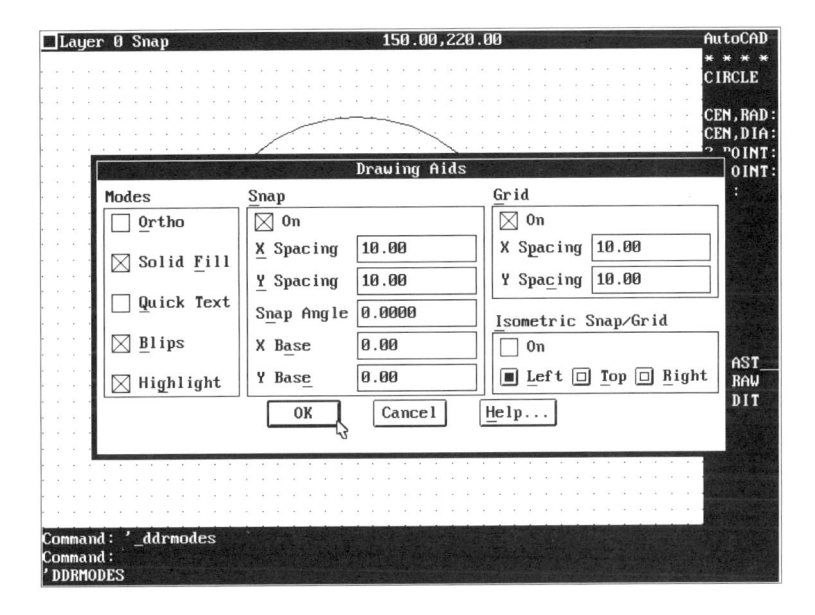

Fig. 3.2.

Click on **OK** to accept the settings and leave the dialogue box. You will return to the drawing editor. The grid is visible, and the cross-hairs will 'snap' to each of the points as if magnetically attracted to them.

Viewing the whole page

To see the drawing sheet you have just set up you must 'zoom—all'. This can be done using the *Screen* menu.

Click on *AutoCAD* at the top of the screen menu. This will ensure that you are at the root menu (that way we both have the same starting position). Now click on *Display* (six lines down). This will lead you to 'page 2' of the screen menu. Near the bottom you will see *ZOOM:*. Click on this, and the zoom options become available.

Note that the command prompt at the bottom of the screen reflects these options also.

Click on *All*. The **ZOOM—ALL** option is now executed. The command prompt is now ready for input again. If you wish to return to the root of the screen menu, pick *AutoCAD* at the top of the screen.

Setting your units

You are now almost ready to start the drawing. Type **UNITS** at the command prompt and press **[enter]**. AutoCAD switches to text mode (the drawing editor is removed for the moment). The drawing will be executed in decimal units, so answer **2** to the first question. The default values for the rest of the questions can be accepted by pressing **[enter]** until the command prompt is presented again. Then press **[F1]** to bring back the drawing editor.

The complete list of options available under the **UNITS** command is shown below.

Command: **UNITS**

UNITS Report formats:	*(Examples)*
1. Scientific	1.55E+01
2. Decimal	15.50
3. Engineering	1'-3.50"
4. Architectural	1-3 1/2"
5. Fractional	15 1/2

With the exception of the 'engineering' and 'architectural' formats, these formats can be used with any basic unit of measurement. For example, decimal mode is perfect for metric units as well as decimal English units.

Enter choice, 1 to 5 <2>:
Number of digits to right of decimal point (0 to 8) <2>:

Systems of angle measure:	*(Examples)*
1. Decimal degrees	45.0000
2. Degrees, minutes, seconds	45d0'0"
3. Grades	50.0000g
4. Radians	0.7854r
5. Surveyors' units	N 45d0'0" E

Enter choice, 1 to 5 <1>:
Number of fractional places for display of angles (0 to 8) <4>:
Direction for angle 0.0000:
East 3 o'clock = 0.0000
North 12 o'clock = 90.0000
West 9 o'clock = 180.0000
South 6 o'clock = 270.0000
Enter direction for angle 0.0000 <0.0000>:
Do you want angles measured clockwise? <N>

Drawing your first entities

Firstly draw the face of the clock. Select *Draw* from the drop-down menu. Select *CIRCLE >*. From the submenu select *Centre, Radius.*

Notice the command prompt response. AutoCAD is waiting for you to pick the centre of a circle. Move the cross-hairs to co-ordinates **200,160** and click the pick button. Move the cross-hairs, and notice the perimeter of the circle rubber-banding. The command prompt indicates that it is waiting for the radius of the circle. Type in a radius of **100** units and press **[enter]**. The circle is instantly drawn by AutoCAD. A small cross marks where you selected the centre of the circle; this is called a 'blip' (remember you switched on the blips in the dialogue box above).

Draw a second circle. This time use the command prompt. Type **CIRCLE** and press **[enter]** (or **[space]**). In response to *<Centre point>* type **CEN**. The cross-hairs will change to a pick box. Pick the perimeter of the circle already drawn. Enter a value of **110** units as the radius. This command prompt sequence is shown below.

Command: **CIRCLE**
3P/2P/TTR/<Centre point>: **CEN**
of
Diameter/<Radius>: **110**

Layers

A drawing can be spread over as many layers as you like. Think of the layers as being like transparent sheets one on top of the other. So far your drawing of the clock has been on the default layer 0. The details of the face of the clock can be placed on a second layer and assigned a different colour.

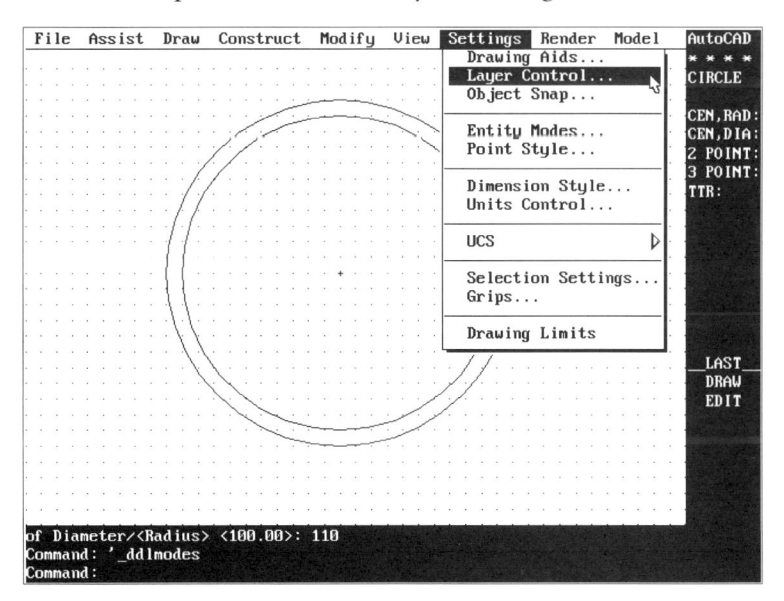

Fig. 3.3.

Using the drop-down menu *Settings,* click on *Layer Control.* The layer dialogue box will be displayed.

To create the new layer for the face type **FACE** in the *EDIT* box and click on *New.* The new layer will be added to the *Layer name* column. The layer will have been assigned the colour white and a continuous line type as default values.

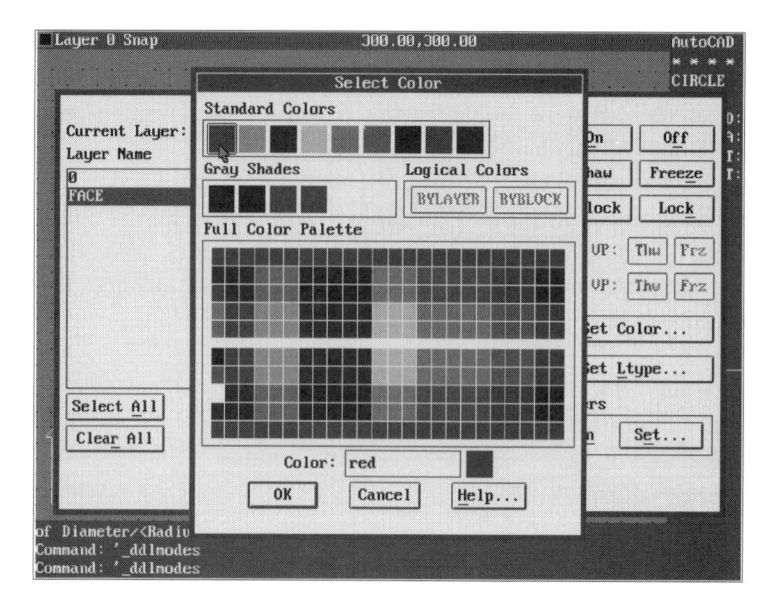

Fig. 3.4.

To assign the colour red to the layer FACE (so that everything drawn on that layer will be in red) click on *white* in the column *Colour* on the row with FACE. The *Select colour* dialogue box will open. Click on *red* on the top row and then on **OK**. Lastly click on *Current*. Click **OK** at the bottom to accept these settings. The drawing editor is returned. Notice that the status line now has the current colour, red, in a small box at the left and *Layer FACE Snap* displayed.

To place the hour markings on the face

Use a 'polyline'. The command sequence is shown below.
To initiate it type **PLINE**.

Command: **PLINE**
From point: **200,230**
Current line-width is 0.00
Arc/Close/Halfwidth/Length/Undo/Width/<Endpoint of line>: **W**
Starting width <0.00>: **3**
Ending width <3.00>   ← Press **[enter]**
Arc/Close/Halfwidth/Length/Undo/Width/<Endpoint of line>: **200,250**
Arc/Close/Halfwidth/Length/Undo/Width/<Endpoint of line>: ← Press **[enter]**
You need twelve of these markings on the face. The 'array' command will copy them for you. Toggle snap off (F9).

Command: **ARRAY**
Select objects: 1 selected, 1 found   ← Pick 12 o'clock marker
Select objects: ← Press **[enter]**

Rectangular or Polar array (R/P): **P**   ← Press **[enter]**
Centre point of array: **CEN**   ← Type CEN and press **[enter]**
of   ← Click on any one of the circles
Number of items: **12**   ← Type 12 and press **[enter]**
Angle to fill (+=ccw, −=cw) <360>:   ← Press **[enter]**
Rotate objects as they are copied? <Y>   ← Press **[enter]**
Command:

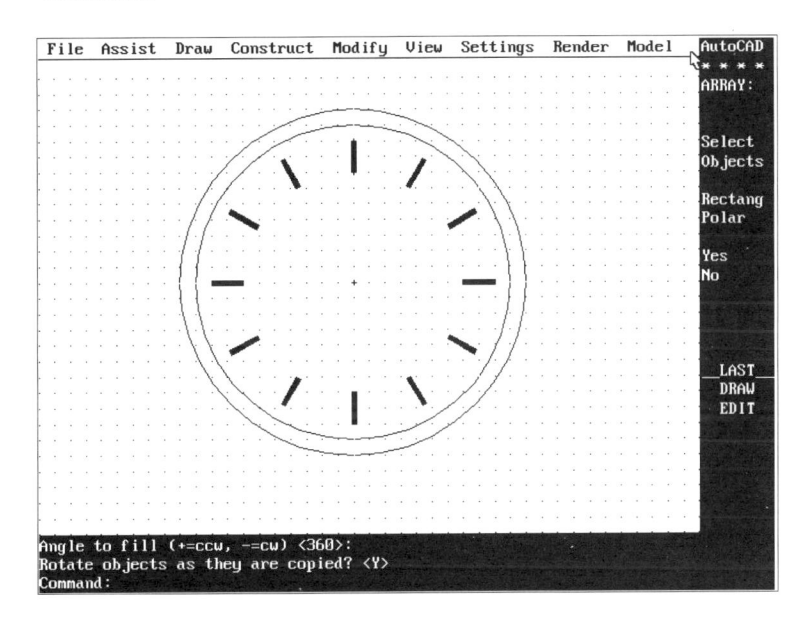

Fig. 3.5. The hours were placed using ARRAY.

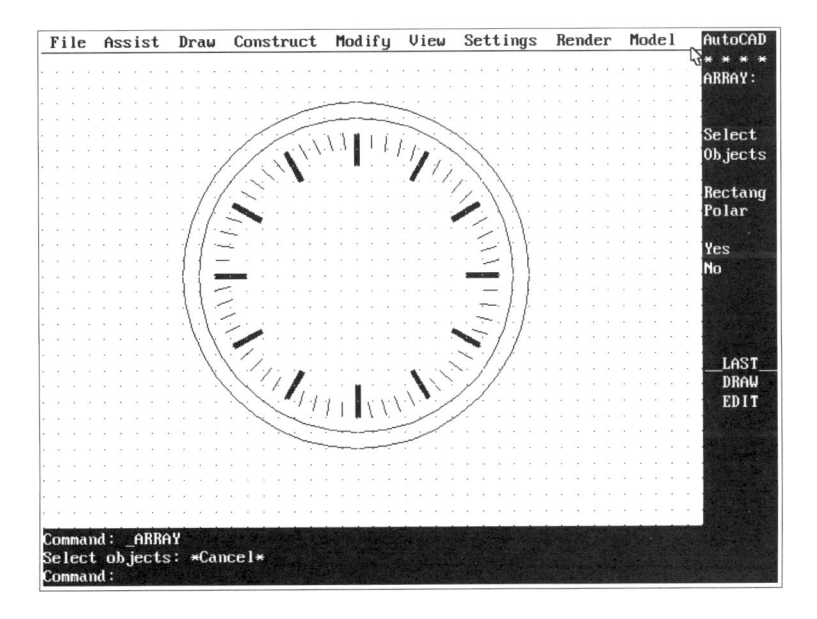

Fig. 3.6.

A TWENTY-MINUTE TOUR OF AUTOCAD   **27**

The minute markings are placed on the face in a similar way. However, the **LINE** command will be used instead of a polyline.

Draw a line from **210,240** to **210,250**. The command sequence is:

Command: **LINE**
From point: **200,250**
To point: **200,260**
To point: ← Press **[enter]**

Now use **ARRAY** to distribute **60** of these around the face.

Command: **ARRAY**
Select objects: ← Click on the minute line
1 selected, 1 found Select objects: ← Press **[enter]**
Rectangular or Polar array (R/P):   ← Type **P** and press **[enter]**
Centre point of array: ← Type **CEN** and press **[enter]**
of   ← Click on any one of the circles
Number of items: ← Type **60** and press **[enter]**
Angle to fill (+=ccw, −=cw) <360>:   ← Press **[enter]**
Rotate objects as they are copied? <Y>   ← Press **[enter]**
Command:

Placing the hands on the clock

The current layer at the moment is **FACE**. This is the layer you are drawing on. To make layer 0 current, bring up the layer dialogue box again from the drop-down menu *Settings* by clicking on *Layer Control*. Highlight the line below *Layer Name* with 0 in it. This is done by clicking once on the line of text. Then click on *Current* and lastly on **OK**.

Check the status line to see that you were successful.

To draw the hour hand, use the **LINE** command with the following co-ordinates:

Command: **LINE**
From point: **200,160**   ← Press **[enter]**
To point: **190,180**   ← Press **[enter]**
To point: **200,220**   ← Press **[enter]**
To point: **210,180**   ← Press **[enter]**
To point: **C**   ← Press **[enter]**
Command: ← Press **[enter]**
From point: **200,160**   ← Press **[enter]**
To point: **190,140**   ← Press **[enter]**
To point: **200,70**   ← Press **[enter]**
To point: **210,140**   ← Press **[enter]**
To point: **C**   ← Press **[enter]**
Command:

Type **REDRAW** and press **[enter]** to refresh the screen. The blips will disappear.

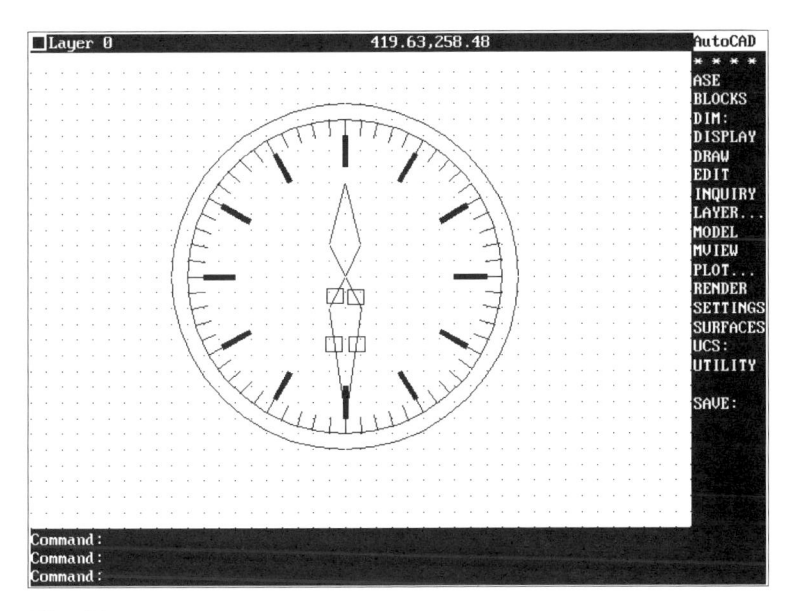

Fig. 3.7.

By rotating one of the hands you can set the time to something other than 12:30. The 'rotate' command lets you pick an entity or group of entities and rotate them around a selected base point. Try rotating the minute hand as follows. After you type **ROTATE** and press **[enter]**, the cursor will display a pick box. Click the pick box on the minute hand, as shown in the diagram.

Command: **ROTATE**
Select objects: ← Click on part of a hand (see fig. 3.★★★)
Select objects: ← Pick part of the hand
1 selected, 1 found
Select objects: ← Pick part of the hand
1 selected, 1 found
Select objects: 1 selected, 1 found   ← Pick part of the hand
Select objects: ← Pick part of the hand
1 selected, 1 found
Select objects: ← Press **[enter]**
Base point: **CEN**
of   ← Pick one of the circles
<Rotation angle>/Reference: **35**

A TWENTY-MINUTE TOUR OF AUTOCAD

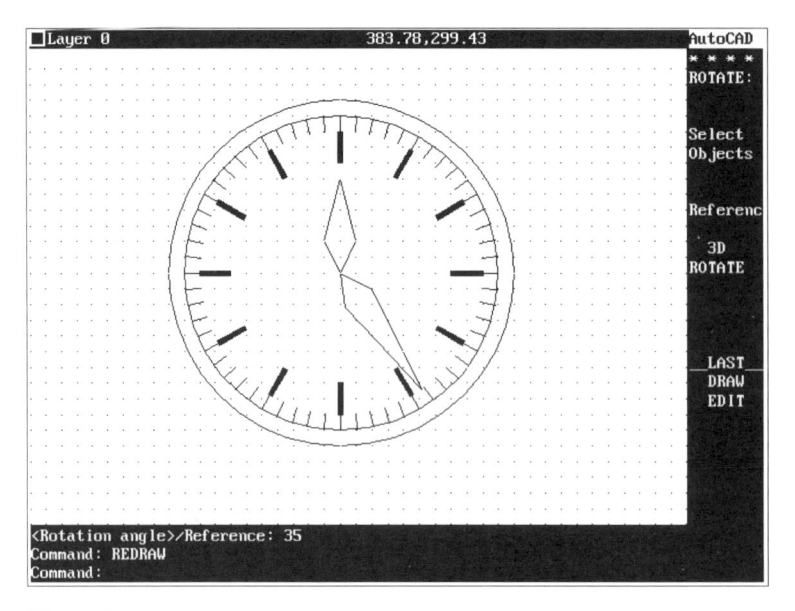

Fig. 3.8.

The time on the clock is shown on the diagram above. Remember that if you make a mistake at any stage you can press **U** (for undo) or **^C** to terminate the command and start again.

Clock outline

The casing will be drawn using a polyline 2 units thick.
Command: **PLINE**
From point: **200,20**
Arc/Close/Halfwidth/Length/Undo/Width/<Endpoint of line>: **W**
Starting width <3.00>: **2**
Ending width <2.00>:   ← Press **[enter]**
Arc/Close/Halfwidth/Length/Undo/Width/<Endpoint of line>: **200,20**
Arc/Close/Halfwidth/Length/Undo/Width/<Endpoint of line>: **400,20**
Arc/Close/Halfwidth/Length/Undo/Width/<Endpoint of line>: **400,90**
Arc/Close/Halfwidth/Length/Undo/Width/<Endpoint of line>: **350,90**
Arc/Close/Halfwidth/Length/Undo/Width/<Endpoint of line>: **290,290**
Arc/Close/Halfwidth/Length/Undo/Width/<Endpoint of line>: **200,290**
Arc/Close/Halfwidth/Length/Undo/Width/<Endpoint of line>: ← Press **[enter]**

Fillet

Some of the corners on the cabinet must now be rounded. This can be done using the 'fillet' command. First the fillet radius must be set.
Command: **FILLET**
Polyline/Radius/<Select first object>: **R**
Enter fillet radius <00.00>: **15**

This fillet radius can be applied to a polyline around part of the clock. Switch off the 'snap' mode by pressing **[F9]** if it is on. This will allow easy selection of the polyline. To apply a fillet to a corner you must select the polyline on both sides of the corner. For example, to fillet the corner between **A** and **B** (see fig. 3.9), pick the polylines at points **A** and **B**. The other suggested points for picking on the polylines are shown in the diagram.

Execute the command now:

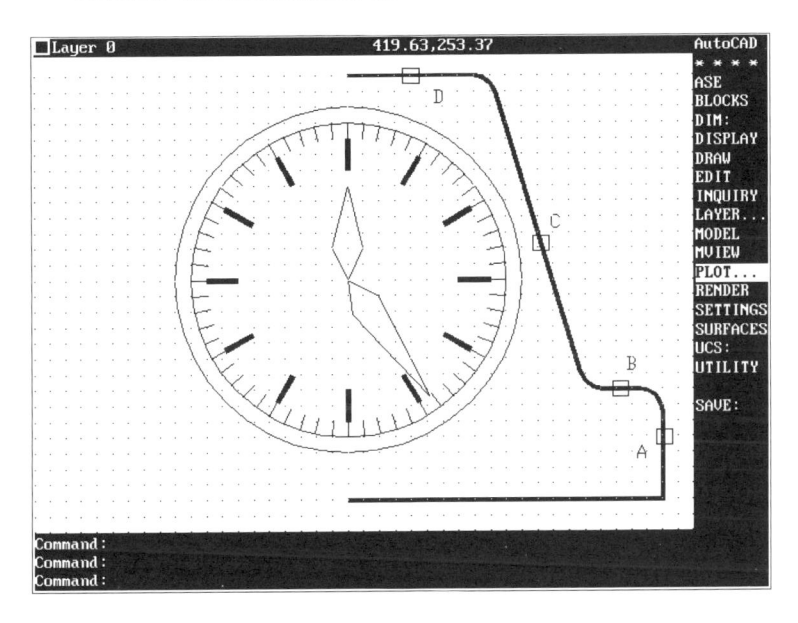

Fig. 3.9.

Command: **FILLET**
Polyline/Radius/<Select first object>: ← Pick section A
Select second object: ← Pick section B

Command: ← Press **[enter]**
FILLET Polyline/Radius/<Select first object>: ← Pick section B
Select second object: ← Pick section C
Command: ← Press **[enter]**
FILLET Polyline/Radius/<Select first object>: ← Pick section C
Select second object: pick section D
Command:

Mirror

The **MIRROR** command can be used to replicate the half of the cabinet produced on the other side. The cabinet polyline will be mirrored across an imaginary mirror axis drawn between the centre of the clock face and the top end of the 12 o'clock mark.

Command: **MIRROR**
Select objects: ← Select the cabinet outline
1 selected, 1 found
Select objects: ← Press **[enter]**
First point of mirror line: **END**
of ← Move the cursor over the top end of the polyline marking 12 and pick

Second point: **CEN**
of ← Pick any of the circles representing the face of the clock

Delete old objects? <N> ← Press **[enter]**
Command:

The polyline should now mirror over into position. If it did not lock into position, type **U** and press **[enter]**. Try the procedure again.

To see the full extent of your drawing, type **ZOOM**, press **[enter]**, then type **E** and press **[enter]**. The clock should sit in the drawing editor like that in fig. 3.★★★.

Command: **ZOOM**
All/Centre/Dynamic/Extents/Left/Previous/Vmax/Window/<Scale(X/XP)>: **E**
Regenerating drawing.
★★Redisplay required by change in drawing extents.

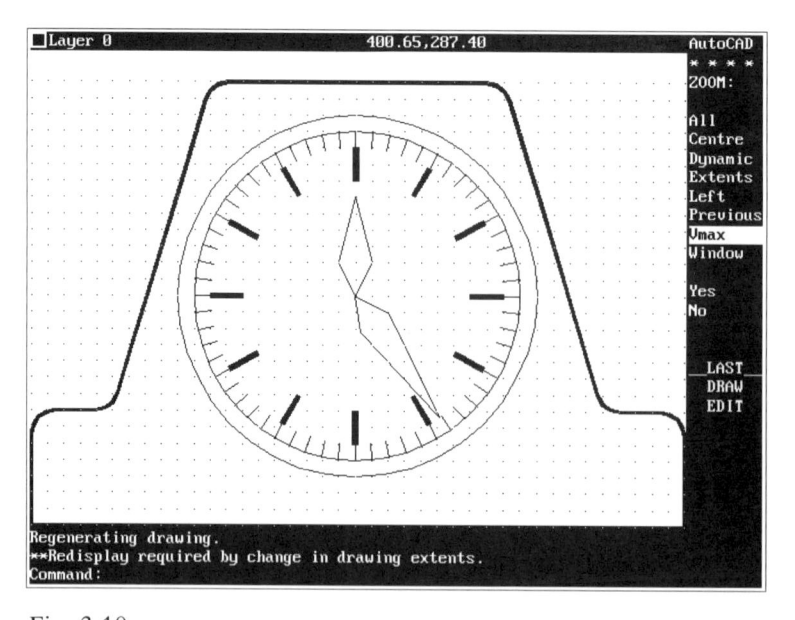

Fig. 3.10.

SUMMARY

You started the drawing of the clock by setting up the size of the electronic sheet to hold the clock in real-world co-ordinates. This was followed by selecting suitable drawing tools, such as SNAP and GRID. ZOOM—ALL was issued to see the full size of the electronic page. Lastly, the UNITS command was used to select decimal units.

The face outline of the clock was drawn using the CIRCLE command. A layer called FACE was set up to hold the digit markings on the face. These were then drawn using the PLINE and ARRAY commands. The hands of the clock were drawn with the line command and rotated into position using the ROTATE command.

Half the casing of the clock was drawn using the PLINE and FILLET commands. The other half was copied using the MIRROR command.

chapter 4

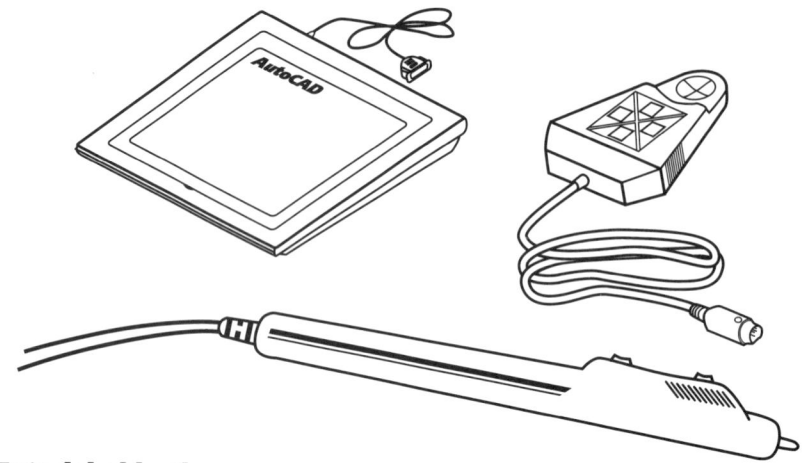

Moving from Traditional Draughting to AutoCAD

Tutorial objectives

By the end of this chapter you should be able to
- compare traditional draughting methods with AutoCAD draughting
- correct mistakes using ^C and ERASE
- start a new drawing
- enter information into the dialogue boxes
- remove entities from a drawing using the ERASE command
- save a drawing using the commands SAVE, QSAVE, and SAVEAS
- end a drawing session with the commands QUIT or END
- understand the advantages and disadvantages of a digitising tablet
- use the three basic methods of issuing commands to AutoCAD
- recover from mistakes
- give a name to a new drawing

The traditional drawing method

Let's take a brief look at how you might set about drawing on paper. When you start a drawing using the traditional draughting methods, the steps involved are at first quite simple. You decide on:

Scale
A drawing of something that in reality is larger than your sheet of paper (such as an extension to your house) must be **scaled down**. Something that is too small to represent comfortably on paper (such as the face of a watch) must be **scaled up**.

Paper size
You choose the size of the paper sheet your drawing will fit on: A4, A3, A2, etc.

Units
The units you use will depend on the conventions expected by the engineers, designers, or builders. You may, for example, work in the imperial or metric systems. Values may be so small that you have to use 'scientific' or exponential notation to dimension the drawing.

Drawing instruments
Drawing tools such as your T-square, pens, erasers and ruler must be close at hand. Precision drawing tools are expensive and need to be maintained and replaced.

Drawing-board
A good board is essential to aid you in the accurate execution of your drawing.

The drawing process
During a draughtsperson's traditional training they learn to draw accurately the basic elements of a drawing: lines, arcs, circles, etc. These are used to construct and edit a drawing.

Let's look at how these problems are solved using AutoCAD.

Drawing with AutoCAD

Scale
The problem of scaling is solved in a very dramatic way: there is simply *no* scaling while you are producing your drawing. All the dimensions you use are entered in real size. AutoCAD refers to this as inputting your drawing in 'real world' co-ordinates. If a table top is 1,300 × 750 mm in reality, you draw it at 1,300 × 750 mm in AutoCAD. Similarly, if a watch component is 0.125 mm in diameter in reality, it is drawn as 0.125 mm in AutoCAD.

The computer will, of course, scale the image up or down to display it on the computer screen.

Paper size

There is no need to concern yourself about paper size while you are drawing on the computer screen. When a paper copy is required (printed by a plotter or printer-plotter) you must then consider the sheet size and scale you wish to present your work on.

While drawing on the computer screen, the command **LIMITS** allows you to set up the size of the area your drawing will occupy. For example, to set up an area on the computer screen to draw a ship of dimensions 210 × 32 m, use the **LIMITS** command to set the drawing limits to 250 × 50 m. This will be enough to accommodate the ship.

Units

This command allows you to set up the units you wish to work with. AutoCAD allows you to change the units you are using at any point in the drawing process. You could, for example, execute your drawing fully or partially in imperial units and then switch to metric units to plot or display the drawing. (See chapter 18.)

Drawing instruments

AutoCAD provides tools to help you draw accurately. The **ORTHO** command, for example, allows the drawing of lines at two pre-determined angles.

The default values for ortho are 0 and 90 degrees. The 'object snap' facility allows you to snap onto objects or entities already drawn on the screen.

Drawing-board

This item has obviously been dispensed with.

The drawing process

CAD drawings are constructed from pre-defined entities such as lines, arcs, and circles. In AutoCAD there is a command for each entity type. During the drawing process the entities are selected and edited using commands. Several entities can be combined into a new single entity called a ***block***.

Some frequently used entities in AutoCAD include:

- lines
- points
- solids
- blocks
- dimensions
- arcs
- text
- shapes
- attributes
- polylines
- circles
- traces

Tutorial 4.1

What to do if you make a mistake

Two types of error frequently occur while you are working with computer-aided design programs: errors in using the program itself, and errors in creating the actual drawing. Both types of error may occupy a considerable amount of a beginner's time. To practise recovering from these errors, start the AutoCAD program now.

The drawing you are presented with here is unnamed.

Assigning a name to a drawing

Three methods of assigning a name to a drawing are outlined below.

(1) *Using the pull-down menu.* Pick *New...* from the *File* drop-down menu. The dialogue box shown in fig. 4.1 will appear.

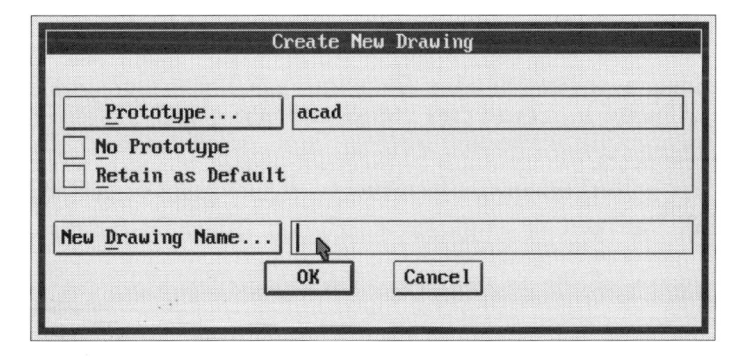

Fig. 4.1. The Create New Drawing dialogue box.

This dialogue box is concerned with the use of a **prototype** drawing and the naming of the new drawing. (The idea of a prototype drawing will be dealt with in chapter 12.)

The edit box following the title *New Drawing Name* displays a flashing cursor. Type in the name of the drawing here: **SANDBOX**. Press **[enter]** or click in the **OK** box with the arrow cursor. The blank drawing editor has now been assigned the name SANDBOX.

If you make a mistake while using a dialogue box, click in the *Cancel* box and start again.

(2) *Using the command line.* Just type the command **NEW** and press **[enter]**. The dialogue box will appear. Fill it in as described above.

(3) *Using the* Screen *menu.* Make sure you are on the root of the screen menu first (click on the word *AutoCAD* at the top of the screen if you are unsure). Click on *UTILITY* and then on *next* and lastly on **NEW...** The dialogue box described above will appear.

The following techniques will help to keep you progressing rapidly through the tutorials.

(i) **^C** (**[control]** plus **C**). This procedure will cancel the instructions you were giving the computer.

Try the following. Assume you wish to draw a line, but instead of typing **LINE** at the command prompt you type **CIRCLE** and press **[enter]**. You can recover the command prompt by typing **^C**.

The command sequence for this exercise is:
Command: **CIRCLE**
3P/2P/TTR/<Centre point>:   ← Now press **^C** to regain the command prompt

Command:

^C can be used at any point during the execution of a command. It will also work to cancel a dialogue box.

(ii) **ERASE**. This command allows you to erase any entity or group of entities in the drawing editor. The command can be accessed from the screen menu by picking *EDIT*. It is found under the drop-down menu *Modify* (in the Windows version it is represented by an icon of an eraser).

Try the following. Use the **LINE** command to draw a few lines from left to right across the screen using the pointing device to pick the end-points of the lines (make sure **ORTHO** (F8) and **SNAP** (F9) are off by checking the status line).

Press **[enter]** when you have picked the last point of the last line entity. Fig. 4.1 shows five such line segments.

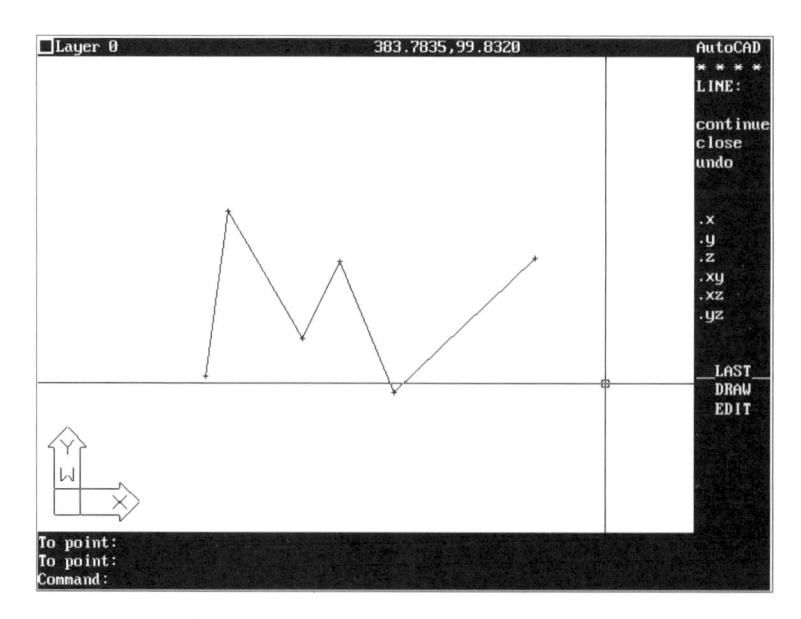

Fig. 4.2. Five lines.

Now use the **ERASE** command to remove the first (leftmost) line segment. Once the command is executed, the cross-hairs change to a 'pickbox'. The pickbox is used to select the entity (or entities) to be removed. Here is the command sequence when it is typed at the command prompt:

Command: **ERASE**
Select objects: ← Pick the first line segment; the line is highlighted

1 selected, 1 found
Select objects: ← Pick another line and press **[enter]**; the line is highlighted

Press **[enter]** again to allow AutoCAD to erase the lines you highlighted.

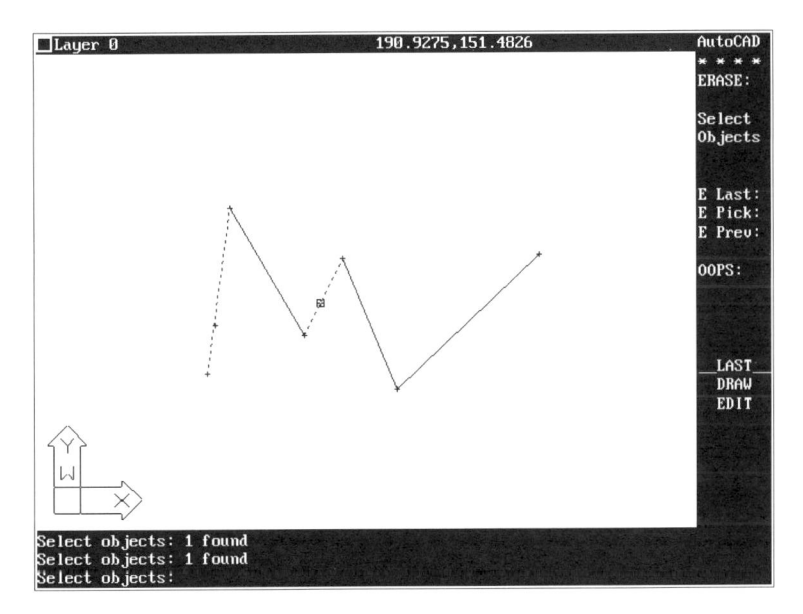

Fig. 4.3. Selected lines highlighted.

Picking ERASE from the pull-down menus
ERASE is found under *Modify*. As it is followed by a small triangle symbol, you can expect a submenu to appear off it when it is selected. This type of menu structure is often called a 'cascading menu'. The options available on the submenu are *Select, Single, Last,* and *Oops!* (see fig. 4.4).

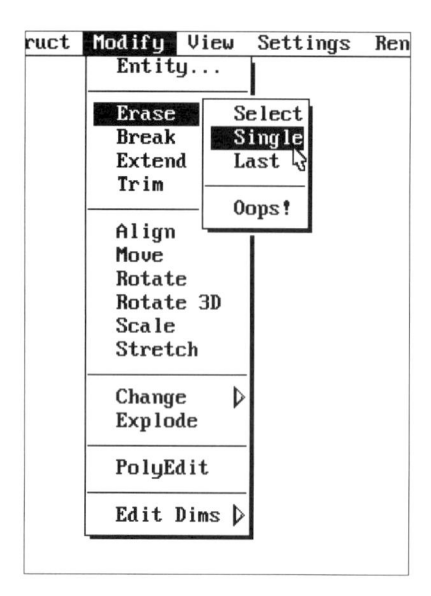

Fig. 4.4. Options on the drop-down menu for ERASE.

Picking *Select* will allow you to highlight the entities you want to erase; pressing **[enter]** after the selection will then erase all the highlighted entities. Picking *Single* will erase an entity immediately on selection; picking *Last* will erase the entity last drawn. Picking *Oops!* will undo the last command you issued. If selecting *Oops!* causes the response **Invalid** then there was nothing to undo at that point. This will occur if you have just saved the drawing.

Picking ERASE from the Screen menu
ERASE can also be selected from the Screen menu under *EDIT*. There are several other erase options available here, which can be explored when your knowledge of AutoCAD has improved.

Exercise
Try drawing and erasing some line entities using the options *Select, Single, Last,* and *Oops!*

Saving a drawing

It is advisable to save the drawing at regular intervals during your work, especially after a major editing session. The simplest way to do this is to type **QSAVE** at the command prompt. AutoCAD will save the drawing and return you to the command prompt. You may then continue editing the drawing.

Type **QSAVE** now and press **[enter]**.

The command **SAVE** will display a *Save Drawing As* dialogue box (see fig. 4.5).

Type **SAVE** now and press **[enter]**. The *Save Drawing As* dialogue box is displayed.

The edit line in this dialogue box will contain the name of your drawing (SANDBOX). Click on **OK** to save it. The drawing is saved to a file with the name you applied when you started the drawing session, and the extension **.dwg** is automatically assigned to it. (Chapter 20 deals with files in more detail.)

Cancel will close the dialogue box without saving the drawing.

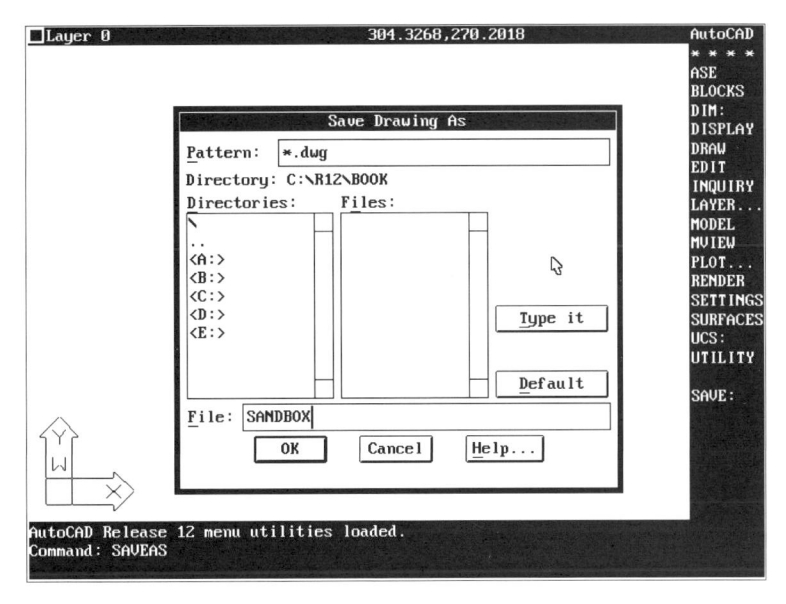

Fig. 4.5. The Save Drawing As dialogue box.

The command **SAVEAS** will call up the same *Save Drawing As* dialogue box. If you enter a new name for the drawing at this stage, the drawing on the screen takes on this new name.

Ending an AutoCAD drawing session

AutoCAD must be closed down using the commands **QUIT** or **END**. The computer must never be switched off while you are still in the drawing editor.

Typing **END** will save the drawing (if you have already given it a name) and finish the drawing session. In a situation where you did not assign a name to a drawing, the **END** command will force the display of a dialogue box titled *Create Drawing File*. This is similar to the *Save Drawing As* dialogue box discussed above. Enter the name of the drawing and click on **OK**. The drawing is then saved and the AutoCAD program is closed down.

The command **QUIT** will allow you to leave AutoCAD if there are no changes to save. If there are changes, a *Drawing Modification* dialogue box (fig. 4.6) is displayed offering the options *Save Changes, Discard Changes,* and *Cancel Command* (see fig. 4.6). Select the appropriate option by picking with the pointing device.

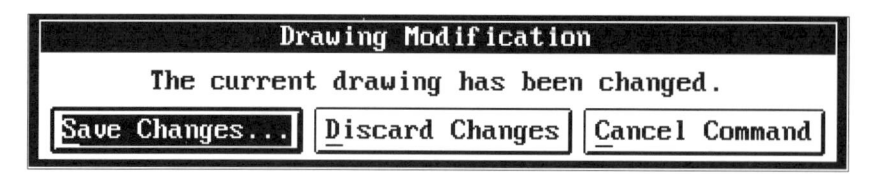

Fig. 4.6. The Drawing Modification dialogue box.

Communicating with AutoCAD

In this tutorial you issued commands to AutoCAD in the following ways:
(1) by typing at the command prompt
(2) by selecting items on the screen menu
(3) by picking with the pointer from the drop-down menus
(4) by using a digitising tablet

The digitising tablet

This is an electronic pad connected to the computer's system unit. Generally the connection is through one of the communications ports (COM1 or COM2). An electronic 'pen' or 'puck' is used as a pointing device to select commands from a template that is placed over the tablet. The AutoCAD 12 template is shown in fig. 4.7.

The template has a screen area; moving the puck or pen in this region produces a corresponding movement on the computer screen. The rest of the template displays icons that represent commands. Picking an icon with the pointing device will execute a command as though it had been typed at AutoCAD's command prompt.

Advantages of a digitising tablet

(1) The movement of the pointing device on the screen area of the tablet translates directly into movements of the cross-hairs on the screen area of the computer. In other words, the position of the pointing device on the tablet is consistent with its position on the computer screen. This suggests a more natural drawing experience.
(2) Many commands can be seen at a glance. This helps users to be more efficient at drawing by exposing them to commands that they may otherwise have forgotten. Using the drop-down and screen menus can often lead to spending time searching for less commonly used commands.
(3) The tablet can be used to **digitise** a drawing. A drawing can be placed on the tablet and traced using the pen or puck. (See chapter 19 for details of this procedure.)
(4) Advanced users of AutoCAD can design their own templates for use with a tablet.
(5) If a puck with several buttons is used, the buttons can be programmed to execute frequently used commands.

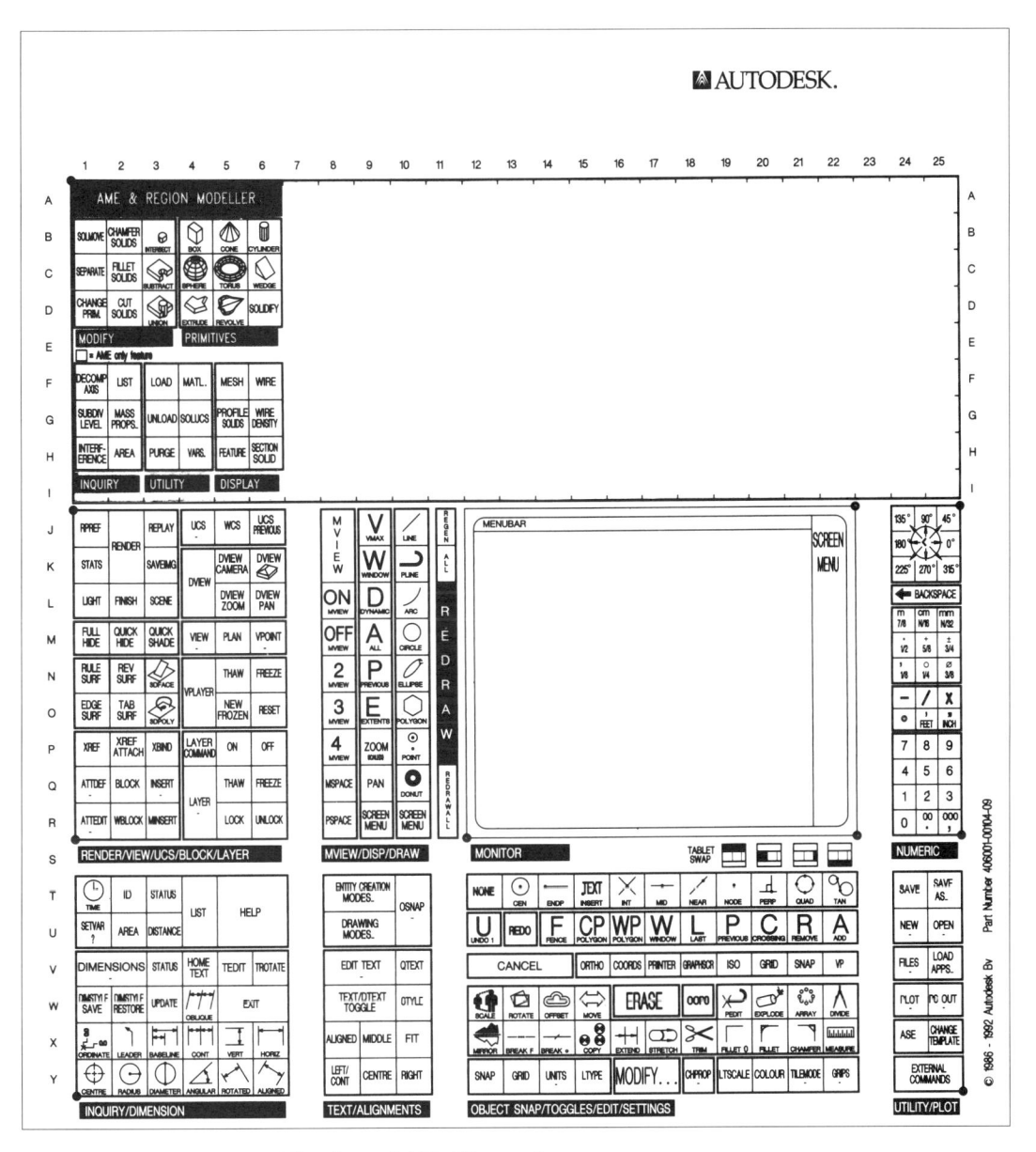

Fig. 4.7. The AutoCAD 12 template.

Disadvantages of a digitising tablet
(1) It is expensive.
(2) It is often only used profitably in CAD programs. A mouse may also have to be purchased to use other types of program.

Advantages of the mouse
(1) It generally produces faster cursor movement on the screen.
(2) It is inexpensive relative to a digitiser.
(3) It can be used with a large variety of other programs.

Disadvantages of a mouse

(1) Its movements are not directly related to the cursor movement on the screen.
(2) It cannot be used to digitise or trace drawings.
(3) It often leads to users employing a limited number of commands for problem solving.

The importance of the command prompt

Regardless of the method of command input, AutoCAD will communicate with you through the command prompt. For example, picking **LINE** from the screen, drop-down menu or digitising tablet will produce a *From point* response at the command prompt. It is essential that you develop the technique of watching the command prompt when working.

Additional information

Drawing names

DOS users are restricted to names of eight characters or less. Some characters cannot be used in a name: for example the stroke (/), reverse stroke (\), full point (.) and space cannot be used. A *path* to a subdirectory can be given while naming the drawing. (See chapter 20 on DOS.)

SUMMARY

AutoCAD allows the user to draw using 'real-world' co-ordinates. Scaling is done, if necessary, only when plotting a drawing on paper. Drawings are constructed from pre-defined entities.

Errors in typing at the command prompt or in selecting commands from the menus can be rejected by typing **^C**. A command can then be repeated. **^C** will also allow you to exit from a command you do not want to complete.

The **ERASE** command is used to erase entities from the drawing editor. Entities on the screen are selected by a 'pickbox'.

'Dialogue boxes' are presented for many commands. They normally have a box (called an 'edit line') that allows the user to input information, such as the name of a drawing.

All AutoCAD commands can be typed in at the command prompt. Many other commands can be selected from the screen menu, drop-down menus, and digitising tablet. If in doubt about how to select a command, try using the command line. The command line also displays AutoCAD's responses to your commands, regardless of how the command was issued.

The digitising tablet has many advantages over the mouse.

The commands used in this chapter were:

NEW: displays the *New Drawing* dialogue box and allows the user to assign a name to a new drawing.

ERASE: will erase selected entities.
QSAVE: saves a drawing quickly and returns you to the drawing editor.
SAVE: displays the *Save Drawing As* dialogue box and allows the user to save the drawing or to assign a new name to the drawing.
SAVEAS: displays the *Save As* dialogue box and allows the user to assign a name to the drawing. This box will also appear if you have not assigned a name to the drawing and the **SAVE** command is issued.
END: automatically saves the drawing (if it already has a name) and closes down AutoCAD.
QUIT: will close down AutoCAD. However, if unsaved changes have been made to the drawing since it was last saved, the *Drawing Modification* dialogue box is displayed, which allows the modified drawing to be saved or discarded.

EXERCISES

1. Write a brief note explaining how AutoCAD deals with scaling.
2. Explain the term 'real-world co-ordinates'. Are such co-ordinates ever used in traditional draughting methods? Give examples.
   The following terms are used with AutoCAD; explain each briefly: (*a*) paper space; (*b*) limits; (*c*) entities; (*d*) dialogue box; (*e*) edit box.
3. State three of the limitations applied to naming a drawing under the DOS version of AutoCAD. What is meant by the term 'default value'?
4. Start a new drawing called EXER4-4. Draw several straight-edged shapes under the following conditions:
   (*a*) with ORTHO and SNAP ON
   (*b*) with ORTHO OFF and SNAP ON
   (*c*) with both ORTHO and SNAP OFF
Use the ERASE command by selecting it from the screen menu, the drop-down menu, and the command prompt.
5. Distinguish between (*a*) SAVE and SAVEAS; (*b*) QUIT and END; (*c*) ERASE and ^C.
6. Which communications port is a digitising tablet attached to? What are the advantages of a digitising tablet over a mouse?

chapter 5

Beginning a New Drawing

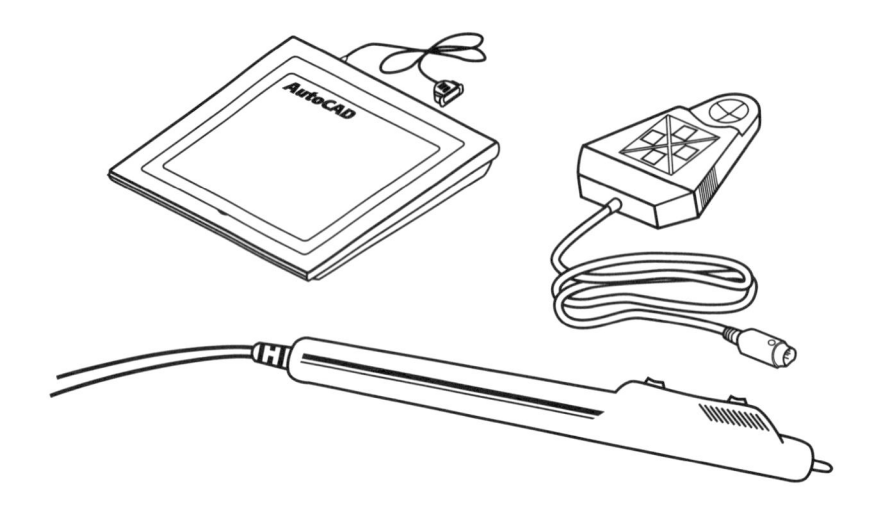

Tutorial objectives

By the end of this chapter you should be able to
- set up AutoCAD to start a drawing
- use the 'limits' command to set the size of the drawing editor
- magnify your drawing using the 'zoom—all' and 'zoom window' commands
- place a grid over the drawing
- tell AutoCAD what units you want to work with
- locate points in the drawing using polar co-ordinates
- use the 'circle' command
- place text on the drawing
- use the 'pline' command to draw lines of varying thicknesses

INTRODUCTION

This is an important chapter. It will show you how to go about setting up AutoCAD to accept a drawing on your terms. You will learn how to tell AutoCAD what units you will draw in, the size of your sheet of paper, and what drawing aids you require. You will then be taken through the process of drawing a simple baseplate. Entering drawing information accurately using polar, Cartesian and absolute co-ordinates is explained in detail. Lastly, there are some assignments for you to practise.

Tutorial 5.1

Drawing a simple baseplate

Target drawing

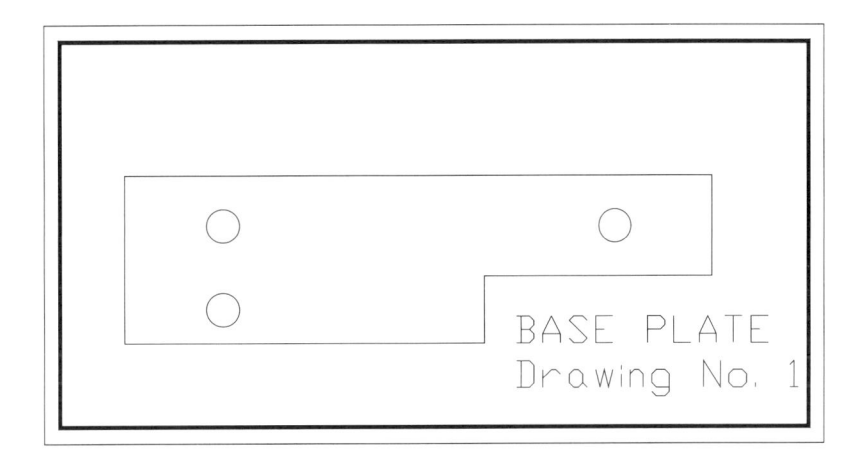

Drawing instructions

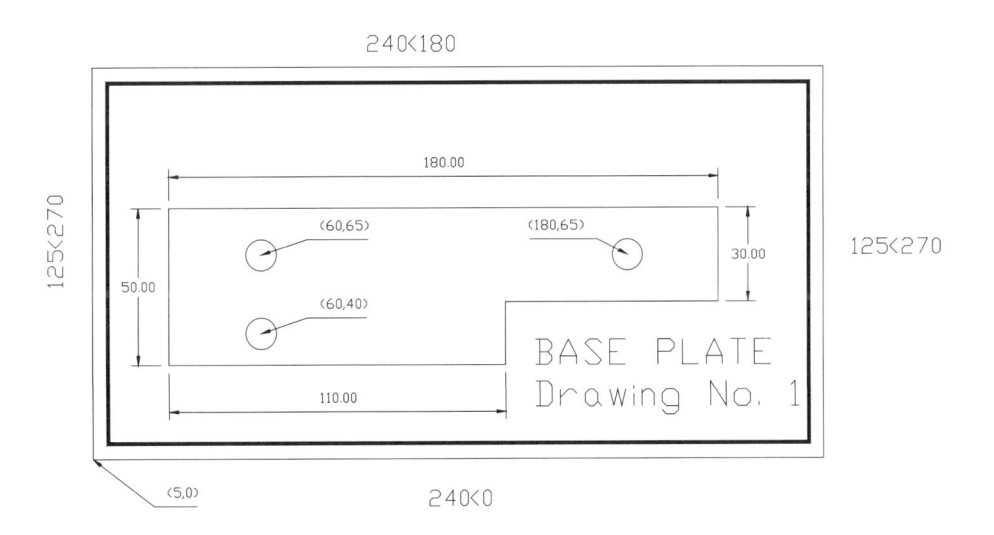

Beginning a new drawing

Execute the AutoCAD program. At the drawing editor select *New...* from the *File* drop-down menu. Enter the name of the drawing, **BPLATE1**, in the edit box and click on **OK**. The drawing editor is returned to your control.

AutoCAD has no idea what units you are going to draw with, nor does it know what size sheet of paper you wanted. What AutoCAD presented you with are its default settings in a ***prototype*** drawing. These setting will now have to be changed to draw the plate successfully.

The drawing will be constructed in decimal units, to two decimal places. The **UNITS** command will enable you to use this system of units. The baseplate is 180 × 50 mm. This can be accommodated on a sheet of size 297 × 100 mm. The **LIMITS** command, in conjunction with the **ZOOM—ALL** and **GRID** commands, will allow you to set up the electronic sheet size.

Drawing instructions
Setting up the drawing sheet
Units

Type **UNITS** at the command prompt and press **[enter]**. AutoCAD switches to text mode (the drawing editor is removed for the moment) and a series of questions concerning the set-up of your drawing will be presented. The drawing will be executed in decimal units, so answer **2** to the first question, *Enter choice 1 to 5 <2>:*

The second question will ask for the *Number of digits to the right of decimal point (0 to 8) <4>:* Type **2** in response and press **[enter]**.

The default values are in the angle brackets and can be accepted for the rest of the questions by pressing **[enter]** until the command prompt is presented again. DOS users must then press **[F1]** to bring back the drawing editor. Windows AutoCAD users will be returned to the graphics screen automatically.

The complete list of options available under the **UNITS** command is given in chapter 3.

Once the drawing editor has been displayed, move the cursor around the screen to check that the co-ordinates in the status line area are responding. Function key F6 switches the co-ordinate readings on and off.

Limits

To set the electronic page size, type **LIMITS** at the command prompt and press **[enter]**. AutoCAD responds with:
Reset Model space limits:
ON/OFF/<Lower left corner><0.00,0.00>
Press **[enter]** to accept the lower left corner as 0,0. AutoCAD now presents you with:
Upper right corner <420.00,297.00>:
Type in **280,150** and press **[enter]**. The electronic page size on the screen has now been set.

Grid

The *grid* was introduced earlier as a drawing aid. It will help you to locate points and to position entities in the drawing editor. The grid is not part of a drawing.

The grid also has the important function of letting you know the size of the sheet you are drawing on. By switching the grid **ON** you can see the size of the limits on screen. In this tutorial, set the **GRID** to 10 units.

The command sequence is:

Command: **GRID**
Grid spacing (X) or ON/OFF/Snap/Aspect <10.00>:

Type **10** and press **[enter]**. The grid is switched *on,* and will cover part of the drawing editor with a spacing between the grid dots of 10 units. The area the grid covers is the size of the sheet you set up with the **LIMITS** command above. If you draw outside this grid you are drawing outside the electronic page size you have just set.

Zoom

The **ZOOM** command changes the magnification at which the drawing is displayed on the screen. There are ten options available when the command is accessed by typing **ZOOM** at the command prompt. The screen menu selection of the command shows eight options, and the drop-down menu under *View, Zoom >* gives access to five options. An option within any AutoCAD command is selected at the command prompt by typing the capitalised letters of the option.

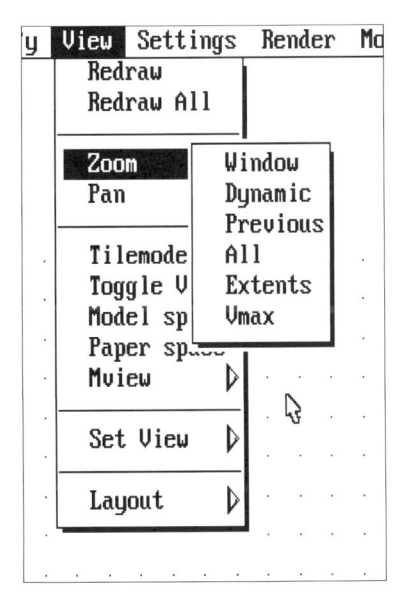

Fig. 5.1. The 'zoom' drop-down options.

Type **ZOOM** at the command prompt now. The ten options available are:
All/Centre/Dynamic/Extents/Left/Previous/Vmax/Window/<Scale (X/XP)>:

At the moment the *All* option is the only one to concern us. Type **A** for 'all' and press **[enter]**. This will cause the drawing editor to be displayed out to the limits you set and as large as possible on the monitor you are using.

If the grid does not fill the screen completely after executing the *Zoom All* command, it simply means that the **aspect ratio** of your screen does not match the aspect ratio of the limits you set.

Fig. 5.2 shows the extent of the grid.

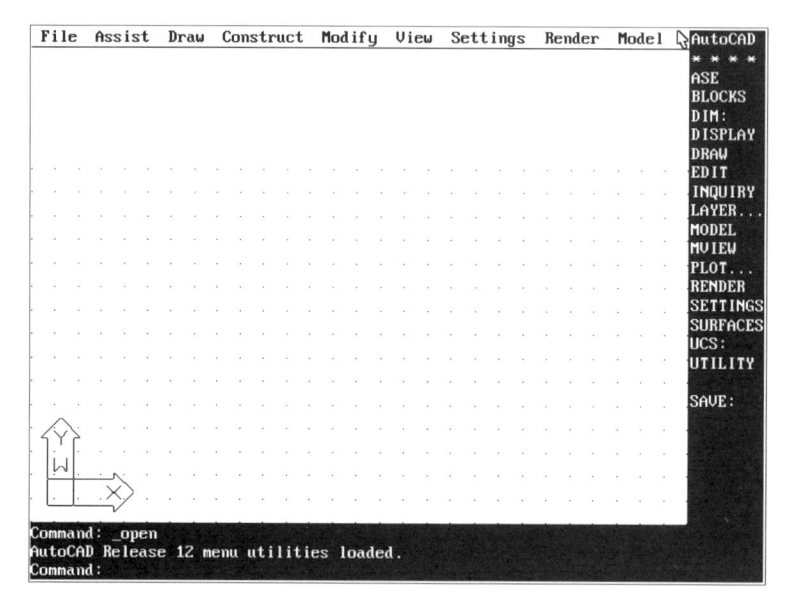

Fig. 5.2. The drawing editor after setting the limits and executing the 'zoom—all' command. Note that the grid does not fill the screen completely in this case.

You are now ready to proceed with drawing the baseplate.

Drawing the baseplate—polar co-ordinates

The outline of the baseplate is drawn using the **LINE** entity with polar co-ordinates. Polar co-ordinates oblige you to give the length of a line and its angle of orientation. Refer to the target drawing and the drawing instructions at the beginning of the tutorial.

The format of polar co-ordinate input is:

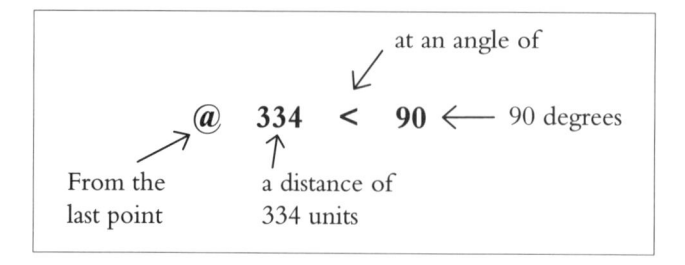

```
                         at an angle of
                              ↙
        @    334    <    90   ←  90 degrees
       ↗      ↑
   From the   a distance of
   last point 334 units
```

The starting points for the baseplate are the co-ordinates **30,30**. Type **LINE** at the command prompt and follow the sequence:

Command: **LINE**
From point: **30,30**   ← Starting point
To point: **@50<90**   ← Vertical side
To point: **@180<0**   ← Top horizontal side
To point: **@30<270**   ← Vertical side
To point: **@70<180**   ← Horizontal side
To point: **@20<270**   ← Vertical side
To point: **C**   ← Closes the shape

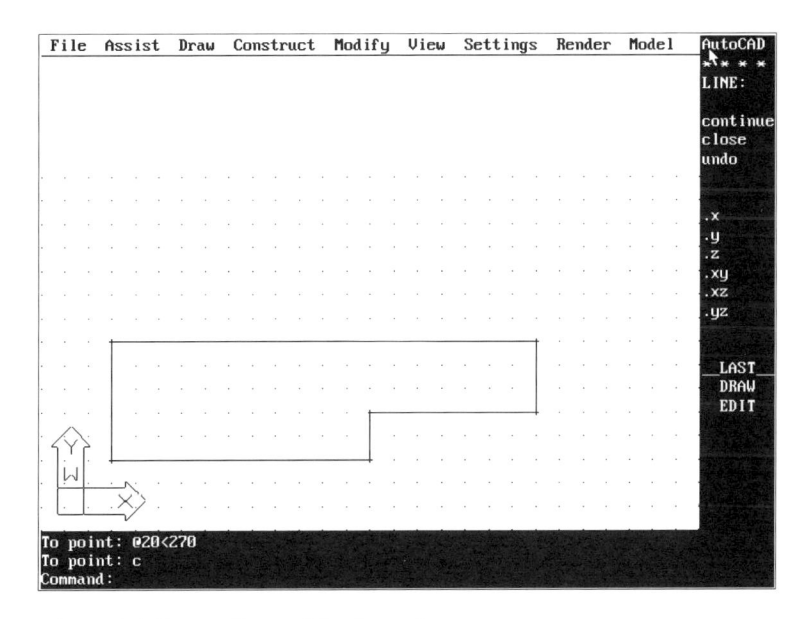

Fig. 5.3. The outline of the baseplate.

You have carried out a major drawing session on the baseplate. It is advisable to **QSAVE** your work at this stage. Type **QSAVE** and press **[enter]**.

Placing the holes in the baseplate

The drawing instructions identify the centre of each of the holes. They are drawn using the **CIRCLE** entity. Four options appear when the **CIRCLE** command is executed, as follows.

Command: **CIRCLE**
3P/2P/TTR/<Centre point>:
3P allows the user to pick three points on the screen through which a circle is transcribed. *2P* works in an identical fashion: two points are picked on the screen and a circle is drawn through them.

TTR asks for two tangent points and the radius of the circle you want drawn through the points.

BEGINNING A NEW DRAWING   **51**

How the command works

In the baseplate drawing the holes are drawn by selecting the centre of the circle. The default option is <*Centre point*> (remember that the default option is always shown in angle brackets). Then the radius is given to describe the circle.

The radius of each of the holes on the baseplate is 5 units. The bottom left hole is placed as follows:

Command: **CIRCLE**

3P/2P/TTR/<Centre point>: **60,40**

The centre point is the default option. The cursor can be used to pick the centre point 60,40, although it would be more accurate to type in the absolute co-ordinates **60,40** and press **[enter]**.

AutoCAD responds with:

Diameter/<Radius>:

The radius is now offered as the default. All the holes have a radius of 5 units, so type **5** and press **[enter]**.

Hole 1 is now complete. Try drawing the other holes yourself and then **QSAVE** the drawing.

The 'text' command

The 'text' command allows you to place text entities onto a drawing. The size, angle of orientation and style of text used are also controlled by the command.

To place the text 'BASEPLATE' as in the target drawing, execute the following:

Command: **TEXT**

Justify/Style/<Start point>:

The default option is in angle brackets, so AutoCAD wants to know where you wish to start the text from. You can pick a point on the screen with the cross-hairs, or type in co-ordinate values. In this case type in the co-ordinates **150,30** and press **[enter]**. The response is:

Height <3.0>: **8**	← Type in **8** and press **[enter]**
Rotation angle <0>: **0**	← 0 degrees runs the text horizontally
Text: **BASEPLATE**	← Type the text in here—note that this is one of the few places in AutoCAD where pressing **[space]** is *not* equivalent to pressing **[enter]**.

After typing in the text 'BASEPLATE' press **[enter]**. The text will appear on the screen.

Placement of the second line of text can be achieved in the following way. Press **[enter]** again to call up the **TEXT** command.

Note: Pressing **[enter]** or **[space]** when you are at the command prompt will always call up the last command you executed.

The options presented again are:

Justify/Style/<Start point>:

If you press **[enter]** at this point the next line of text will be placed directly under the previous 'BASEPLATE'. Press **[enter]** now and type in the text 'Drawing No. 1'. Press **[enter]** to see its placement on screen.

Type **REDRAW**, or select it from the drop-down menu *View* to refresh the screen and remove the blips.

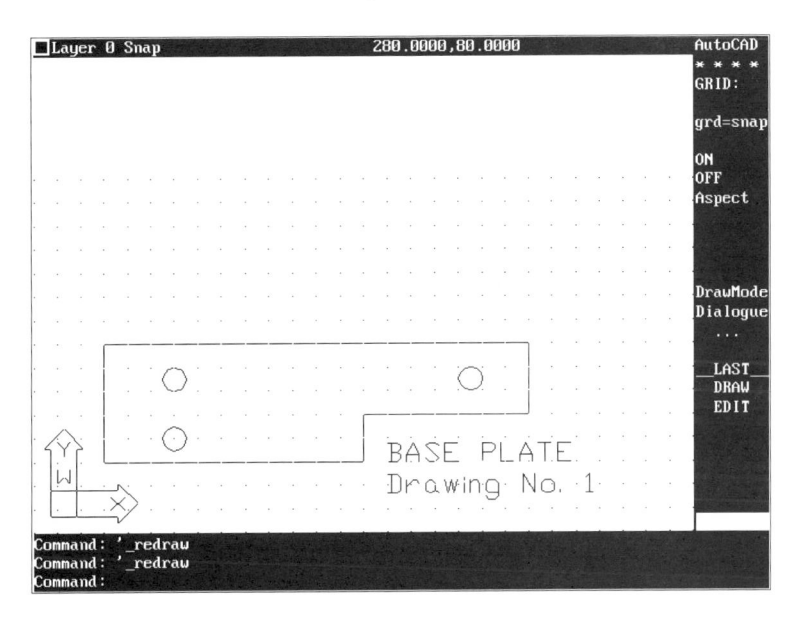

Fig. 5.4. The baseplate with the holes and text in place.

Placing a border around the drawing

A double border will now be placed around the drawing using the **LINE** and **POLYLINE** entities. The **PLINE** command will allow you to draw polylines with a user-specified thickness, which can be seen on the screen.

Switch the grid (F7) and snap *on* (F9) if they are off, and set both to a value of 5 to help you draw the border. To do this you must follow the command sequence below.

Command: **GRID**
Grid spacing (X) or ON/OFF/Snap/Aspect <10.0000>: **5**
Command: **SNAP**
Snap spacing or ON/OFF/Aspect/Rotate/Style <5.0000>: **5**
Command:

Polylines are special lines and are treated by AutoCAD with special editing commands. The command **PEDIT** is used to edit polylines. Type **PLINE** now.

Command: **PLINE**
From point: ← AutoCAD asks you for the first point of the polyline. Move the cross-hairs to 10,5 and pick the point.
Seven options are now presented:
Arc/Close/Halfwidth/Length/Undo/Width/<Endpoint of line>:

The *Width* option is used to set the width of the polyline. Press **W** to select it.

Starting width <0.00>: **1** ← Type 1 and press **[enter]**
Ending width<1.00>: ← Press **[enter]** to accept the default

The seven options reappear. The default option *Endpoint of line* can now be followed. Type in the following co-ordinates for each *Endpoint of line*:

240,5 ← Press **[enter]**
240,120 ← Press **[enter]**
10,120 ← Press **[enter]**
10,5 ← Press **[enter]**

A polyline border with a thickness of 1 is now complete. Press **[enter]** to terminate the command.

The outer border will now be drawn using the **LINE** command in conjunction with the co-ordinate reading on the status line. You may have noticed that the reading on the status line gives the *x* and *y* values for the position of the cross-hairs. However, as soon as a drawing command is issued the reading takes on the form [*distance*] < [*angle*] if the system variable **COORDS** is set to **2**.

The system variables

System variables are variables that hold specific values or settings that affect many different aspects of AutoCAD. By changing a variable you can change such features as the size of the pickbox at the cross-hairs or how the co-ordinate read-out appears on the status line. (Appendix A contains a complete listing of all the variables.)

To ensure that your co-ordinate reading on the status line is the same as that used in this tutorial, assign a value of 2 to the variable COORDS.

To do this, execute the following at the command prompt:

Command: **COORDS**
New value for COORDS <1>: **2** ← Input a value of 2
Command:

This value of 2 will be saved with the drawing.

To continue drawing the border, execute the **LINE** command, and in response to *From point* type in the co-ordinates **5,0**. Now move the cross-hairs until the co-ordinate reading on the status line is *240<0*. Pick this point. Continue drawing the line with the following values (don't forget to read them from the status line):

125<90
240<180
125<270

The outer border is now drawn. Press **[enter]** to finish the command.
QSAVE the drawing, or type **END** to finish your drawing session.

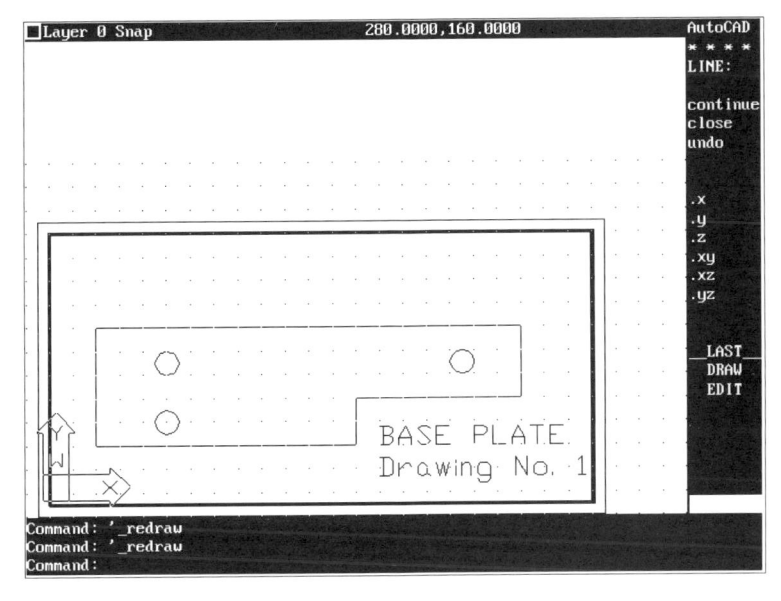

Fig. 5.5. The completed baseplate.

SUMMARY

The drawing editor was opened and the new drawing named. The **UNITS** command was used to set the drawing units. The **LIMITS** command defined the size of the electronic sheet to hold the drawing—remember that the drawing was input using *real-world co-ordinates*. The **ZOOM—ALL** command forced AutoCAD to display the full area of the electronic page on the computer screen. The grid and snap drawing tools were switched on to help you with part of the drawing. Accuracy of input was obtained by using *polar co-ordinates*. Text was entered with the command **TEXT**. A border was drawn using a *polyline* and a line. The last command executed can be called up by pressing [ent/⁄/⏎] or [space]. Lastly, the screen display was refreshed and the *blips* removed by typing **REDRAW**.

Additional information

Below is a more detailed reference description of some of the commands used in the tutorial.

Zoom
All/Centre/Dynamic/Extents/Left/Previous/Vmax/Window/<Scale(X/XP)>:

/All—fits the drawing pages on the screen out to the **LIMITS.**
/Centre—allows you to specify a new centre around which the zoom command will operate. The new centre can be chosen by picking with the pointing device or by typing in a co-ordinate. AutoCAD will ask for a *Magnification or Height <default value>:*. The default value represents the present magnification of the zoom. Try picking the centre of one of the

baseplate holes as the centre and give a magnification of 50 units.

/Dynamic—allows you to both pan (slide around the drawing) and zoom at the same time. A window will appear, which you can place over the drawing. Pressing **[enter]** will select that area of the drawing for magnification.

/Extents—will zoom the drawing to the extents of the drawing. The bottom left of the drawing is placed at the bottom left corner of the screen.

/Left—This option is similar to centre, except that the point chosen becomes the bottom left of the screen display when you zoom.

/Previous—AutoCAD remembers your zooms. Selecting *Previous* will return you to the previous zoomed display.

/Vmax—allows you to zoom out as far as possible without a regeneration of the drawing occurring.

/Window—allows you to pull a rectangular window around part of the drawing. The entities contained within the windows are zoomed to fill the screen.

<Scale (X/XP)>: The X option implies that you can enter a number by which the drawing will be displayed. For example, **.2** will zoom out from the drawing, while **2** will double the size of the drawing. The XP option implies that a value such as 5× will magnify the drawing to five times its current display size.

Grid

Grid spacing (X) or ON/OFF/Snap/Aspect <default>:

<default>—A value, in drawing units, can be input to set a new spacing for the grid. AutoCAD will always present you with the last value as the default.

/Grid spacing (X)—The X allows you to set the grid spacing to a multiple of the snap setting. If the snap setting was 10 units, a value of 2× will set the grid to 20 units.

/ON—switches the grid on.

/OFF—switches the grid off.

/Snap—By typing **S** the grid is set up to follow to the snap setting.

/Aspect—The aspect option refers to the aspect ratio of the vertical grid spacing to the horizontal spacing. AutoCAD will ask for the X and Y spacing.

Circle

3P/2P/TTR/<Centre point>:

/3P—Select three points, or type in their co-ordinates, and AutoCAD will draw a circle through the selected points

/2P—Select two points, or type in their co-ordinates, and AutoCAD will draw a circle through the selected points.

/TTR—allows you to select two tangent points and the radius of a circle you want to be described through the points.

/<Centre point>:—Select the centre point for the circle.

Text
/Justify—Selecting J will open a further submenu.
/Style—You can create a style for the particular font you are working with.
/<Start point>:—Select the point where the text will be inserted.

Polyline
From point:
Arc/Close/Halfwidth/Length/Undo/Width/<Endpoint of line>:
/Arc—used for the creation of arcs using polylines.
/Close—This is similar to close in the LINE command.
/Halfwidth—an alternative method for determining the width of a polyline.
/Length—allows the user to specify the length of a polyline segment.
/Undo—allows a segment of the polyline to be removed.
/Width—used to determine the width of a polyline.

ASSIGNMENTS

Assignment 1

Produce the following drawing of a book.

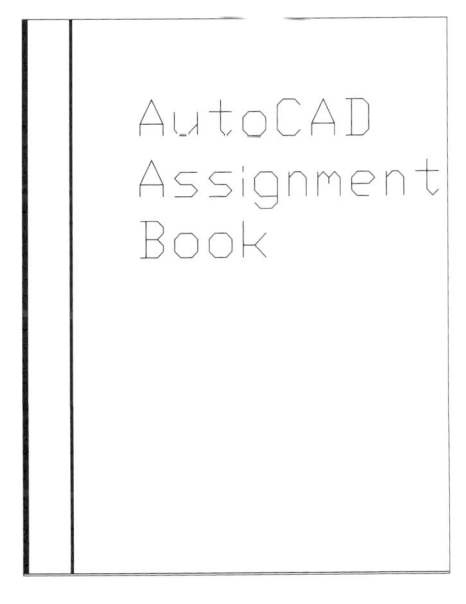

Target drawing

BEGINNING A NEW DRAWING **57**

Drawing instructions

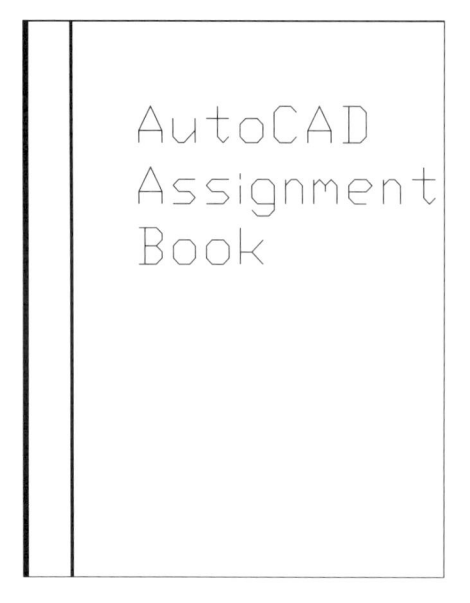

```
AutoCAD
Assignment
Book
```

Use a LINE to draw the top, bottom and right-hand edges of the book. Use a PLINE to draw the spine.
Units: decimal, no decimal places.
GRID = 1, SNAP = 1, LIMITS = 0,0 to 30,30.
Text height = 1.5.

Assignment 2

Construct the following shapes using the LINE command. Suggested LIMITS for exercise (a) are 0,0 to 100,30. Choose appropriate LIMITS for the other exercises yourself. Work with suitable GRID and SNAP settings to help you with the shapes. Use polar co-ordinates.

(a)

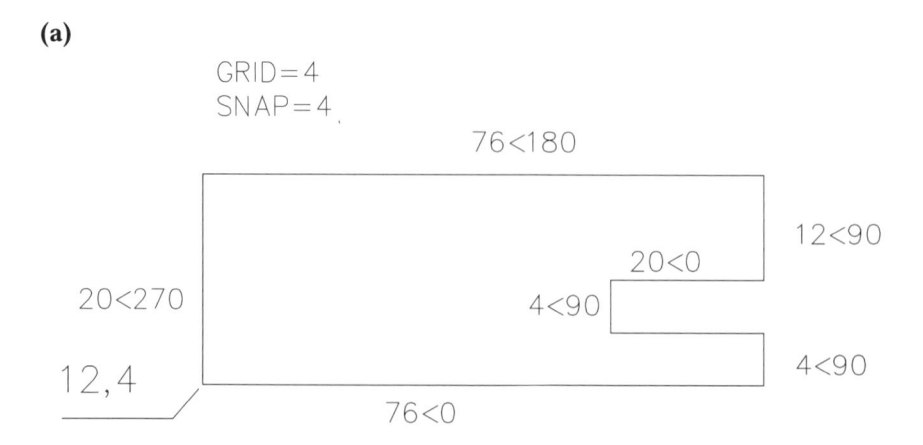

GRID=4
SNAP=4

76<180
12<90
20<270
20<0
4<90
12,4
76<0
4<90

(b)

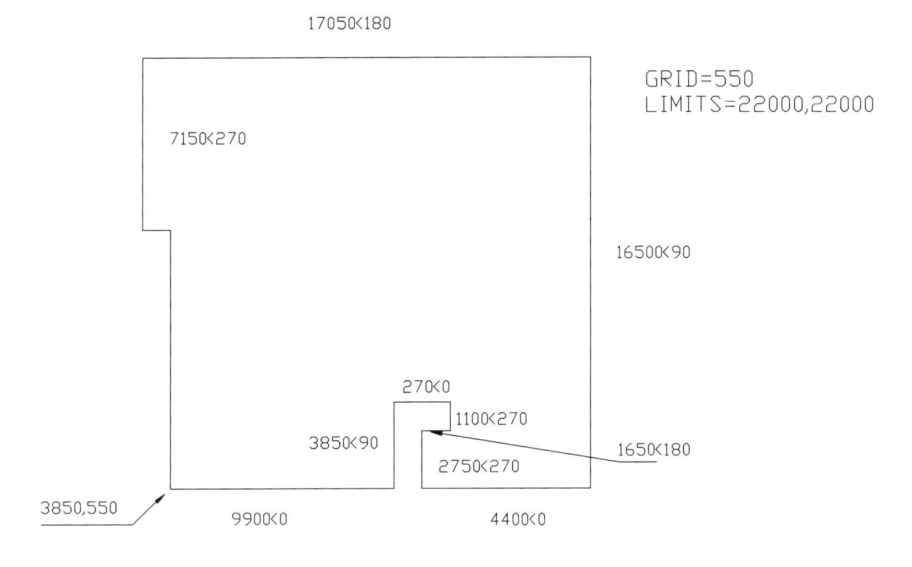

17050<180

7150<270

GRID=550
LIMITS=22000,22000

16500<90

270<0
1100<270
3850<90
2750<270
1650<180

3850,550

9900<0   4400<0

(c)

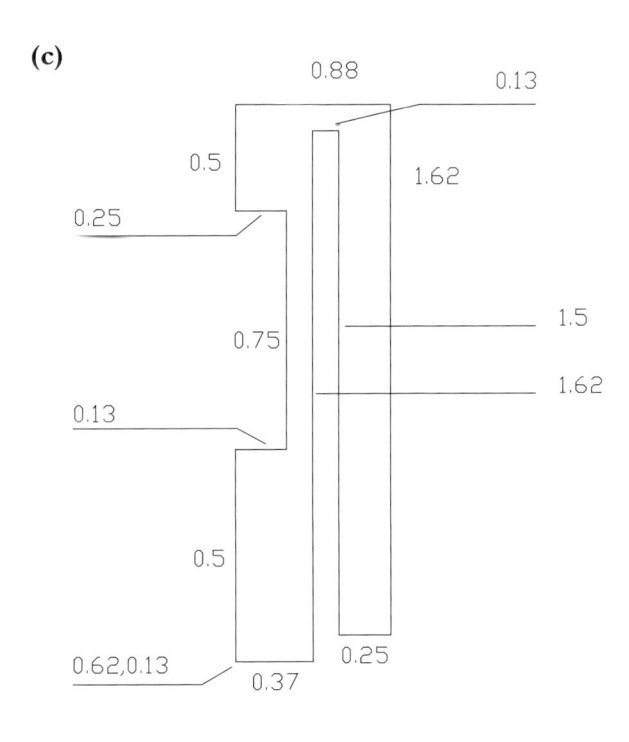

0.88   0.13

0.5

1.62

0.25

0.75

1.5

0.13

1.62

0.5

0.62,0.13   0.25
0.37

BEGINNING A NEW DRAWING   **59**

Assignment 3

Drawing instructions

This drawing can be executed quickly with appropriate settings for a GRID and SNAP. The outline of the elevation is drawn with the polyline entity.

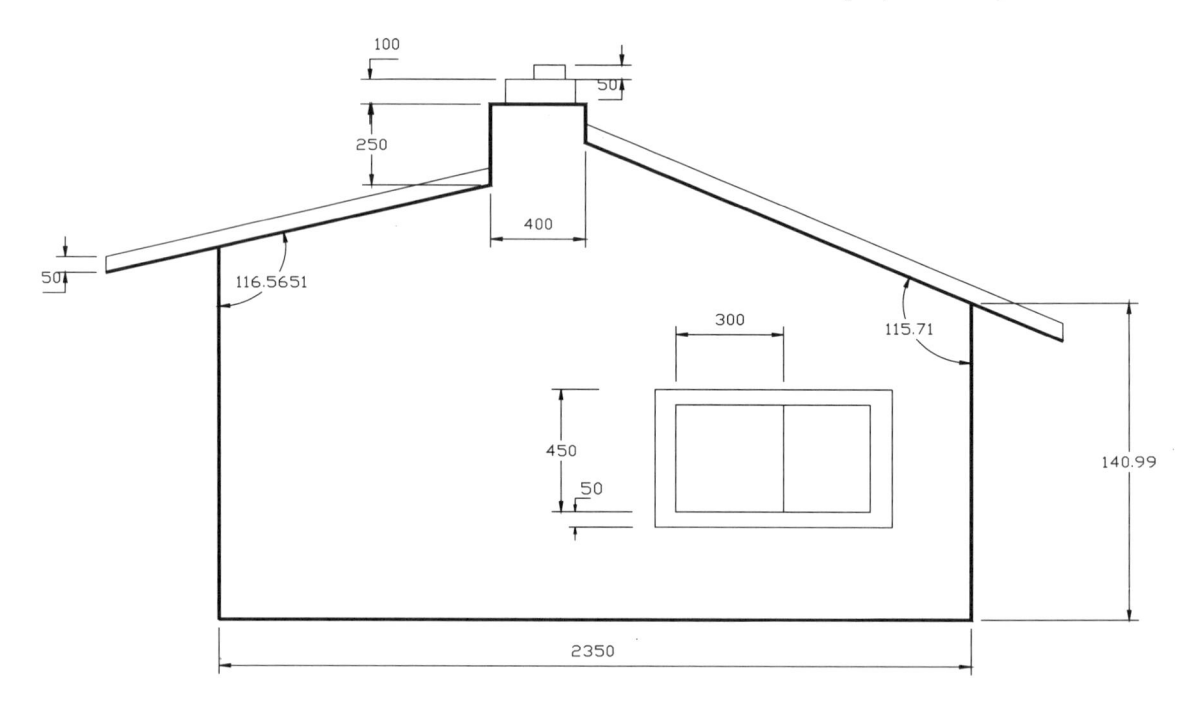

Target drawing

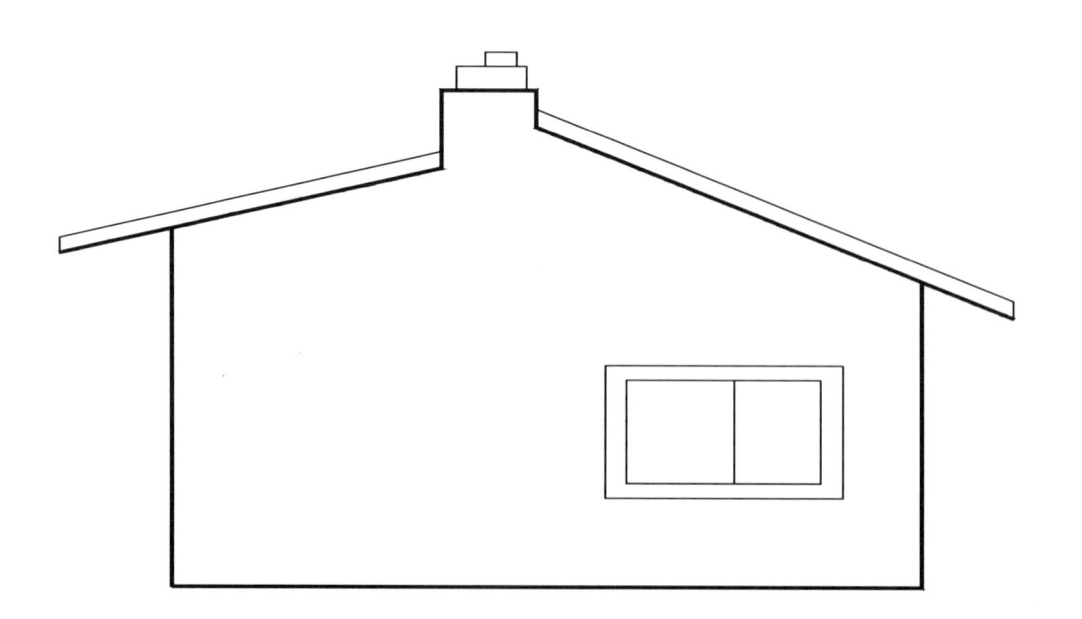

Assignment 4

Drawing instructions

Align the plan view with the side elevation, using the GRID and SNAP.

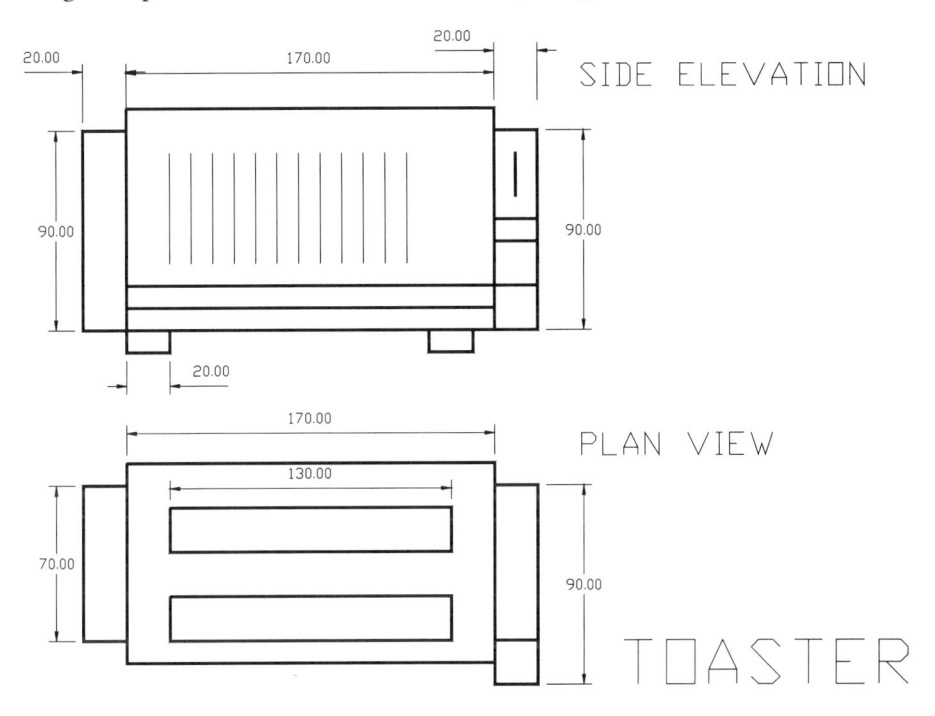

Target drawing

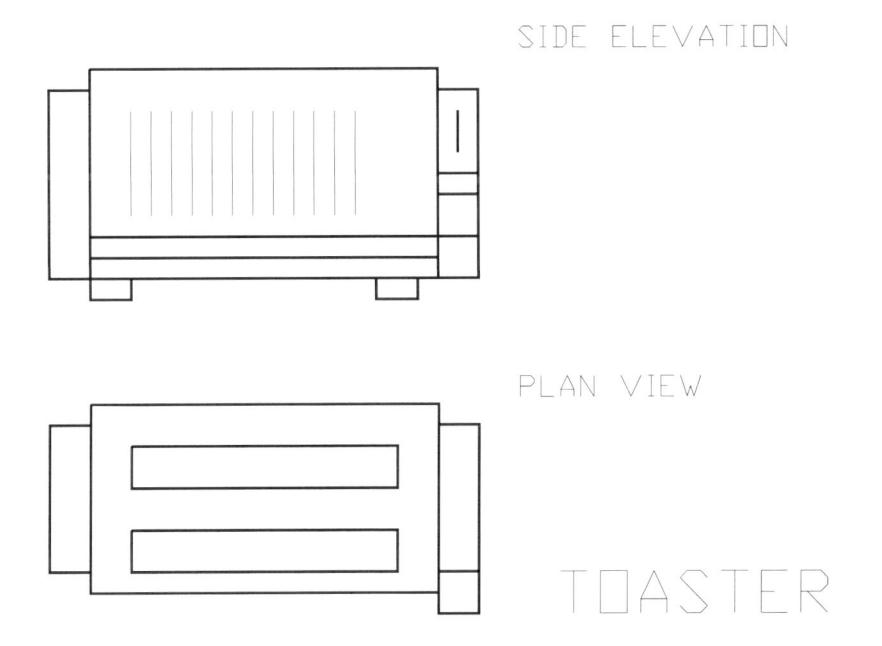

Assignment 5

Drawing instructions

    GRID = 10.
    SNAP = 10.
    Polyline width = 5.

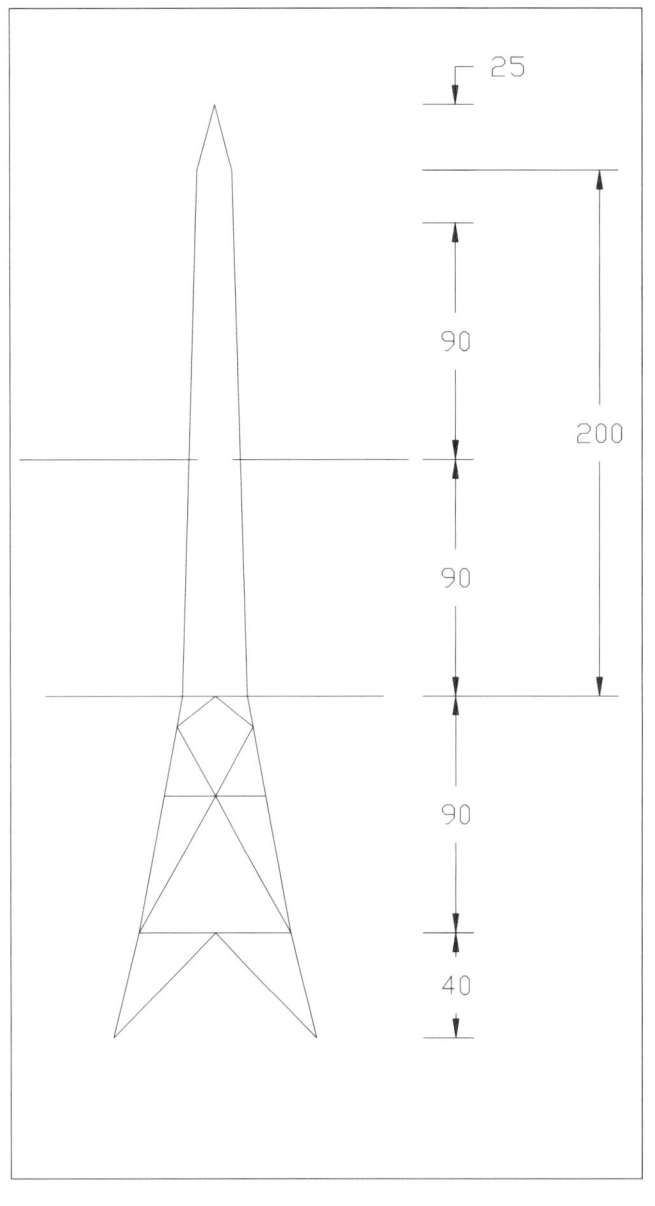

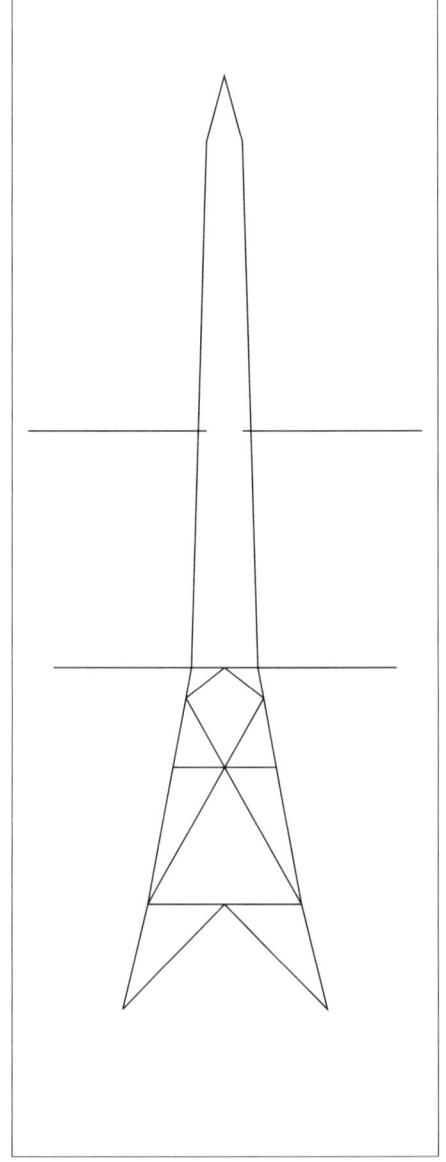

Target drawing

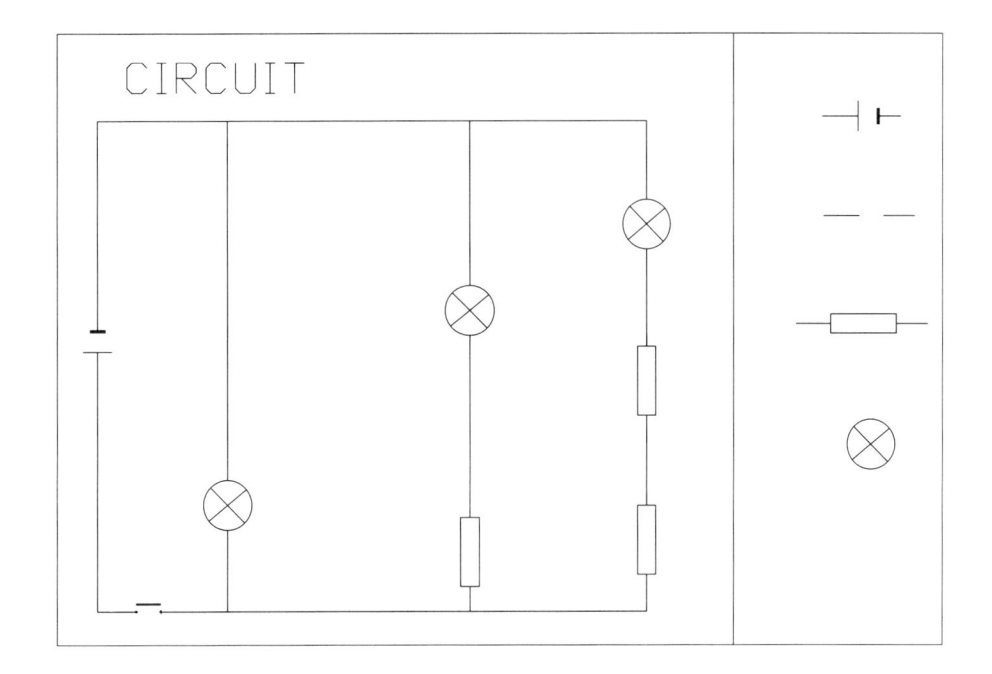

Assignment 6

chapter 6
Relative and Absolute Co-ordinates

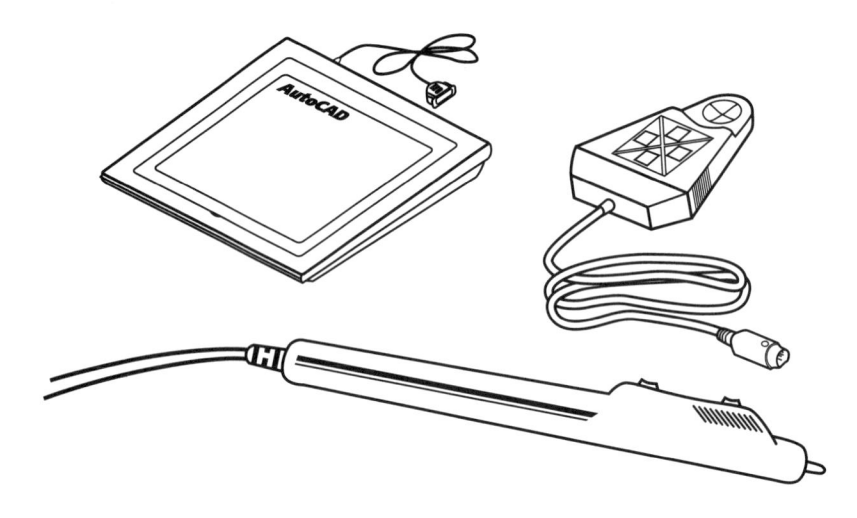

Tutorial objectives

By the end of this chapter you should be able to
- input points using relative co-ordinates
- input points using absolute co-ordinates
- use the **FILLET** command to round corners
- apply straight edges to corners—the **CHAMFER** command
- magnify a small area using the **ZOOM—WINDOW** command
- calculate the area inside a perimeter—the **AREA** command
- get help while working on AutoCAD—the **HELP** command

INTRODUCTION

Tutorial 5.1 in the last chapter concentrated on the drawing of entities using polar co-ordinates as the principal method of input. In this tutorial, relative and absolute co-ordinates will be used to construct a more complicated drawing of a 3.5 inch diskette. Two new commands are introduced: **FILLET** and **CHAMFER**. The **FILLET** command is used to put a round corner between two intersecting entities (or entities that would intersect if extended). **CHAMFER** is used to construct a straight edge between entities.

Placing detail into a drawing is done with the aid of the **ZOOM** command, using the sub-option *Window*. A window is drawn around the area you need to work on in detail. AutoCAD will then magnify that windowed area.

Tutorial 6.1

Construction of a 3.5 inch diskette

Target drawing

Drawing instructions

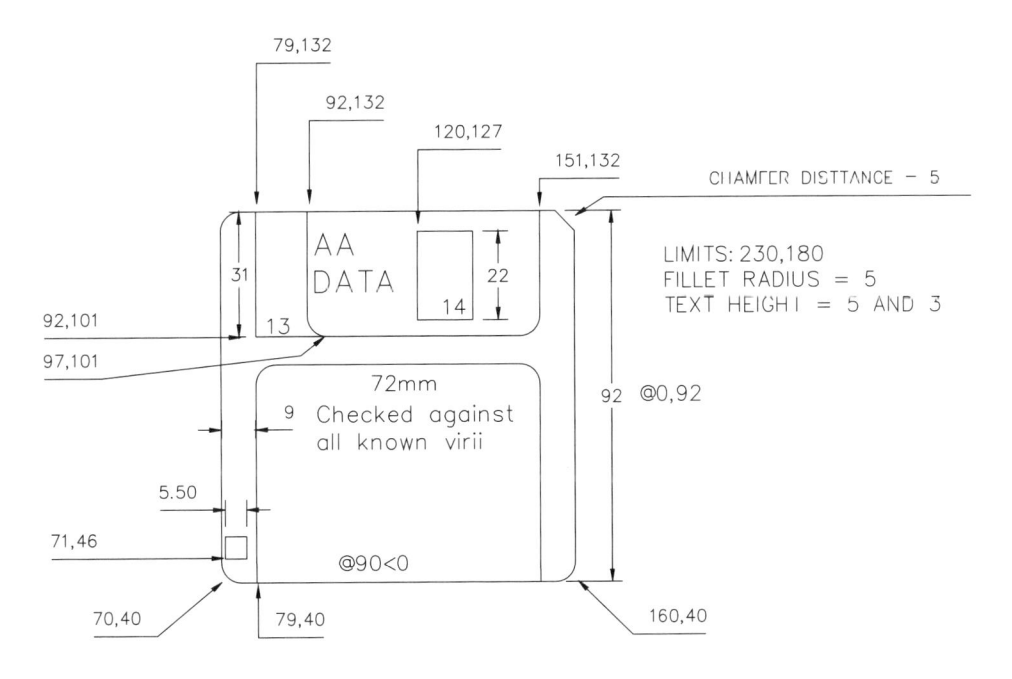

Start AutoCAD. Open a new drawing and name it **DISK35**.
Apply the following settings:
Units: decimal
Limits: 0,0 to 230,180
Snap: off
Grid: off
Don't forget to do a **ZOOM—ALL** before you proceed.

RELATIVE AND ABSOLUTE CO-ORDINATES

Drawing the disk outline

Start at the bottom left-hand corner and work around the perimeter in an anticlockwise direction.

Absolute co-ordinates

These co-ordinates are typed in using the standard Cartesian notation, using x and y distances from the origin 0,0. The x and y values must be separated by a comma.

Pick *DRAW* from the screen menu. Pick **LINE** from the menu. AutoCAD now asks *LINE From point*. Respond by typing the absolute co-ordinate **70,40**. This is the bottom left-hand corner of the disk. In response to *To point* type the absolute co-ordinates **160,40**. You have drawn the bottom edge of the disk using the absolute co-ordinates.

Relative co-ordinates

Again you position the point in the drawing editor by giving the x and y values, but relative to the last position picked rather than the origin 0,0.
The format of a relative co-ordinate input is as follows:
@0,92
Continue with the **LINE** command by responding to the prompt *To point* with **@0,92**. Then,
To point: **@–90,0**   ← The minus draws the line from right to left.
To point: **C**   ← C closes the shape.
You have now completed the outline of the disk. Press **[enter]** to terminate the command.

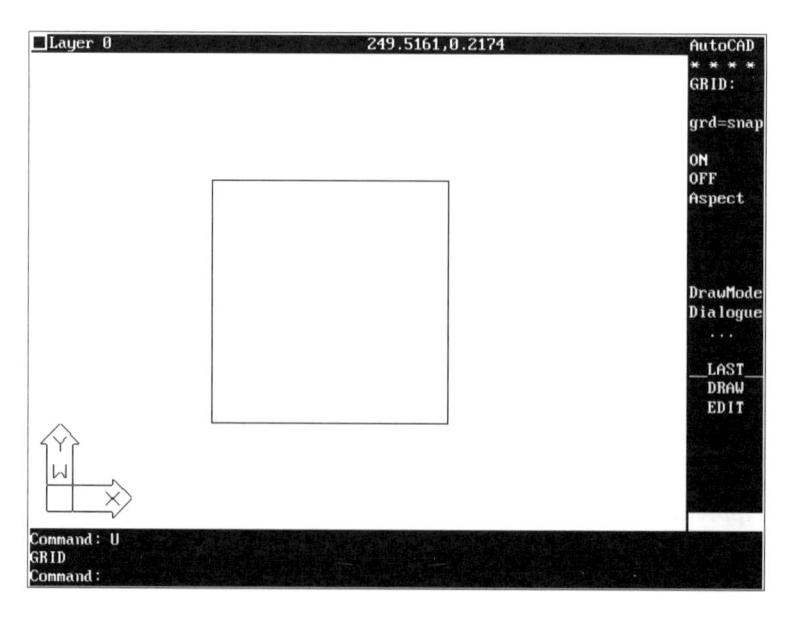

Fig. 6.1. Basic outline of the diskette.

The 'fillet' command

The corners of the disk need to be rounded. This is achieved by using the **FILLET** command. The command creates a smooth arc between lines, polylines, arcs, and circles. The radius of the arc that the **FILLET** command draws is determined by the draughtsperson.

How the command works

The intersecting entities are trimmed back the specified distance, and an arc is described to connect them. Once the command is issued, the pick box can be used to select the entities to fillet. On selection of the entities, the fillet arc is inserted without having to press **[enter]** (most other AutoCAD commands require you to press **[enter]** after selecting entities). Fig. 6.2 shows how AutoCAD inserts the fillet arc.

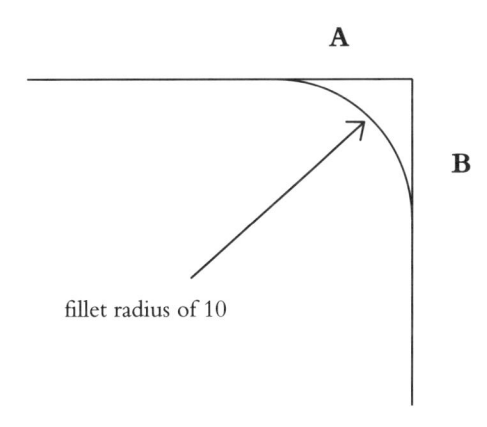

Fig. 6.2. The original straight lines A and B
and trimmed back and a fillet radius (arc) of 10 units is constructed.

To fillet the corners of the disk, type **FILLET** at the command prompt. The options available are:
Polyline/Radius/<Select two objects>:
You cannot use the polyline option here, as the disk perimeter is drawn with line entities only. The default is to *'Select'* two objects to fillet. However, before you do this you will need to set the fillet radius.
Type **R** to input the radius, and press **[enter]**. AutoCAD responds with:
Enter fillet radius<0.000>:   ← The default here is 0.000; your
                                      default value may be different.
Respond by typing **5** and pressing **[enter]**. At this stage you are returned to the command prompt, even though you have not had the opportunity to apply the fillet radius of 5 to the disk. You must call up the fillet command again by pressing **[enter]** or **[space]**.
Command: **FILLET**
Polyline/Radius/<Select two objects>:
As you have just set the radius to 5, you can proceed and select the two sides of the disk you want the fillet to connect (see fig. 6.3).

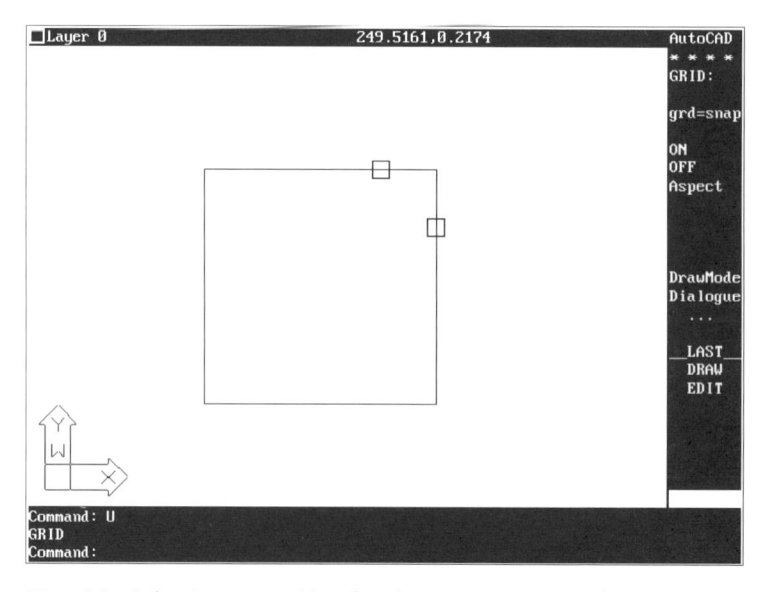

Fig. 6.3. Selecting two sides for the construction of a fillet arc.

Call up the command again and proceed to fillet the other three corners. After this major editing session it is advisable to **QSAVE** the drawing.

The 'zoom' command

The **ZOOM** command allows you to magnify parts of the drawing and then to continue editing and drawing. In this tutorial, zoom will be selected from the drop-down menu *Display*. When the *'Zoom window'* option is selected, AutoCAD will ask you to select the *First* and *Other* corners of a window or box. The part of the drawing in this window will be magnified to fill the screen. The size of the window you select is determined by how much you move the cross-hairs after you pick *First corner*.

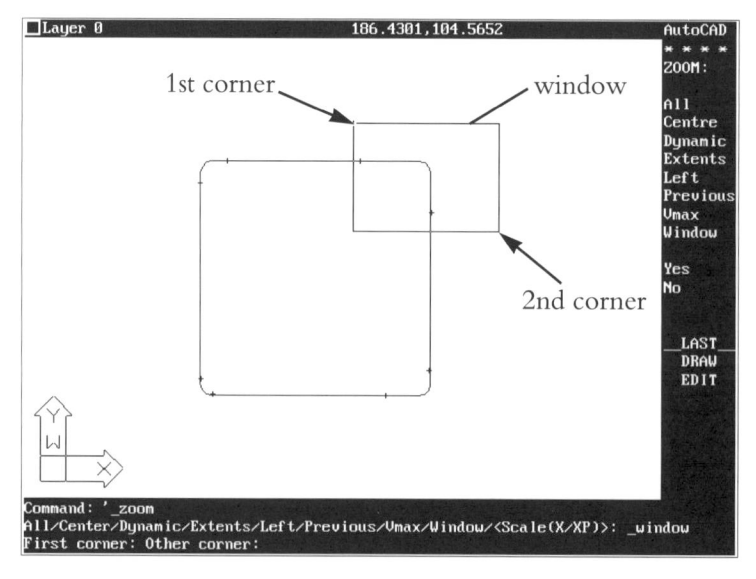

Fig. 6.4. How to select the size of the window.

Try this now. Highlight *Display* on the drop-down menu. Select the *Zoom window* option. In response to *First corner* select a point near 140,140 (check the co-ordinates reading on the status line). In response to *Other corner* pick a point near the co-ordinates 180,112. Your screen should now show a detail of the top right-hand corner of the disk.

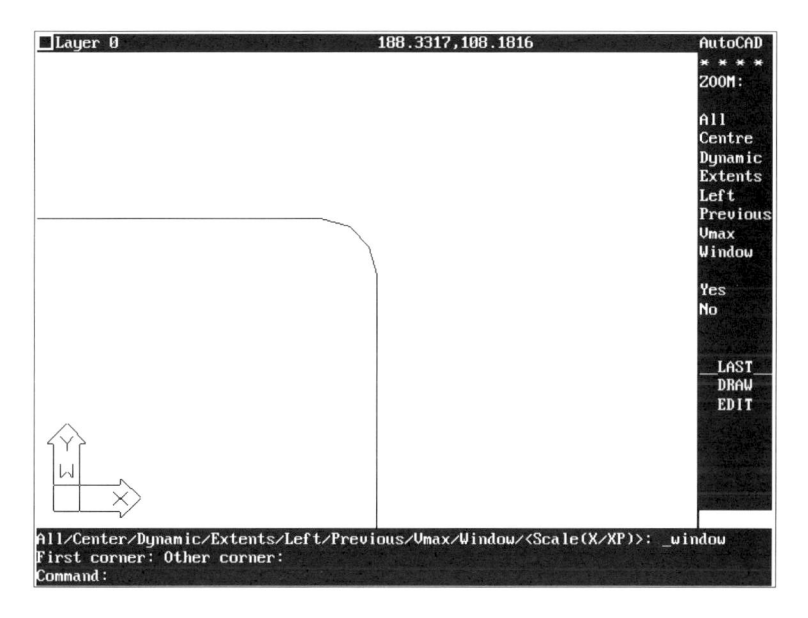

Fig. 6.5. The result of the 'zoom—windows' option.

The 'chamfer' command

If you examine the top right-hand corner of a 3.5 inch diskette you can see that it is not rounded but instead has a small straight edge. This straight edge can be put in using the **CHAMFER** command.

Before the chamfer can be applied it is necessary to remove the fillet by using the 'erase' command. To do this:

Command: **ERASE**

Select objects: ← The cross-hairs will have changed to a small pick box

Move the pick box in over the fillet arc and select it by clicking the *Pick* button. The arc will be highlighted. Press **[enter]** to terminate the command, and the arc will be erased. The **CHAMFER** command will now be used to insert a line at the corner.

How the command works

The **CHAMFER** command is similar in function to the **FILLET** command. It has the effect of trimming back the two lines a specified distance (the chamfer distance) and then joining the two trimmed lines with a straight line. You can input a chamfer distance first and then apply the chamfer to the selected entities.

Type **CHAMFER** at the command prompt. The command sequence is:
Command: **CHAMFER**
Polyline/DISTANCE/<Select first line>: **D**
Enter first chamfer distance<0>: **5**
Enter second chamfer distance<5.000>: **[enter]**

The chamfer distances have been set. To apply them to the two lines near the corner press **[enter]** or **[space]** again to call up the command.
Command:
CHAMFER Polyline/Distance/<Select first line> ← Pick one of the lines—it becomes highlighted

Select second line: ← Pick the second line—the chamfer is constructed

The result is shown in fig. 6.6.

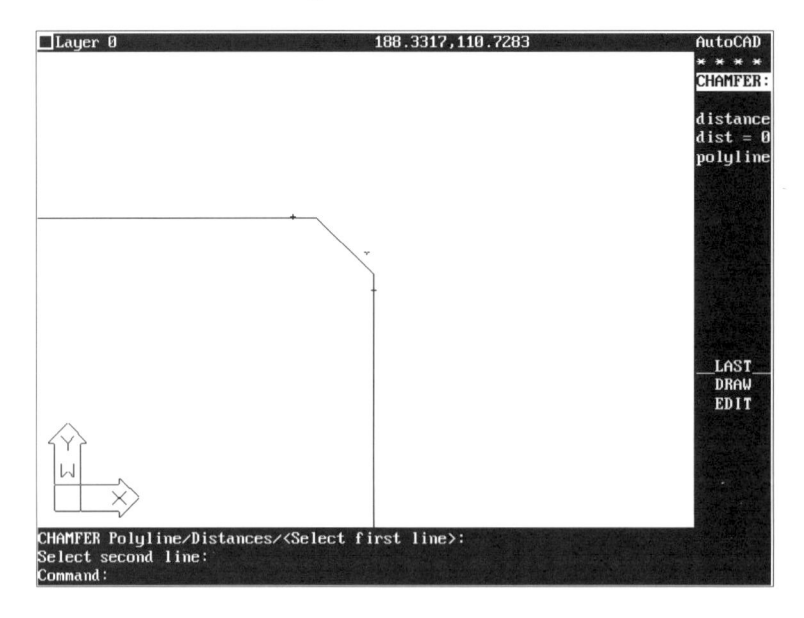

Fig. 6.6. The chamfer.

ZOOM—ALL before you proceed (or use the zoom option *previous* to zoom to the previous view).

Drawing the disk label

The label outline is represented by a line that starts 9 mm in from the edge of the disk at co-ordinates 79,40. It is 54 mm in height and 72 mm wide. The finishing point is at 151,40. The top two corners are filleted; the fillet radius is 5.

Try drawing the label now. Here is an outline of the procedure.
Command: **LINE**
From point: **79,40**
To point: **@54<90**
To point: **@72<0**

To point: **151,40**
Press **[enter]** to terminate the command.
Now fillet the top corners of the label.
Command: **FILLET**
Polyline/Radius/<Select first object>:   ← As the last fillet radius was 5 you can proceed to select the two lines you wish to fillet.

Type **REDRAW** to refresh the screen. The disk should now look like fig. 6.7.

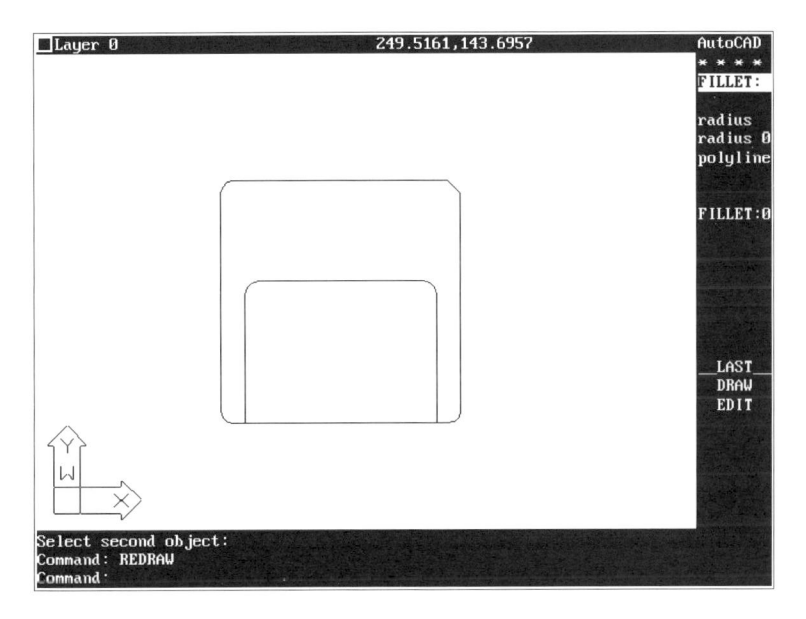

Fig. 6.7. The filleted label.

Drawing the read/write window

To draw the outline starting at the co-ordinates 92,132 in an anticlockwise direction, execute the following:
Command: **LINE**
From point: **92,132**
To point: **@31<270**
To point: **151,101**
To point: **@31<90**
To point: **[enter]**   ← To finish the command
Now fillet the bottom two corners of the read/write cover:
Command: **FILLET**
Polyline/Radius/<Select first object>:   ← As the last fillet radius was 5, you can proceed to select the two lines you wish to fillet.

The small window in the read/write cover can now be put in place using a line.
Command: **LINE**
From point: **120,127**

To point: **@22<270**
To point: **@14<0**
To point: **@22<90**
To point: **C**
Lastly, to finish the depression that the cover is in:
Command: **LINE**
From point: **79,132**
To point: **@31<270**
To point: **97,101**
Press **[enter]** to terminate the command.
Press **[enter]** to call up the **LINE** command again. The small write-protect hole requires the following input:
Command: **LINE**
From point: **71,46**
To point: **@5.5<0**
To point: **@5.5<90**
To point: **@5.5<180**
To point: **C**
'Redraw' to remove the blips (see fig. 6.8).

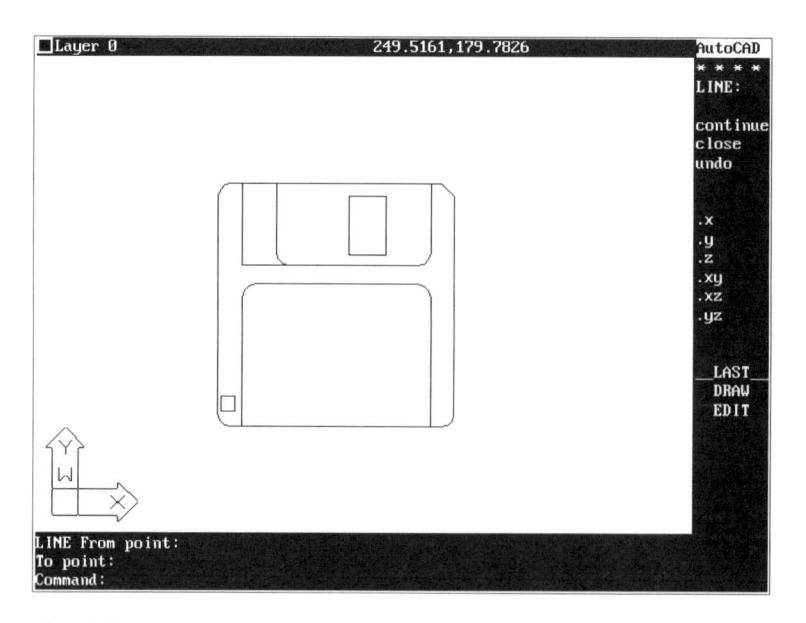

Fig. 6.8.

Use the 'text' command to place the text on the disk. The position of the text is not critical (see the target drawing at the beginning of this section).
Type **END** to save the drawing and exit AutoCAD.

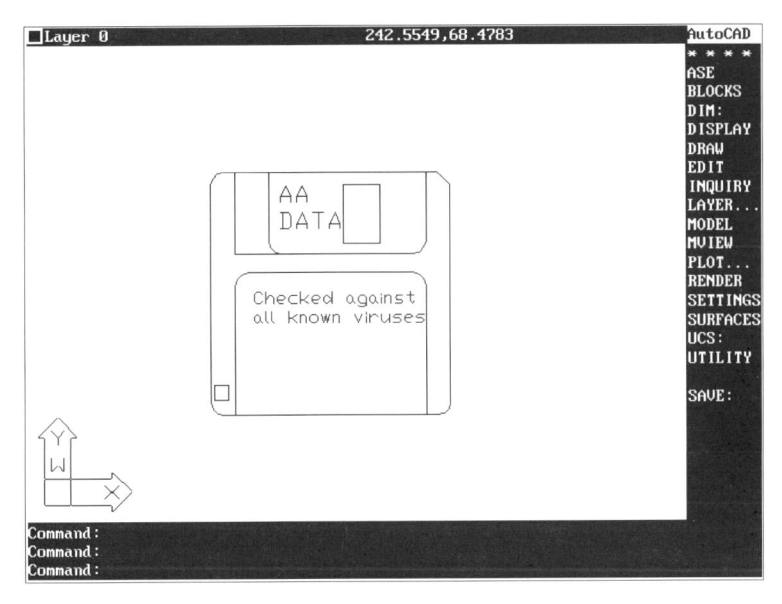

Fig. 6.9. The completed drawing.

Additional information

More on 'fillet'

In the drawing in this tutorial the **FILLET** command was applied to two lines that intersected. The command may be applied to almost any two lines, whether they intersect or not (provided they are not parallel). The **FILLET** command can also be applied to circles, arcs, and polylines, and many combinations of each, for example a line and a circle, two circles, a polyline and an arc, and so on.

The fillet arc can be removed by typing **U** for undo, or by setting the radius back to 0 and selecting the required entities. Two lines that do not intersect can be forced to meet at a point if a fillet radius of 0 is applied to them.
The fillet arc radius can be set by picking two points on the screen. The distance between the points is taken by AutoCAD to be the required radius.

More on 'chamfer'

The **CHAMFER** command can be applied to any two lines whether they meet or not (provided they are not parallel). You are asked to input two chamfer distances. The chamfer distance is the distance from the point of intersection (imagined or real) back to where the lines are cut. A straight line is then used to join the two ends. The distances can be input by picking with the pointing device on the screen. The distance between the two selected points is the chamfer distance.

If you input two different chamfer distances, be careful about which line you select first. The first selected line has the first chamfer distance applied to it, the second selected line has the second chamfer distance applied.

If two lines do not meet, then a chamfer distance of 0 will cause them to intersect.

The 'area' command

This command calculates the area of regions enclosed by a perimeter or picked using the pointing device. The command will also give you the length of the perimeter of the enclosing boundary.

The command is found on the drop-down menu under *Assist* and then *Inquiry*. The available options are:

<*First point*>/*Entity*/*Add*/*Subtract:*

First point is the default option. On selecting a point, AutoCAD will continue asking *Next point*. When you have marked out the required perimeter press **[enter]**. AutoCAD will display an area and perimeter calculation.

Selection of the *Entity* option will invoke the response *Select circle or polyline*. On selection, the area and perimeter length are displayed.

The *Add* option allows you to add several areas without leaving the *Area* command.

The following command sequence calculates the total area of four circles. Note that *Add* was selected first and then the *Entity* option was applied.

Command: **AREA**
<*First point*>/*Entity*/*Add*/*Subtract:* **E**
<*First point*>/*Entity*/*Subtract:* E
(ADD mode) Select circle or polyline:
Area = 785.40, Circumference = 99.35
Total area = 785.40
(ADD mode) Select circle or polyline:
Area = 785.40, Circumference = 99.35
Total area = 1570.80
(ADD mode) Select circle or polyline:
Area = 2827.43, Circumference = 188.50
Total area = 4398.23
(ADD mode) Select circle or polyline:
Area = 785.40, Circumference = 99.35
Total area = 5183.63
(ADD mode) Select circle or polyline:
<*First point*>/*Entity*/*Subtract:*
The *Subtract* option works in a similar way.

The 'help' command

The **HELP** command will provide help on the use of any of the AutoCAD commands. To call up the *Help* dialogue box type **HELP** at the command prompt. Enter the command you need help with in the edit box, and press **[enter]**. Clicking on *OK* will return you to the drawing editor.

SUMMARY

This tutorial involved the used of editing commands almost exclusively. A considerable amount of drawing was carried out using the 'line' command, but the necessary editing introduced the **FILLET** and **CHAMFER** commands. **ZOOM** was used as a drawing aid to help you work on detail. The drawing was executed in an efficient manner. This type of drawing efficiency should be at the forefront of your mind when you approach a new drawing. The more commands you are familiar with in AutoCAD the more efficient the drawing process will be.

Information was input using relative and absolute co-ordinates. Inputting data in this way gave you accurate and easy control over the placement of points.

ASSIGNMENTS

Assignment 1

The **FILLET** and **CHAMFER** commands can be used extensively in this assignment. The square, screwdriver and chisel require the use of polylines.

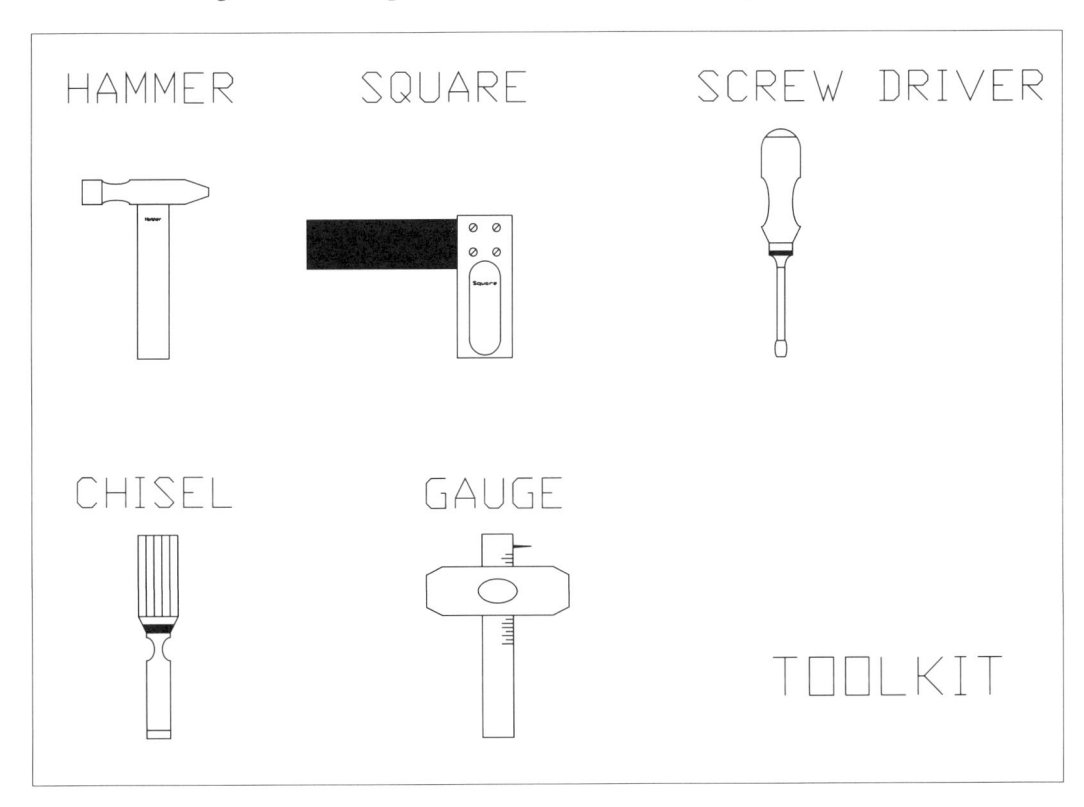

Assignment 2

Target drawing

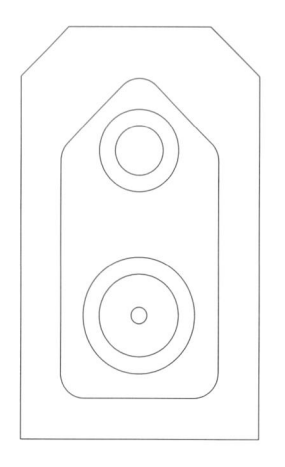

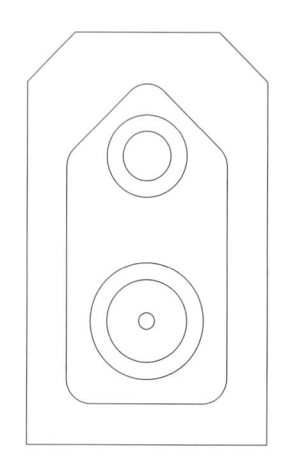

TWO WAY STEREO SPEAKERS

Drawing instructions

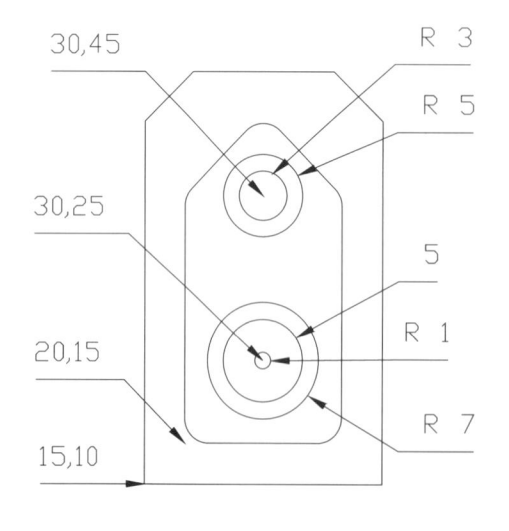

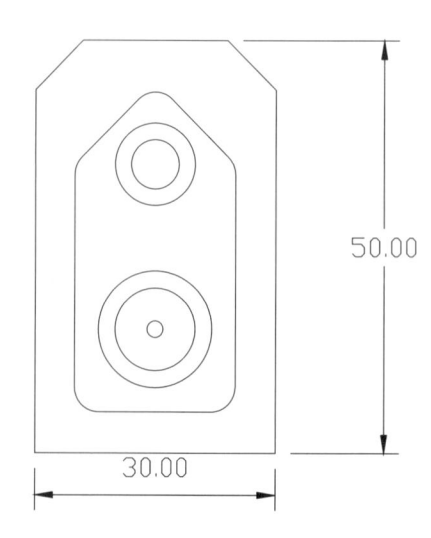

TWO WAY STEREO SPEAKERS

CHAMFER DISTANCE=6
FILLET RADIUS = 3

30,45
R 3
R 5
30,25
5
R 1
20,15
R 7
15,10

50.00
30.00

Assignment 3

Target drawing

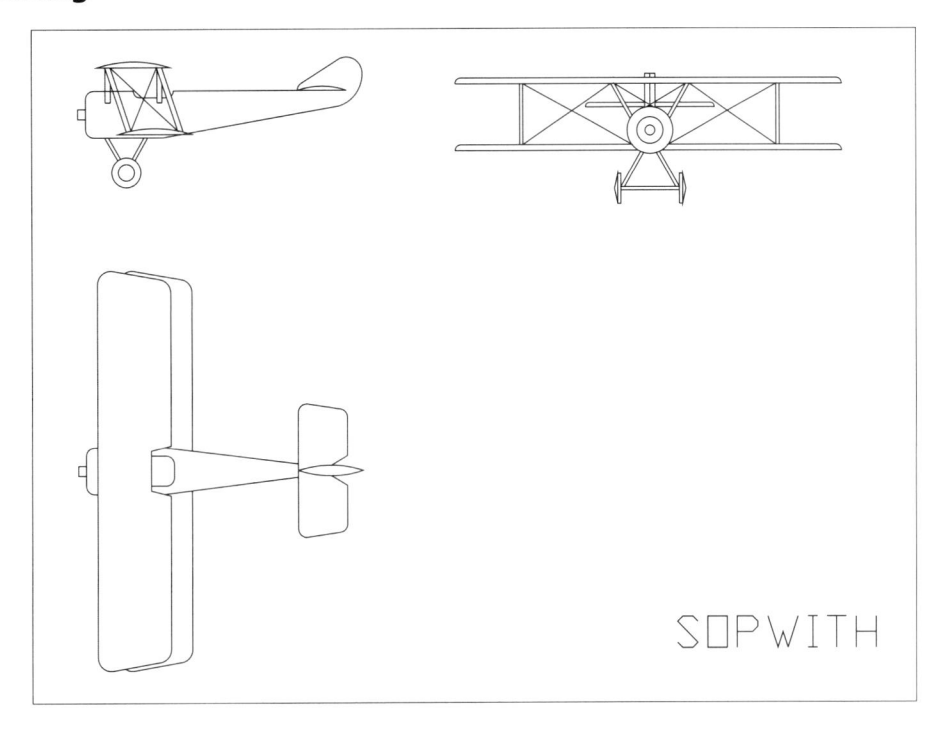

Drawing instructions

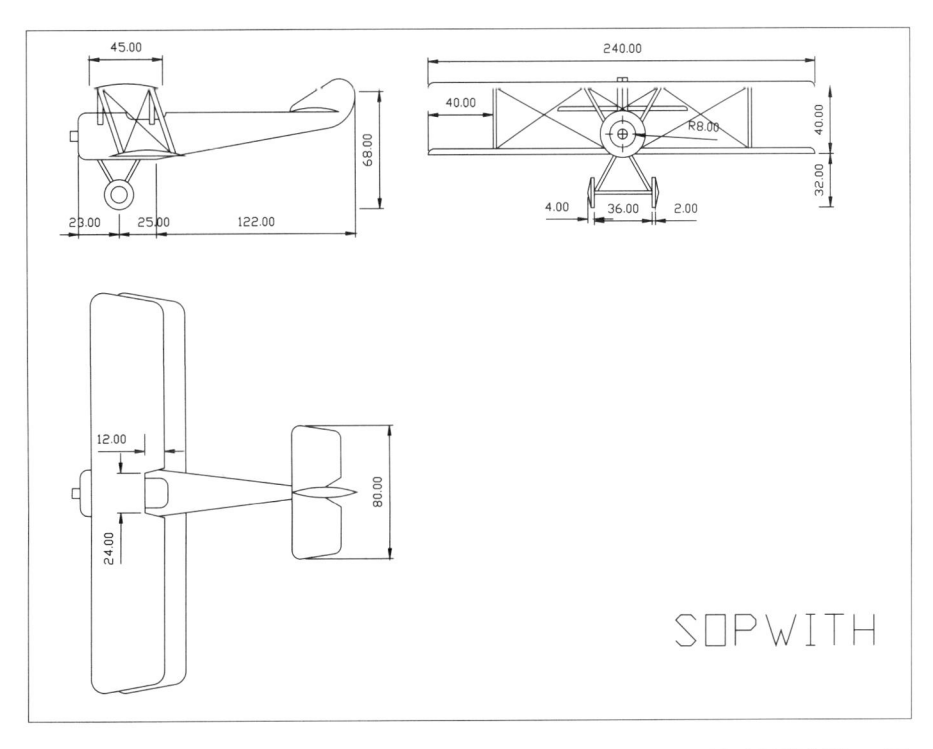

RELATIVE AND ABSOLUTE CO-ORDINATES

Assignment 4

Target drawing

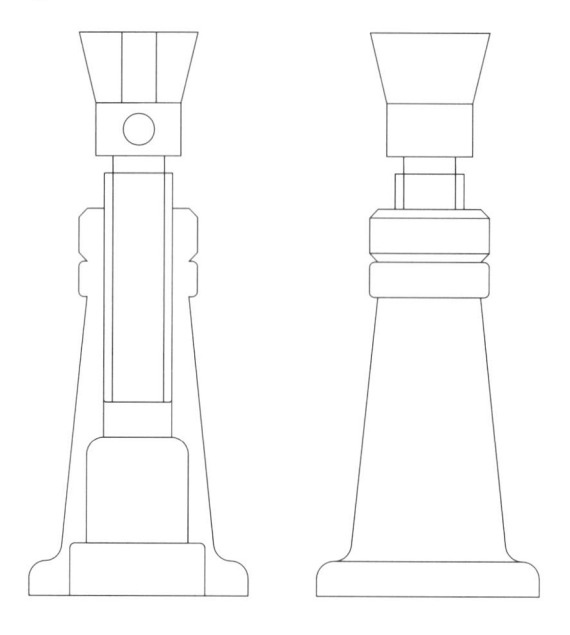

OUTLINE OF
A JACK

Drawing instructions

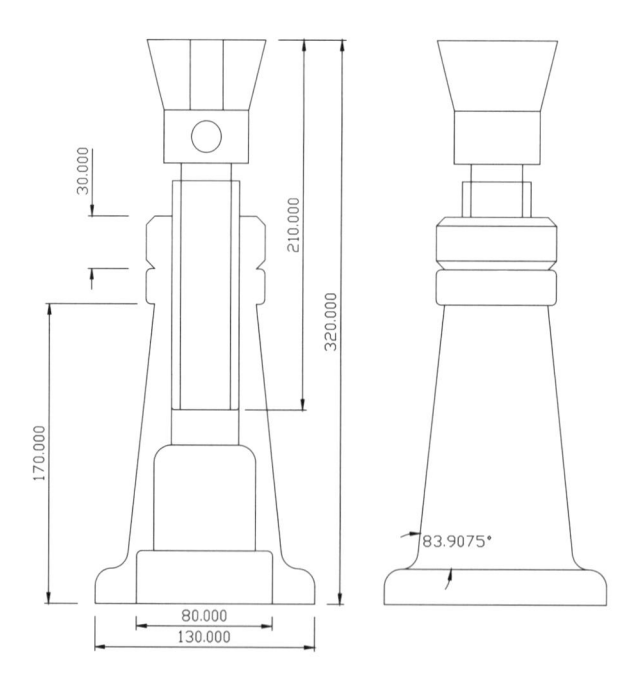

OUTLINE OF
A JACK

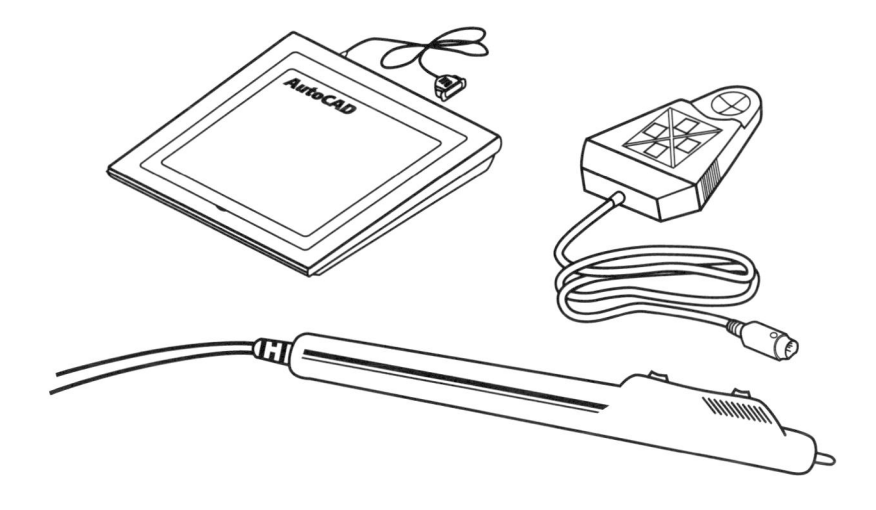

chapter 7
Speeding Up the Drawing Process

Tutorial objectives

By the end of this chapter you should be able to
- use the *Drawing aids* dialogue box
- duplicate entities using the OFFSET command
- snap onto different parts of entities using the object snap modes
- use the VIEWRES command to help in detailed work or to speed up drawing display
- duplicate entities using the COPY command
- produce multiple copies of entities in rows or circles using the ARRAY command
- select entities by pulling a window around them
- distinguish between the REGEN and REDRAW commands
- decide whether to use the REGENAUTO command or not
- use the TRACE command to draw a line with specified width
- issue a second command while in the middle of another

Tutorial 7.1

Target drawing

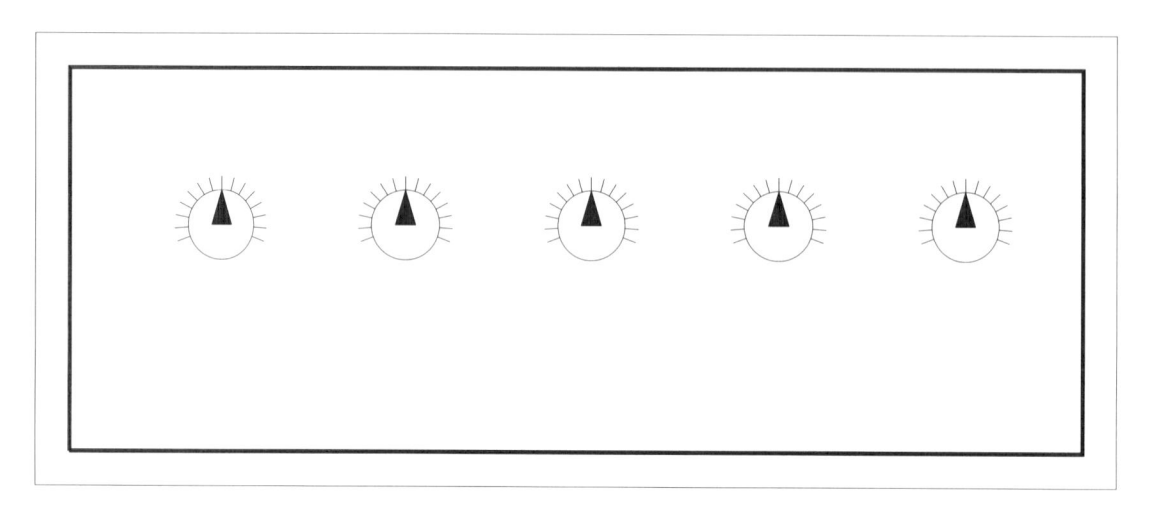

Drawing instructions

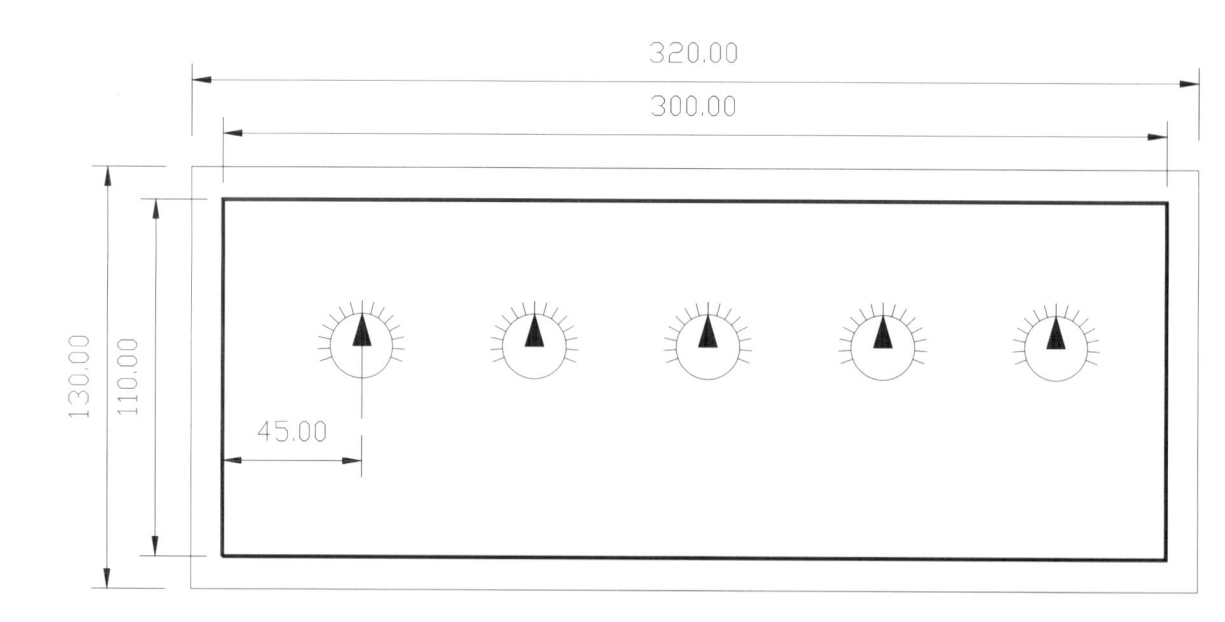

INTRODUCTION

Tutorial 7.1 introduces three commands that speed up the drawing process considerably: **OFFSET**, **COPY**, and **ARRAY**. To use these commands efficiently you must plan the drawing procedure carefully. For example, four of the knobs on the amplifier in the target drawing are identical in structure. One of the knobs, with all the required detail, should be drawn first, and this can then be copied to the other positions.

The **OFFSET** command is frequently used to form construction guides. The entities offset can then be erased when they have served their function.

Start a **NEW** drawing, called AMP. Set the following values:

UNITS = decimal
LIMITS = **420,297**

Call up the *Drawing Aids* dialogue box by selecting *Settings* from the drop-down menu and clicking on *Drawing Aids...* Select the items shown in fig. 7.1. Settings are made by clicking with the pointer in the appropriate box. An item is selected if there is an X in the box.

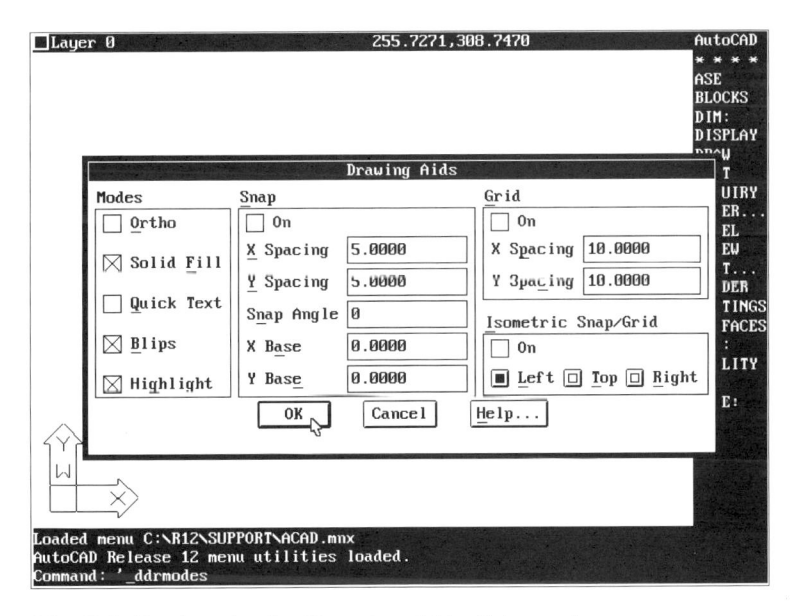

Fig. 7.1. Settings in the Drawing Aids dialogue box.

Note: The **GRID** and **SNAP** are set to OFF.

SPEEDING UP THE DRAWING PROCESS 81

Drawing the outline

Draw an outline using the **LINE** command. Start at the bottom left corner using 50,30 as the starting co-ordinates. The polar co-ordinates are as follows (working anti-clockwise): **@320<0**, **@130<90**, **@320<180**, **@130<270**.

The polyline command **PLINE** will be used to draw a bevelled rim inside the outline, and later a polyline will also be used to design a simple logo to identify the product.

PLINE can be found on the drop-down menus under *Draw* and then *Polyline >*. Two-dimensional and three-dimensional options are offered: the 2D option is the only one you require at the moment. On the screen menu you must pick *DRAW,* then *next,* and finally **PLINE**. To call the command from the command prompt type **PLINE** and press **[enter]**.

Using a polyline, start the outline at the bottom left corner at co-ordinates 60,40. The base of the bevelled rim is 300 mm wide and 110 mm high. Use the *w* option to set the width of the polyline to 1 unit. The command sequence is:

Command: **PLINE**
From point: **60,40**
Arc/Close/Halfwidth/Length/Undo/Width/<Endpoint of line>: **W**
Starting width: <0.0000> **1**
Ending line width: <1.0000> ← Press **[enter]** to accept this default value
Arc/Close/Halfwidth/Length/Undo/Width/<Endpoint of line>: **@300<0**
Arc/Close/Halfwidth/Length/Undo/Width/<Endpoint of line>: **@110<90**
Arc/Close/Halfwidth/Length/Undo/Width/<Endpoint of line>: **@300<180**
Arc/Close/Halfwidth/Length/Undo/Width/<Endpoint of line>: **@110<270**
Arc/Close/Halfwidth/Length/Undo/Width/<Endpoint of line>: ← **[enter]**

The polyline outline should now appear as in fig. 7.2.

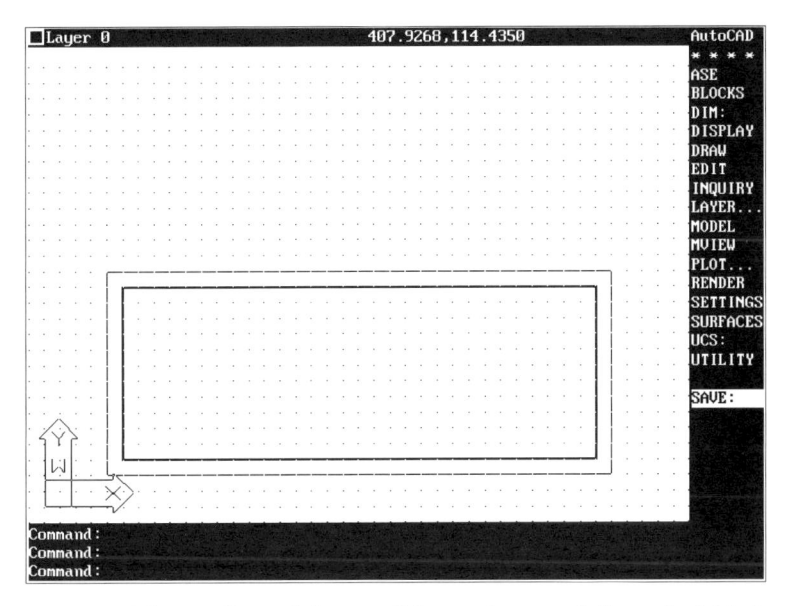

Fig. 7.2. The outline of the amplifier, using a polyline of width 1 unit.

Drawing the knobs

The knobs are constructed from circles. The centres of the circles are 55 mm down from the top of the amplifier face. The distance between each of the knobs is also 55 mm. The **OFFSET** command will be used to help locate the centres of the knobs.

The 'offset' command

OFFSET makes a copy of an entity parallel to and a specified distance from the original entity. If a polyline entity is **OFFSET**, the specified distance is measured from the central axis of the polyline. **OFFSET** is available under the drop-down menu *Construct,* under the screen menu *Edit,* and then *next.* It is called up at the command prompt by typing **OFFSET**.

How the command works

(1) You are first asked for the *Offset distance* or *Through.* The offset distance can be indicated by picking a distance with the pointing device or by typing in a value.

(2) The *Through* option allows you to specify a point that the offset entity will attempt to intersect. (Remember that because **OFFSET** makes copies of entities parallel to the original one, points can be selected through which **OFFSET** entities cannot cross.)

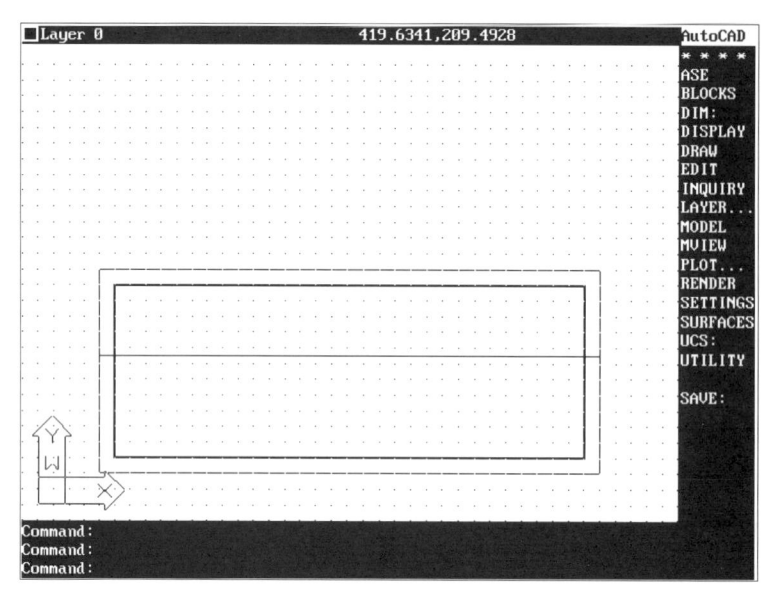

Fig. 7.3. The top line offset a distance of 55 mm.

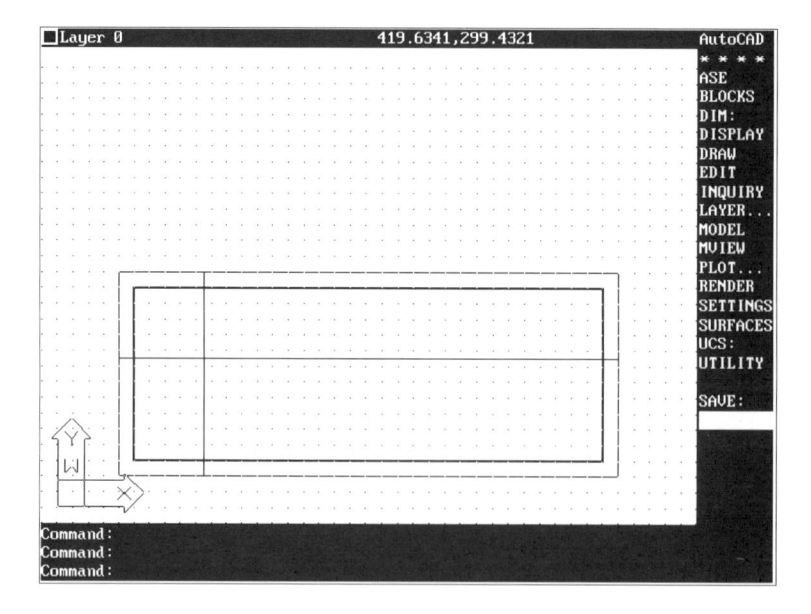

Fig. 7.4. The end line offset a distance of 55 mm.

Type **OFFSET** and press **[enter]**. The command sequence is outlined below.

Command: OFFSET	
Offset distance or Through<current>:	← Type **55** and press **[enter]**
Select objects to offset:	← Select anywhere on the top LINE
Side to offset?	← Select anywhere below the selected line (see fig. 7.3)
Select objects to offset:	← Select the vertical line on the left

Side to offset?	← Select anywhere to the right of the vertical line (see fig. 7.4)
Select objects to offset:	← Select this newly offset vertical line
Side to offset?	← Select to the right
Select objects to offset:	← Select this newly offset vertical line
Side to offset?	← Select to the right
Select objects to offset:	← Select this newly offset vertical line
Side to offset?	← Select to the right
Select objects to offset:	← Select this newly offset vertical line
Side to offset?	← Select to the right (see fig. 7.5)

Press **[enter]** to end the **OFFSET** command.

At this point save your work with **QSAVE**. The construction lines are now in place to help with locating the centre of the knobs.

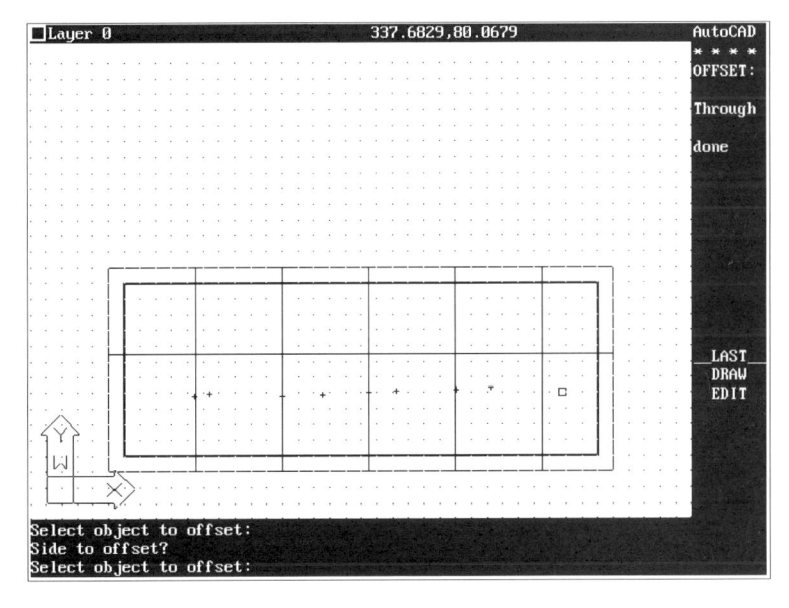

Fig. 7.5. Construction lines created with the OFFSET command.

The blips show the points selected during **OFFSET**. The pickbox is also visible in this screen image. The size of the pickbox can be changed (see the 'Additional information' section at the end of the chapter).

The 'object snap' modes

When the **SNAP** and **GRID** are switched on, entities can be locked onto the grid points on the screen. AutoCAD also allows the user to snap on to entities or objects in the drawing. You could, for example, snap on to the mid-point of a line or the centre of a circle. The object snap modes are found under the four asterisks (****) beneath the word *AutoCAD* on the screen menu or on the drop-down menu under *Assist* and then *Object snap>*.

The modes do not exist as commands in their own right but can be called up as a sub-option within any command that requires you to pick a point on a previously drawn entity.

Try selecting the object modes now by picking the four asterisks on the screen menu. Return to the root menu by picking the word *AutoCAD* at the top of the screen. The object snap modes are available at all times during your work.

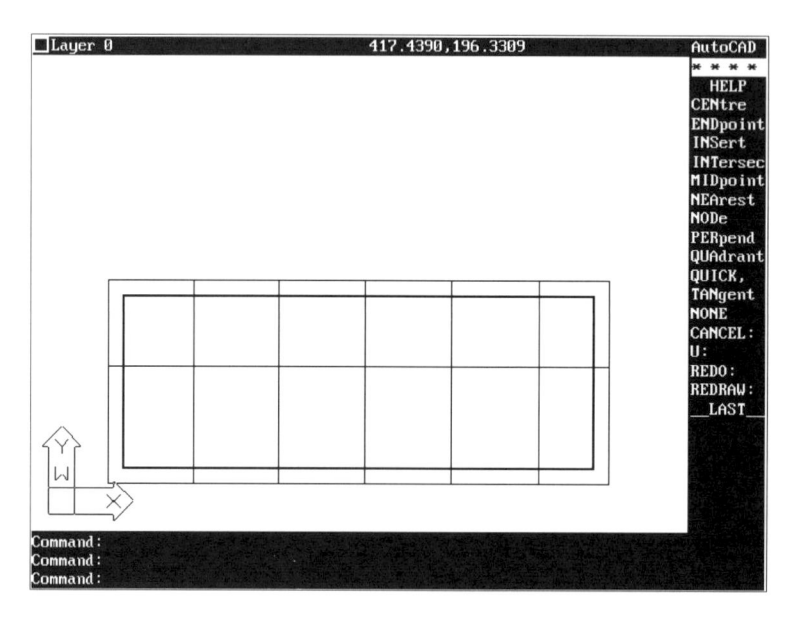

Fig. 7.6. The construction lines in place.

The leftmost knob will now be positioned over the intersection of two of the offset lines using the **CIRCLE** entity and the object snap mode **INTersec**.

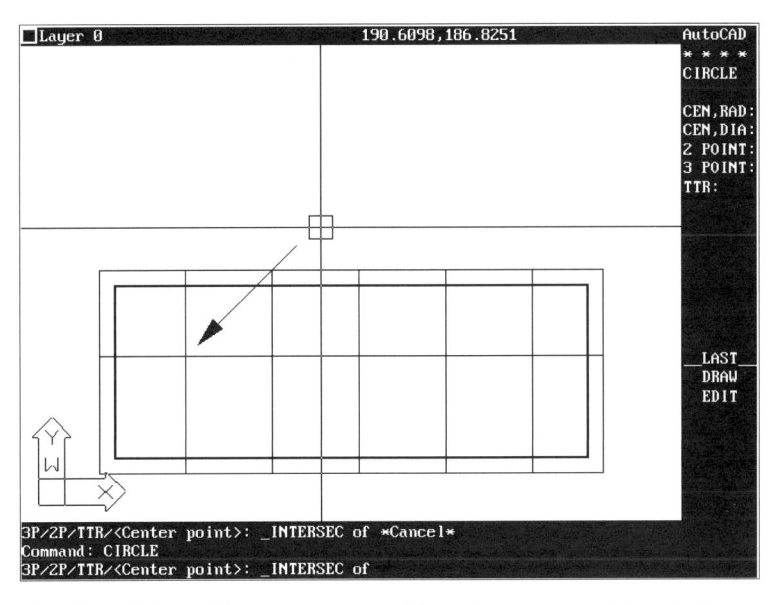

Fig. 7.7. Using object snap to position the centre of the circle.

Execute the **CIRCLE** command from the command prompt as follows.

Command: **CIRCLE**

3P/2P/TTR/<Centre point>: ← Select INTersec from the object snap mode or type **INT**; note how the cross-hairs have changed to a target box.

AutoCAD responds with
_INTERSEC of ← Move the target box in over the intersection illustrated in fig. 7.7 and press the pick button.

Diameter/<Radius>: **10** ← Enter the radius value of 10 units and then **[enter]**.

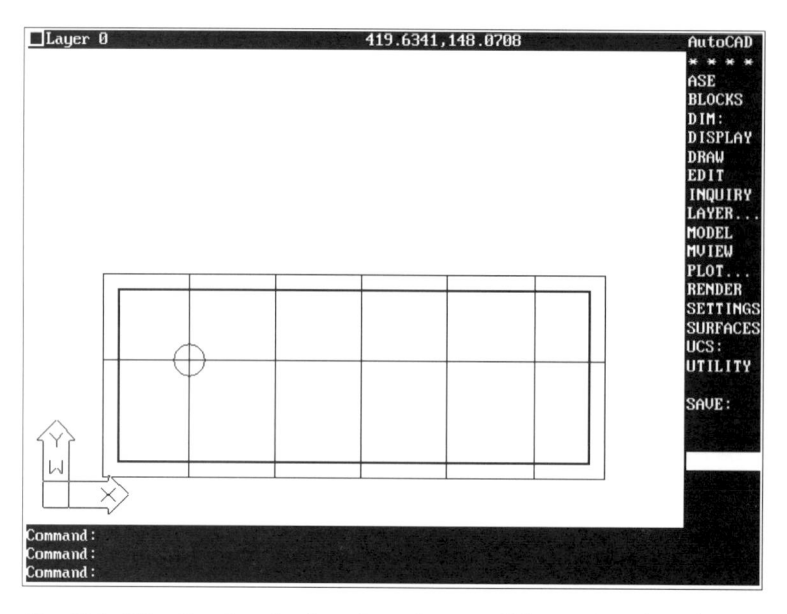

Fig. 7.8. The first knob placed on the amplifier, using the object snap mode intersection.

Placing the details on the knob

The 'viewres' command

The **VIEWRES** command controls the display resolution of arcs, lines, and circles. The illustrated explanation of the command here may not work on your version of AutoCAD because of a previous setting of the **VIEWRES** variable on your computer.

ZOOM in on the knob using the **ZOOM—Window** option to produce an image similar to that in fig. 7.9 opposite.

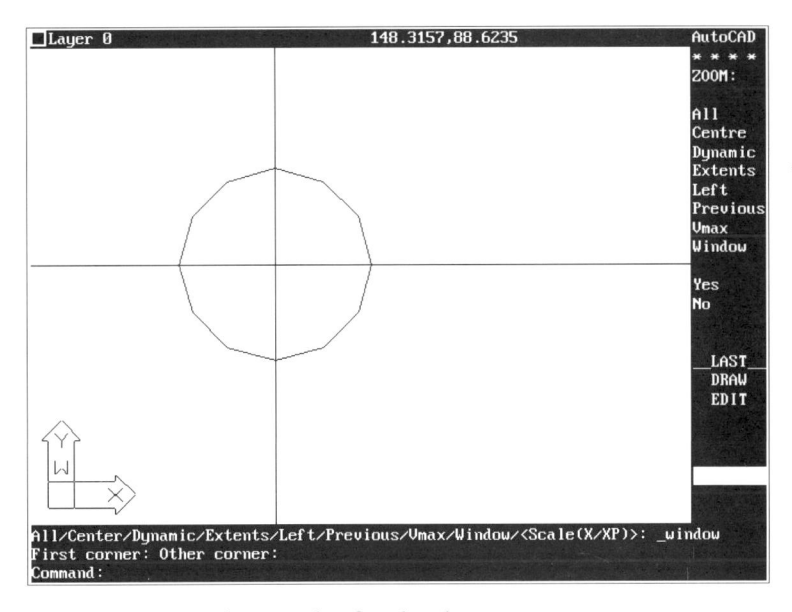

Fig. 7.9. Zoomed in on the first knob.

The circle here looks at though it is composed of several straight lines, instead of having a smooth perimeter. AutoCAD draws circles at this resolution for speed; the circles will plot with a smooth perimeter regardless of how they appear on the screen.

How the command works

Type **VIEWRES** at the command prompt or select *DISPLAY* from the screen menu and then **VIEWRES** from the submenu (it is not available from the drop-down menus).

AutoCAD responds with *Do you want fast zooms?<Y>:* If you answer NO to this, all subsequent ZOOMs (also PANs and restored VIEWs) will bring about a regeneration. Regenerations can be very slow on complex drawings.

Press **[enter]** to accept the default YES. AutoCAD now responds, *Enter circle zoom percent (1–20000<100>:*.

Values between 1 and 20000 can be entered. Type in **500** and press **[enter]**. The drawing will be automatically regenerated and the circles will take on a smooth appearance.

ERASE the vertical construction line running through the centre of the circle before proceeding.

The 'array' command

The **ARRAY** command allows you to copy an entity or group of entities several times to produce a circular or rectangular arrangement of the entities. The command is found on the screen and tablet menus under **EDIT**. The command is executed from the command prompt by entering **ARRAY**.

How the command works
The command gives a great deal of control to the user in how the array is constructed. Consequently AutoCAD will ask a lot of questions before it proceeds to draw.

Select the entities you want to array in the usual way. AutoCAD will then ask whether the array is to be **POLAR** (in a circle) or **RECTANGULAR** (in rows and columns).

If polar array is selected, AutoCAD will need to know the centre point around which the entities will be copied, then the number of items you want in the array (this number includes the entity you are copying). Finally you must tell it through how many degrees it must be spread, and whether or not the objects making up the array are to keep their present orientation on the screen or if they should also rotate as they are copied. AutoCAD will then draw the array in an anti-clockwise direction.

If rectangular is selected, AutoCAD will need to know the number of columns and rows that are required for the construction of the array. Once these values are entered, you must supply the distance between each row and column. AutoCAD will then construct the array.

Drawing the graduations around the knob

Draw a line from 105,115 to 105,119. Then execute the array command as follows:

Command: **ARRAY**
Select objects: ← Select the vertical line just drawn
1 found
Select objects: ← Press **[enter]**
Rectangular or Polar array (R/P) <R>: **P**   ← Type **P** and press **[enter]**
Centre point of array: **CEN**   ← This is the object snap mode
CENTRE of   ← Pick the circle by clicking over
                                                  the perimeter
Number of items: **8**   ← Eight copies of the entity
Angle to fill (+=ccw, −=cw) <360>: **110**   ← 110 degrees anti-clockwise
Rotate objects as they are copied? <Y>   ← Accept yes by pressing **[enter]**

The array is constructed in an anti-clockwise direction, because the angle entered was positive. See fig. 7.10.

Exercise
Produce the array clockwise. See fig. 7.11.

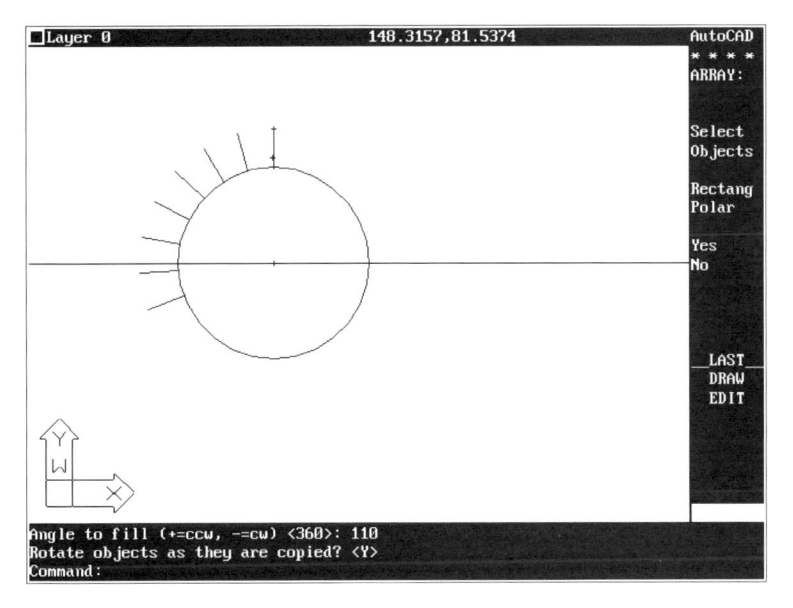

Fig. 7.10. The graduated markings on one side of the knob.

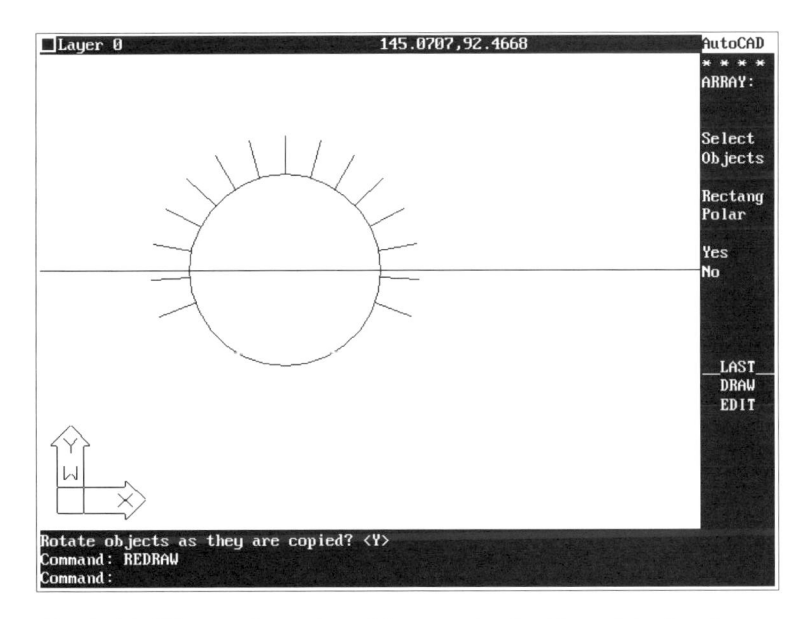

Fig. 7.11. The graduated markings on both sides of the knob.

Placing a marking on the knob

The *width* option of the polyline command asks for a *Starting width* and an *Ending line width*. With two different values, a polyline can be made to taper from one end to the other. A pointer on the knob can be constructed using this idea.

SPEEDING UP THE DRAWING PROCESS

To draw a tapering polyline (a width of 6 units at one end and 0 units at the other) from the centre of the circle to the end of the vertical graduated line, execute the following.

Command: **PLINE**
From point: **CEN**   ← The object snap mode can be typed
of   ← Pick the perimeter of the circle
Current line-width is 1.0000
Arc/Close/Halfwidth/Length/Undo/Width/<Endpoint of line>: **W**
Starting width <1.0000>: **6**
Ending width <6.0000>: **0**
Arc/Close/Halfwidth/Length/Undo/Width/<Endpoint of line>: **END**
                                   Object snap mode ↲
of   ← Click towards the end of the line nearest the circle
Arc/Close/Halfwidth/Length/Undo/Width/<Endpoint of line>: ← **[enter]**
Command:
ZOOM—All to see your work.

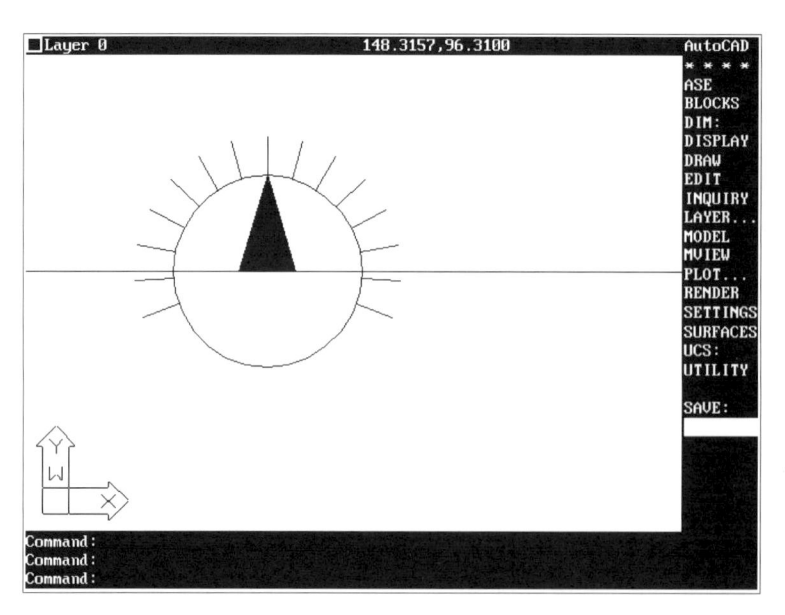

Fig. 7.12.

The 'copy' command

COPY will copy an entity or group of entities to a new position on the drawing editor. The original entity or group of entities will remain unaffected by the procedure. The command allows you to make single or multiple copies.

How the command works

AutoCAD will ask you to select the entities you want to copy. Once selection has been made you must specify the *Base point or displacement*. Think of the base point as a handle by which you pick up the entity or group of entities. This point can be specified using the object snap or by just clicking on or outside the object or objects.

Lastly, AutoCAD will ask for the *Second point of displacement*. (The displacement option is discussed in the 'Additional information' section at the end of this chapter.)

The **COPY** command will be used to copy one of the knobs to the other four intersections of the offset lines. The *Base point or displacement* will be the centre of the circle that constitutes the knob (use the object snap **CEN**), and the *Second point of displacement* will be the intersection of the offset lines. The complete knob can be selected using the window sub-option. Pull a window around the knob in a similar fashion to a zoom window.

Here is the command sequence:

Command: **COPY**
Select objects: **W**   ← This is for the windows selection method

First corner:
Other corner:
17 found
Select objects: ← Press **[enter]**
<Base point or displacement>/Multiple: **CEN**   ← The object snap mode
of   ← Click on the perimeter of the circle

Second point of displacement: **INT**   ← The object snap mode
of   ← Click on the intersection of the lines

Continue in this way to copy the knob to all the points of intersection to produce a result similar to that in fig. 7.13. Erase the offset lines. END the drawing.

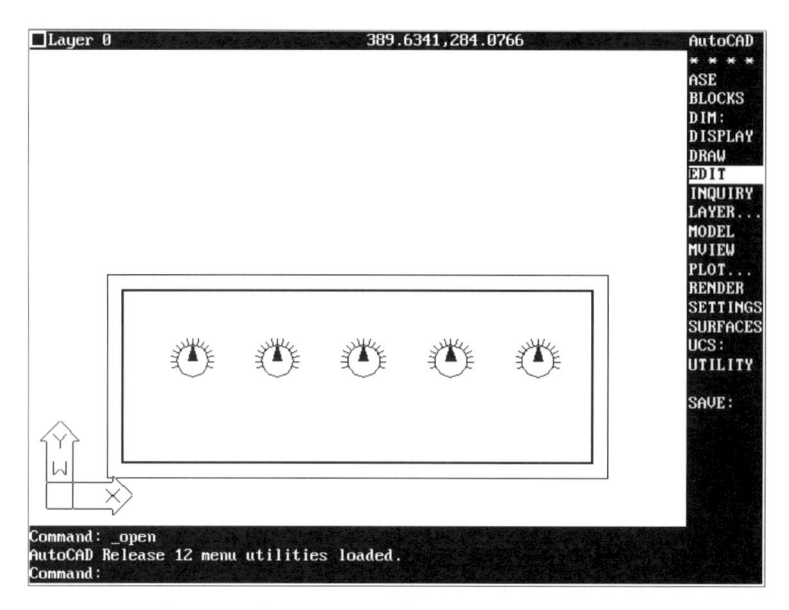

Fig. 7.13. The completed target drawing.

ADDITIONAL INFORMATION

The 'array' command

Polar arrays
In the tutorial above, the number of objects in the polar array was specified (eight in each case). If the angle between the objects in the array is more important to you than the actual number, you may respond to *Number of items* by just pressing **[enter]**. AutoCAD will then proceed to ask *Angle to fill (+=ccw, −=cw) <360>:* and *Angle between items*. Type in the angle you want, and AutoCAD will calculate the number of items for you.

When AutoCAD asks you for the *Centre point of the array* you can respond by picking any point on the screen with the pointing device.

Polar array exercise
(1) Draw a single line on the screen and make an array with an angle of 12° between each entity. The centre point of the array can be selected by picking any point on the screen with the pointing device. The command sequence is given below.

Command: **ARRAY**
Select objects: 1 found
Select objects:
Rectangular or Polar array (R/P) <R>: **P**
Centre point of array:
Number of items:
Angle to fill (+=ccw, −=cw) <360>:
Angle between items: **12**
Rotate objects as they are copied? <Y>

(2) Execute the command again, but this time answer N to the question *Rotate objects as they are copied?* <Y>. See fig. 7.14.

Rectangular arrays

The *R* option allows the generation of a rectangular array. The rectangular array is constructed using rows and columns. AutoCAD asks for the number of rows and columns and the distance between each. A positive value causes AutoCAD to generate the rows and columns upwards and to the right of the chosen entities. The row and column calculations are taken from the bottom left of the group of selected entities.

Rectangular array exercise

Draw a square near the centre of the screen. Using both positive and negative distance values, create two sets of arrays of the square. Use the windows method to select the arrays. See fig. 7.15.

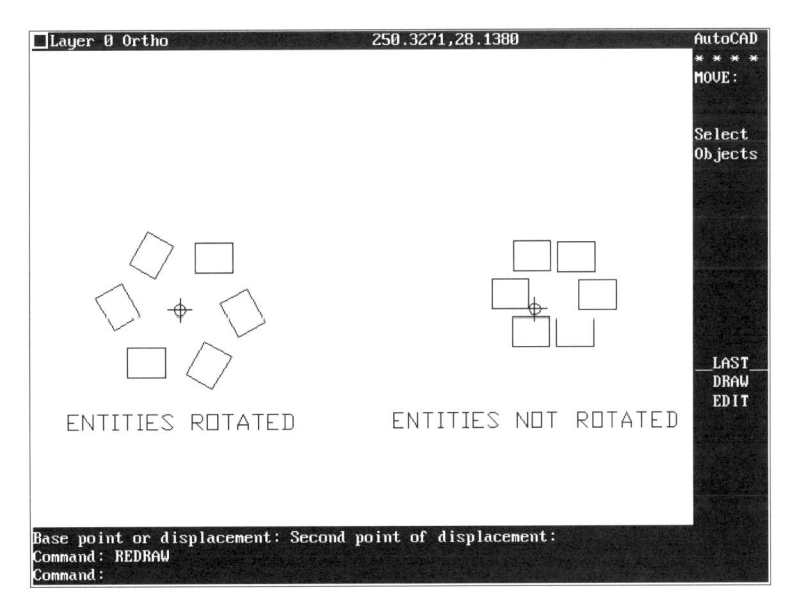

Fig. 7.14. Polar array.

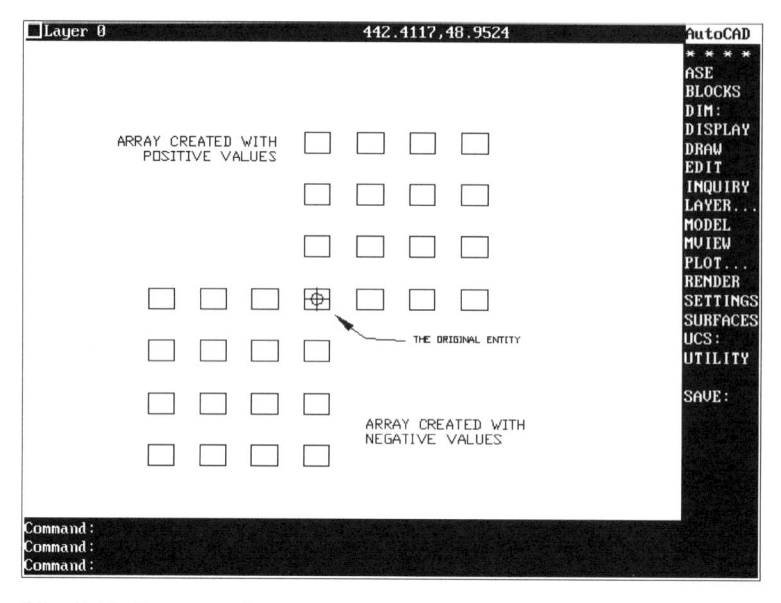

Fig. 7.15. Rectangular array.

The 'copy' command

The multiple option
COPY also allows **multiple** copies to be made of entities while executing the command once. To do this, select the option **M** from the prompt <*Base point or displacement*>/*Multiple:*. AutoCAD will then keep asking for a second point of displacement until you terminate the command by pressing **[enter]**.

Below is a sequence of commands to copy an entity six times.

Command: **COPY**
Select objects: 1 found
Select objects:
<Base point or displacement>/Multiple: **M**
Base point:
Second point of displacement: ← First copy made
Second point of displacement: ← Second copy made
Second point of displacement: ← Third copy made
Second point of displacement: ← Fourth copy made
Second point of displacement: ← Fifth copy made
Second point of displacement: ← Sixth copy made
Command:

The displacement option

In response to <*Base point or displacement*>/*Multiple:* you may type in a value in *x* and *y* co-ordinates. This value will then move the selected entities relative to the selected base point when you press **[enter]** in response to *Second point of displacement*. The command sequence below moves the selected

entity 50 units up the *x* axis and 50 units along the *y* axis.
Command: **COPY**
Select objects: 1 found
Select objects:
<Base point or displacement>/Multiple: **50,50**
Second point of displacement: ← Press **[enter]**
Command:

REDRAW, REGEN, and REGENAUTO

During the tutorials you used the **REDRAW** command. **REDRAW** refreshes the display by refreshing the pixels on the screen. It was used to remove the temporary blips that were left after picking points on the screen. Switching the grid *on* refreshes the screen in the same way as **REDRAW**. Some other AutoCAD commands (such as snap) will also force a redraw.

The **REGEN** command seems to work in a similar way to **REDRAW**. However, before it updates the screen it recalculates the position of all the entities in the drawing. This can take a considerable time (perhaps as much as thirty minutes) if the drawing is complex. While the **REGEN** is taking place you cannot proceed with drawing or editing. It is advisable to avoid REGENs if at all possible. Some of AutoCAD's commands (such as **PAN**, **ZOOM**, and **VIEW**) can force a **REGEN** under specific conditions. A **REGEN** can be stopped using **^C**.

The command **REGENAUTO** can be used to control how frequently AutoCAD will attempt to automatically regenerate a drawing after commands like **ZOOM** and **PAN** (or in fact any command that greatly modifies entities in the drawing). The format of the command is as follows:
Command: REGENAUTO
ON/OFF <On>:
OFF switches the automatic regeneration mode off. AutoCAD will ask, *About to regen—proceed?<Y>* if the setting is off and a command is trying to force a **REGEN**. *On* is the default value.

The commands **REGENALL** and **REDRAWALL** refer to a screen that contains 'viewports'. This topic is covered in chapter 10.

Transparent commands

Many of AutoCAD's commands can be executed while you are in the middle of another command. These are referred to as 'transparent commands'. To execute a command transparently you must precede it with an apostrophe ('). Once the transparent command is executed, control is returned to the original command.

The command sequence below starts with the **LINE** command. After you select the first point, the transparent command **ZOOM** is invoked. After you have used the **ZOOM—Window** option AutoCAD automatically reverts to the LINE command.

Command: **LINE**
From point:
To point: '*ZOOM*
>>Centre/Dynamic/Left/Previous/Vmax/Window/<Scale(X/XP)>: **W**
>>First corner: >>Other corner:
Resuming LINE command.
To point:

The symbol >> reminds you that a transparent command is being executed. A command will not be executed transparently if it requires a regeneration of the drawing.

The 'trace' command

TRACE is used to draw a thick line. It can be used as an alternative to **PLINE** in some situations.

The command is not available on the drop-down menus. On the screen menu it is found under *DRAW* and then *next*. This menu also displays the options **FILL ON** and **FILL OFF**. These options determine whether the **TRACE** is filled with a solid colour or not. The command sequence is:

Command: **TRACE**
Trace width <10.00>:
From point:
To point:
To point:
Command:

The trace width can be calculated by selecting two points on the screen with the pointing device. The width cannot be varied along its length.

TRACE works in a similar way to the **LINE** command: it will continue asking *To point* until the command is terminated. If a series of connecting **TRACE** line segments is drawn, the **UNDO** command will not undo the segments individually: the complete sequence of segments executed in one command sequence will be removed.

The **UNDO** command cannot be applied to **TRACE**.

Exercise

Try drawing a few trace lines, and experiment with the following options:
- Indicating the trace width using the pointing device
- Setting the FILL to ON and OFF

SUMMARY

The **OFFSET** command was used to draw construction lines to help in locating the centres of the knobs. It was also used to help design the on-off button. The object snap modes enabled you to snap on to existing entities. Various points on entities, such as the centre of circles or the mid-point or intersection of lines, could be selected with ease. The four asterisks (****) on the screen menu could be called up at any stage during the drawing process to make the modes available. The modes could also be typed in (just the capitalised letter were necessary).

The **VIEWRES** command allowed you to control the display resolution of ARCS and CIRCLES. The lower the resolution, the faster the drawing would regenerate.

The **ARRAY** command gave control over repeating entities in circular or rectangular fashion. Lastly, the **COPY** command allowed you to make multiple or single copies. Window selection of entities was introduced during the copy command.

The **REGEN** command causes a recalculation of the position of all the entities on the screen. This can take a considerable time. **REDRAW** refreshes the screen without a recalculation having to be done. It is much faster than a **REGEN**. **REGENAUTO** switches the **REGEN** mode on or off.

The **TRACE** command was used with the options to fill in the trace thickness with or without a colour.

ASSIGNMENTS

Assignment 1

Suggested procedure

Draw one side of the valve accurately and use the COPY command to move the entities to the other side.

Use the object snap mode END to join the lines.

The border should be drawn with the TRACE entity, with Fill on.

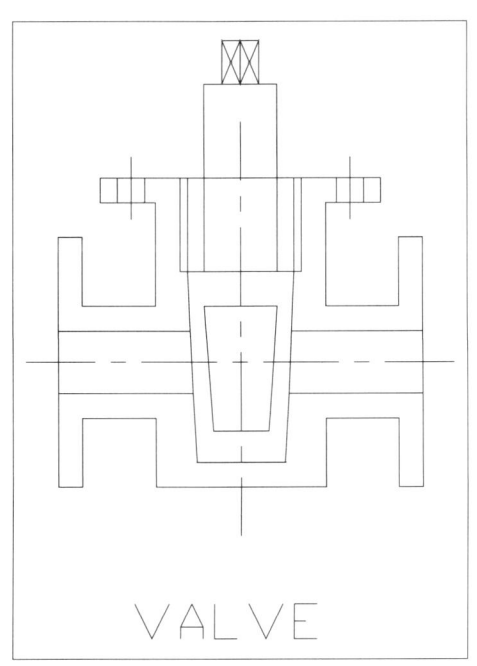

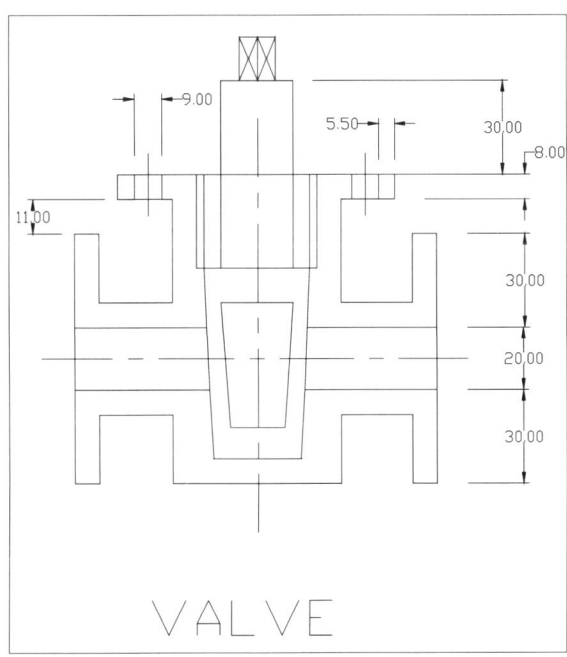

SPEEDING UP THE DRAWING PROCESS

Assignment 2

Suggested procedure
Set up suitable limits. Try to execute the drawing without a setting for GRID and SNAP. Use OFFSET to create the grid for the keys. Then draw a single key and, using object snap, lock it into position with the 'multiple' option.

Alternatively, place the keys using the ARRAY command.

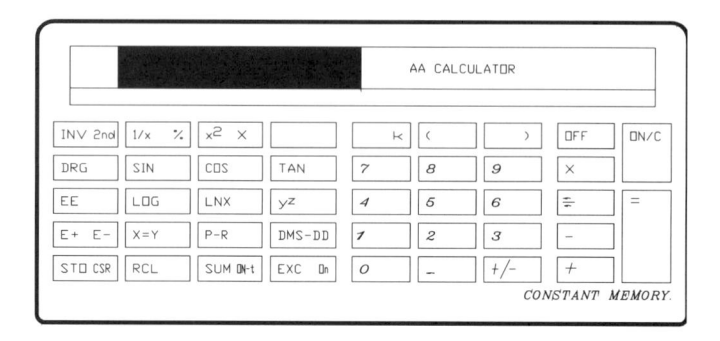

CALCULATOR DESIGN

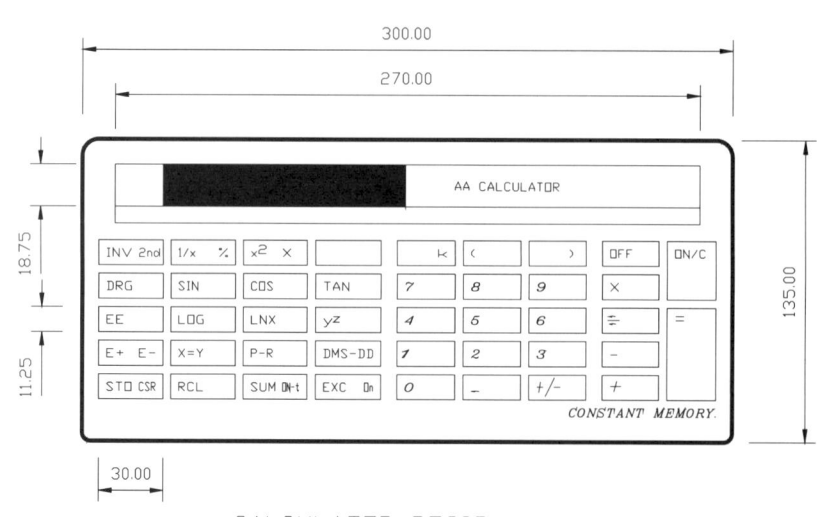

CALCULATOR DESIGN

Assignment 3

Suggested procedure
Draw the large circle first. Construct two lines from its centre, using the object snap mode CEN: one line vertically and the other horizontally (switch ORTHO on to help).

In conjunction with OFFSET, locate the centre of the other circles.

The straight edges of the perimeter of the plate are drawn using the object snap mode TAN.

BASE PLATE

BASE PLATE

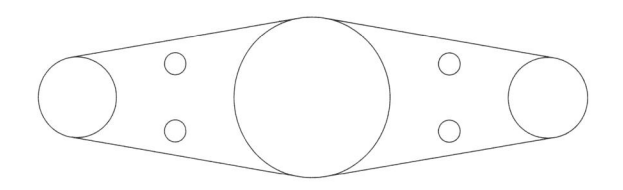

Assignment 4

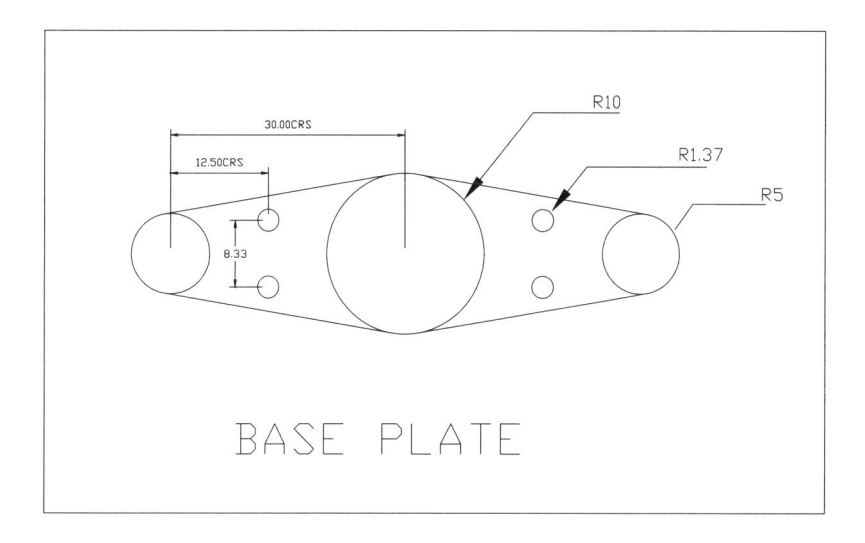

Suggested procedure

Construct inner and outer circles first. Place a single cog on each, and use the POLAR ARRAY command to draw the rest.

Target drawing

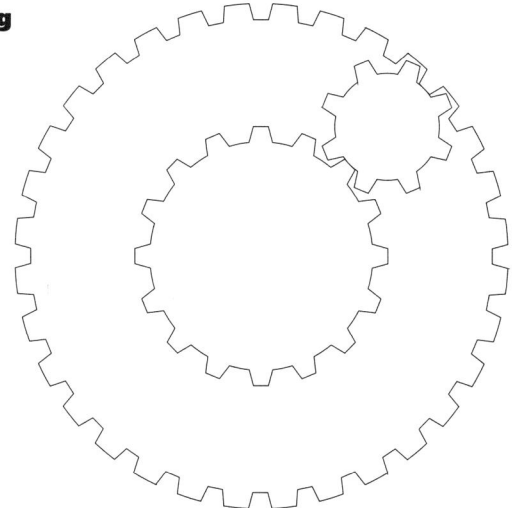

SPEEDING UP THE DRAWING PROCESS

Drawing instructions

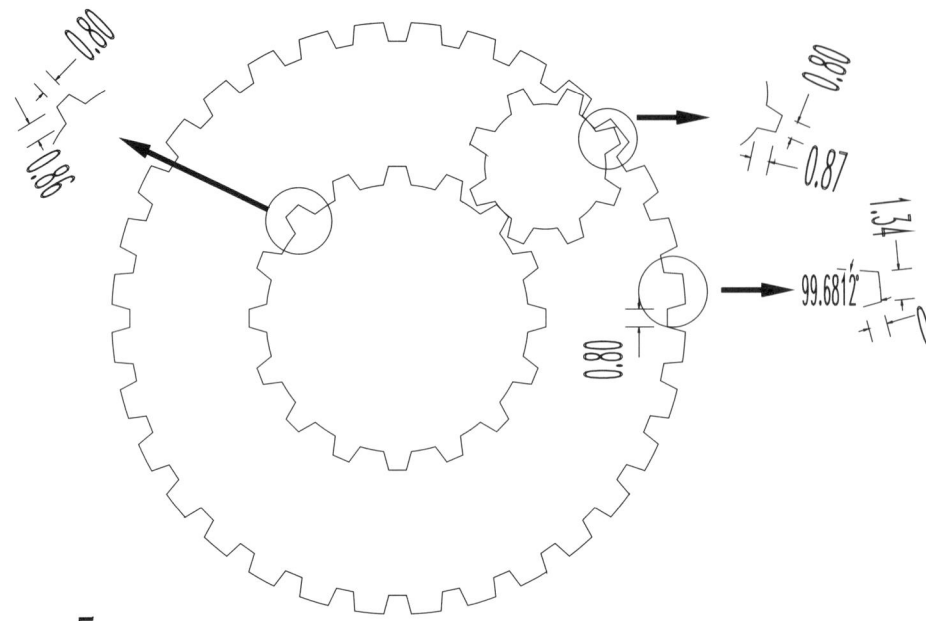

Assignment 5

Suggested procedure

The five circles with diameter 0.50 are positioned using the ARRAY command. The outer circle (diameter 3.50) can be obtained by offsetting the inner circle (diameter 3.20). The tips of the armature can be constructed from arcs or straight lines to which a fillet is applied.

The cogs are constructed from straight lines and arcs.

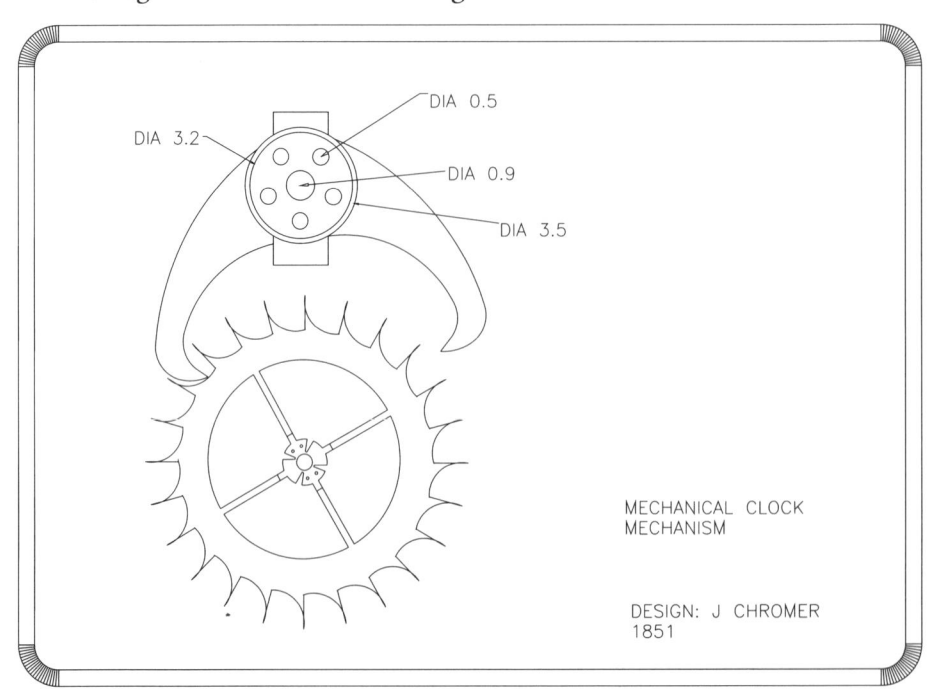

MECHANICAL CLOCK MECHANISM

DESIGN: J CHROMER
1851

chapter 8

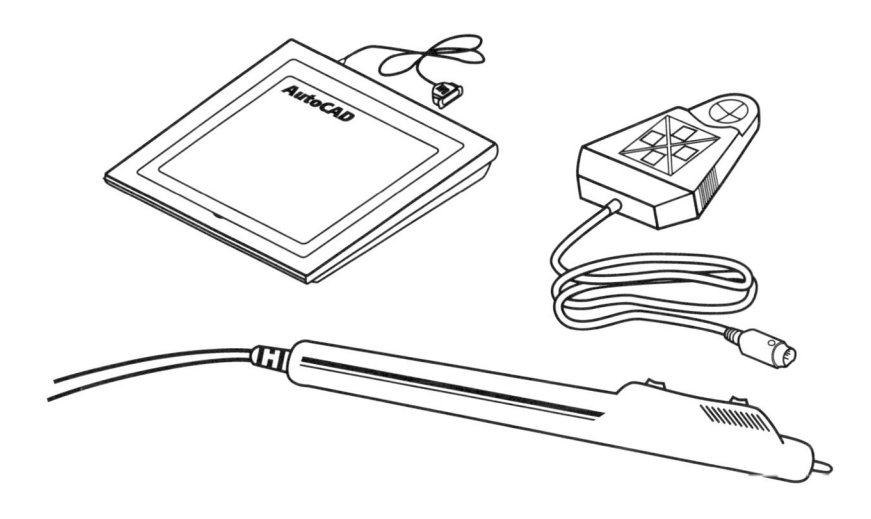

Major Drawing and Editing Commands

Tutorial objectives

By the end of this chapter you should be able to
- change the size of entities in a drawing using the SCALE command
- draw circles using the DONUT command
- justify text using the centre option of the TEXT command
- change the size of the object snap aperture box using the APERTURE command
- change the size of the select entity pickbox using the PICKBOX command
- rotate entities using the ROTATE command
- use the ZOOM options Dynamic and Extents—very useful in large complicated drawings
- move around a drawing without using the ZOOM command—the PAN command
- draw solid filled shapes using the SOLID command
- draw ellipses using the ELLIPSE command
- insert polygons (inscribed or circumscribed) using he POLYGON command
- draw arcs using some of ARC's many options
- specify whether solids should be filled in or not—the FILLMODE Variable

Tutorial 8.1

Open the drawing AMP, which you started in the last chapter.

The volume control on an amplifier is usually larger in diameter than the other knobs, for easy manipulation. The **SCALE** command can be used to scale up one of the knobs.

The 'scale' command

The SCALE command is used to increase or decrease the size of an entity or group of entities. A scale factor is given by the user; AutoCAD will then calculate the new size of the selected entities. Scaling is executed with reference to a user-specified base point, and is applied equally to both the x and y axis of the object. The selected entities can be dragged until they are the size the user requires.

How the command works

SCALE can be typed in at the command prompt. It is also found on the screen menu under *EDIT* and on the drop-down menu *Modify*. When the command is invoked you must select the entities for scaling. Selection can be made with a pickbox or by using a window.

AutoCAD will then require the user to select a base point. This is the point from which AutoCAD will do all its scaling calculations. The base point can be selected by picking a point using the pointing device, or by using the object snap modes. Lastly, AutoCAD asks *<Scale factor>/Reference:*. If a value is given as the scale factor, then values greater than 1 will increase the entity's size and less than 1 will decrease it.

To scale up the second-last knob from the right, execute the following:

Command: **SCALE**
Select objects: **W**   ← Pull a window around the knob
First corner:
Other corner:
17 found
Select objects: ← Press **[enter]**
Base point: **CEN**   ← For the centre object snap mode
of   ← Click on the perimeter of the selected circle

<Scale factor>/Reference: **2**   ← A value of 2 will double the size
Command:

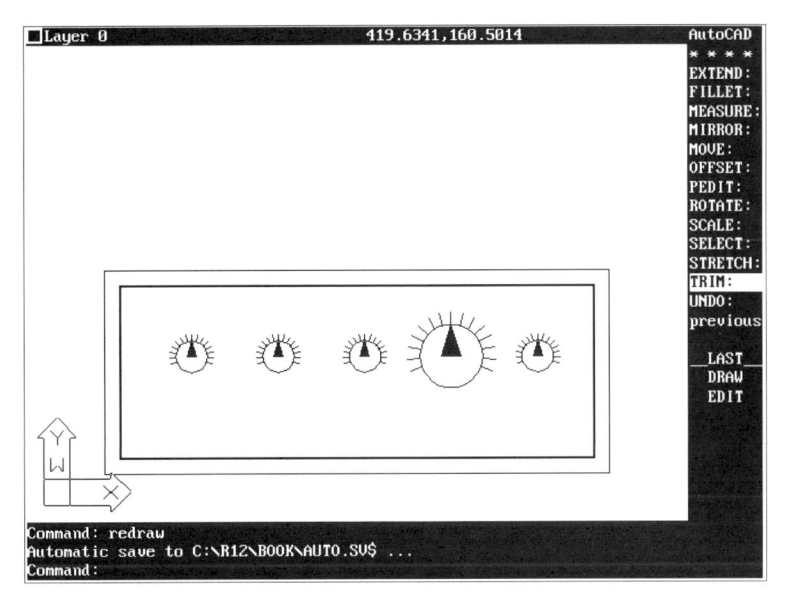

Fig. 8.1. The scaled-up knob.

Zoom—All to see the complete drawing.

The 'donut' command

To draw the on-off switch you use the DONUT command, which allows you to draw a circle with a specified thickness for the perimeter.

'Donuts' are polylines. They are found on the screen and drop-down menus under *DRAW*, and can be called up at the command prompt by typing **DONUT** or **DOUGHNUT**.

How the command works

AutoCAD looks for an inside and outside diameter. These determine the width of the polyline making up the circle. These diameters can be given as a number or by picking points on the screen. Picking points on the screen can be done with the aid of the object snap mode. The command sequence below places a doughnut at co-ordinates 105,55. This represents the power button on the amplifier.

Command: **DONUT**
Inside diameter <0.5000>: **7**
Outside diameter <1.0000>: **9**
Centre of doughnut: **105,55**
Centre of doughnut:
Command:

Positioning TEXT on the drawing

The text will be positioned below the knobs. This will give a better overall appearance to the drawing. It can be accomplished using a newly drawn construction line, which is then offset.

(1) Draw a construction line 17 units long from the centre of a small knob at an angle of 270°. OFFSET this line to the other small knobs (**OFFSET** distance is 55 units). Use this line to centre the text.

Here is the command sequence:

Command: **LINE**
From point: **CEN**
of   ← Pick the perimeter of the knob
To point: **@17<270**
To point: ← Press **[enter]**
Command: **OFFSET**
Offset distance or Through <Through>: **55**
Select object to offset: ← Click on the line just constructed
Side to offset?   ← Click to the right of the line

Repeat the process to offset the line to all the knobs.

(2) Inserting the text. The text can be 'justified' so that the centre of each word lies directly at the end of the construction line. To place the word 'BASS' under the first small knob, execute the following:

Command: **TEXT**
Justify/Style/<Start point>: **J**   ← This calls up the justify text options
Align/Fit/Centre/Middle/Right/TL/TC/TR/ML/MC/MR/BL/BC/BR: **C**
Centre point: **END**
of   ← Pick the end of the construction line
Height <current>: **3**
Rotation angle <0>:
Text: **BASS**
Command:

Insert the text 'TREBLE', 'BALANCE' and 'AUX' on the other small knobs. The larger knob is for the volume settings. To create a construction line for this, add a line 10 units long to the end of the short construction line. Then place the text at the end of this new line. The command sequence is given below.

Command: **LINE**
From point: **END**
of   ← The existing short construction line
To point: **@10<270**
To point:
Command: **TEXT**
Justify/Style/<Start point>: **J**
Align/Fit/Centre/Middle/Right/TL/TC/TR/ML/MC/MR/BL/BC/BR: **C**

Centre point: **END**
of   ← The long construction line
Height <3.0000>:
Rotation angle <0>:
Text: **VOLUME**
Command:

Making the entity selection first

In all your editing work up to this stage you proceeded by selecting a command and then selecting the entities you wanted to execute the command on. AutoCAD allows you to work in reverse order also. You can pick the entities when the command prompt line is blank and then issue the command.

Try this procedure now to **ERASE** all the construction lines. Make sure the command prompt line is blank. Move the pickbox at the centre of the cross-hairs in over the construction lines, and pick each one. Note the special way they highlight. The little boxes that mark out the selected entities are called 'grips'. Now type **ERASE** at the command prompt and press **[enter]**. The selected entities are erased. **REDRAW** would refresh the screen.

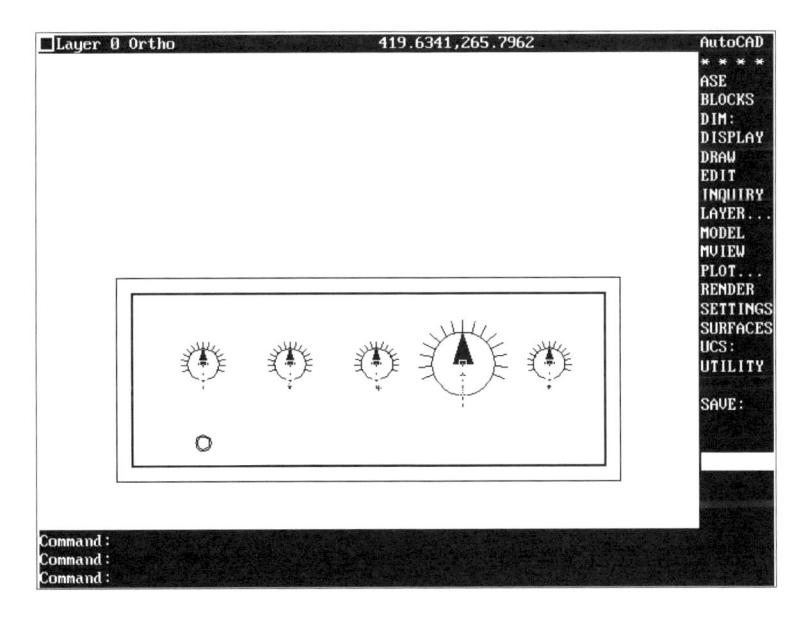

Fig. 8.2.

Adding the logo

The logo consists of two polylines, a line, and a circle. The leftmost polyline that makes up the logo has a beginning thickness of 4 and an ending thickness of 0.

Zoom in on the amplifier and execute the following:
Switch **ORTHO** on (F8 key)

Command: **PLINE**
From point: **285,55**
Current line-width is 4.0000
Arc/Close/Halfwidth/Length/Undo/Width/<Endpoint of line>: **W**
Starting width <4.0000>: **0**
Ending width <0.0000>: **4**
Arc/Close/Halfwidth/Length/Undo/Width/<Endpoint of line>: **300,55**
Arc/Close/Halfwidth/Length/Undo/Width/<Endpoint of line>: ← **[enter]**
Command: **COPY**
Select objects: ← Pick the polyline. Note that the pickbox must be at the edge of the polyline.

1 found
Select objects: ← **[enter]**
<Base point or displacement>/Multiple: END   ← Object snap mode END
of   ← Click near the thin end of the wedge

Second point of displacement: **313,55**
Switch **ORTHO** off.
Command: **LINE**
From point: **END**
of   ← Pick the thick end of the left wedge
     ← Note how the line attaches to the middle of the width of the polyline

To point: **END**
of   ← Pick the thin edge of the right wedge

To point: ← **[enter]**
Command: **CIRCLE**
3P/2P/TTR/<Centre point>: **MID**
of   ← Pick the line
Diameter/<Radius> <5>:
Command:

Exercise: CHAMFER and FILLET

FILLET the top corners of the amplifier with a fillet radius of 10 units. A fillet radius of 0 will produce an intersection of two straight lines. Apply a **CHAMFER** with distances of 5 and 15 units to the bottom left and right corners.

The 'rotate' command: turn up the volume

This command allows you to rotate an entity or group of entities about a specified point. The angle of rotation can be input by rubber-banding or by entering a value. If the value is positive, the rotation occurs in an anti-clockwise direction.

Rotate is available from the drop-down and screen menus under *Modify* and *DRAW*, respectively.

How the command works

The **ROTATE** command will ask you to *Select objects* and then prompt for the rotation *Base point* and the rotation angle. The 'base point' is the point around which the rotation will take place.

The command sequence below is used to rotate the volume knob around the centre point (**CEN**).

Command: **ROTATE**
Select objects: ← Select the wedge marker on the large knob

1 found
Select objects: ← Press [enter]
Base point: **CEN**
of ← Pick the perimeter of the knob
<Rotation angle>/Reference: ← Use the rubber banding effect to select a rotation angle

Command:

The reference angle option permits you to rotate the entities by referring to another entity's angle or the present angle of the entity you want to rotate. In the example below, the marker on the 'treble' knob is set at 90°. This can be rotated back to 0°, as follows.

First select the marker and then execute the command **ROTATE** by typing it.

Command: **ROTATE**
1 found
Base point: **CEN**
of ← The circle
<Rotation angle>/Reference: **R** ← For the reference option
Reference angle <0>: **90** ← This is the angle the marker is at
New angle: 0 ← This is the angle it will be rotated to

Command:

Place the word 'AMPLIFIER' below the small knobs. The position of the text is not critical.

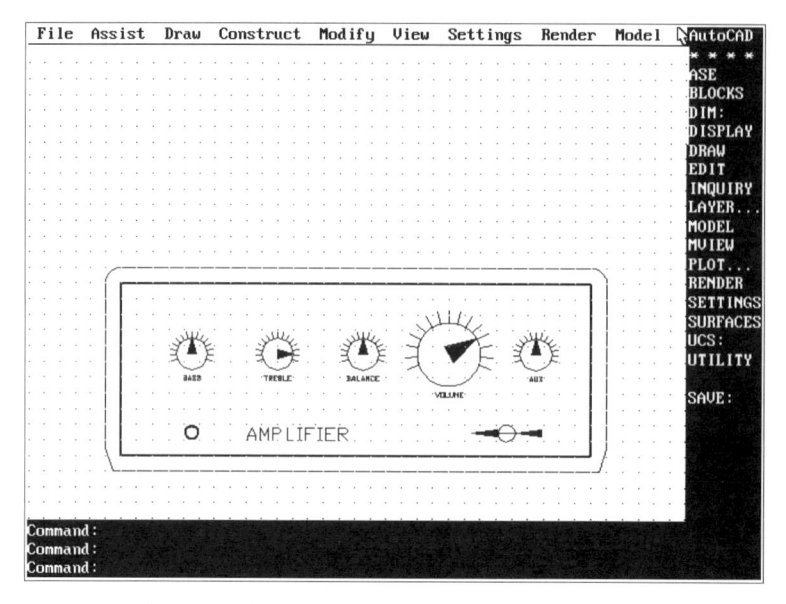

Fig. 8.3. The amplifier with the rotated knobs.

The 'zoom' command

The **ZOOM—window** and **ZOOM—all** options have been used up to now. (An outline of all the ZOOM options was given at the end of chapter 5.) The options **ZOOM—Extents** and **ZOOM—Dynamic** will now be examined in more detail.

ZOOM—Extents

This option will magnify the drawing as much as possible, while displaying everything in the drawing. If you draw outside the electronic page set by the limits, **ZOOM—Extents** will incorporate the entities into the display. **ZOOM—All** will leave them out, because they are outside the drawing limits.

Try doing a **ZOOM—Extents** on the drawing of the amplifier now; the view you obtain should be similar to that in fig. 8.4. The drawing fills the screen as much as possible.

Note: If the command fails to display the drawing on the screen as much as you expected, it may be because some small entities you accidentally drew are positioned some distance from the drawing. Look for these, and erase them if necessary.

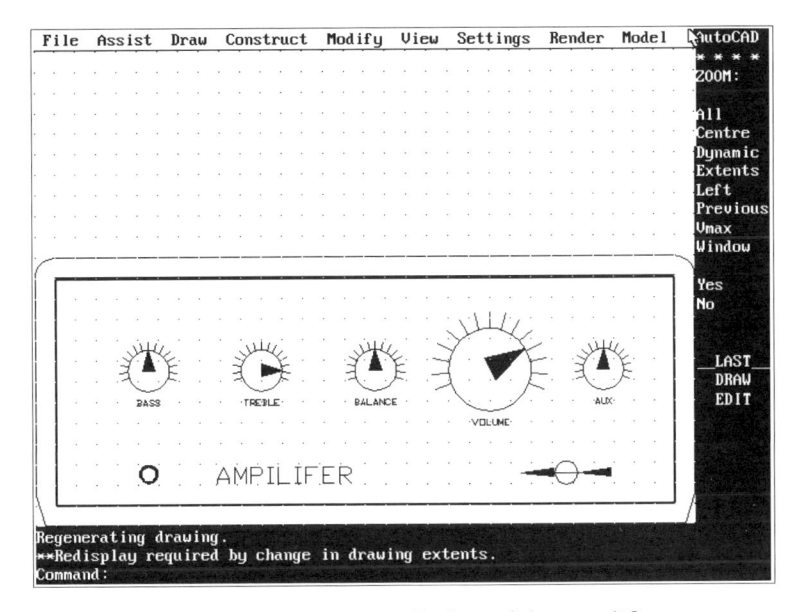

Fig. 8.4. The ZOOM—Extents display of the amplifier.

ZOOM—Dynamic

ZOOM—All before you proceed. **ZOOM—Dynamic** is very useful if you have a large complex drawing. Executing the command will display a complete view of the drawing and then allow you to pull a window over the part of it you want to see in detail.

How the command works

When **ZOOM—Dynamic** is selected, the current drawing screen is cleared. The new screen displays the complete drawing and a small box termed the 'view box'. This box can be moved (panned) around the screen and positioned by picking with the pointing device. Once [enter] is pressed, the computer will display the area the view box was over.

Try the following. **ZOOM—Window** around the volume knob. Now do a **ZOOM—Dynamic**. The screen should look like fig. 8.6.

MAJOR DRAWING AND EDITING COMMANDS **111**

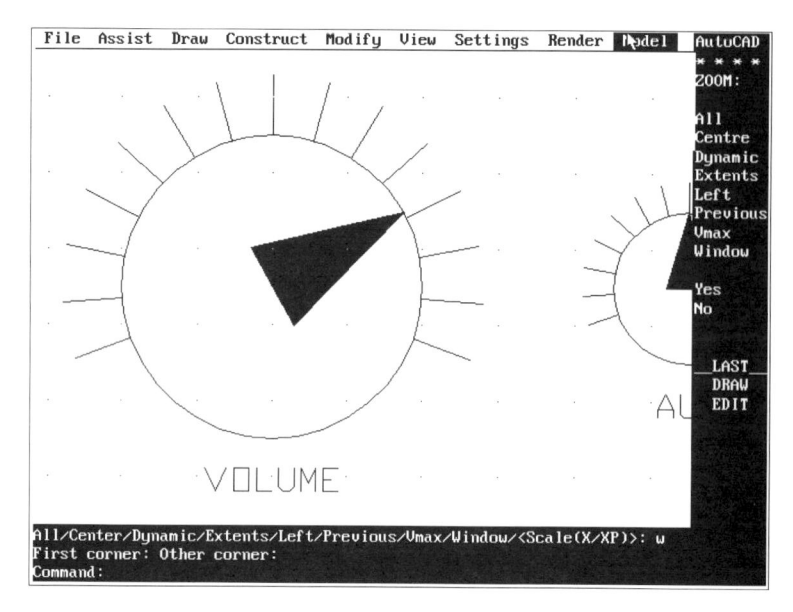

Fig. 8.5. ZOOMed in on the volume knob.

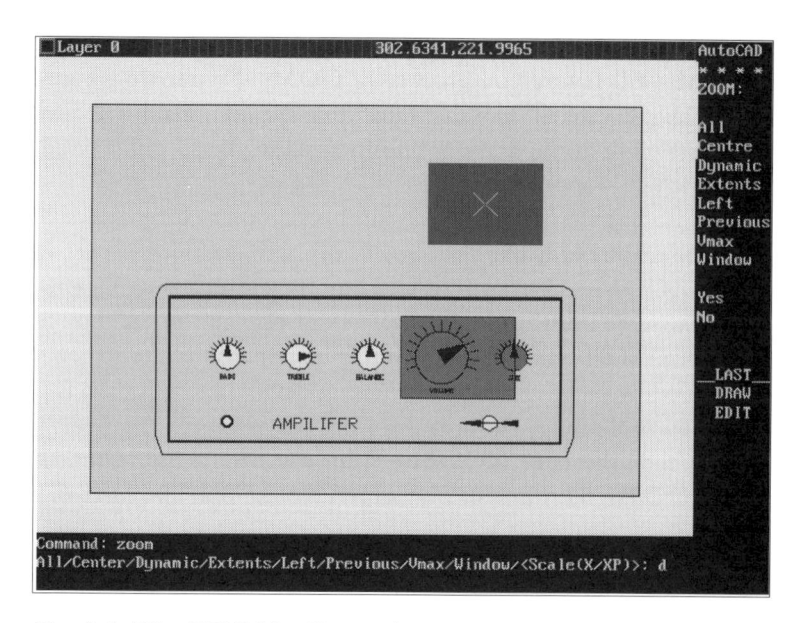

Fig. 8.6. The ZOOM—Dynamic screen.

This screen has several rectangular areas displayed.
(1) Move the pointing device around. You will see a box with an X at the centre moving with you. This is the view box.
(2) Another rectangle on the screen is composed of a dotted border (green on colour monitors). This shows the view displayed on the screen before you executed the **ZOOM—Dynamic** command.
(3) The outermost solid rectangle is the current drawing extents. To zoom in on the bass knob, move the view box in over it and pick with the pointing

device. An arrow will appear at the right-hand side of the view box. This allows you to size the box. Press **[enter]**. The bass knob will be displayed.

The 'pan' command

The **PAN** command allows you to slide the image of the drawing around on the screen. Imagine that your screen is just a small window looking down on a large drawing. By executing the **PAN** command you can move to another area of the drawing without zooming. The problem with the **PAN** command is that you must know where you are going.

How the command works

On executing **PAN** you are asked for *PAN Displacement*. After picking a point on the screen you are asked for a *Second point*. If the second selected point is to the right of the first one, you pan to the left. If **ORTHO** is switched on, your pans will be vertical or horizontal. The command sequence summary is given below.

Command:
PAN Displacement: ← Pick a point on the screen
Second point: ← Pick a second point on the screen
Command:

Finishing the drawing

Complete the drawing by adding a polyline border and a title block with your name, date and '100 W AMPLIFIER'. **END** to save the drawing and exit AutoCAD.

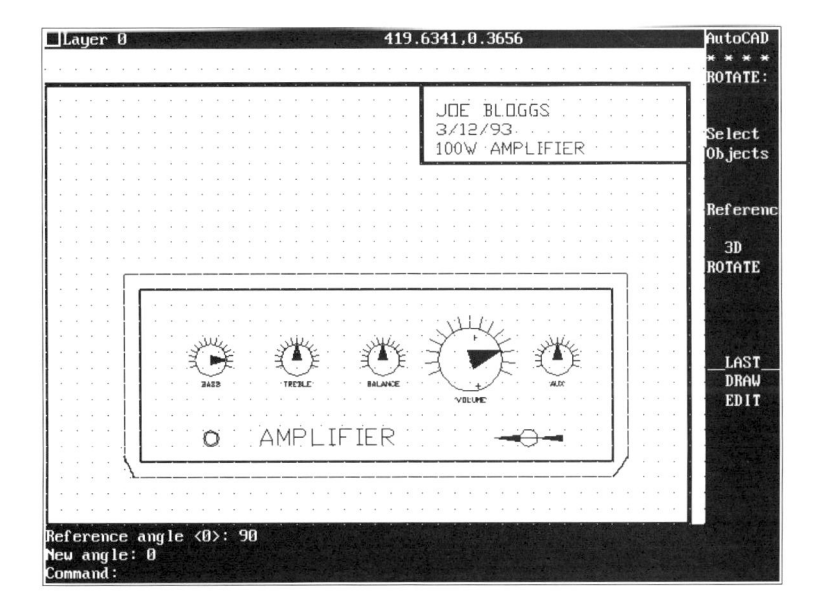

Fig. 8.7. The completed drawing.

ADDITIONAL INFORMATION

Start a new drawing, called TESTC8. Set the **LIMITS** from 0,0 to 50,30. Test the following commands before you start the assignments at the end of this chapter.

The 'aperture' variable

The size of the target box used when in the object snap mode can be changed using the APERTURE command.

How the command works

Type **APERTURE** at the command prompt. AutoCAD responds with *Object snap target height (1–50 pixels) <10>*. (A pixel is a single dot of colour on a screen. All entities are drawn in pixels.) Values of 1 to 50 are acceptable. The larger the value, the bigger the target box. AutoCAD will remember the size you enter until a further change is made to the value.

Object snap

Object snap modes will not work when typed in directly at the command prompt. They are used as a drawing or editing aid within a drawing or editing command. An object snap mode can be called up by typing the capitalised letters found in the screen menu listing under ★★★★.

CENtre	**NODe**
ENDpoint	**PERpend**
INSert	**QUADrant**
INTersec	**QUICK**
MIDpoint	**TANgent**
NEArest	**NONE**

The 'pickbox' variable

This command controls the size of the pickbox used when selecting entities for editing.

How the command works

Typing **PICKBOX** at the command prompt calls up the response *New value for PICKBOX <3>*. A larger value increases the size of the box. Decrease the size of the pick box if you are editing a detailed drawing.
Command: **PICKBOX**
New value for PICKBOX <3>: **6**
Command:

The 'arc' command

The command is found on the drop-down menu under *Draw*. Ten options are available:

3-point
Start, Cen, End
Start, Cen, Angle
Start, Cen, Length
Start, End, Angle
Start, End, Radius
Start, End, Dir
Cen, Start, End
Cen, Start, Angle
Cen, Start, Length

These ten options are also available from the screen menu.

3-point: three points selected on the screen will have an arc described through them.

Start refers to the start point of the arc. It can be selected by using the pointing device or using object snap modes or co-ordinates.

Centre refers to the arc's centre point. It can be selected by using the pointing device if you are using object snap modes or co-ordinates.

End is used to select the ending point of the arc. Again it can be selected by using the pointing device if you are using object snap modes or co-ordinates.

Angle describes an arc's length. The angle can be indicated using the pointing device or by typing in a value. The angles are measured anti-clockwise.

Length refers to the length of the arc's chord. The length can be indicated using the pointing device or by typing in a value.

Dir means 'direction'. Normally this is indicated by using the pointing device. The ORTHO command may be useful in conjunction with this option.

Radius refers to the arc's radius. The radius can be indicated by using the pointing device or by typing in a value.

To illustrate the drawing of arcs, the *Start, Cen, Angle* option will be used. Draw a horizontal line 10 mm from 6,22 to 16,22 to represent a door. An arc will be attached to the line to indicate the direction in which the door opens.

Select the option *Start, Cen, Angle* from the drop-down menu (*S, C, A* from the screen menu).

Command: _arc Centre/<Start point>:   ← Pick the right end of the line
Centre/End/<Second point>: _c Centre: ← Pick the left end of the line
Angle/Length of chord/<End point>: _a
Included angle: **A**
Requires valid numeric angle or second point.
Included angle: **90**
Command:

The 'ellipse' command

The ellipse is constructed from a polyline. The ellipse command is found under *DRAW* on the screen and drop-down menus and under *Display/Draw* on the tablet. The command **ELLIPSE** can be typed in at the command prompt.

There are various ways AutoCAD can help you to draw an ellipse. An ellipse has a **major axis** and a **minor axis**.

The axis and eccentricity method

Using this technique you specify the beginning point of one of the axes. This axis can then become the major or minor axis (depending on your next step).

You then specify the *other axis distance,* which is the distance from the centre of the first axis you have drawn. The *other axis distance* describes the ellipse's eccentricity.

The command syntax is:

Command: **ELLIPSE**
(Axis endpoint 1)/Centre: **33,14**
Axis endpoint 2: **43,14**
(Other axis distance)/Rotation: **38,16**
Command:

In this case the first axis you drew became the major axis.

Now try this one:

Command: **ELLIPSE**
(Axis endpoint 1)/Centre: **33,14**
Axis endpoint 2: **43,14**
(Other axis distance)/Rotation: **38,22**
Command:

In this case the first axis became the minor axis.

You can also rotate a circle into the third dimension, to give it the appearance of an ellipse.

Draw a line from 6,10 to 16,10. Execute the following:

Command: **ELLIPSE**
<Axis endpoint 1>/Centre: **END**
of   ← Pick the left end of the line
Axis endpoint 2:   ← Pick the right end of the line
<Other axis distance>/Rotation: **R**
Rotation around major axis: **75**
Command:

Exercise

The maximum angle of rotation is 89.4°. Try rotating the ellipse 0° and then 90°.

Specifying the centre and the two axes

Use the pointing device to select the centre and the end-points of the two axes.

Command: **ELLIPSE**
(Axis endpoint 1)/Centre: **C**
Centre of ellipse: ← Pick a point
Axis endpoint : ← Pick a point
(Other axis distance)/Rotation: ← Pick a point
Command:

Your screen should now contain these ellipses.

Ellipses are also drawn in the tutorial on isometric drawing in chapter 16.

The 'solid' command

'Solids' are areas filled with colour. The **SOLID** command is found under *DRAW, next* and **SOLID:** on the *Screen* menu (for the moment ignore the FILL ON, FILL OFF options). On the tablet it is under the *Display/Draw* icons. At the command prompt you can just type **SOLID**.

When the command is issued, AutoCAD will ask for four points. The first and third points must lie on the same side if you want to draw a rectangular object.

In fig. 8.8 below, the solids have their points marked and numbered. Notice how in all the rectangular shapes the points 1 and 3 are always on the same side. By selecting the points in clockwise or anti-clockwise directions, a 'bow tie' is produced. Terminating the command after the third point will produce a triangle. This can be used extensively in the assignment of the compass drawing.

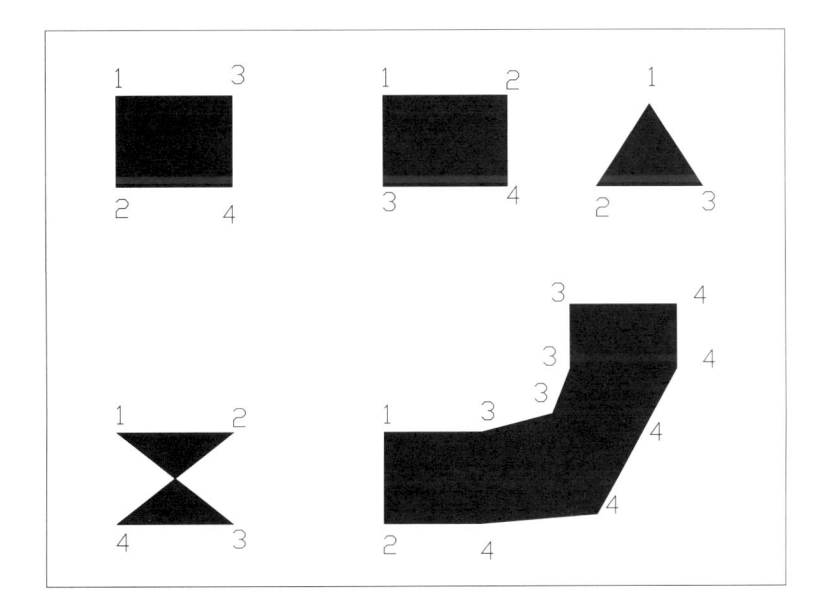

Fig. 8.8. Solids produced by selection of points.

Here are some examples:
Command: **SOLID**
First point: ← Pick or type 2,26
Second point: ← Pick or type 2,20
Third point: ← Pick or type 8,26
Fourth point: 8,20
Third point: ← Press **[enter]**.
Execute the command again by pressing **[enter]**.
Command: **SOLID**
First point: ← Pick or type 14,26
Second point: ← Pick or type 21,26
Third point: ← Pick or type 14,20
Fourth point: **21,20**
Third point: ← Press **[enter]**.
Execute the command again by pressing **[enter]**.

 This sequence produces the 'bow-tie' effect:
Command: **SOLID**
First point: **4,9**
Second point: **10,9**
Third point: **10,4**
Fourth point: **4,4**
Third point: ← Press **[enter]**
Command:

 In the above exercises, AutoCAD continues to ask for a third point when it is finished drawing the shape. If a point is selected, a fourth point is requested. AutoCAD uses the previous third and fourth points as a first and second point for the continuing solid. For example:
Command: **SOLID**
First point: **22,9**
Second point: **22,3**
Third point: **28,9**
Fourth point: **28,3**
Third point: **31,9**
Fourth point: **37,5**
Third point: **34,13**
Fourth point: **40,13**
Third point: **34,19**
Fourth point: **40,19**
Third point: ← Press **[enter]**.
Command:

The 'polygon' command

This command uses polylines to draw polygons. **POLYGON** is found under *DRAW* on the screen and drop-down menus and under *Display/Draw* on the tablet.

After specifying the number of sides in the polygon (from 3 to 1,024), you can draw it in one of two basic ways:
(1) Define one side of the polygon, and AutoCAD will construct the rest.
(2) Give the centre point, and AutoCAD will ask if you want the polygon inscribed or circumscribed around an imaginary circle. The second method is the default.

Example 1
This polygon will have five sides and will be inscribed in an imaginary circle of radius 4 units. The centre of the polygon can be chosen using any of the co-ordinate input methods, or using object snap modes.
Command: **POLYGON**
Number of sides: **5**
Edge/(Centre of polygon): **8,23**
Inscribed in circle/Circumscribed about circle (I/C): **I**
Radius of circle: **4**
Command:
The illustration below shows the way the radius is defined for inscribed and circumscribed circles.

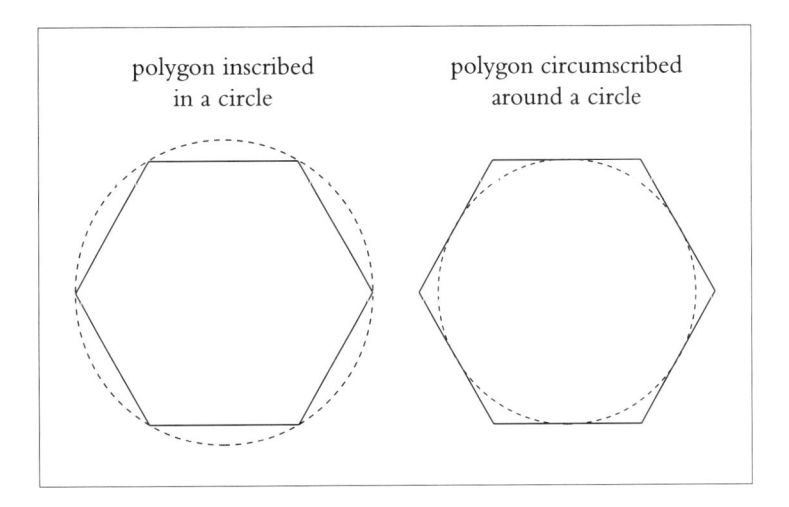

Fig. 8.9. Defining the radius of inscribed and circumscribed circles.

Example 2
In this example the polygon will again have 5 sides but is defined on the basis of a circumscribed circle.
Command: **POLYGON**
Number of sides: **5**
Edge/(Centre of polygon): **8,12**
Inscribed in circle/Circumscribed about circle (I/C): **C**
Radius of circle: **4**
Command:

Example 3
This example illustrates the case where one side of the polygon is defined. AutoCAD then uses this to construct the shape.
Command: **POLYGON**
Number of sides: **8**
Edge/(Centre of polygon): **E**
First endpoint of edge: **25,24**
Second endpoint of edge: **22,24**
Command:

The 'fillmode' variable

This variable allows you to determine whether entities such as **SOLIDS** and **POLYLINES** are filled in with a colour or not. A setting of 1 is on and 0 is off. It is often a valuable time-saver (from the point of view of REGENS) to develop the drawing with this mode switched off. Before plotting the drawing, the value can be returned to 1.
The command sequence is:
Command: **SETVAR**
Variable name or ?: **FILLMODE**
New value for FILLMODE : **1**
Command: **REGEN**
Regenerating drawing.
Command:

SUMMARY

A complete drawing or selected entities within it can be scaled up or down using the **SCALE** command. Text can be placed and justified on a drawing using the **TEXT** command. The commands **APERTURE** and **PICKBOX** are system variables that control the size of the cursor pickbox for the selection of entities and the aperture used for selecting entities when the object snap modes are active. The DONUT command draws circles using the polyline entity. Entities may be rotated around a selected base point using the ROTATE command. The PAN and ZOOM—Dynamic commands are useful for moving around large drawings.

Areas of solid fill are drawn with the command SOLID. The variable FILLMODE controls whether the solids are filled in with colour or not. The command ELLIPSE is used to draw the ellipse entity. A polygon of 3 to 1,024 sides can be drawn using the command POLYGON. It can be drawn in one of two basic ways: (*a*) define one side of the polygon, and AutoCAD will construct the rest; (*b*) give the centre point, and AutoCAD will ask if you want the polygon inscribed or circumscribed around an imaginary circle. This latter method is the default.

Lastly, arcs may be drawn using a variety of options.

ASSIGNMENTS

Assignment 1

Suggested procedure

Use the **ARC** command and its options to draw the crockery. A suitable SNAP mode will help to keep the curvature of the ARCs consistent.

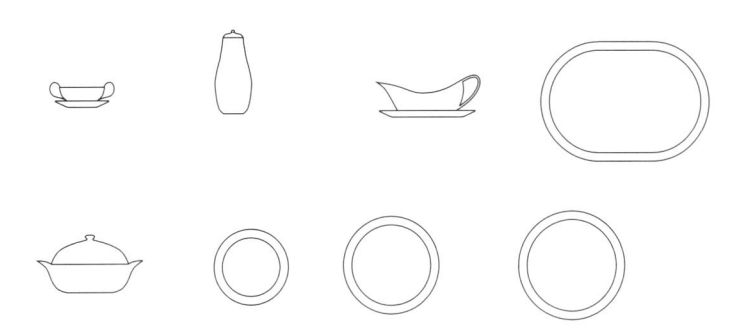

Assignment 2

Drawing instructions

Use the **SOLID** command to construct the compass rose.

Assignment 3

Suggested procedure

Use standard dimensions in drawing the plan view of the apartment. The walls (exterior) can be drawn using a polyline with FILL off.

Examine the drawing carefully to see which elements are repeated (the chairs, for example), and use the COPY command to replicate them. The

OFFSET command should be used in drawing the draining-board and stairs. The bathroom fittings require the use of FILLET extensively. ARCs should be used to indicate the door sweep.

Draw the border and title block with FILL off. Complete the title block.

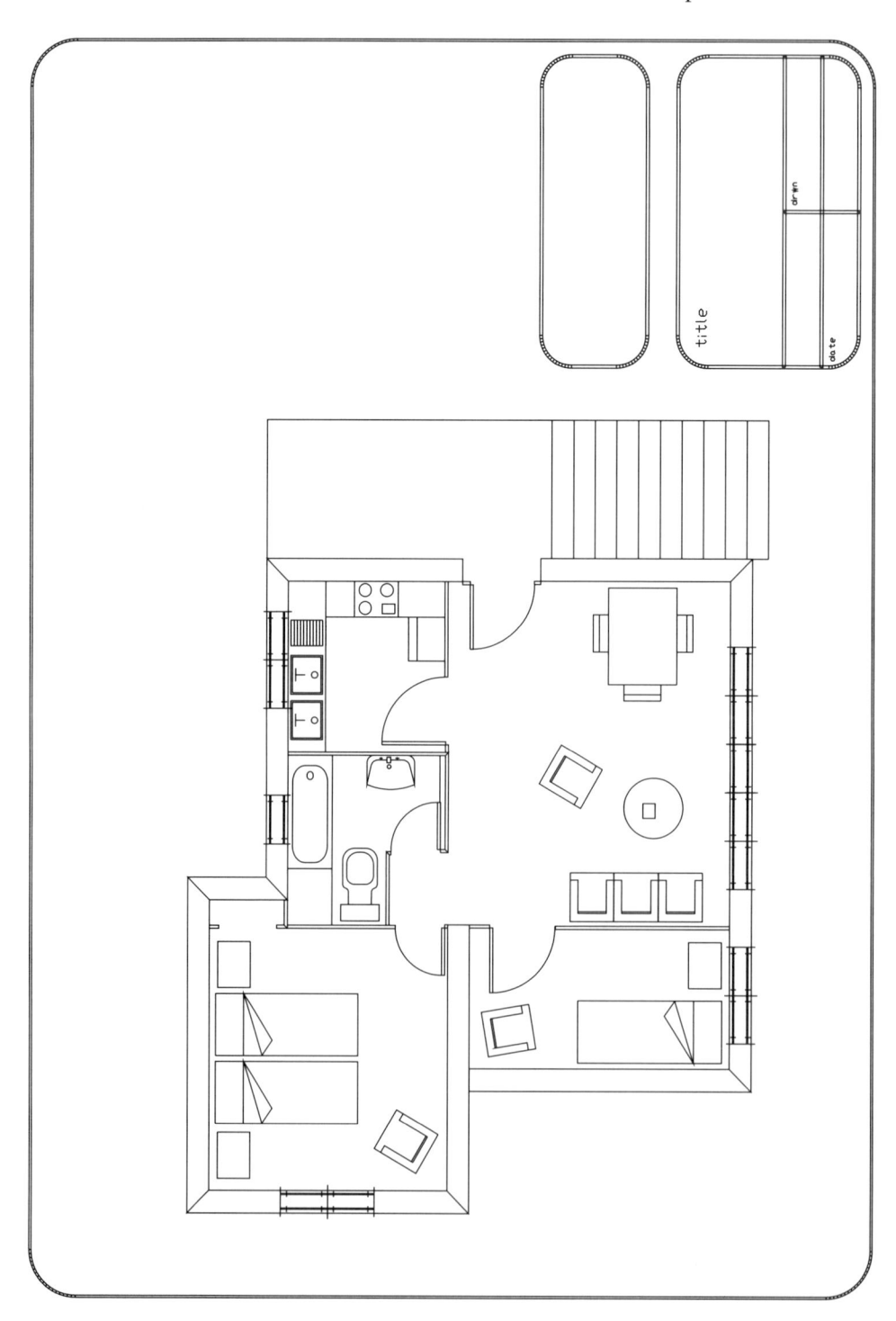

Assignment 4

Suggested procedure

All curved surfaces should be drawn using the **ARC** command.

Target drawing

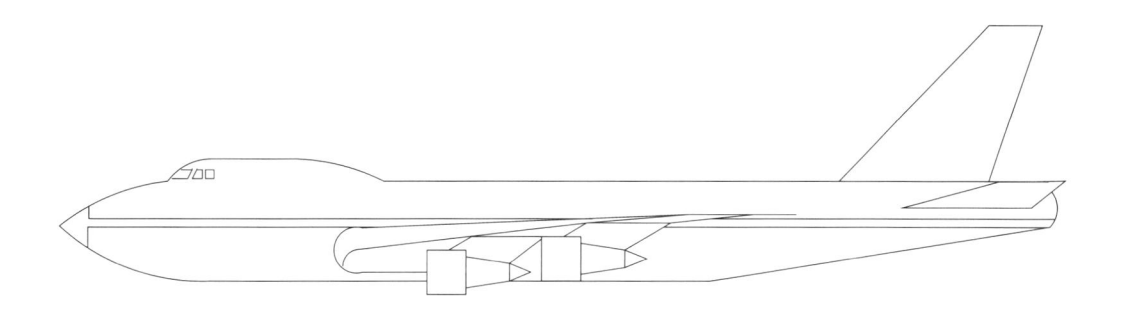

Drawing instructions

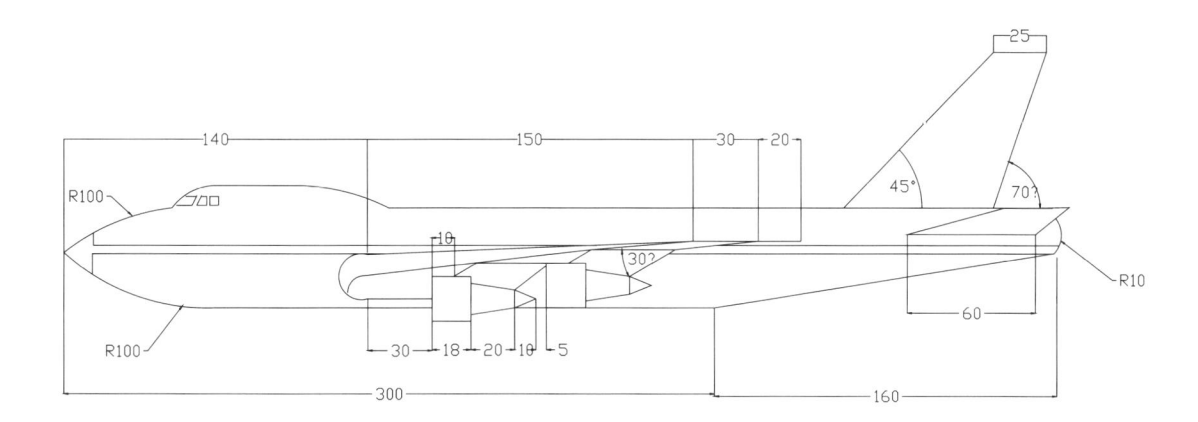

Assignment 5

Target drawing

TAILSTOCK

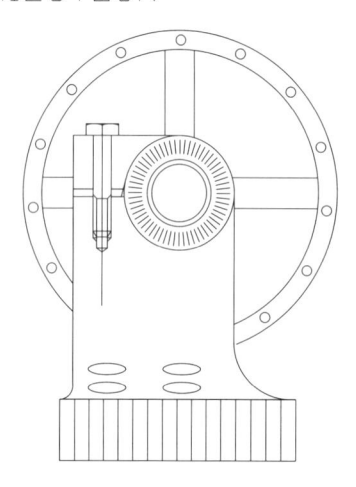

Drawing instructions

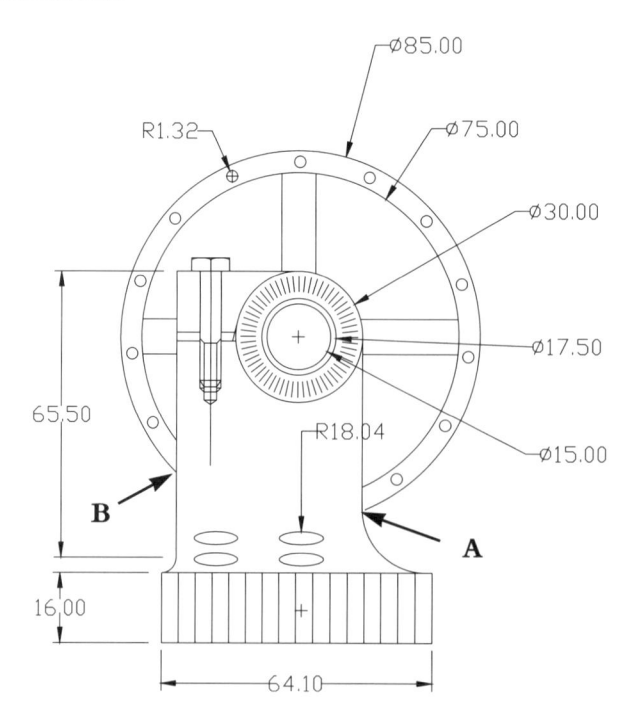

Suggested procedure

Draw the inner circle first. The ARRAY (polar) can be used to place the markings on the central axis. The outer two circles should be constructed from arcs using the centre option to pick a centre at the axis. Use the object snap mode NEAR to position the arcs at A and B.

chapter 9

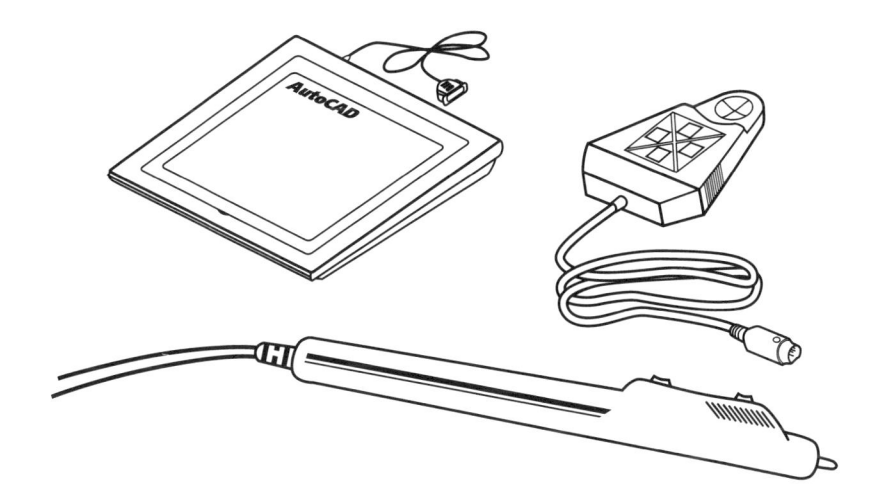

Linetypes and Further Editing

Tutorial objectives

By the end of this chapter you should be able to
- cut back an entity using the TRIM command
- place POINT entities into a drawing
- use different LINETYPEs in a drawing
- use the LTSCALE command to change the scaling on linetypes
- extend the length of linear entities using the EXTEND command
- CHANGE the properties of selected entities
- produce mirror images of selected entities using the MIRROR command
- control how text is mirrored using the MIRRTEXT system variable

Tutorial 9.1

Target drawing

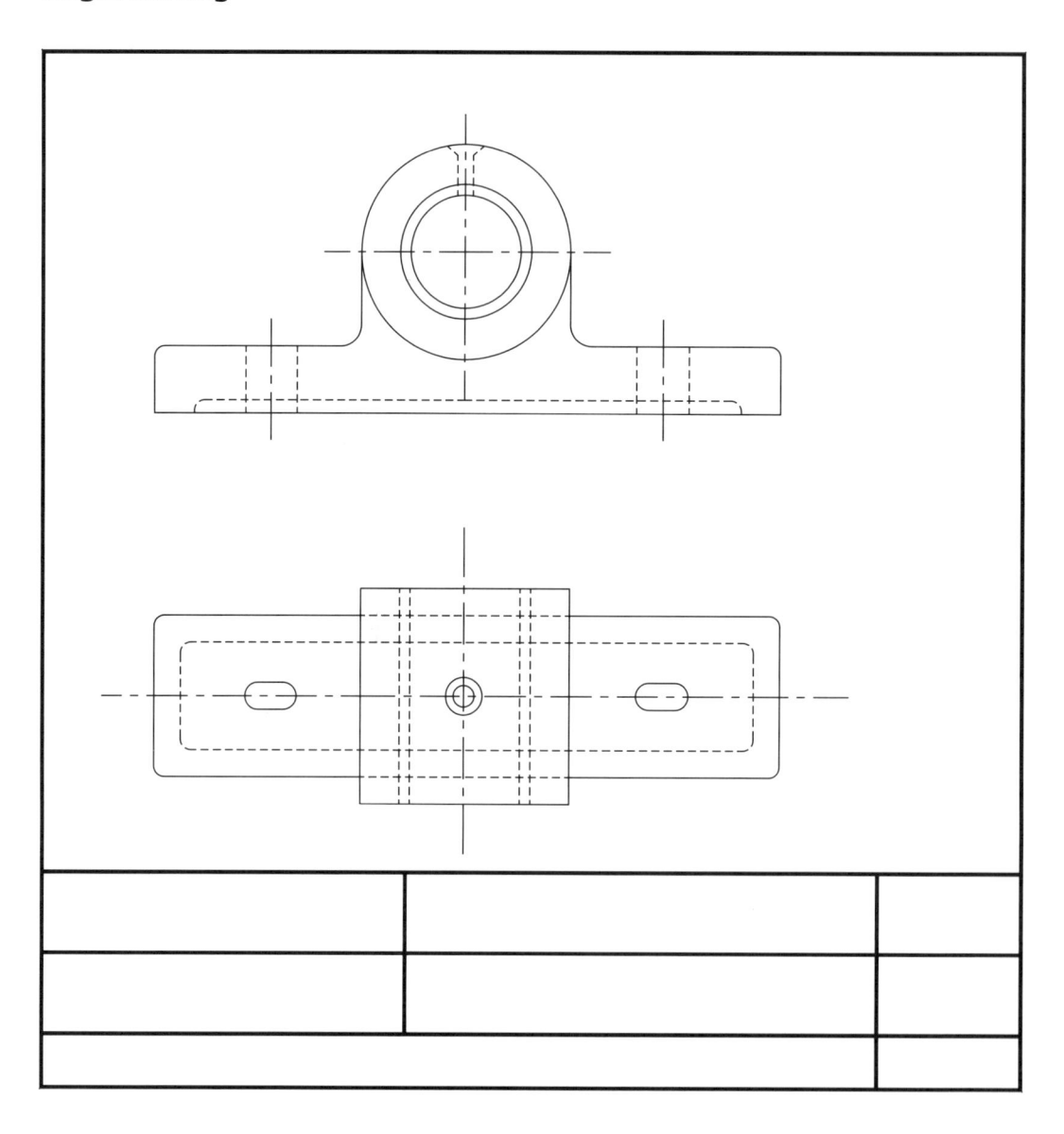

Drawing instructions

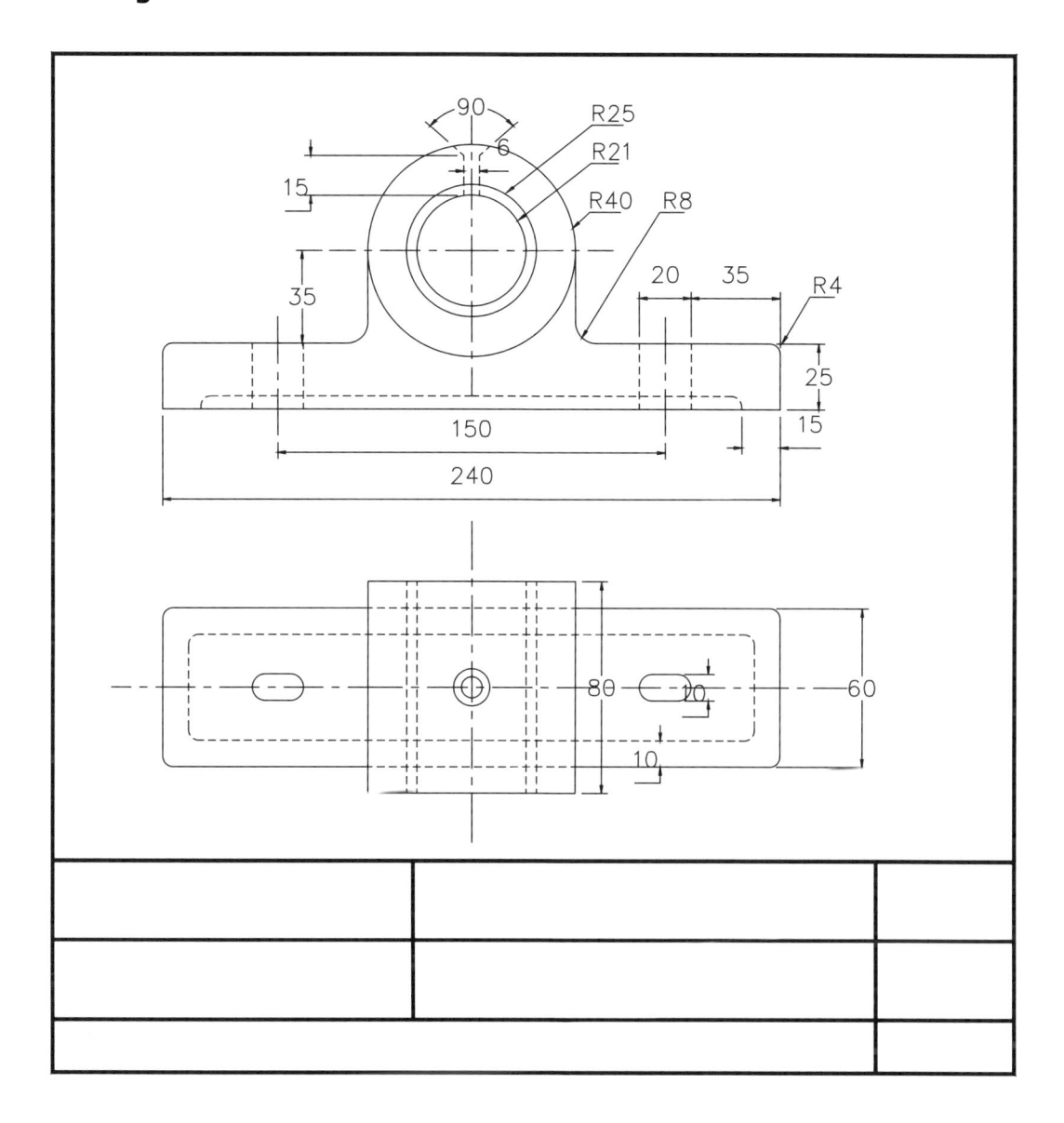

Working with linetypes

Setting up a new drawing
The drawing shows two views of a bushed bearing. Open a new drawing and call it **BEARINGS**. The settings are as follows:
UNITS: Decimal, no decimal places. Angle measurement must also be in decimals, to 0 decimal places.
LIMITS: 0,0 to 500,420.
GRID: ON and set to 10 units.

SNAP: ON and set to the grid value.

Don't forget to **ZOOM—All** to display the sheet to the limits. Draw the sectioned view first with continuous linetype. A suggested drawing sequence is outlined below.

Step 1: Draw the three concentric circles with 260,340 as their centre point.

Step 2: Draw a line 120 units long (half the length of the base) from the centre of a circle at 0°. **OFFSET** this line 35 units down to form the top of the base, and further **OFFSET** this line 25 units down to form the baseline of the base.

Step 3: Draw the end vertical line (marked *A* in fig. 9.1) and the bearing support line from the outer circle to the top of the base (marked *B* in fig. 9.1). The object snap modes **END** and **INT** will be useful in aiding the construction of these lines.

Zoom in on the drawing using the window option.

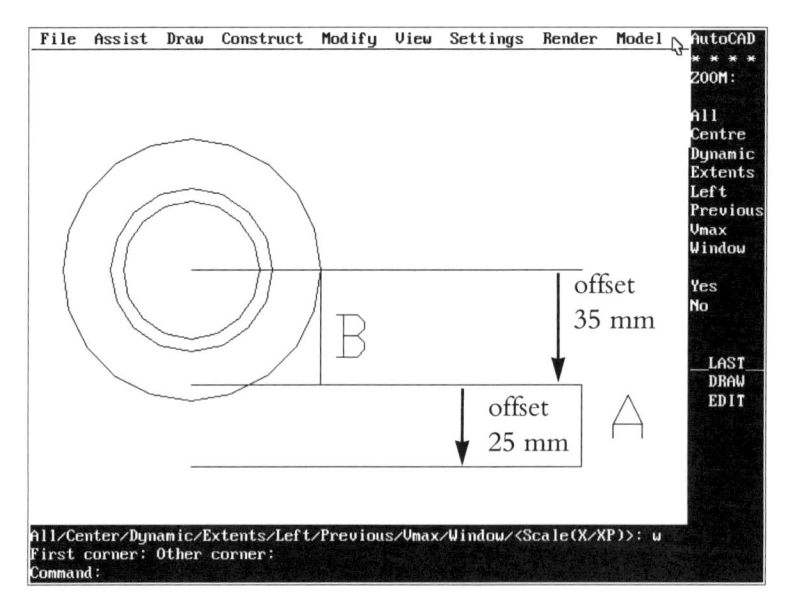

Fig. 9.1. Construction of the bearing ring and its base.

Step 4: Trim the top line that forms the base to where it intersects with line *B* using the **TRIM** command.

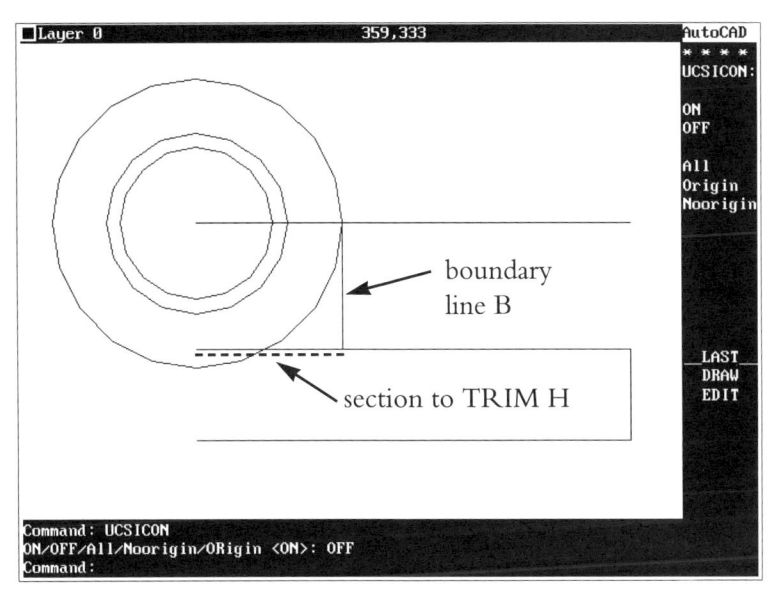

Fig. 9.2. Using the TRIM command.

The 'trim' command

TRIM will remove parts of entities back to a boundary. It is found on the *'Modify'* drop-down menu and under EDIT on the screen and tablet menus.

How the command works

The command first asks for the boundary you need to trim back to. Select it with the pick box. Several different boundaries or *cutting edges* can be selected at once. It then asks you for the entity you want to trim. Boundaries can be polylines, lines, arcs, and circles.

Here is the command sequence:

Command: **TRIM**
Select cutting edge(s)... ← Pick the vertical line B
Select objects: 1 found
Select objects: ← Press **[enter]**
<Select object to trim>/Undo: ← Select the horizontal line H
<Select object to trim>/Undo: ← Press **[enter]**
Command:

Step 5: It is necessary to mark the location of the beginning of the vertical hidden line that indicates the hidden bore. This point is 35 mm in from the end of the base. **OFFSET** the end line 35 mm (see fig. 9.3). The intersection between this offset line and the top line (marked *X* in fig. 9.3) is the edge of the bore. This point can be marked using a **POINT** entity.

LINETYPES AND FURTHER EDITING **129**

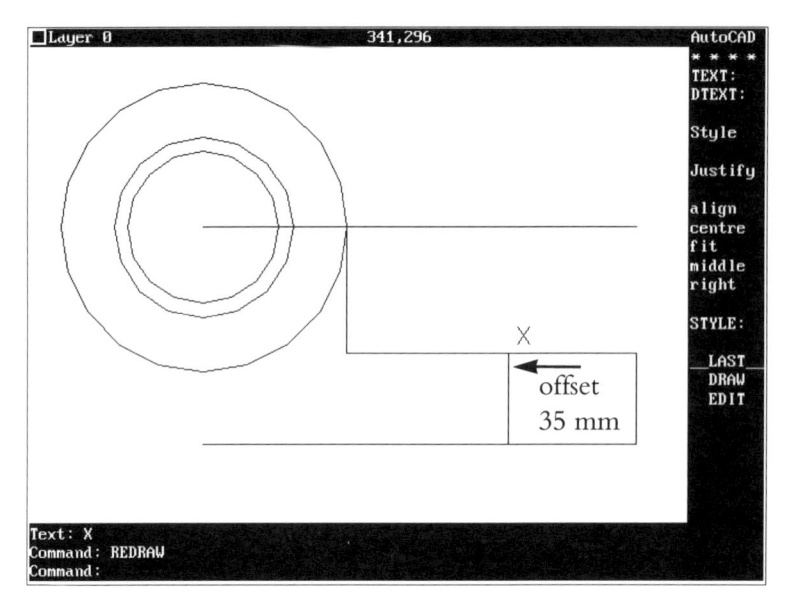

Fig. 9.3. Positioning the edge of the bore.

The 'point' command

Points can be positioned anywhere in a drawing. They may be used to attach entities to at a later stage, or just left as visual markers. The object snap modes can be used to position points (as well as the cross-hairs, and the absolute and relative co-ordinates). **POINT**s can be located at a later stage by the object snap modes **NEArest**, **CENtre**, and **NODe**.

Types of points
AutoCAD has twenty different point types. These can be selected and sized to suit the drawing.

How the command works
The **POINT** command is found on the drop-down, screen and tablet menus under *'DRAW'*. When the command is selected, AutoCAD will prompt *'Point'*. Pick the position on the drawing for the insertion of the point.

When the command is executed, the screen menu will display the *'Type and Size'* option. Selecting this option will display the *'Point Style'* box. This contains all the available points.

Inserting a point into the bearings drawing
Pick a point from the drop-down menu. Pick *'Type and Size'* from the screen menu. The following screen is displayed.

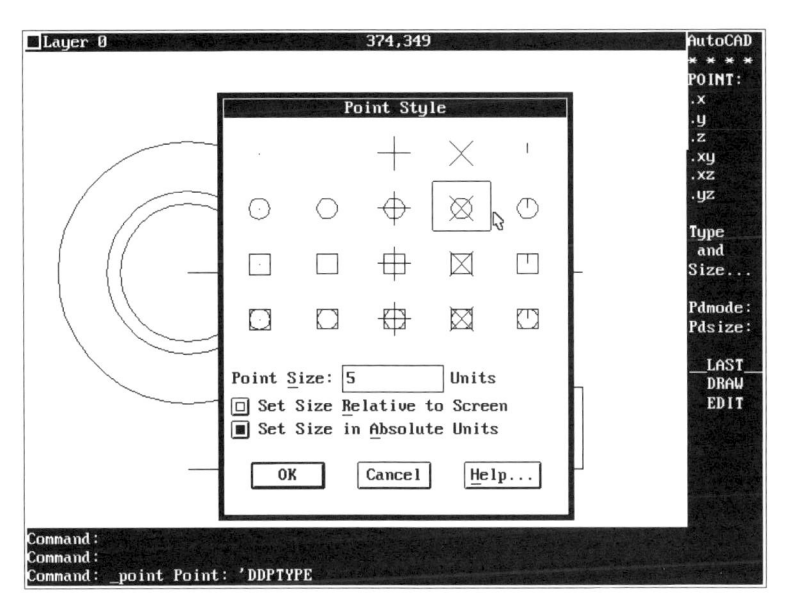

Fig. 9.4. The 'Points Style' box.

Select the point highlighted and insert a value of 5 in the *'Point size:'* edit box. Switch on the radio button *'Set in Absolute Units'*. Click on **OK** and insert the **POINT** into the drawing using the object snap mode **INT** to find the intersection between the offset vertical line and the top of the base (marked X in fig. 9.3).

Delete the vertical line which was used to position the point at X. See fig. 9.3.

Command: **_POINT**
Point: 'DDPTYPE Point: **INT**
of   ← Pick point X
Command:

Step 6: Apply fillets of 8 mm and 4 mm to the two corners, and erase the offset line below the point. See the drawing instructions on page 127.

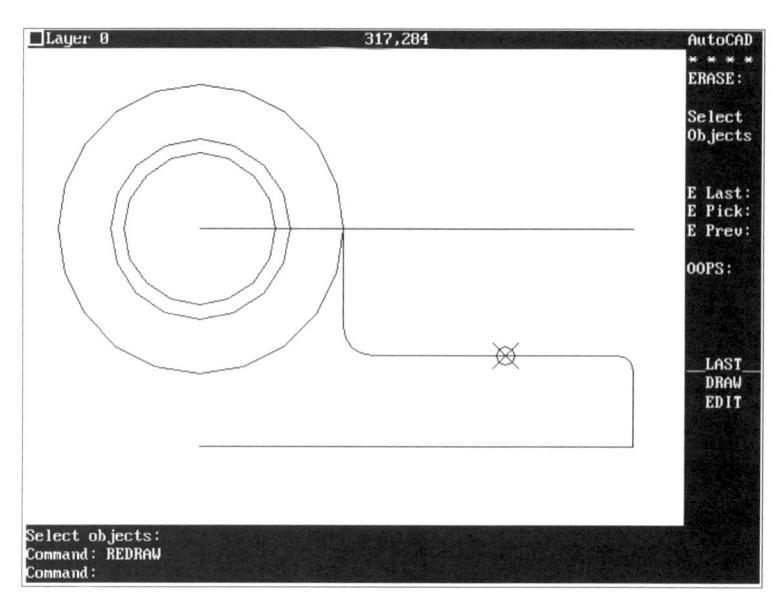

Fig. 9.5. The drawing after the insertion of a point.

Step 7: Change the linetype. This is explained below.

Using different linetypes

In many disciplines, including architecture and engineering, different linetypes are used to communicate information about the drawing. Up to now only the *continuous* linetype has been used in drawings. This is the default setting.

Eight other standard linetypes are supplied with AutoCAD. These are stored in a file called *ACAD*.

The LINETYPE command

A linetype has to be loaded into memory first from the ACAD file and then made current. Once a linetype has been made current, all entities drawn from then on will be in that linetype. The **LINETYPE** command is used to load and make current a linetype.

A list of the available linetypes can be called up in the following way:
Command: **LINETYPE**
?/Create/Load/Set: ← Type **?** and press **[enter]**
The *'Select Linetype file'* dialogue box is displayed (see fig. 9.6).

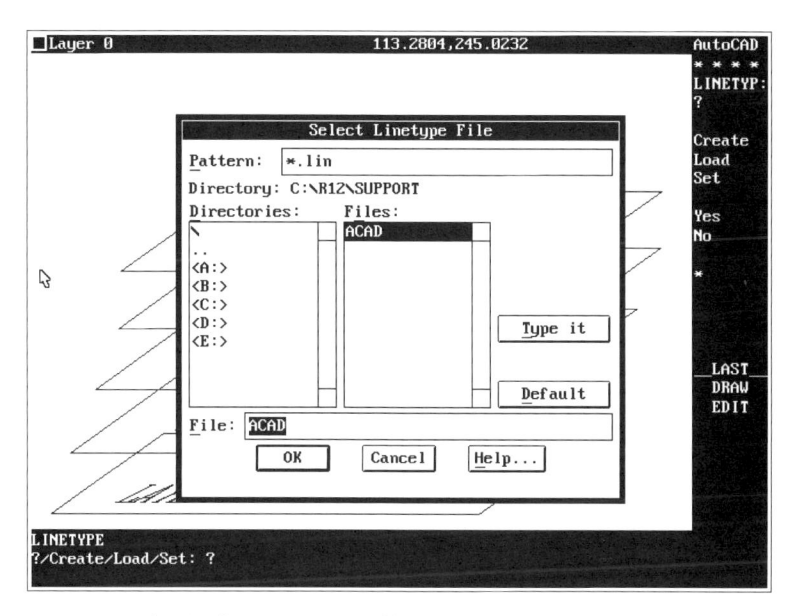

Fig. 9.6. The 'Select Linetype file' dialogue box.

If *ACAD* is in the edit box then click on **OK** or press **[enter]**. The contents of this file are then loaded. AutoCAD switches to text mode and the list of linetypes is displayed.

Note that the description of the linetypes is not very accurate (see how some of the dots are above the lines). The selected linetype will, however, be rendered with complete accuracy within AutoCAD's drawing editor.

There are three versions of each type of line, for example HIDDEN, HIDDEN2, and HIDDENX2. The HIDDENX2 is double the scale of HIDDEN, and HIDDEN2 is half its scale.

How to use a linetype within your drawing

As an example, the **HIDDEN** linetype will be loaded and made current. There are two steps involved in doing this:
(1) Load the linetype from a file.
(2) Make the linetype you want the current one.

The 'load' option
Select **L** for load. AutoCAD will respond with *Linetype(s) to load:*. Enter the linetype name **HIDDEN** and press **[enter]**. The *'Select Linetype file'* dialogue box reappears. If *ACAD* is in the edit box, click on **OK** or press **[enter]**. Select **S** for set. This will allow you to set a linetype as current.
New entity linetype (or ?) <BYLAYER>: HIDDEN
?/Create/Load/Set: ← Press **[enter]** to terminate the command
Command:

LINETYPES AND FURTHER EDITING   **133**

Any drawing from now on will be executed using the hidden linetype. To revert to continuous linetype simple *'Set'* it.

Draw a line from the inserted **POINT** (use the object snap **NODe** to select the **POINT**) **PERPendicular** to the opposite side.

Step 8: Scale the linetype.

The 'ltscale' command

The lengths of the dashes and the spacing between the dashes may not suit you. Fortunately this can be controlled using the **LTSCALE** command. **LTSCALE** is a global command. It affects all the different linetypes in the drawing.

Change the **LTSCALE** on your drawing to 0.5. Here is the command sequence:

Command: **LTSCALE**
New scale factor <1.0000>: **.5**
Regenerating drawing.
Command:

If the line still appears to be continuous, try a value of 0.75.

Step 9: OFFSET the hidden line 20 units to the left. Erase the **POINT**, as it is not needed any more.

Step 10: The centre line can be placed in the bore between these two hidden lines by (*a*) OFFSETting the left hidden line 10 units and then (*b*) OFFSETting the top and bottom lines of the base, (*c*) extending this centre hidden line a little beyond the base, using the **EXTEND** command, and lastly (*d*) using the **CHANGE** command to convert the hidden line to a centre line.

(*a*) OFFSET the right hidden line 10 units to the left.
(*b*) OFFSET the top and bottom lines of the base by 10 units (see fig. 9.7).

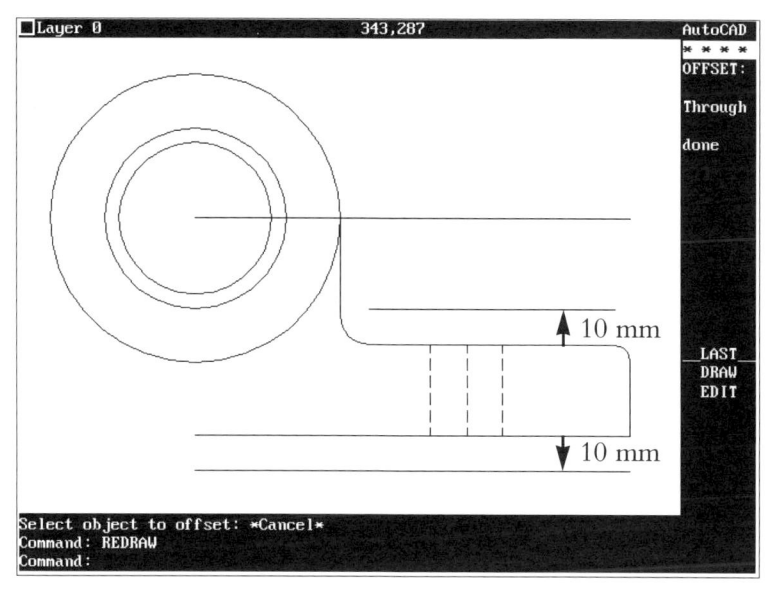

Fig. 9.7. The offset lines for the construction of the centre line.

(c) The centre hidden line can now be extended using the **EXTEND** command.

The 'extend' command

A boundary edge must be selected to show AutoCAD where to extend an entity to.

How the command works
The command can be accessed from *'Modify'* on the drop-down menu and under *'EDIT'* on the screen and tablet menus.

The command first asks for the boundary you want to extend to. It then asks for the entity you want to extend. Boundaries can be polylines, lines, arcs, and circles. By selecting two boundaries, an entity can be extended in two different directions. This is the case in this drawing.

To extend the centre hidden line, execute the following:

Command: **EXTEND**
Select boundary edge(s)...
Select objects: ← Select the top offset line
1 found
Select objects: ← Select the bottom offset line
1 found
Select objects: ← Press **[enter]**
<Select object to extend>/Undo: ← Pick the centre line near its top end
<Select object to extend>/Undo: ← Pick the centre line near its bottom end
Command:

Now erase the top and bottom offset lines.

Step 11: Convert the hidden line to a centre line: the **CHANGE** command.

The 'change' command

CHANGE allows you to change colours, elevations, thicknesses, linetypes, layers, and text. Some of these options are covered in later chapters.

How the command works

The command can be accessed from the screen and tablet menus under *'EDIT'* and under *'Modify'* on the drop-down menu. When the command is executed, AutoCAD will ask you to select the entities for changing. You will then be prompted for *'Properties/<Change point>:'*. The default option can be selected by just pressing **[enter]**. This will allow you to change the insertion point, style, height, rotation angle and content of text.

To change the linetype, select **P** for properties. From the options, select **LT** for linetype.

Here is the command sequence.

Command: **CHANGE**
Select objects: ← Pick the centre hidden line
1 found
Select objects: ← Press **[enter]**
Properties/<Change point>: **P**
Change what property (Color/Elev/LAyer/LType/Thickness) ? **LT**
New linetype <HIDDEN>: **CENTRE**
Change what property (Color/Elev/LAyer/LType/Thickness) ? ← Press **[enter]**
Command:

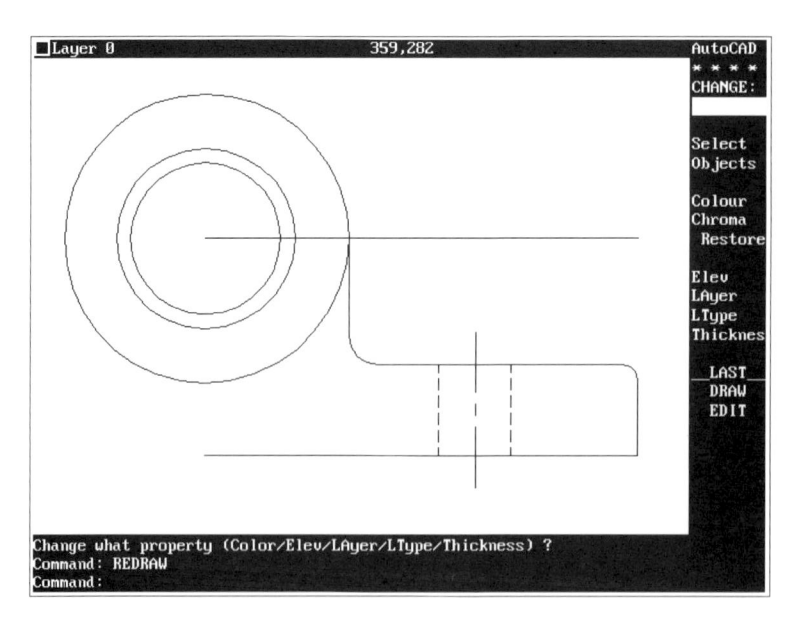

Fig. 9.8. The centre and hidden lines in position.

Step 12: Draw the hidden line showing the recess in the base. To do this, **OFFSET** the base line up 5 mm. **OFFSET** the end vertical line 15 mm.

Use **TRIM** to remove parts of lines C and D and the ends of the hidden lines that extrude below D (see fig. 9.9). (Tip: the **FILLET** command can be used with a radius of 0 to achieve the same effect.)

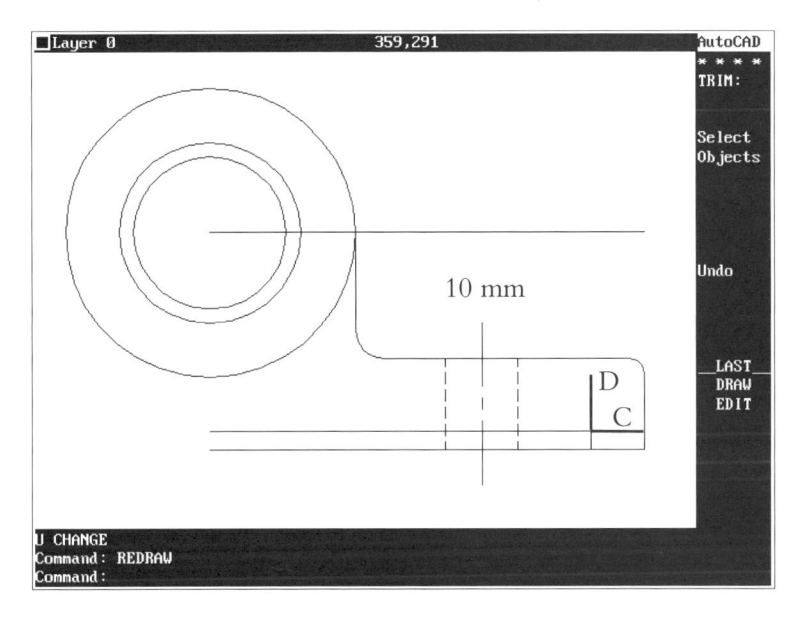

Fig. 9.9.

Step 13: Convert what remains of D and C to a hidden linetype using the **CHANGE** command. **FILLET** this hidden line with a radius of 4 mm.
Step 14: Set the linetype to **CENTRE** to make it current. Switch **ORTHO** on (F8 key). Draw a centre line from the end of the hidden line D to a few millimetres off the top of the circle (see fig. 9.10).

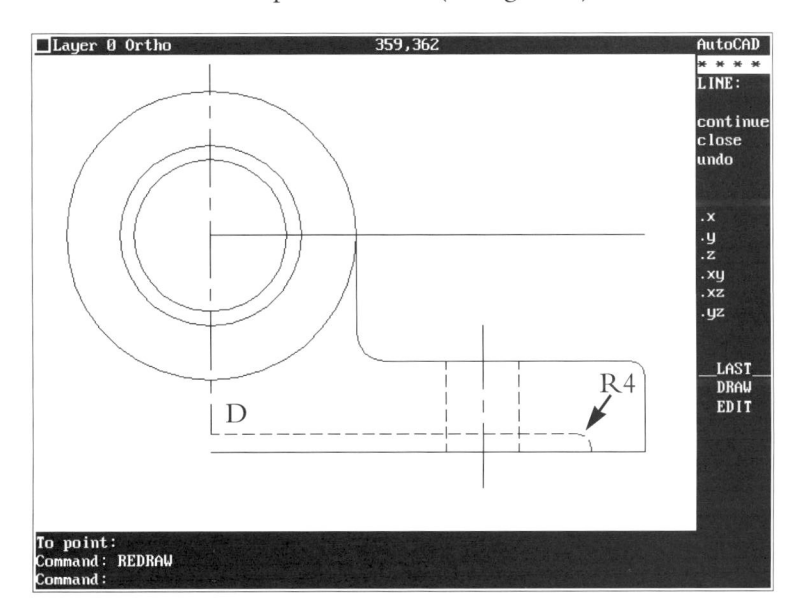

Fig. 9.10.

Step 15: Mirror all the drawing (except for the circles), using the **MIRROR** command.

The 'mirror' command

MIRROR produces a mirror image of selected entities across a mirror axis. During the command, AutoCAD will allow you the option of retaining or deleting the entities that are being mirrored. The **ORTHO** mode can play a valuable part during the execution of the command.

How the command works

The command is found under *'EDIT'* on the screen and tablet menus and under *'Construct'* on the drop-down menu. On execution you are asked to select the entities you want to mirror. AutoCAD will then want to know where the mirror axis is. This can be defined by picking two points on the screen. The mirror axis does not have to exist visually on the screen as an axis. Lastly you will be offered the option to *'Delete old objects?'*.

Using 'mirror' on the drawing

Switch off ORTH mode if it is on. Type **MIRROR**, and use a window to select all the entities on the screen apart from the circles. When asked for the mirror axis, use the object snap mode END to pick one end of the centre line. The image will then 'rubber-band'.

Use object snap END again to pick the other end of the centre line. The mirrored image will lock into position. Answer **N** to *'Delete old objects?'*.

Here is the command sequence:

Command: **MIRROR**
Select objects: **W** ← Pull a window around the entities
First corner: Other corner: 13 found
Select objects: ← Press **[enter]**
First point of mirror line: **END**
of ← Pick one end of the centre line
Second point: **END**
of ← Pick the other end of the centre line
Delete old objects? <N> ← Press **[enter]**
Command:

Zoom-All to see the effect. Then use **Zoom-Window** to obtain a view similar to fig. 9.11.

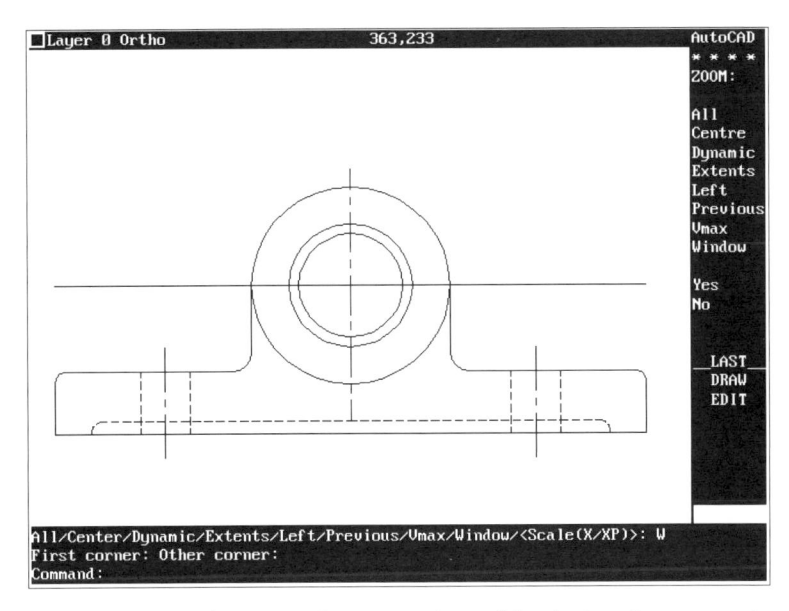

Fig. 9.11. The drawing after execution of the 'mirror' command.

Step 16: Use the **CHANGE** command to convert the horizontal lines that run through the centre of the circles to a centre line. **OFFSET** the vertical centre line 55 mm to the left and right. Then use these vertical offsets to **TRIM** the horizontal centre line. Lastly, erase the offsets.

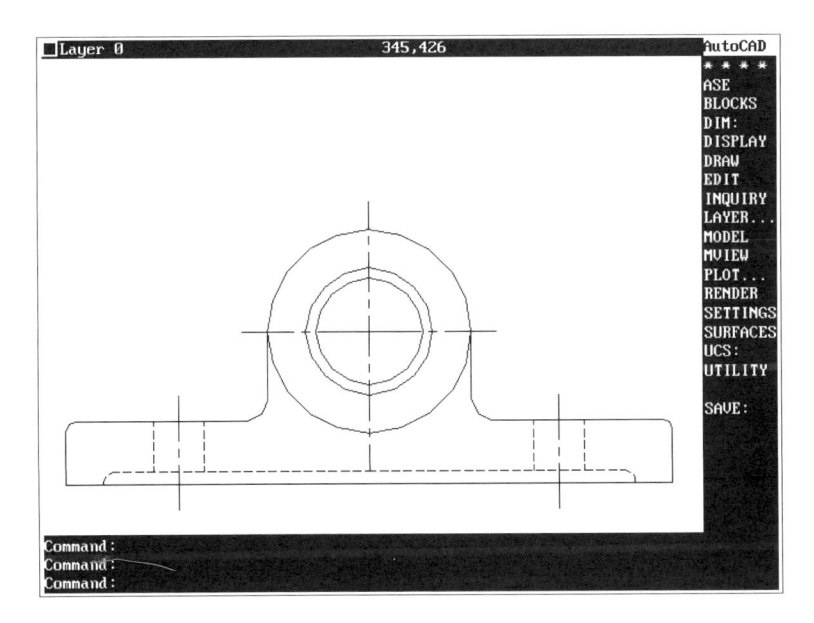

Fig. 9.12. The finished drawing.

Exercise

Try drawing the oil hole at the top of the circles. Suggested technique: use continuous linetype; offset the centre line 3 mm to the right; offset the inner circle out 6 mm; trim the offset centre line; draw the opening using a polar value of **@10<45**; change to hidden linetype, and mirror the completed structure.

ADDITIONAL INFORMATION

Changing the size of a point

The system variable PDSIZE is used to change the size of a point entity. Points with a PDMODE value of 0 and 1 are not affected by the PDMODE settings (PDMODE 0 = a dot and PDMODE 1 = nothing).

The PDSIZE variable affects the size of the point in three ways:
(1) If the values assigned to PDSIZE are positive, the point size is calculated by AutoCAD as an absolute size (in drawing units).
(2) If the values assigned to PDSIZE are negative, the point size is calculated by AutoCAD as a percentage of the height of the viewport size.
(3) A PDSIZE value of 0 displays points 5 per cent of the height of the graphics display.

Exercise

Draw a few points, and vary the **PDSIZE** settings to see the effect.

Note on using linetypes in a drawing

The HIDDEN and CENTRE linetypes are the most commonly used in drawings (apart from the continuous linetype). Hidden lines are used to indicate part of a structure that cannot be seen from the view in the drawing: for example hidden outlines or edges or other unseen profiles.

The centre linetype usually indicates symmetry. In accordance with the BS 308 ruling, the centre linetype will start and end with a long dash. Take care that they extend just a little beyond the structure they are assigned to. One difficulty that CAD programs have with centre lines is the inability to control how they cross: they should cross at a line and not a space. Rather than ignoring that feature, you can generally solve the problem by using the **MOVE** command in conjunction with ORTHO to move one of the centre lines the appropriate distance to provide the intersection.

Although the linetypes supplied with AutoCAD do not follow the BS 308 standard exactly, they are in fact good enough. The use of one of the three options (such as CENTRE2, CENTREX2, and CENTRE) in conjunction with LTSCALE should serve most people's needs. Assigning a pen thickness to a linetype will be covered in the chapters on LAYERS and PLOTTING.

Construction lines

Construction lines that need to be left in a CAD drawing are drawn as dotted lines.

Freehand lines

Freehand lines are often used to indicate an interruption or partial view of a section. In AutoCAD the command **SKETCH** is used to create freehand lines. (See chapter 16.)

The 'mirrtext' system variable

The **MIRRTEXT** variable controls how text is mirrored. If text is mirrored when the variable is set to 1 (the default value), the text will appear inverted (exactly as it would appear in a mirror). If the **MIRRTEXT** variable is set to 0, the text will appear normal.

Try both **MIRRTEXT** settings to see this for yourself. The command sequence to change the variable is:

Command: **SETVAR**

Variable name or ?: **MIRRTEXT**

SUMMARY

An entity can be cut back using the **TRIM** command. A cutting edge must be selected to show AutoCAD where to trim an entity back to. POINTs are simple entities that can be placed as markers in a drawing. The command POINT places the entities into the drawing. AutoCAD is supplied with a small library of different linetypes. These must be loaded and set to be current before they are used. The command LINETYPE offers to load and set current options. The spacing between the dots and dashes in a linetype may not be suitable for a drawing. The command **LTSCALE** allows the length of dashes and spaces in a linetype to be scaled up or down until they suit the drawing.

The length of some entities can be extended using the **EXTEND** command. A boundary edge must be selected to show AutoCAD where to extend to.

CHANGE allows you to change colours, elevations, thicknesses, linetypes, layers, and text. **MIRROR** produces a mirror image of selected entities across a mirror axis. During the command, AutoCAD will allow you the option of retaining or deleting the entities that are being mirrored. The **ORTHO** mode can play a valuable part during the execution of the command. The **MIRRTEXT** variable controls how text is mirrored. If text is mirrored when the variable is set to 1 (the default value), the text will appear inverted (exactly as it would appear in a mirror). If the **MIRRTEXT** variable is set to 0, the text will appear normal.

ASSIGNMENTS

Assignment 1

Target drawing

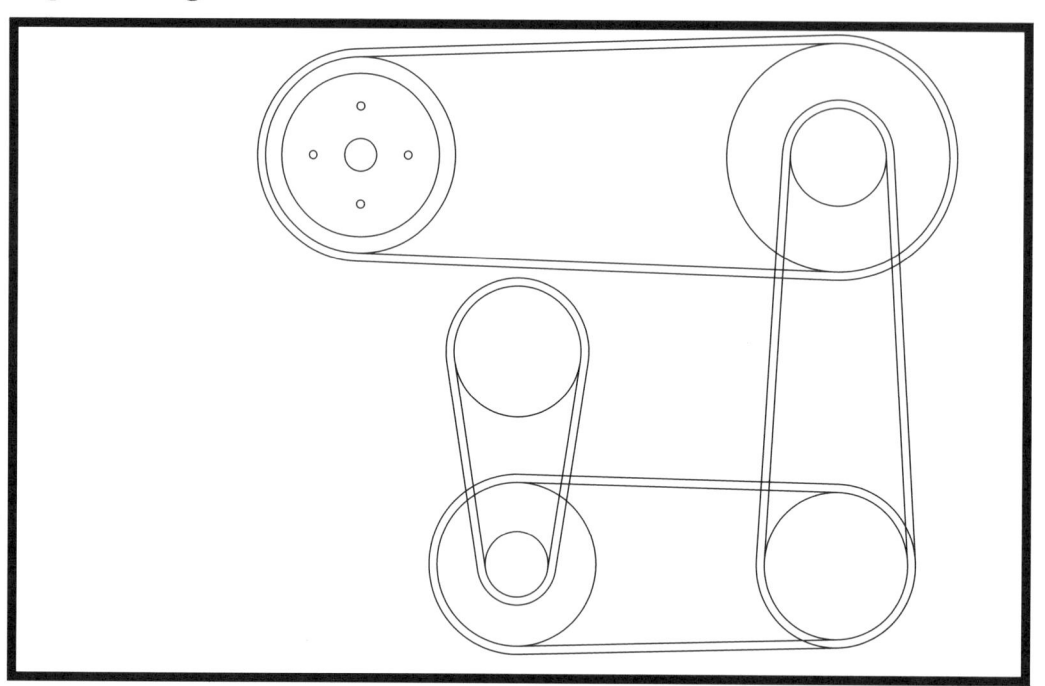

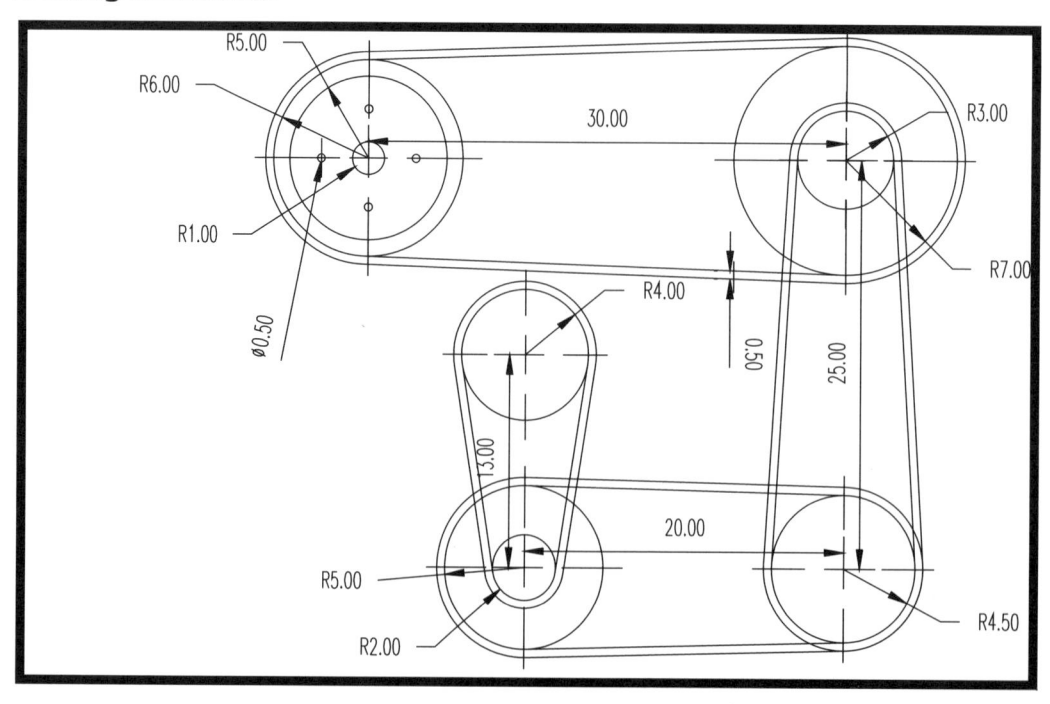

Drawing instructions

142 AUTOCAD ASSIGNMENTS

Assignment 2

Start the drawing with the elevation view. Placement of many of the entities will require the use of construction lines, using the OFFSET command. TRIM and EXTEND will be needed extensively.

Target drawing

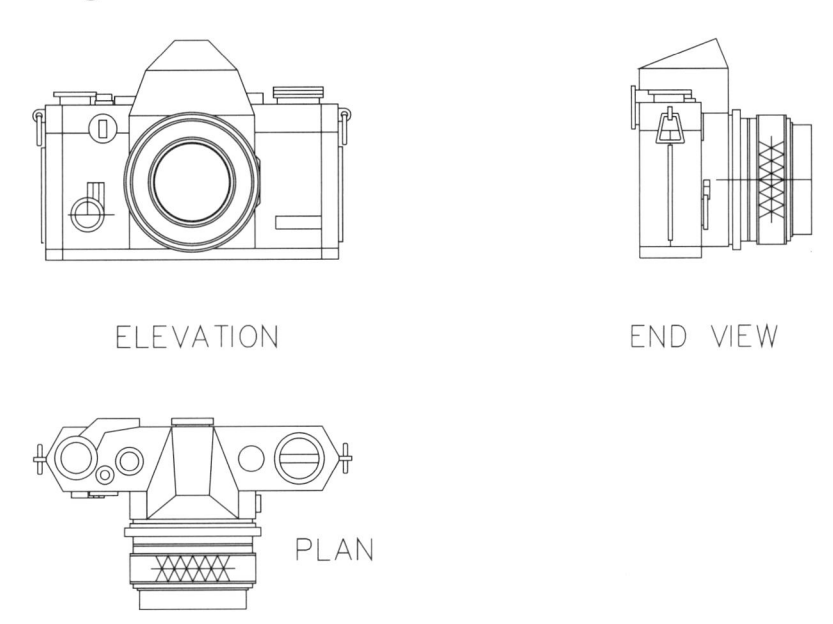

ELEVATION

END VIEW

PLAN

Drawing instructions

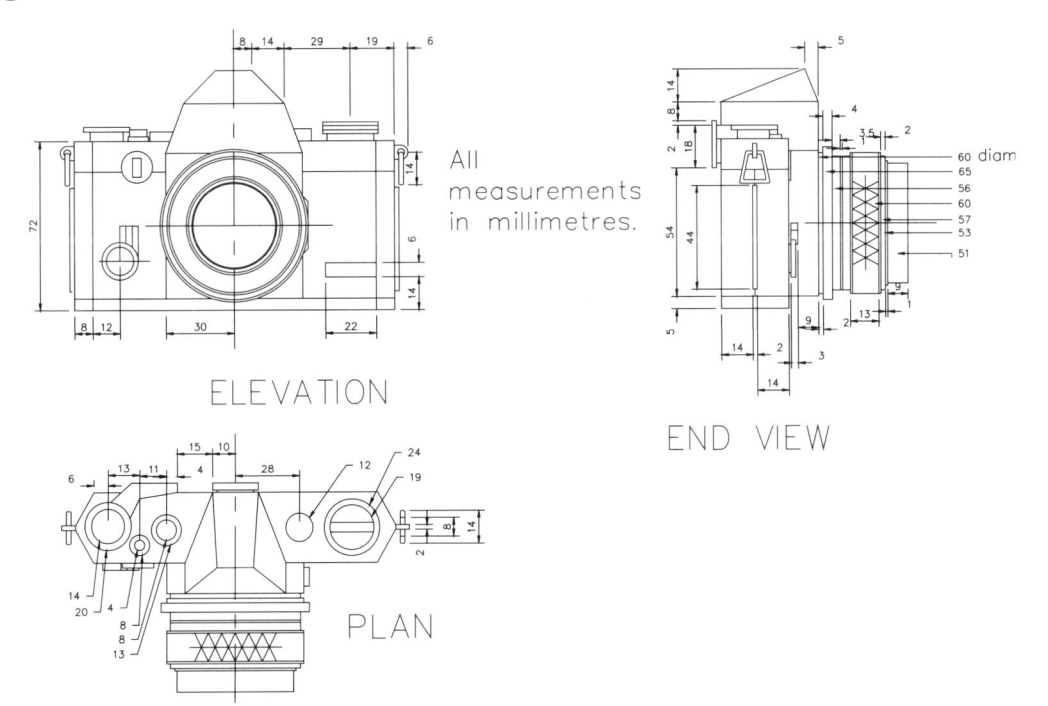

All measurements in millimetres.

ELEVATION

END VIEW

PLAN

LINETYPES AND FURTHER EDITING

Assignment 3

Target drawing

Drawing instructions

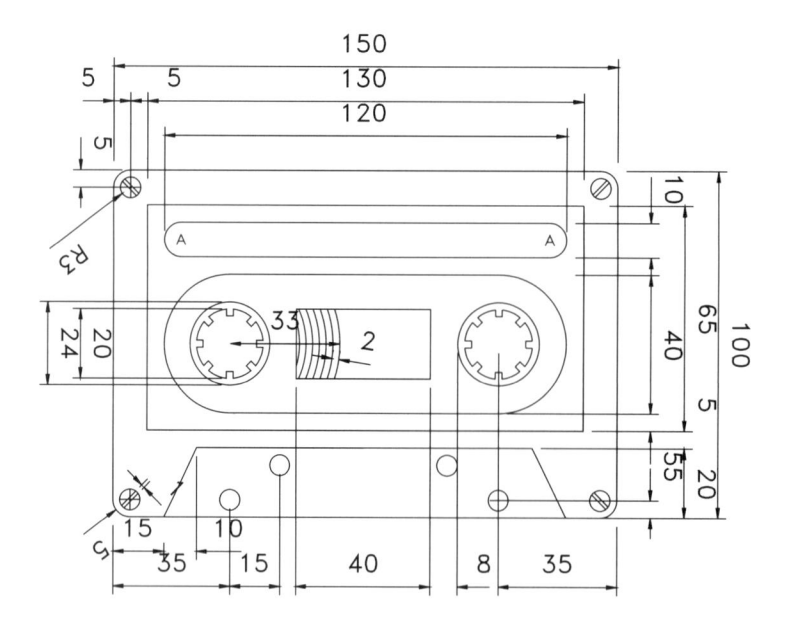

Assignment 4

Target drawing

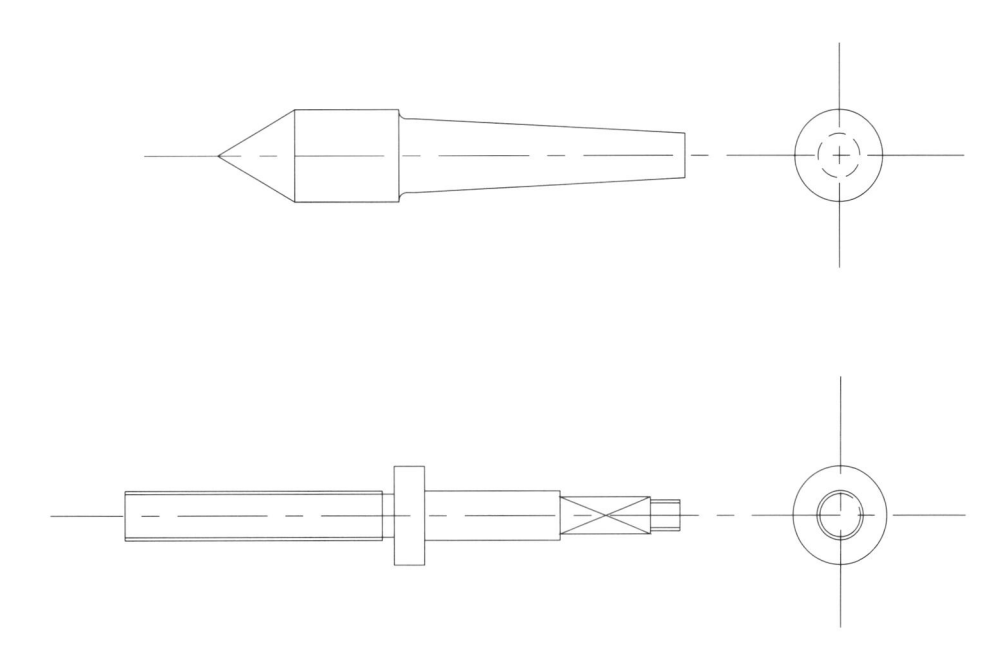

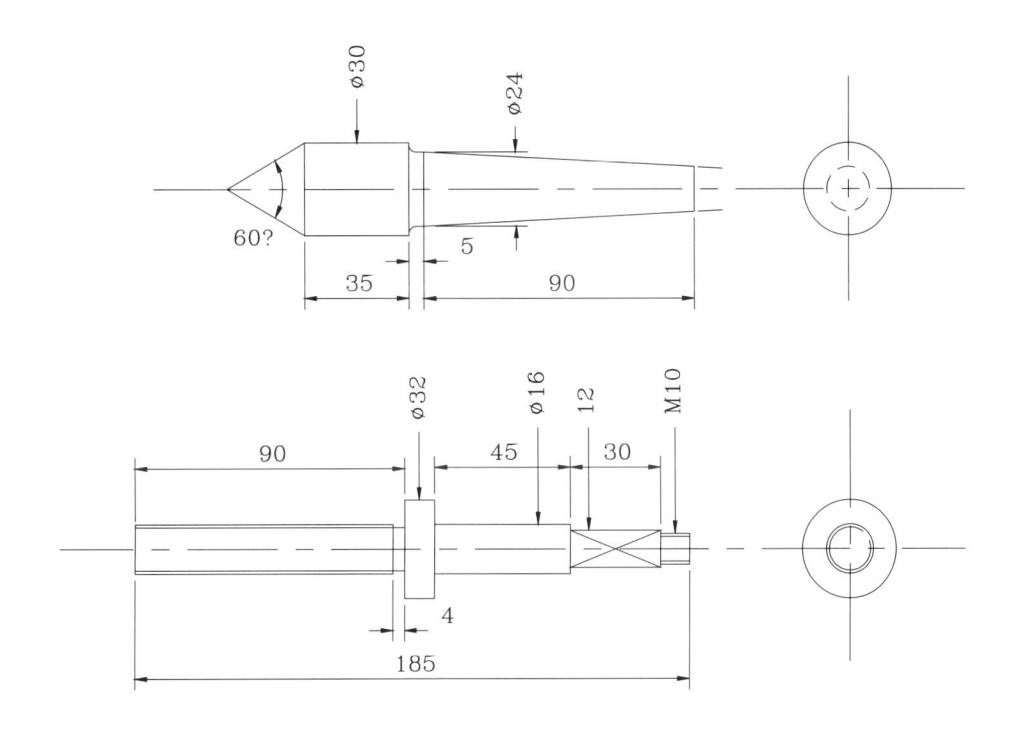

Drawing instructions

LINETYPES AND FURTHER EDITING

chapter 10
Viewports, Breaking and Extending

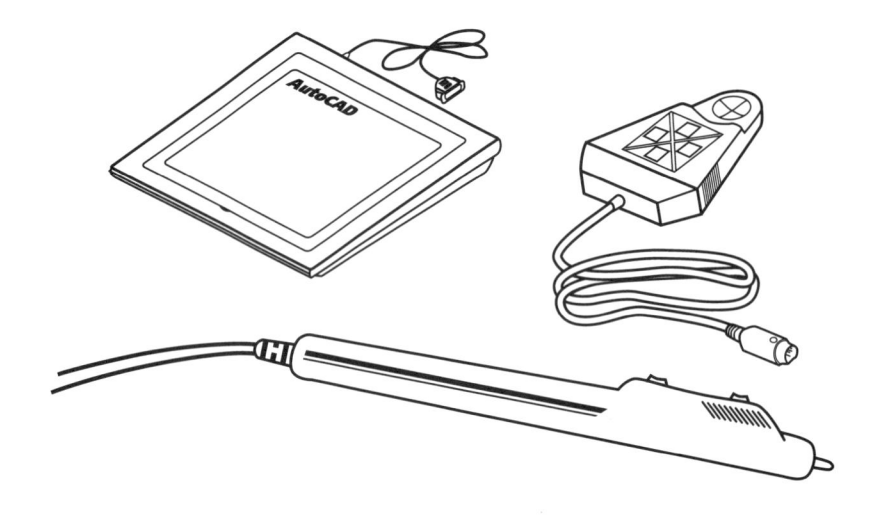

Tutorial objectives

By the end of this chapter you should be able to
- set up different views of a drawing using the VPORTS command
- make two entities from one—the BREAK command
- save views of a drawing—the VIEW command
- extend linear entities—the EXTEND command
- draw a polygon—the POLYGON command
- display the co-ordinates of a point—the ID command
- find the length of a line—the DIST command

Tutorial 10.1

Load the **BEARINGS** drawing that you completed in chapter 9. Check that the current linetype is continuous.

Target drawing

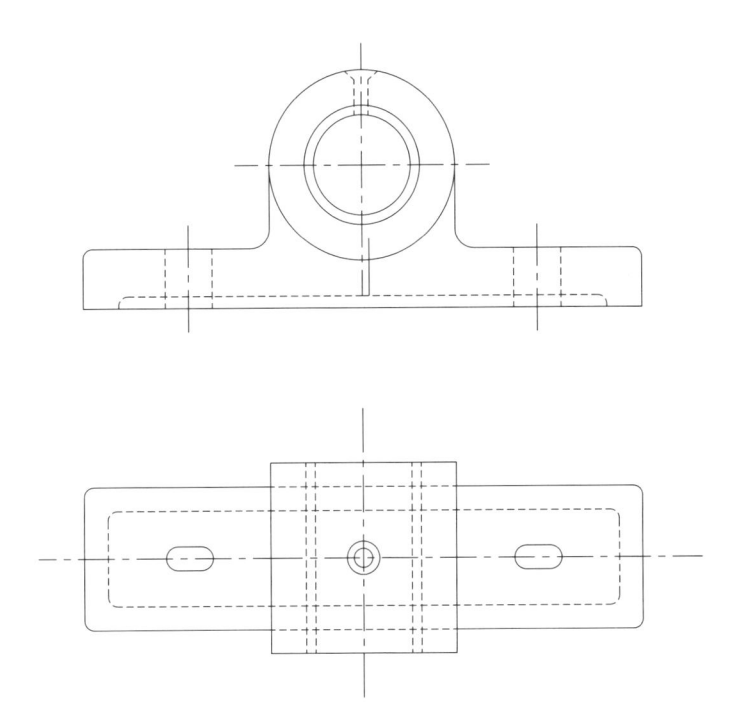

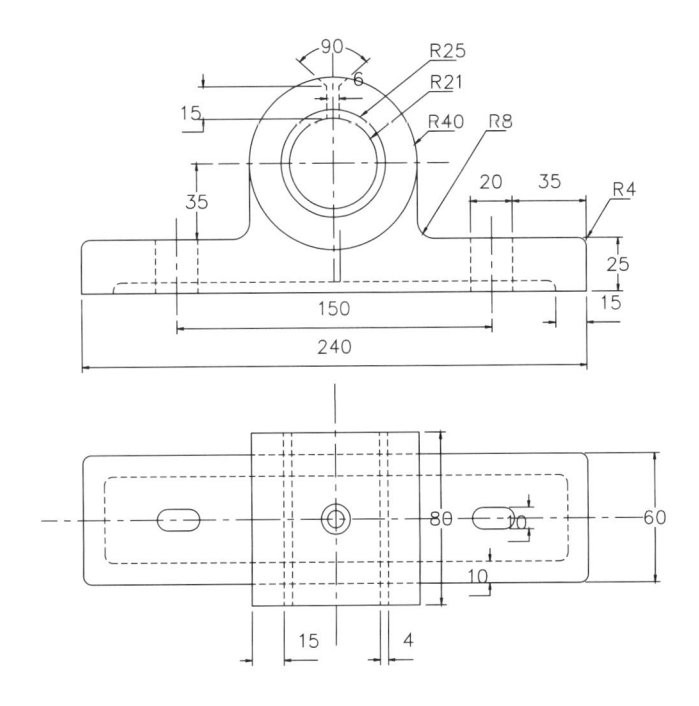

Drawing instructions

The 'vports' command—viewports

All your work up to now was executed while you had a single view of the drawing. The **ZOOM** and **PAN** commands allowed you to move around this view to help in editing or the accurate placement of entities.

AutoCAD release 12 (and later versions) allows you to set up several views of a drawing at once. This is done by setting up two or more 'viewports'. Each viewport can hold a different view of the drawing. The arrangement of some of these viewports is shown in fig. 10.1.

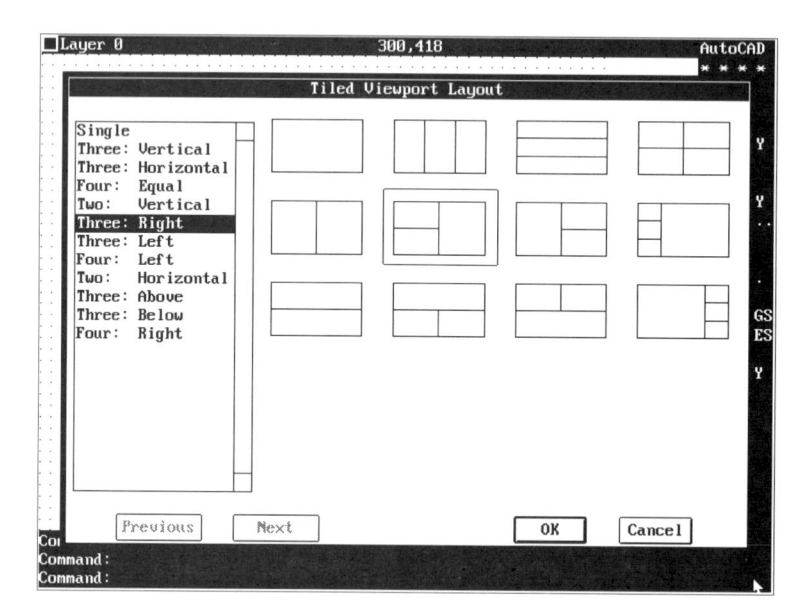

Fig. 10.1. Some of AutoCAD's viewport configurations.

Up to sixteen views (on DOS computers) of a drawing can be on screen at any time. You can only work in a single view by setting it 'current'.

Many of AutoCAD's commands can be executed across viewports: that is, a command can be started in one viewport and completed in another.

How the command works

The command is found on the screen menu under *'View'*, *'Layout'*, and finally *'Tiled Vports ...'* The icon menu in fig. 10.1 will be displayed. Selection of a viewport arrangement is made by clicking in the appropriate box and then selecting **OK**. The drawing will regenerate immediately after the viewports are displayed.

If the command is executed from the command prompt, the following options are displayed:

Save/Restore/Delete/Join/SIngle/?/2/<3>/4:

- Number of viewports: The default number of viewports is three.
- Save and restore: An arrangement of viewports can be saved with a name and restored at a later stage.
- Delete allows a saved viewport name to be deleted.

- Join will merge two viewports into a single one.
- SI will revert to a single viewport display.
- ? will display a list of saved viewports.

If the default of three viewports is selected, AutoCAD will ask you for the display arrangement of the ports on the screen.

Horizontal/Vertical/Above/Below/Left/<Right>:

If *Horizontal* or *Vertical* are selected, the three viewports occupy the same area of the screen in a horizontal or vertical display.

When *'Above/Below/Left/<Right>:'* are selected, one of the viewports is made larger than the other two. The larger port can be positioned above, below, left or right on the screen, with the two smaller, equal-sized viewports beside it. These arrangements can be see in fig. 10.1.

Setting up viewports and making a port current

Select viewports from the drop-down menu, as described above. Select the three vertical viewports (second from the left on the top row), and click on **OK**. The screen displayed should resemble that in fig. 10.2.

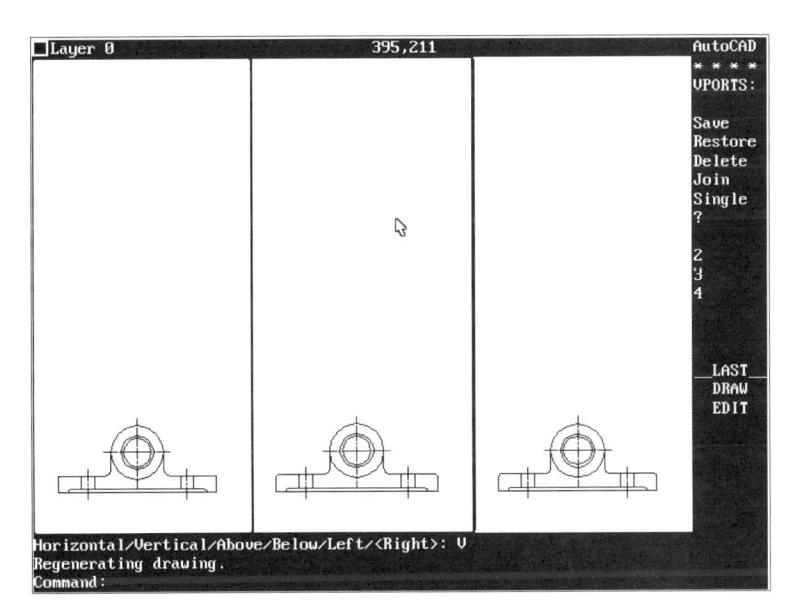

Fig. 10.2. Three vertical viewports.

Move the pointing device. The viewport with the cross-hairs is the *current* port. You can draw and edit in this port. Only one viewport can be current at a time.

Try moving into another viewport. Once the cross-hairs are moved into another viewport they change to an arrow. Click on the pick button to make the viewport current.

Execute the **VPORTS** command at the command prompt and select the *'Save'* option. In response to *'?/Name for new viewport configuration:'* give the name **FIRST**.

Here is the command sequence:
Command: VPORTS
Save/Restore/Delete/Join/SIngle/?/2/<3>/4: **S**
?/Name for new viewport configuration: **FIRST** ← This is name you are giving
the three-viewports set-up

Command:

Executing a command between viewports

Make the rightmost viewport current, and then **ZOOM—Extents**. Set the middle viewport current and Zoom in, as shown in fig. 10.3. If the circles are not smooth, set the **VIEWRES** value to **2000**.

Set the leftmost viewport current, and **ZOOM Window** on the right slot. Your display should be similar to that in fig. 10.3. Execute the **VPORTS** command at the command prompt and select the *'Save'* option again. In response to *'?/Name for new viewport configuration:'* give the name **SECOND**.

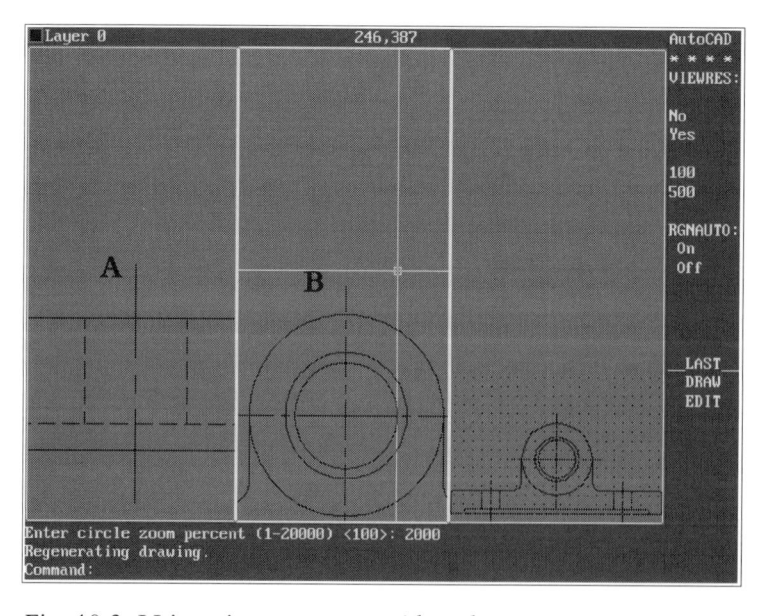

Fig. 10.3. Using viewports as an aid to drawing.

To draw a line from the top of the centre line in the left viewport to the top of the centre line in the middle viewport, follow these steps:
(1) Make the left port current and execute the **LINE** command.
(2) Use the object snap mode **END** to select the top of the centre line A in fig. 10.3.
(3) Move the cross-hairs into the middle viewport and click on the pick button to set the port as current. The line will appear attached to the cross-hairs.
(4) Use the object snap mode **END** to attach the line to the top of the centre

line B in fig. 10.3. Press **[enter]**. Note how the rightmost viewport displays the line.
(5) Execute **REDRAWALL** to refresh the three viewports.
(6) Make the middle viewport current.
(7) Execute the **VPORTS** command at the command prompt line.
(8) Select SI to return to a single viewport.
Command: VPORTS
Save/Restore/Delete/Join/SIngle/?/2/<3>/4: **SI**
Regenerating drawing.
   Note that the viewport that was current is displayed when you return to a single screen.
(9) **ZOOM—All**.
(10) **ERASE** the line you just drew.

Restoring the saved viewports

During your work you saved two viewport set-ups. These can be called up at any time. If you have forgotten the names of the views you saved, the **?** will list them. For example, to check what views you saved and to restore the SECOND view, execute the following:
Command: **VPORTS**
Save/Restore/Delete/Join/SIngle/?/2/<3>/4: **?**
Viewport configuration(s) to list <*>:   ← Press **[enter]**
Current configuration:
**
id# 2
corners: 0.0000,0.0000 1.0000,1.0000
Configuration FIRST:
0.6667,0.0000 1.0000,1.0000
0.0000,0.0000 0.3333,1.0000
0.3333,0.0000 0.6667,1.0000
Configuration SECOND:
0.0000,0.0000 0.3333,1.0000
0.3333,0.0000 0.6667,1.0000
0.6667,0.0000 1.0000,1.0000
Command: ← Press **[enter]** to call up the command again
VPORTS
Save/Restore/Delete/Join/SIngle/?/2/<3>/4: **R**
?/Name of viewport configuration to restore: **SECOND**
Regenerating drawing.
Command:

Note: The values you are presented with may differ from those above.

Some characteristics of the viewports

- A command can be started in one viewport and completed in another.
- SNAP and GRID can be switched on in one viewport and off in another, i.e. the viewports can hold different drawing settings.
- The REDRAW and REGEN commands will only apply to the current viewport. REDRAWALL and REGENALL will apply the commands to all the viewports on the display.
- When you return to a single-screen display the current viewport is the one that is displayed on the single screen.

Do not **SAVE** any changes you made during this tutorial. **QUIT** AutoCAD or proceed to the next tutorial.

Tutorial 10.2

Load the section of the **BEARINGS** drawing as completed in tutorial 10.1. The plan view will now be added to the drawing. Use **ZOOM** and **ORTHO** wherever you think they will help you in this assignment.

Open a single viewport if you have not already done so and **ZOOM—All**.

Drawing the plan view

Tip: Draw the complete structure in continuous linetype and then convert the required lines to hidden or centre linetype.

Step 1: The construction of the plan can be started by drawing a line from the bottom left corner of the section view (marked A in fig. 10.4) a distance of 120 mm at 270°. The end of this line (marked B in fig. 10.4) can then be used to construct the plan view.

Draw the outline of the plan view from B. Erase the construction line AB.

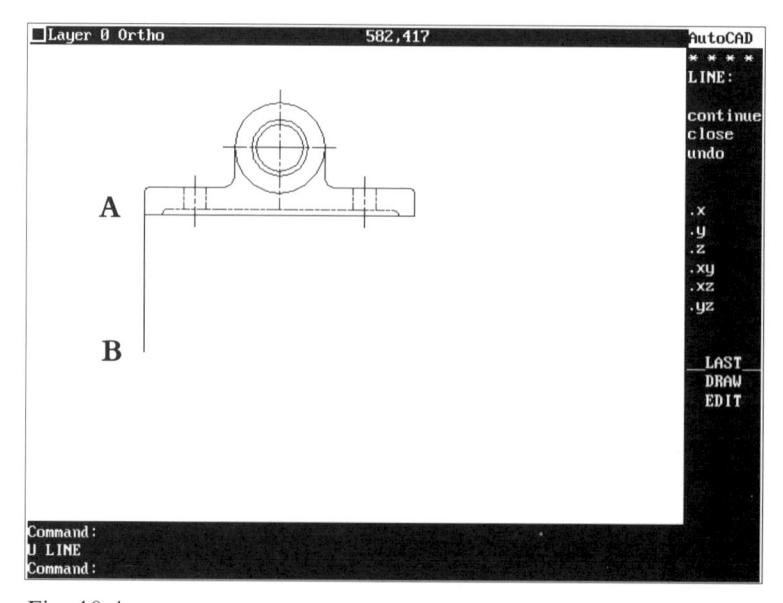

Fig. 10.4.

Step 2: **FILLET** the outline ($r = 4$).
Step 3: **OFFSET** the straight edges of the outline inwards 10 mm (do not offset the fillet arcs) to form the inner rectangle.
Step 4: Fillet the corners of this inner rectangle (fillet radius = 4).
Step 5: Construct square C with sides of 80 mm (see fig. 10.5 and 10.6). Start by taking construction lines down from the plan view a length of approximately 280 mm. These construction lines are shown in fig. 10.5.

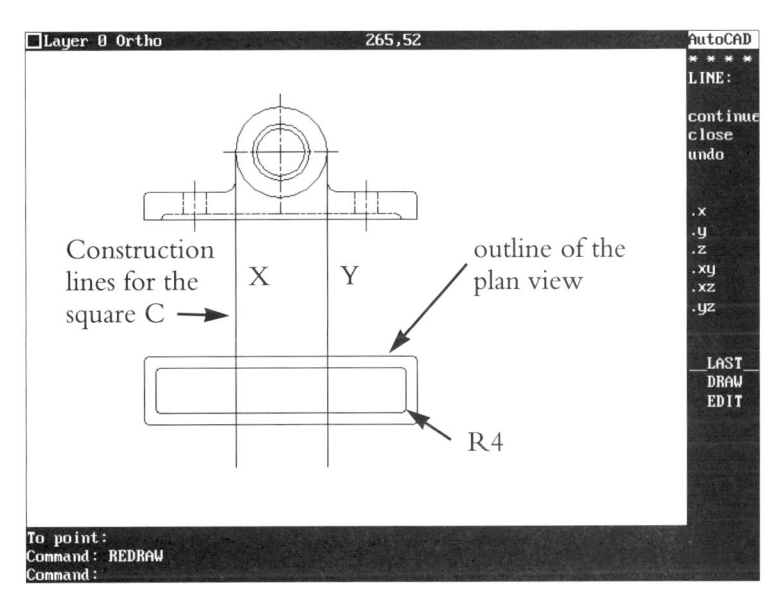

Fig. 10.5. Creation of construction lines.

Offset the upper and lower lines of the plan view (marked U and L, respectively) of the plan view 10 mm (fig. 10.6).

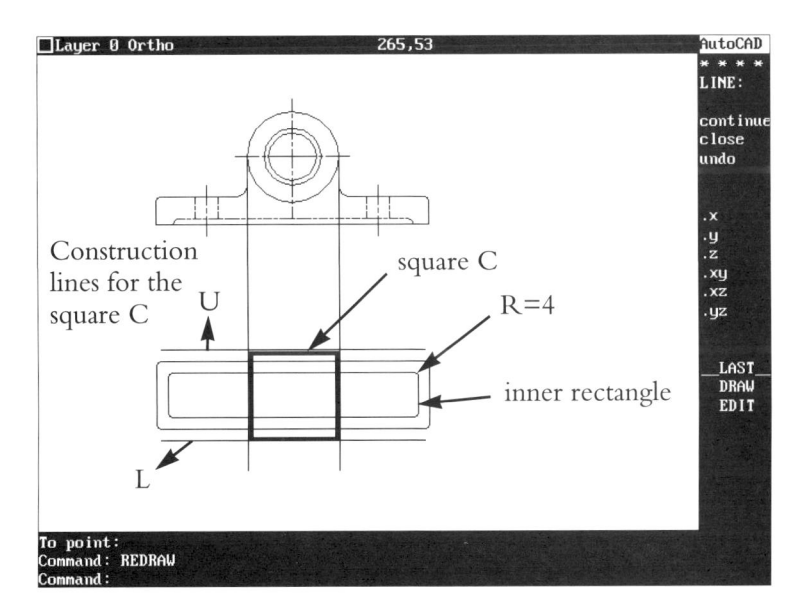

Fig. 10.6. Offset lines in position.

Step 6: **TRIM** the vertical construction lines X and Y in fig. 10.5. Offset the vertical sides of square C 15 mm and 4 mm, respectively (see fig. 10.7). Change these vertical lines to the hidden linetype. Also change the inner offset rectangle D (fig. 10.7) to hidden linetype (don't forget to select the fillet arcs at the corners).

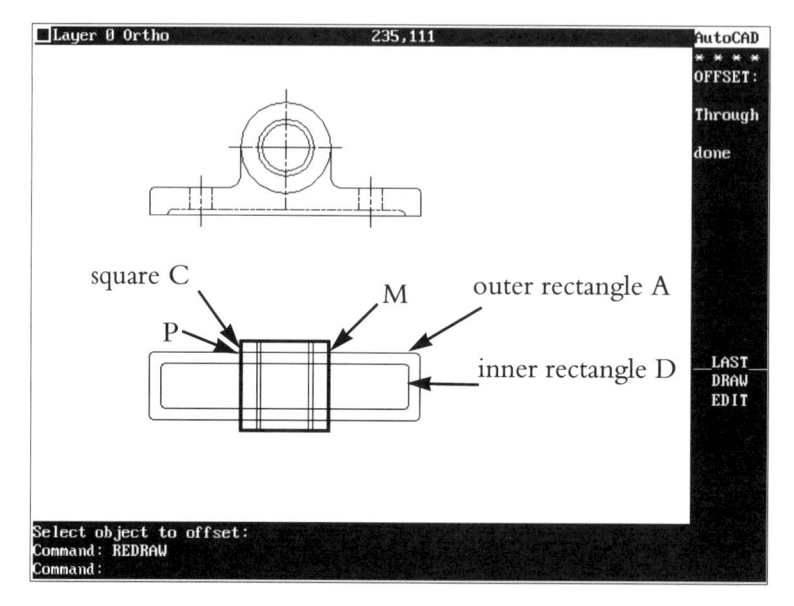

Fig. 10.7.

Step 7: **TRIM** lines U and L in fig. 10.6 to finish square C. Part of the outer rectangle A must be shown in hidden linetype. It is not possible to convert part of a line to a different linetype. To overcome this problem, each of the upper and lower sides of rectangle A can be broken into three lines, using the **BREAK** command.

The 'break' command

BREAK allows you to break entities or remove pieces of them. A line can be broken into two line entities. Only one entity can be broken at a time. Lines, circles, arcs and polylines can be edited with the **BREAK** command. An entity can be broken with a gap placed in it, or an invisible break can be made that functions to divide the entity into two entities.

How the command works

The command is found under *'Modify'* on the drop-down menu and under *'EDIT'* on the screen and tablet menus. When the command is executed, an entity is selected. The point at which the entity is selected can be the first break point. This is followed by a request for the second break point. If the two selected points are at different positions on the entity, AutoCAD will break the object by removing the portion of entity between these points. If the two points are the same, AutoCAD produces an invisible break in the entity. This latter case of applying an invisible break will be used here.

Execute the BREAK command.

Command: **BREAK**
Select object: ← Pick the line PM in fig. 10.7
Enter second point (or F for first point): **F**
Enter first point: **INT**
of   ← Pick the point P in fig. 10.7
Enter second point: **@**
Command:

This has created two line entities from a single line by inserting an invisible break at point P. To break the line again at point N, call up **BREAK** by pressing **[enter]**.

Command: **BREAK**
Select object: ← Pick the line PM in fig. 10.7
Enter second point (or F for first point): **F**
Enter first point: **INT**
of   ← Pick the point M in fig. 10.7
Enter second point: **@**
Command:

The line between P and M is now a separate line entity. The **CHANGE** command can be used to convert it to hidden linetype.

Exercise
BREAK the equivalent line on the other side and **CHANGE** it to hidden linetype (see fig. 10.8).

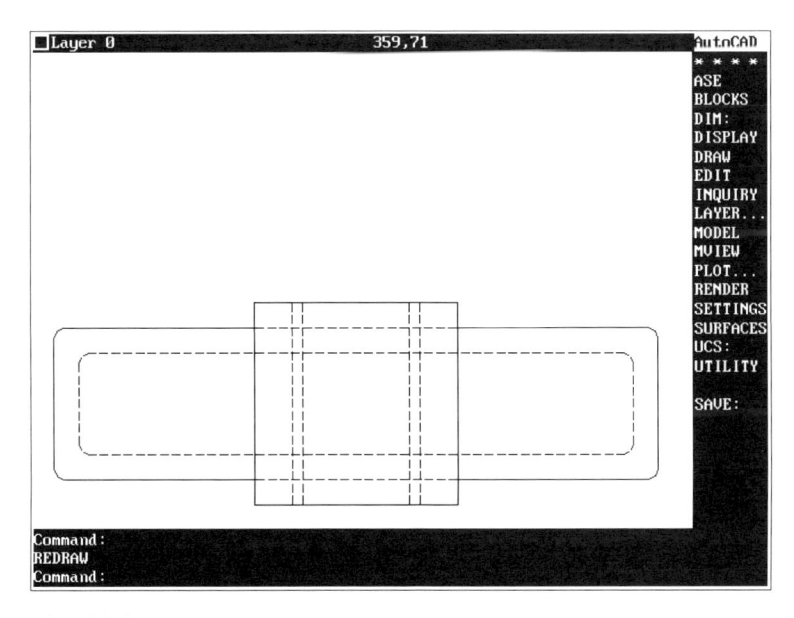

Fig. 10.8.

Step 8: Place the centre lines and the circles representing a plan view of the oil hole. To do this, switch **ORTHO** on. Draw a line from the centre of any one of the circles in the section view through the plan view (marked E in fig. 10.9). Draw a centre line F through the plan view horizontally. The object snap mode **MID** may help here (see fig. 10.9).

Using the intersection of these lines, place the two circles at the centre of the plan (radii of 4 and 7 units).

TRIM or **BREAK** the construction line F to form a centre line, and use the **CHANGE** command to convert it to the centre linetype. The drawing at this stage is illustrated in fig. 10.9.

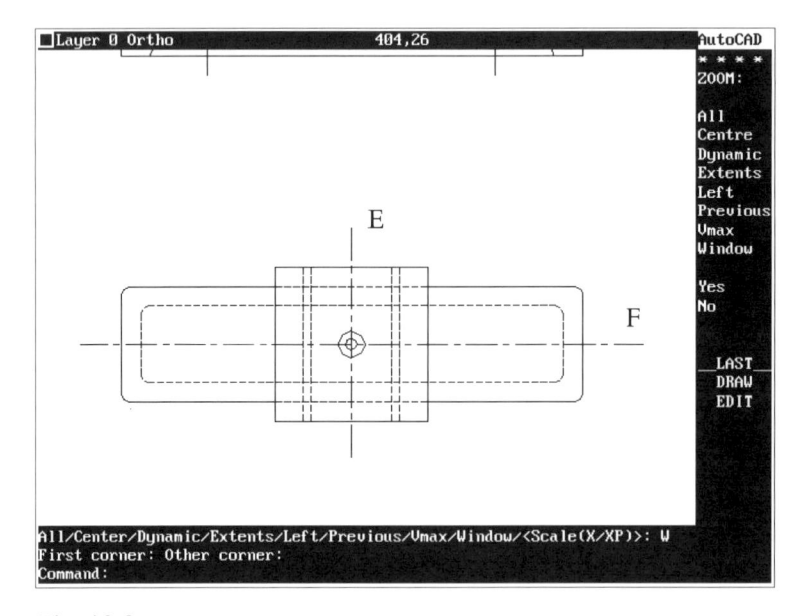

Fig. 10.9.

Step 9: Draw the slots. Set up three viewports, as shown in fig. 10.10. Set your linetype to continuous.

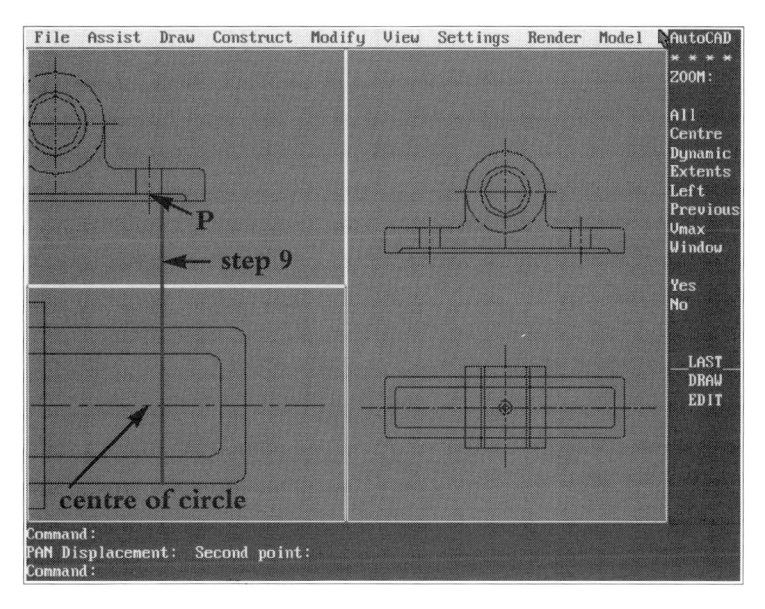

Fig. 10.10.

Draw a construction line from the rightmost hidden line in the sectional view of the slot (marked P in the top left viewport) down to the plan view (bottom left viewport). The semicircles that compose the slot have a radius of 5 mm.

To construct the semicircle, offset the construction line just drawn 5 mm to the left. The intersection of this offset line and the centre line in the plan view will define the centre of a circle. Draw the circle ($r = 5$) with the centre at this intersection indicated as point H in fig. 10.11.

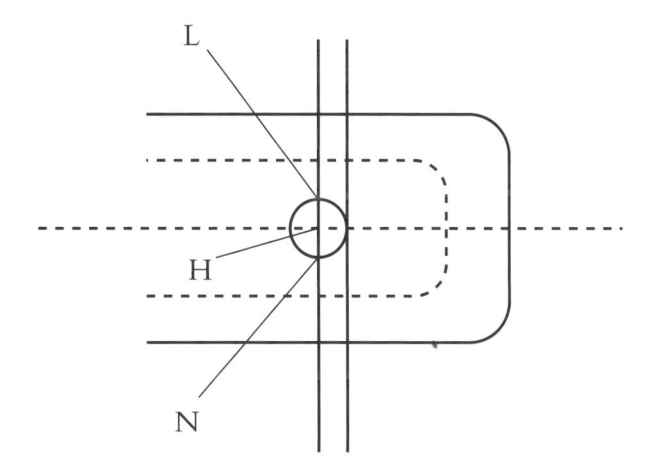

Fig. 10.11. Bottom left viewport.

Forming a semicircle with the 'break' command

Zoom in on the circle in the bottom left viewport. The left half of the circle will now be removed to leave the right semicircle in place. This will form the right side of the slot.

Command: **BREAK**
Select object: ← Pick anywhere on the circle
Enter second point (or F for first point): **F**
Enter first point: **INT**
of   ← Pick the top intersection L in fig. 10.11
Enter second point: **INT**
of   ← Pick the bottom intersection N in fig. 10.11
Command:

The semicircle is now formed.

Draw a line from the centre line of the slot in the section view in the top left viewport, through the slot in the plan view (bottom left viewport). Zoom previous in the bottom left viewport and **MIRROR** the semicircle, using this axis as the mirror line.

Join the two semicircles with straight lines. The slot is drawn. Erase all the construction lines.

Make the right viewport current, and mirror the slot to the left side of the plan view. Delete your construction lines and return to a single viewport.

ADDITIONAL INFORMATION

The 'break' command

The **BREAK** command can be used to remove the tail end of a line (this is illustrated in fig. 10.12). The line A is to be terminated at 'x'. Issue the **BREAK** command. In response to *'Select object'*, pick the point 'x'. As a second point pick the point 'y' off the end of the line. The segment of the line after 'y' will be removed.

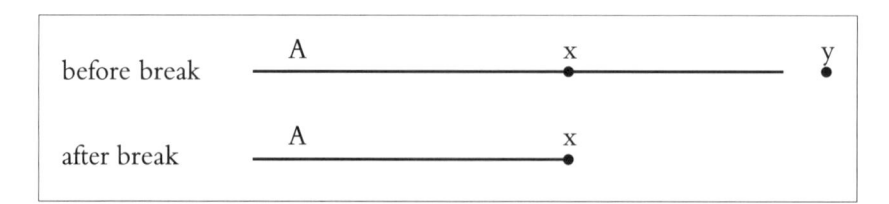

Fig. 10.12. The 'extend' command.

The 'view' command

This command allows you to save and later recall saved views of a drawing. It is found on the drop-down menu under *'Render', 'Views...'*

The command is especially useful in large drawings that occupy a large area. Normally you may have used the **ZOOM** and **PAN** command to move back and forth to frequently used areas of the drawing. The **VIEW** command allows you to save these views and recall them when required. A large map might have views of the NORTH, SOUTH, EAST and WEST saved as views.

The procedure to save a NORTH view is:
- ZOOM in on the view you want, and
- issue the VIEW command to save it.

The command sequence to save a NORTH view is:
Command: **VIEW**
?/Delete/Restore/Save/Window: **S**
View name to save: **NORTH**
To recall the view type:
Command: **VIEW**
?/Delete/Restore/Save/Window: **R**
View name to restore: **NORTH**
Command:

The dialogue box 'view control' can be called up from the command prompt by typing **DDVIEW**.

Views can be selected with a window and saved in the normal way. Saved views can also be plotted using the **PLOT** command (see chapter 18).

The 'extend' command

This command enables you to extend the length of entities up to an already existing boundary. The entity you are extending and the boundary it is extending to must be visible on the screen.

The **EXTEND** command can be accessed from the drop-down menu under *'Modify'* and on the screen menu under *'EDIT'*.

How the command works

The command first asks for the boundary you want to extend to. It then asks for the entity you wish to extend. Boundaries can be polylines, lines, arcs, and circles.

The command syntax is:
Command: **EXTEND**
Select boundary edge(s)...
Select objects:
Select objects:
Select object to extend:

The *'Select boundary edge(s)...Select objects:'* prompt is asking you to pick the boundary you want your entity or entities to extend to.

An entity such as a line may be extended in two directions during a single execution of the command.

The 'polygon' command

This command uses polylines to draw polygons. **POLYGON** is found under *'DRAW'*, *'next'*, on the Screen menu and under *'Draw'* on the tablet and drop-down menus.

After you specify the number of sides in the polygon (from 3 to 1,024), it can be drawn in one of two basic ways:
(1) define one side of the polygon, and AutoCAD will construct the rest;
(2) give the centre point, and AutoCAD will ask if you want the polygon inscribed or circumscribed around an imaginary circle. This latter method is the default.

The examples below illustrate this.

Example 1
In this case the polygon will have five sides and will be inscribed in an imaginary circle of radius 4 units. The centre of the polygon can be chosen using any of the co-ordinate input methods or using object snap modes.
Command: **POLYGON**
Number of sides: **5**
Edge/(Center of polygon): **8,23**
Inscribed in circle/Circumscribed about circle (I/C): **I**
Radius of circle: **4**
Command:

The diagram illustrates the way the radius is defined for inscribed and circumscribed circles.

Example 2
In this example the polygon will again have five sides but is defined on the basis of a circumscribed circle.
Command: **POLYGON**
Number of sides: **5**
Edge/(Center of polygon): **8,12**
Inscribed in circle/Circumscribed about circle (I/C): **C**
Radius of circle: **4**
Command:

Example 3
This example illustrates the case where one side of the polygon is defined. AutoCAD then uses this to construct the shape.
Command: **POLYGON**
Number of sides: **8**
Edge/(Center of polygon): **E**
First endpoint of edge: **25,24**
Second endpoint of edge: **22,24**
Command:

The 'ID' command

The command **ID** will list a point's *x, y* and *z* co-ordinates. The command is found under *'Assist'* and then *'Inquiry'* on the drop-down menus and under *'INQUIRY'* on the screen menu.

The command sequence is:

Command: **ID** ← Now pick a point on the screen; use an object snap mode if you like

Point: X = 205.00 Y = 85.00 Z = 0.00

Any point can be picked on the screen using the point device or any of the object snap modes. The command can be issued transparently.

The 'dist' command

The command is found under *'Assist'* and then *'Inquiry'* on the drop-down menus and under *'INQUIRY'* on the screen menu. Its principal function is to provide you with the distance between two points; however, it also supplies the angle in the XY plane and the angle from the XY plane.

Here is the command syntax:

Command: **DIST**
First point: Second point:
Distance = 196.02, Angle in XY Plane = 354.1440, Angle from XY Plane = 0.0000
Delta X = 195.00, Delta Y = -20.00, Delta Z = 0.00

The command can be issued transparently.

SUMMARY

The **VPORTS** command was used to allow you to set up different views of your drawing. A viewport must be made current before you can draw in it. Drawing and editing commands can be executed across viewports. This has the advantage of allowing detailed work on a large drawing without continually having to **ZOOM** and **PAN**. Viewports can also be saved and restored. The **BREAK** command can be used to remove parts of entities. An invisible break can be inserted into an entity using the **@** symbol. Entities can be extended to meet already existing entities using the **EXTEND** command. The command **POLYGON** can be used to draw polygons either by defining one side of the polygon and allowing AutoCAD to calculate the size and position of the others or by picking the centre of an imaginary circle and allowing AutoCAD to inscribe or circumscribe a polygon around it.

The utility commands **DIST** and **ID** provide information on the length and co-ordinates of entities in a drawing.

ASSIGNMENTS
Assignment 1

Target drawing

Drawing instructions

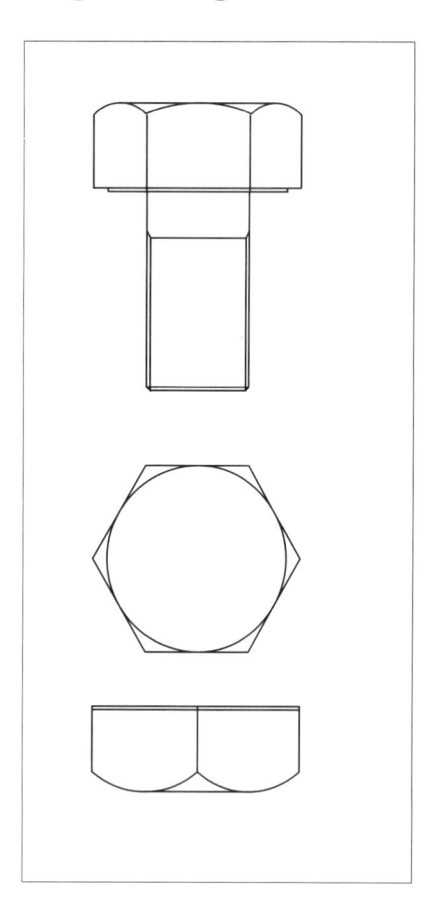

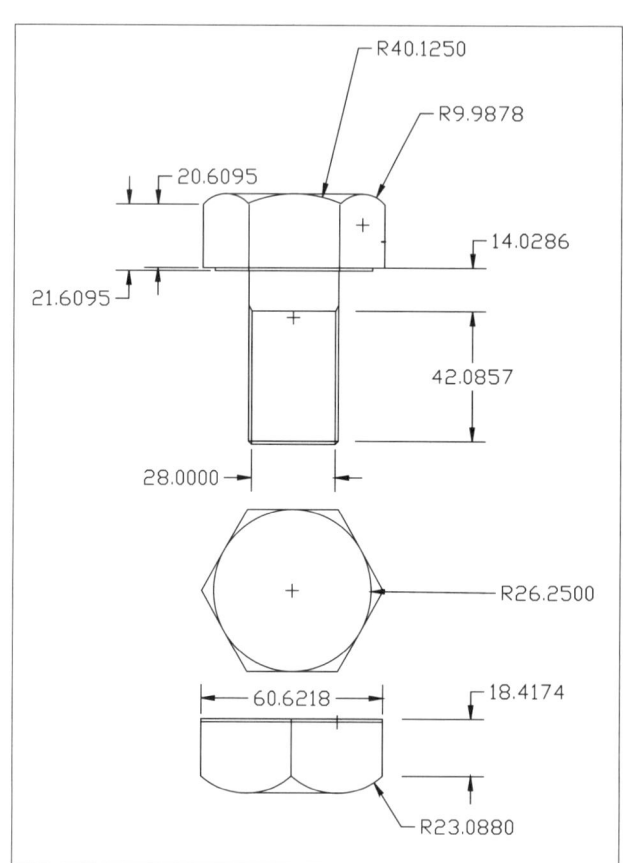

Suggested procedure

The plan view of the nut is constructed from a polygon, and a circle is inscribed inside it. The curved surfaces on the nut and bolt can be constructed from arcs. The **OFFSET** command will also be useful. Use three viewpoints.

Assignment 2

Target drawing

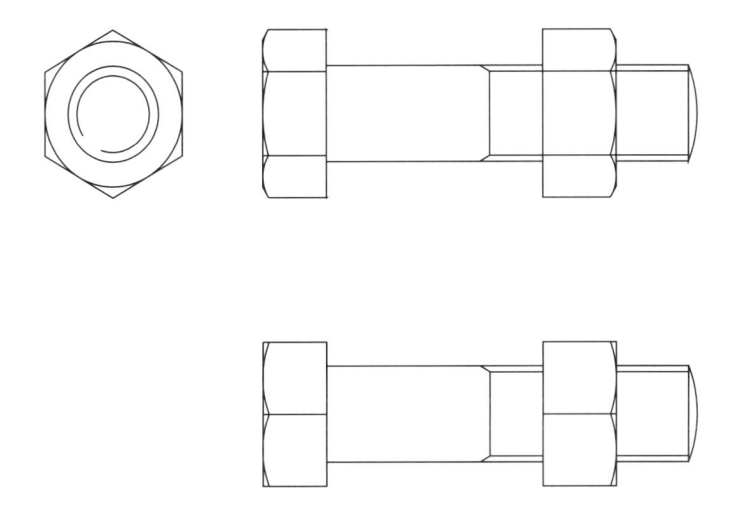

Drawing instructions

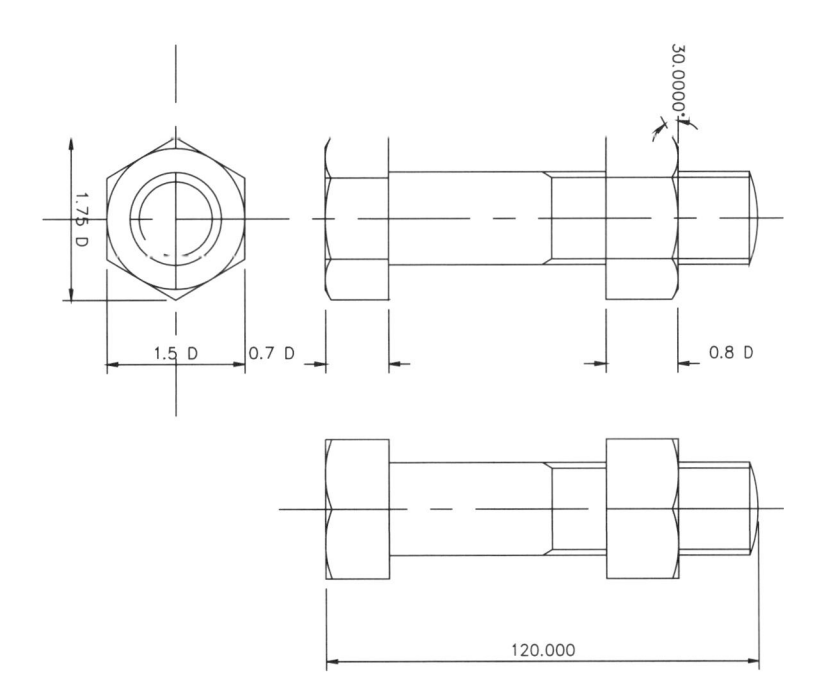

Suggested procedure

The procedure and commands are similar to those of assignment 1.

Assignment 3

Target drawing

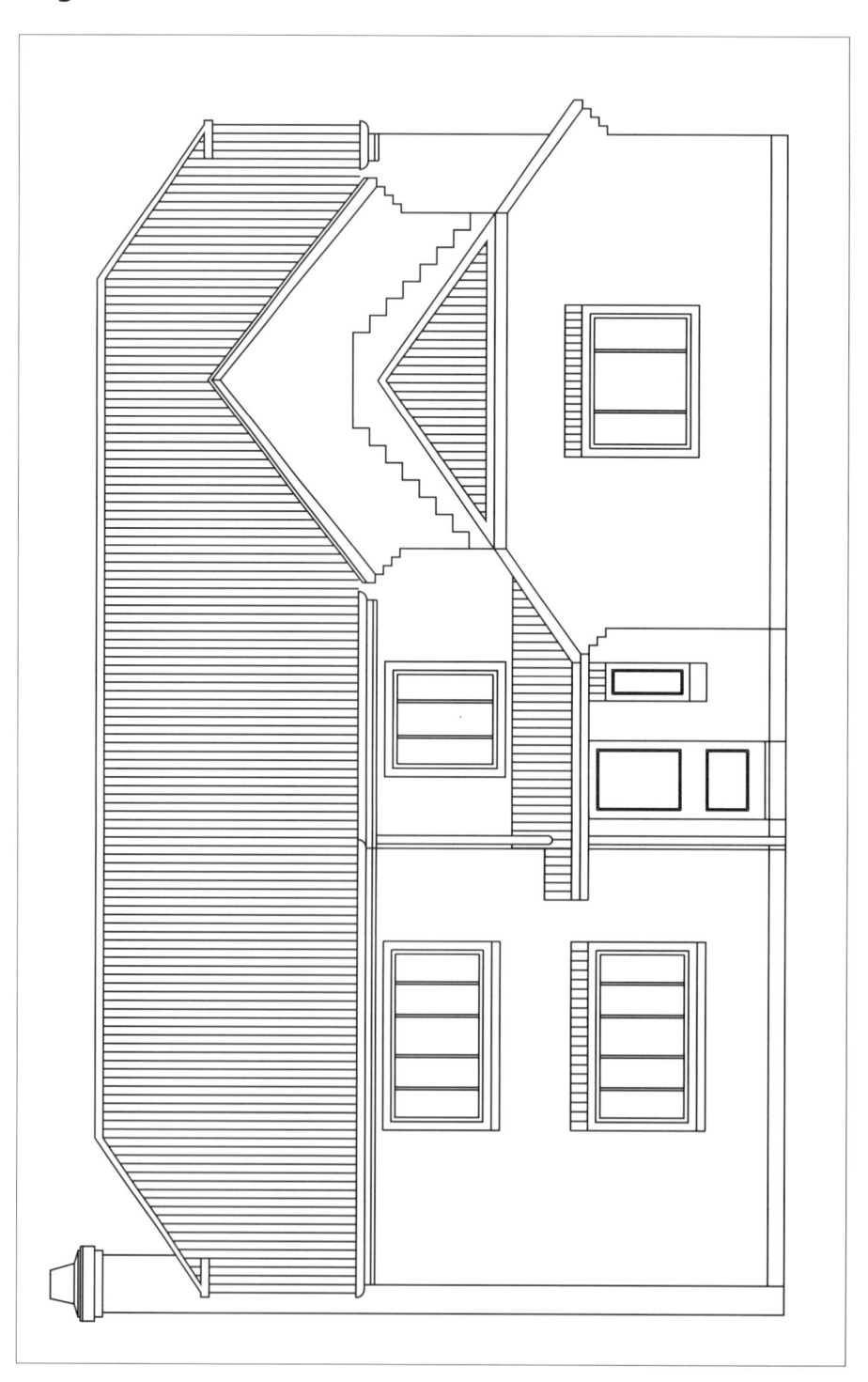

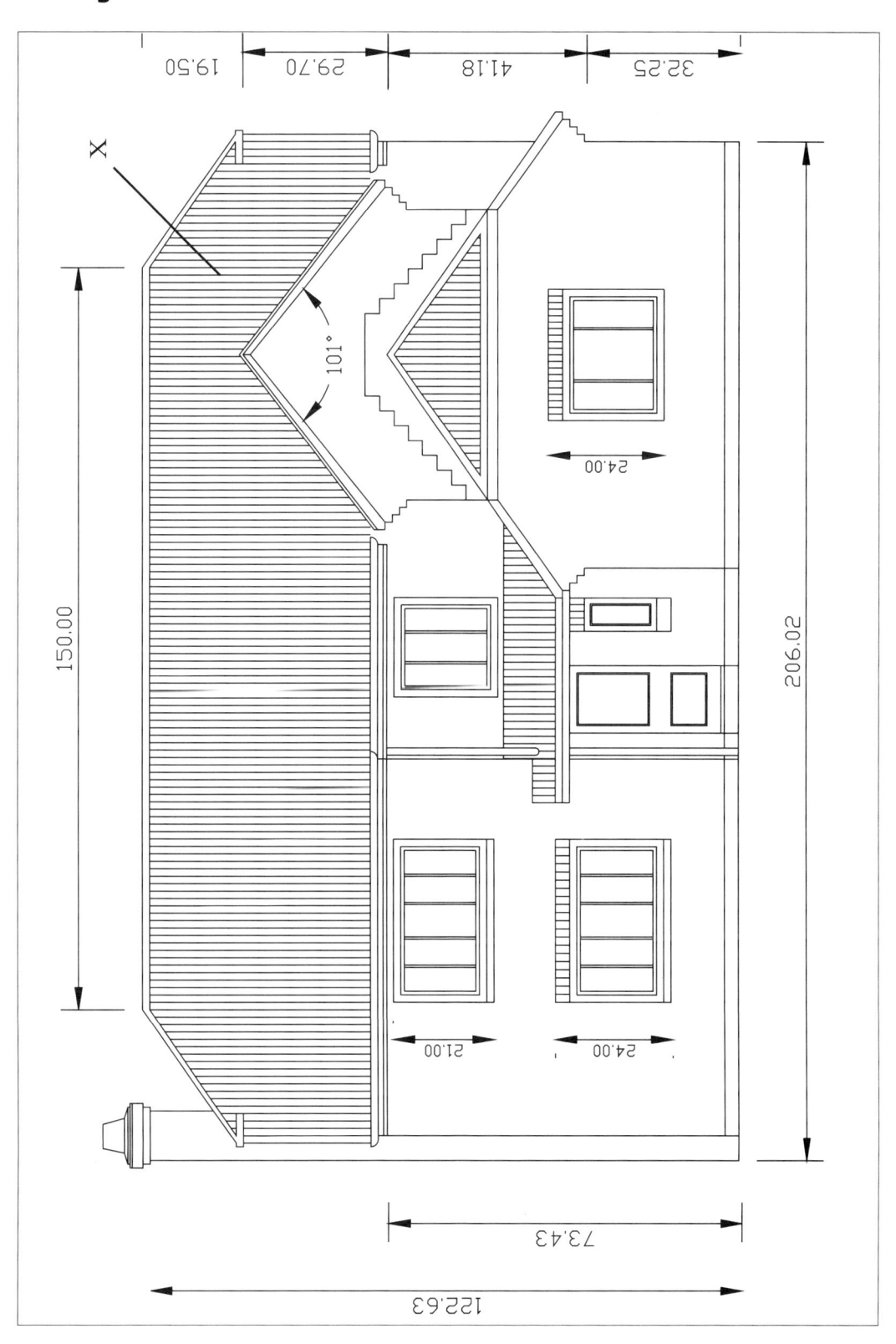

Drawing instructions

VIEWPORTS, BREAKING AND EXTENDING

Suggested procedure

The windows will need the use of the **TRIM**, **OFFSET** and **BREAK** commands. The tiling on the roof can be constructed in the following way:
(1) Draw the line marked X first.
(2) Offset this to the left and right across the roof.
(3) Use the **EXTEND**, **TRIM** and **BREAK** commands to tidy up their placement.

Assignment 4

Target drawing

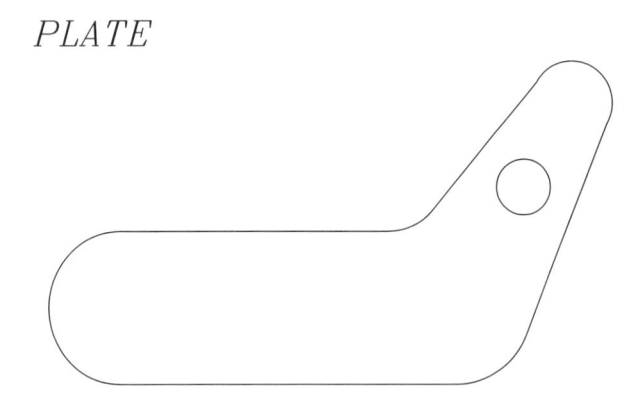

PLATE

Drawing instructions

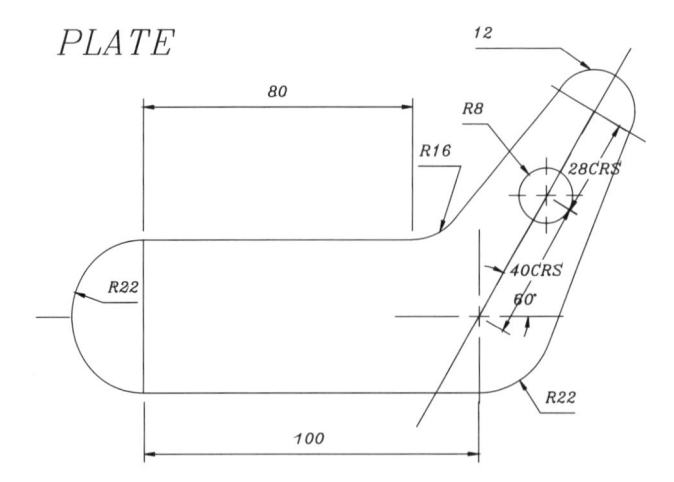

PLATE

Suggested procedure

Draw the outline of the plate first. Use circles for the curved ends of the plate and use the **BREAK** and **TRIM** commands to edit them. The placement of the hole in the plate should be left until last.

Assignment 5

Target drawing

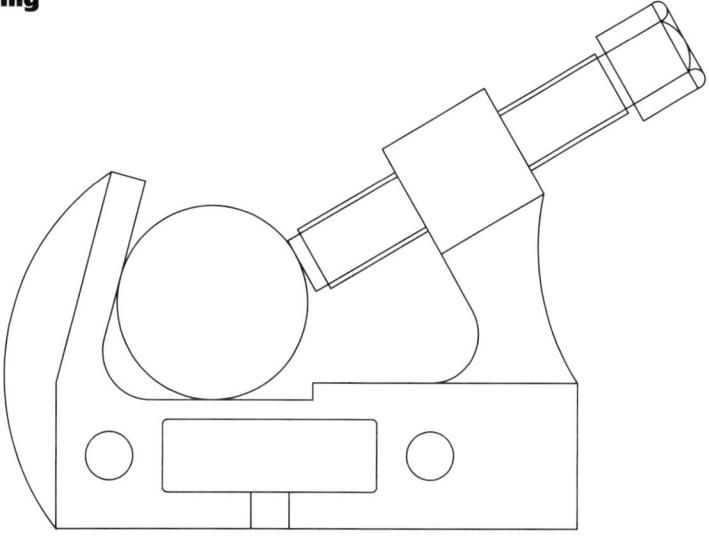

Drawing instructions

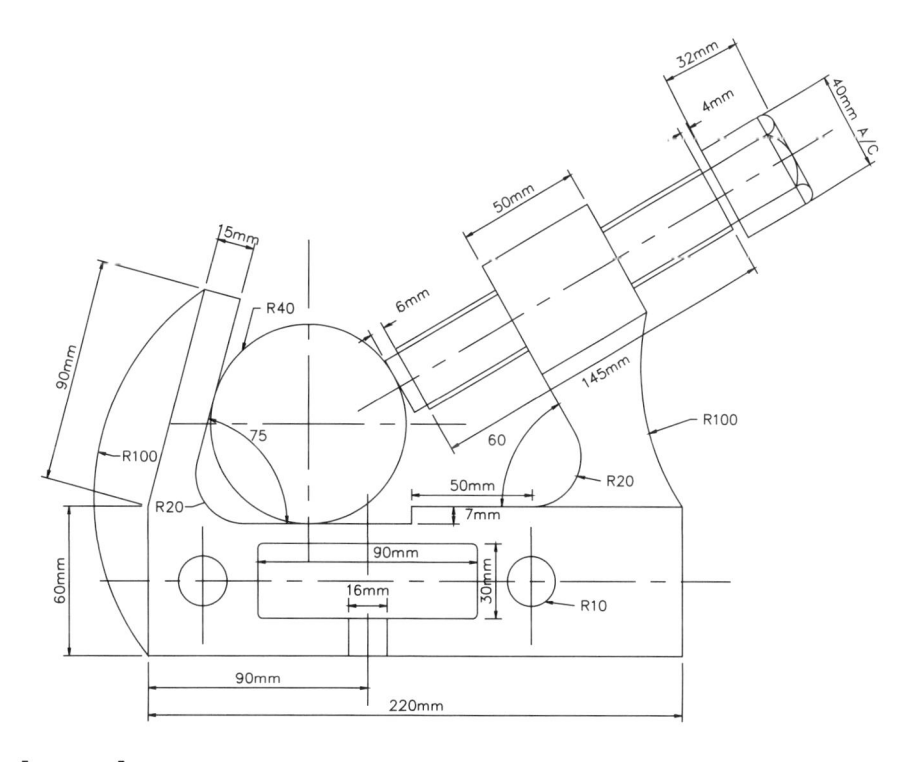

Suggested procedure

The bar-vice will require the use of nearly all the commands you have encountered so far. Use the assignment to explore the use of the object snap modes.

chapter 11

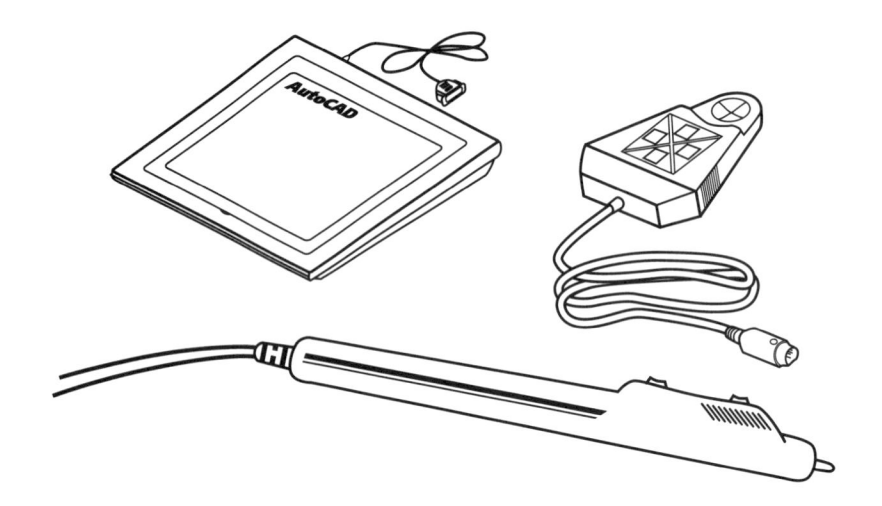

Layers, Basic Dimensioning and Hatching Patterns

Tutorial objectives

By the end of this chapter you should be able to
- create layers for use in a drawing
- name layers and control their display
- make a layer current
- freeze layers to help speed up the drawing process
- use basic dimensioning commands
- place hatching patterns into a drawing

Tutorial 11.1

Load the **BEARINGS** drawing created in the last tutorial. The drawing will be developed further in this tutorial with the insertion of dimensions and the creation of layers.

Target drawing

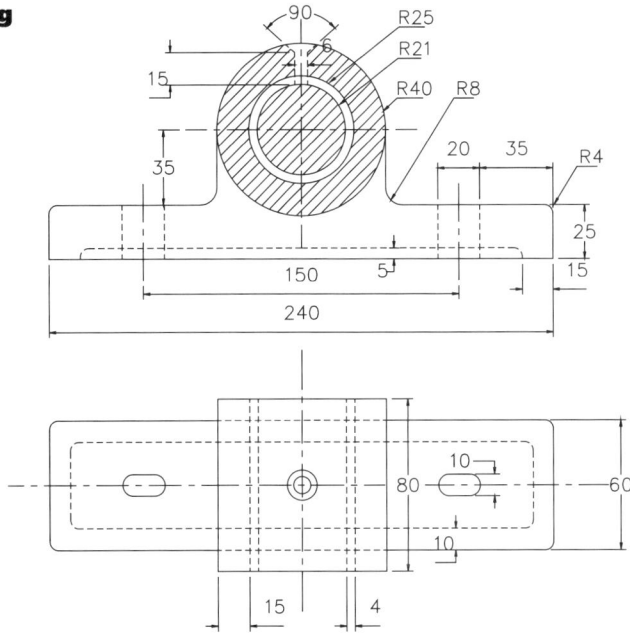

Layers in CAD drawings

AutoCAD drawings can be constructed on different layers.

A layer can be thought of as equivalent to a sheet of transparent acetate. Part of the drawing (the walls of a building, say) can be constructed on this acetate sheet. Slip another acetate sheet in over the first one and draw the windows or indicate the dimensions.

The two sheets represent two layers. The drawing is distributed between them and can be viewed as a whole, or each layer can be viewed separately. Layers are always directly above or below each other.

AutoCAD allows the creation of as many layers as necessary: there is no limit to the number that can be used in a drawing. There is also no limit to the number of entities that can be placed on a layer.

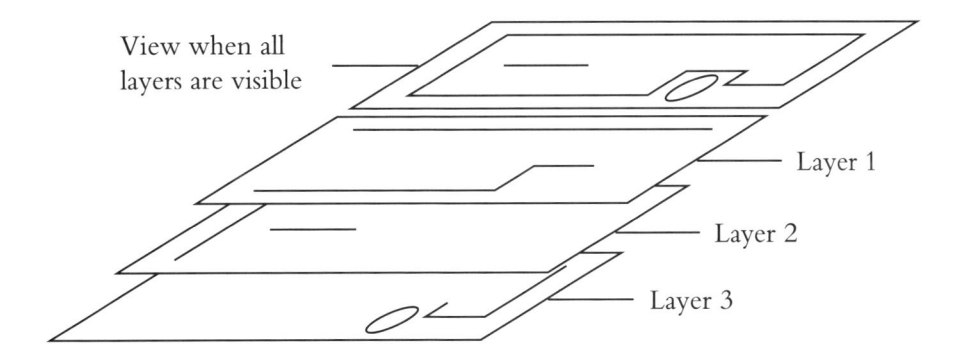

Fig. 11.1. Different elements of a drawing can be spread over several layers.

When a new AutoCAD drawing is started you are provided with layer 0. Layer 0 has some special properties. All the tutorials up to this were created on the default layer 0. Before proceeding you should set the drawing to a single viewport, and **Zoom—All** if you have not already done so.

Some properties of layers

- Layers can be made visible or invisible.
- Linetypes and colours can be assigned to different layers.
- The drawing process can be speeded up by preventing layers that are not in use from regenerating.

The 'layer' command

The command can be executed from the command prompt and the screen menu; however, by executing it from the drop-down menus the *'Layer Control'* dialogue box is displayed. This allows easy access to all the layer subcommands.

Select *'Layer Control…'* from the *'Settings'* drop-down menu. The dialogue box displayed is shown in fig. 11.2.

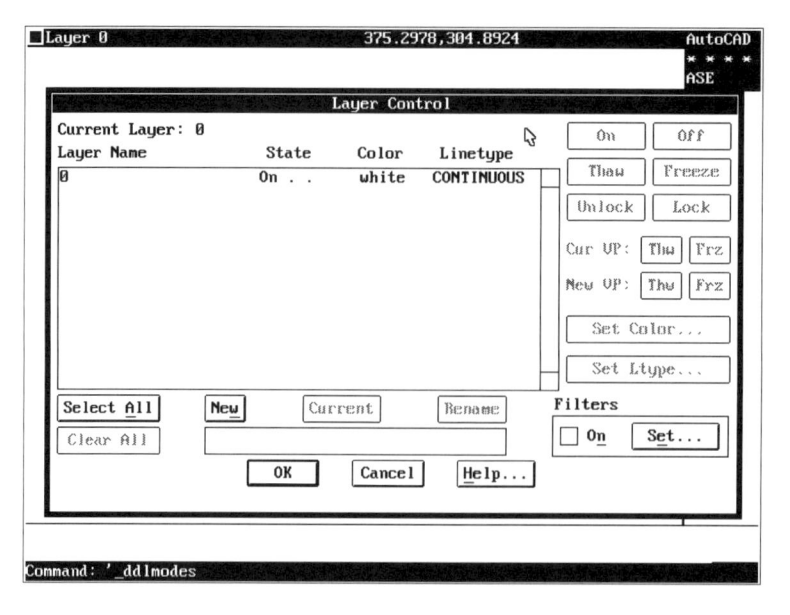

Fig. 11.2. The 'Layer Control' dialogue box.

Some of the titles in the dialogue box are 'ghosted', while others appear in their normal type. This feature is used to distinguish options in the dialogue box that are available and those that are unavailable. The ghosted options are unavailable. The available options are now described.

Layer name

The default layer 0 is present under the *'Layer name'* column.

State
A layer can be on or off. These options indicate whether a layer is visible on screen or not. Several layers can be visible (on) or invisible (off) at once.

Colour
A colour can be assigned to a layer or layers. All entities drawn on the layers take on the specified colour. This is referred to as assigning a colour *BYLAYER*.

Linetype
A linetype can be assigned to a layer in a similar fashion. All entities drawn on the layer or layers take on the specified linetype. This is referred to as assigning a linetype BYLAYER.

Select all
This selects all layers for a variety of subcommands, such as applying a colour or a linetype to all layers.

New
New will create a new layer. Layer names can be up to 31 characters; however, they must not contain a space.

Filter
See additional information at the end of this chapter.

OK, Help, and Cancel
These function in the normal way.

Creating a new layer

By default, the cursor is flashing in the edit box. Type the name of the layer to be created in this box. In this case enter **DIMENSIONS** and click with the arrow cursor in the *'New'* box. The layer is created and appears in the list of layers in the dialogue box. This new layer is set to the default values *'On…'* (i.e. visible), *'white'* colour, and *'CONTINUOUS'* linetype.

Assigning a colour to a layer

Select the layer you want to change the colour on. In this exercise move the arrow cursor onto the word **DIMENSIONS** under *'Layer Name'* in the dialogue box and click on the pick button once. This action is termed 'selecting the layer'.

The **DIMENSIONS** layer name and default values will be highlighted. Several of the previously ghosted command sub-options are now made available for this selected layer. Click in the *'Set Color'* box. The *'Select Color'* dialogue box is displayed.

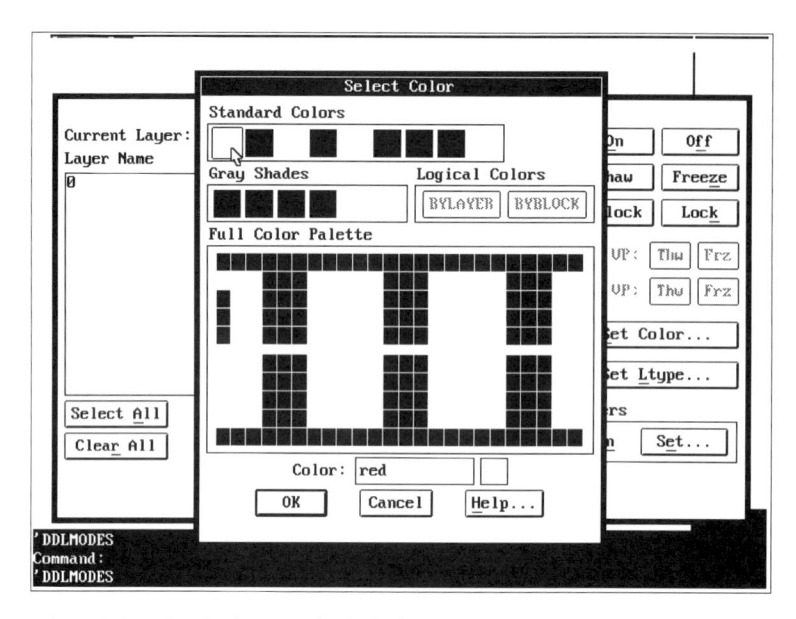

Fig. 11.3. The 'Select Color' dialogue box.

There are several ways to set the colour. For the moment use the *'Standard Colors'* at the top of the dialogue box. Click on the colour **red** (the leftmost colour for those using a monochrome display). Pick **OK** to return to the *'Layer Control'* dialogue box. Note that **'red'** is now attributed to the **DIMENSIONS** layer. All entities drawn on this layer will be displayed in red. Deselect the **DIMENSIONS** layer by clicking on it again. The highlighting will be removed.

Exercise 1
Create the following layers with the attributed colours:

Layer	Colour
Section	blue
Plan	green
Text	cyan
Border	magenta

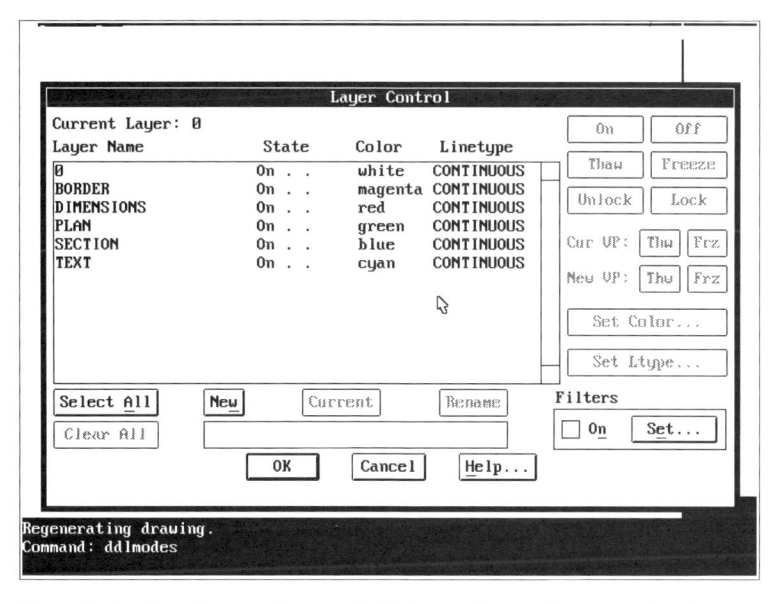

Fig. 11.4. The 'Layer Control' dialogue box after exercise 1.

Making a layer current

To draw on a layer, you must first make it current.

Highlight the **BORDER** layer and then select the *'Current'* box. If the *'Current'* box is ghosted it means that you must have more than one layer selected. Deselect the other layers and make sure that only **BORDER** is highlighted.

Click on **OK** to return to the drawing editor. Check the status line to see if **BORDER** is current and **MAGENTA** is the assigned colour. All drawing and editing will now take place on this layer.

Note: The status line will only display the first eight characters of a layer name on standard VGA screens. Draw the border and title box illustrated in the target drawing at the beginning of the chapter. Positioning and size of the title box are not critical.

Making layers visible and invisible

To see the effect of switching layers on and off, try the following exercises.
(1) To switch off layer 0: Select the layer by highlighting it in the dialogue box. Click on **OFF**. Click on **OK**. When the drawing editor is redisplayed, the plan and section views of the drawing are not displayed. The layer 0, which the drawings were constructed on, is now invisible.

Switch layer 0 on before you proceed.
(2) To switch off the **BORDER** layer: The **BORDER** layer is current. It is not recommended that you switch off a layer that is current. AutoCAD will allow you to do so, but the message *'Warning: the current drawing layer is turned off'* will appear in an alert box.

Make the layer 0 current first and then switch off the **BORDER** layer. The border will disappear and the drawing is displayed.

Switching a layer off will allow you to work on an uncluttered screen. Individual layers can also be plotted. (See chapter 18 on plotting.)

Lock
A layer that is locked is visible on the screen but it cannot be either drawn on or edited.

Unlock
Frees a locked layer or drawing for editing.

Set Ltype
A linetype can be assigned to a layer in a similar fashion to a colour. A linetype must be loaded before it can be assigned to a layer. The loaded linetypes are listed in the *'Select Linetype'* dialogue box.

Rename
Layers can be renamed. To do this, select a layer and change or edit the old name in the edit box and then click on *'Rename'*.

Select All
This option allows the selection of all created layers.

Clear All
This option will deselect all selected layers.

Using the 'layer' command from the command prompt

Use of the **LAYER** command from the prompt does not display the *'Layer Control'* dialogue box. However, nearly all the options on the dialogue box are still available. The command prompt calls up twelve options.

Command: **LAYER**
?/Make/Set/New/ON/OFF/Color/Ltype/Freeze/Thaw/LOck/Unlock:

The ? lists the created layers. If the command is issued now, the layers created in the dialogue box are displayed. The command sequence is:

Command: **LAYER**
?/Make/Set/New/ON/OFF/Color/Ltype/Freeze/Thaw/LOck/Unlock: ?
Layer name(s) to list <*>:

The asterisk (*) is a global replacement character (sometimes called a 'wild card'), and is used to denote all the existing layers. To view several selected layers, type the name of the layers, separated by a comma. For example BORDER, DIMENSIONS will list only those two layers.

Press **[enter]** to accept the asterisk to view all the layers.

Layer name	State	Color	Linetype
0	On	7 (white)	CONTINUOUS
BORDER	On	6 (magenta)	CONTINUOUS
DIMENSIONS	On	1 (red)	CONTINUOUS
PLAN	On	3 (green)	CONTINUOUS
SECTION	On	5 (blue)	CONTINUOUS
TEXT	On	4 (cyan)	CONTINUOUS

Current layer: BORDER

Set makes a layer current. AutoCAD responds with *'New current layer <default>:'*. Enter the layer you want current.

Make is a combination of *New* and *Set*. It will create a new layer and set it current at the same time.

Color assigns a colour to a layer (all entities on the layer will be drawn in the selected colour). You can respond by typing the name of the colour or its number. The standard AutoCAD colours are listed below:

1 Red   5 Blue
2 Yellow   6 Magenta
3 Green   7 White
4 Cyan

If you are using a light background in the drawing editor, colour 7 will be replaced with black, although it will be referred to as **WHITE** and number **7**. The other eight options function in a similar manner to those presented in the *'Layer Control'* dialogue box.

The use of the 'change' and 'chprop' commands with layers

The **CHANGE** command was used in chapter 9 to change the 'linetype' properties of selected entities. A more efficient way to change the properties of entities is to use the CHPROP command. The command allows entities to be moved from one layer to another. To move the plan view of the drawing to the layer PLAN, issue the CHPROP command and use a window to select the plan view and 'LA' to select the LAyer sub-option. AutoCAD will ask for the *'New layer <current>:'* to move the entities to. Enter PLAN and press **[enter]**.

The command sequence is shown below.

Command: **CHPROP**
Select objects: **W**
First corner: Other corner: 36 found
Select objects:
Change what property (Color/LAyer/LType/Thickness)? **LA**
New layer <0>: **PLAN**
Change what property (Color/LAyer/LType/Thickness)?
Command:

If the plan view was successfully moved to the **PLAN** layer, the entities will take on the layer's colour green.

Exercise 2

Move the section view to the **SECTION** layer. It should take on the colour **BLUE**.

Exercise 3

Make the TEXT layer current and place the text in the target drawing on it.

Naming of layers

The layout and organisation of layers in complex drawings is very important, not only for the drawing process itself but as an aid to later editing and plotting of work. The naming of layers should provide information about the drawing in an unambiguous and coherent way.

You may have noticed that the layers you set up in this tutorial were listed alphabetically in the *Layer Control* dialogue box. This is a feature of AutoCAD, and useful to keep in mind when naming layers.

A layer name should give the following characteristics as a minimum:
- a clear indication of what to expect to find on the layer, e.g. a section view, text, or the dimensions of a part;
- the pen weight and colour that will be used for plotting.

The layer names assigned to the **BEARINGS** drawing above could more usefully have been named as follows:

Old name	New name
BORDER	BORD-5-1
DIMENSIONS	DIM1-2-1
PLAN	PLAN-2-1
SECTION	SEC1-1-1
TEXT	TXT1-1-1

The first four characters are a descriptive guide to what is on the layer. The number after the first hyphen describes the pen weight for that layer, and the last digit refers to the colour.

A system like this leaves room for expansion. For example, additional text can be placed on a layer named *TXT2* with its own pen weight and colour. If a drawing contains several sections they can be assigned to layers *SEC2, SEC3,* etc. A layer name can be up to 31 characters long.

Exercise 4

Rename all the named layers in the **BEARINGS** drawing, as described above.

INTRODUCTION TO DIMENSIONING

Before you proceed, make the **DIM1-2-1** layer current.
AutoCAD gives the user complete control over how a drawing is dimensioned. A good knowledge of the dimension command will allow you to fine-tune AutoCAD to your own specialised needs.

Some of the terms used in conjunction with dimensioning are illustrated in figs. 11.5 and 11.6.

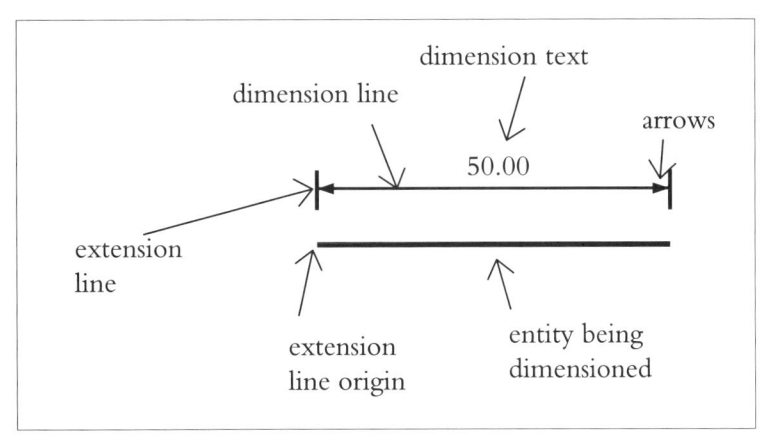

Fig. 11.5.

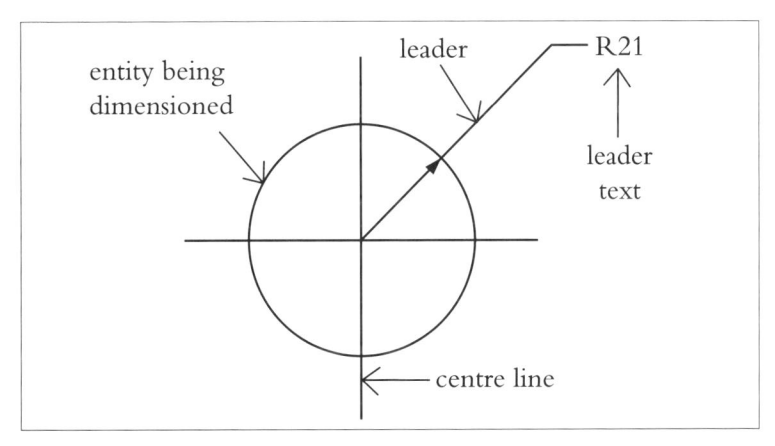

Fig. 11.6. Terms associated with dimensioning circles.

Entering the 'dim' mode

Typing **DIM** at the command prompt brings you into dimensioning mode. The *'Dim'* prompt appears, and you are in effect working in a self-contained program within AutoCAD.

This tutorial will be carried out using the screen menu options.

Select DIM: from the root of the screen menu. The first page of the submenu lists the following:

DIM:
Aligned
Angular
Diameter
Horizntl
Leader
Ordinate
Radius
Rotated
Vertical

Dim Styl
Dim Vars
next
Exit

The command prompt has been replaced by the *Dim* prompt. Many of AutoCAD's normal drawing and editing commands will not function when you are in the Dim prompt.

To leave Dim mode and return to the command prompt, type EXIT or press ^C.

This tutorial will use the dimensioning options *Horizntl, Leader,* and *Vertical*. **EDIT** will call the edit page of the screen menu, and *DRAW* will display the draw entities, while *_LAST_* will call up the last page of screen menu that was used.

The horizontal option

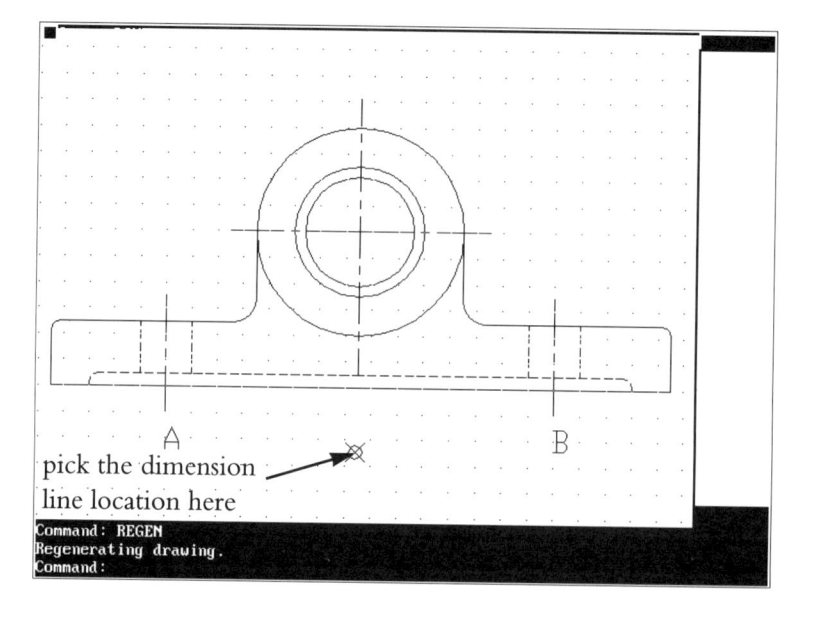

Fig. 11.7. Use the object snap mode to help you measure from the centre lines A and B.

Dimensioning a horizontal line

The distance between the two centre lines marked A and B in fig. 11.7 will now be dimensioned.

How the command works

Click on *Horizntl*. AutoCAD asks for the point you wish to measure from with *'First extension line origin'*. Use the object snap mode **END** to help you select point A. The response is then to ask for *'Second extension line origin'*. Again use **END** to pick point B. Lastly AutoCAD will need to know where to position the dimension line itself. The position can be indicated by picking a point on the screen (see fig. 11.7) to show how far from the object being dimensioned the dimension line is to be constructed.

The distance between the two points is given as a default value. To accept this, press **[enter]**.

Here is the full command sequence to dimension the horizontal line when DIM: is selected from the screen menu:

Command: **_DIM**
Dim: **_HORIZONTAL**
First extension line origin or RETURN to select: **_ENDPOINT**
of   ← Pick the bottom of the centre line at A

Second extension line origin: **_ENDPOINT**
of   ← Pick the bottom of the centre line at B

Dimension line location: ← Pick a point near the POINT in fig. 11.7.

Dimension text <150>:   ← **[enter]**
Dim:

The dimension entity is drawn in red.

The vertical option

The vertical endline is dimensioned in a similar manner. Select 'Vertical' from the screen menu. Remember that the top corner is constructed from a fillet arc. To dimension it accurately select the endpoint of the top horizontal line and the endpoint of the vertical line (marked C and D, respectively, in fig. 11.8). The **ZOOM** command can be used transparently while in the *DIM mode*. Zoom in on the end of the section view to obtain a display similar to fig. 11.8.

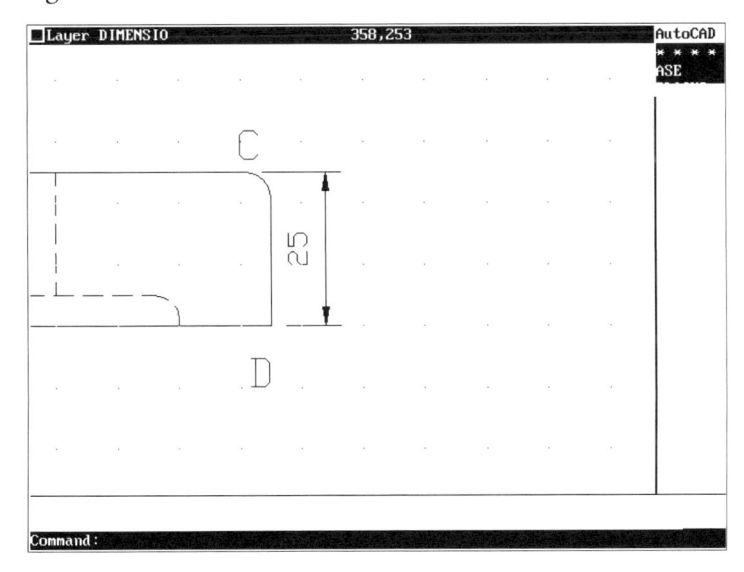

Fig. 11.8. The vertical dimension.

The full vertical dimension line command sequence is as follows:
Command: **_DIM**
Dim: **_VERTICAL**
First extension line origin or RETURN to select: **END**
of   ← Pick near point C
Second extension line origin: **END**
of   ← Pick near point D
Dimension line location:
Dimension text <25>:
Dim:

The leader option

The leader option allows you to place annotations in a drawing. The leader start point is assigned an arrowhead by AutoCAD (although this can be changed: see chapter 15).

The *'To point'* prompts can be responded to in a similar way to the identical prompt in the **LINE** command.

To indicate the radius of the inner section circle using the leader, try the following example.

Do a transparent **ZOOM—Previous** if you zoomed in while dimensioning the vertical line. Pick *'Leader'* from the screen menu.

Command: **_DIM**
Dim: **_LEADER**
Leader start: ← Pick near the inner circle
To point: ← Bring the leader out to
                            the right and pick a point
To point: ← Bring the leader out
                            horizontally and pick a point
To point: ← Press **[enter]**
Dimension text <>:   ← Type **R21** and press **[enter]**
Dim:

Exercise 5
Finish dimensioning the BEARINGS drawing to bring it up to the standard of the target drawing.

HATCHING
Tutorial 11.2

Create a new layer in the **BEARINGS** drawing, called **HATCH**, and assign the colour yellow to it. Make it current, and switch off the DIM1-2-1 layer.

The 'bhatch' command

Hatching is often used in drawings to show a sectional view. The **BHATCH** command in AutoCAD eliminates all the tedious hatching work often associated with hand draughting. A library of 53 hatching patterns is supplied with AutoCAD. Additional patterns can be purchased from independent suppliers, or designed yourself. Hatching can only be executed in an enclosed area.

The command **BHATCH** can be executed from the *'Draw'* drop-down menu and screen menu or by typing **BHATCH** at the command prompt. Fig. 11.9 shows the Boundary Hatch dialogue box.

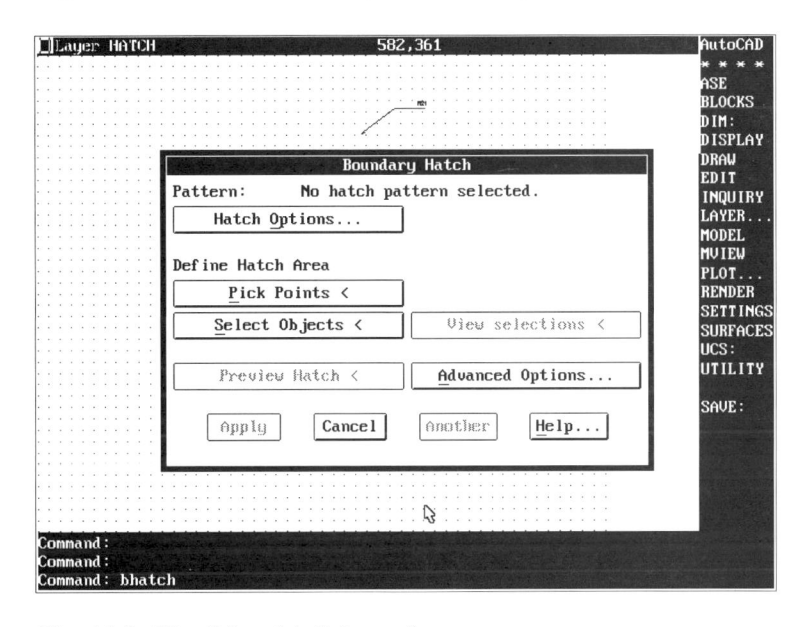

Fig. 11.9. The 'bhatch' dialogue box.

Opening the boundary hatch dialogue box

Select *'Hatch'* from the *'Draw'* drop-down menu, or type **BHATCH** at the command prompt.

Select *'Hatch Options…'* from the dialogue box. The *'Hatch Options'* dialogue box is displayed.

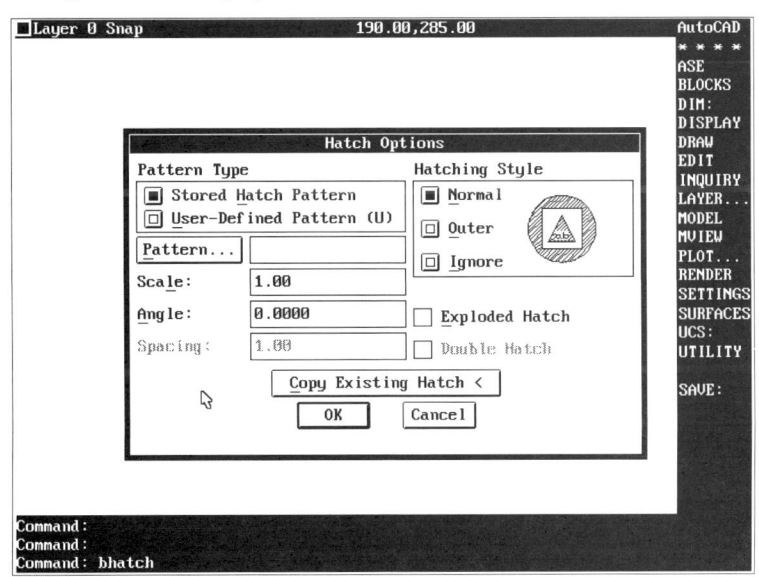

Fig. 11.10. The hatch options dialogue box.

LAYERS, BASIC DIMENSIONING AND HATCHING PATTERNS   **181**

Under the heading *'Pattern Type'* are the titles *'Stored Hatch Patterns'* and *'User-Defined Pattern'*, preceded by two 'radio buttons'. Clicking on a radio button selects that option for use. Click on *'Stored Hatch Patterns'* if it is not already selected.

To the right under the heading *'Hatching Style'* an icon shows visually the types of hatching style available. Try clicking on each of the radio buttons to see the effect. The *'Normal'* style will be used on the **BEARINGS** drawing, so select that option before you proceed. The *'Scale'* and *'Angle'* options dictate the density and angle of orientation of the pattern when it is inserted into the drawing. Input values of **50** and **0**, respectively.

Clicking on *'Pattern…'* will open up the *'Choose Hatch Pattern'* dialogue box. Clicking on *'Next'* will display another page of patterns. Move through the pages until you find *'steel'*. Select it by clicking on it.

You will then be returned to the *'Hatch Options'* dialogue box, and *'steel'* will appear in the *'Pattern…'* box.

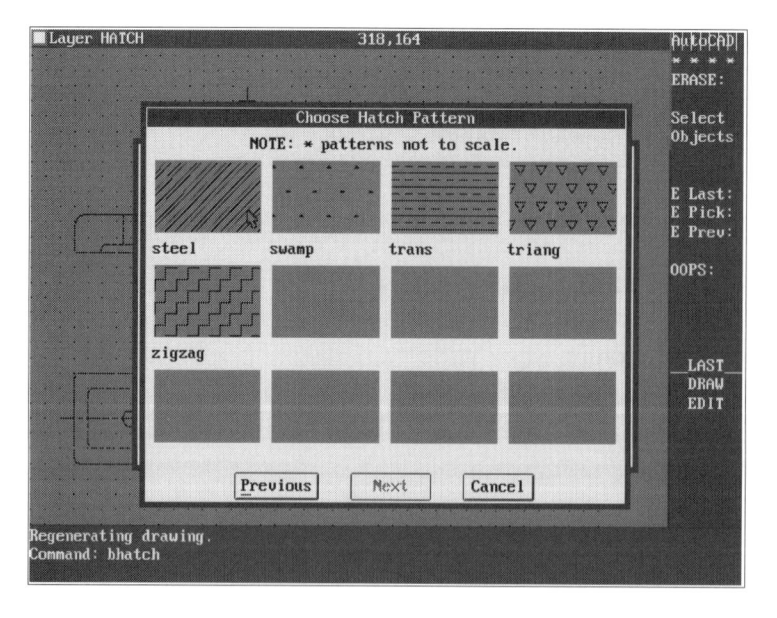

Fig. 11.11. Selecting 'steel' from the 'Choose hatch pattern' dialogue box.

Click on **'OK'** to return to the *'Boundary Hatch'* dialogue box. To select the objects for hatching in your drawing, pick *'Select Objects'*. You will be returned to the drawing. Select the three circles in the section view of the bearings, and press **[enter]**. The dialogue box is redisplayed. Click on *'Apply'*. The circles in the drawing will be hatched in the *NORMAL* style.

'Preview Hatch' can be used to get a preview of the area being hatched and the style that will apply to it. This is particularly useful if you intend to hatch a large area.

Marking hatching boundaries

The circles were an easy example to hatch, because they have an 'unbroken perimeter'. In many situations within a drawing the boundaries may have gaps or may consist of boundaries that overlap. AutoCAD will not be successful in hatching in such an area: often the hatching will leak out of the area you wished to hatch. Fig. 11.12 shows incorrect hatching. To overcome this problem, try one of the following techniques.
(1) Use the *'Pick Points <'* subdialogue box from the *'Boundary Hatch'* dialogue box and click inside the area you want to hatch. AutoCAD will create a boundary for you and apply the hatching when *'Apply'* is selected.
(2) Draw a new boundary over the old one (say with a polyline) and hatch inside that boundary. The polyline can then be removed when the hatching is complete.
(3) Use the **BREAK** command with the *@* option to create invisible breaks.

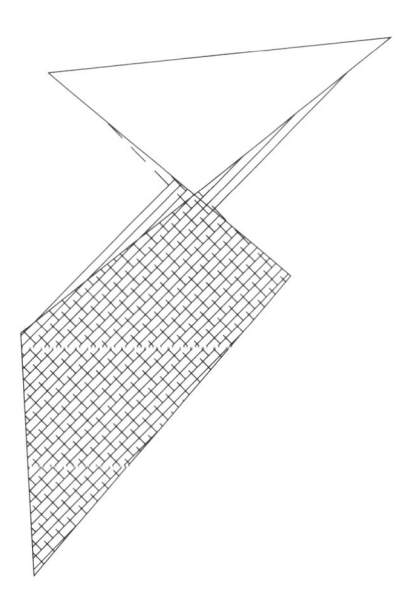

Fig. 11.12. Poor selection of a hatching boundary.

Method 1 above usually works. Methods 2 and 3 ensure that complete entities mark out the boundary of the area being hatched. A hatching pattern is a single entity (just as an associative dimension is). However, the commands **TRIM**, **BREAK** and **EXTEND** can be applied to it after the command **EXPLODE** has been used on it. This command will turn the hatching into many separate entities. The command syntax is:
Command: **EXPLODE**
Select objects: 1 found
Select objects:
Command:
 A hatching pattern that is exploded will take on the colour of the default layer 0.

The 'hatch' command

This command is issued from the command prompt and screen menu. When **HATCH** is issued at the command prompt, the following options are presented:

Command: **HATCH**
Pattern (? or name/U,style):

If you respond with the question mark, a list of available hatching patterns stored within AutoCAD is displayed. Some of these patterns are listed below;

Some of AutoCAD's stored hatching patterns

ANGLE	Angle steel
ANSI31	Iron, brick, stone masonry
ANSI32	Steel
ANSI33	Bronze, brass, copper
ANSI34	Plastic, rubber
ANSI35	Firebrick, refractory material
ANSI36	Marble, slate, glass
ANSI37	Lead, zinc, magnesium; sound, heat and electrical insulation
ANSI38	Aluminium
ARB816	8 × 16 block elevation stretcher bond
ARB816C	8 × 16 block elevation stretcher bond with mortar joints

By responding to the request *'Pattern (? or name/U,style):'* with one of these names, you load the pattern into the drawing for use.

The other options are:

★Style: respond with
N = Normal (invert in odd areas)
O = fill outermost areas
I = fill through internal structure
★U: this option allows the user to define a simple hatching pattern.

The command syntax is:
Command: **HATCH**
Pattern (? or name/U,style): **U**
Angle for crosshatch lines <0>: **45**
Spacing between lines <1.0000>:
Double hatch area? <N>
Select objects:

If the response **'Y'** is given to *'Double hatch area?'* a second set of hatching lines is drawn at 90° to the first set.

ADDITIONAL INFORMATION

The *'Layer Control'* dialogue box can be called up at the command prompt by typing **DDLMODES**. It can also be used transparently by using the apostrophe ('DDLMODES). The **DIM1** option returns you to the command prompt after the execution of a single dimension option.

The filter option in the 'Layer Control' dialogue box
The filter option allows you to control which layers you want listed in the *'Layer Control'* dialogue box. For example, you may decide to list all layers assigned the colour green or all layers that are locked. The *'Set…'* option in the filters subdialogue box allows you to set the parameters that control these listings. The filters you set can be switched on by placing a tick in the *'On'* subdialogue box.

SUMMARY

The chapter introduced the use and properties of layers. Layer creation and the visibility of layers as an aid to efficient drawing were discussed. The layer a drawing is being executed on is the 'current layer'. A layer can be assigned a colour. AutoCAD can cope with any number of layers. A suggestion was made about the naming of layers in a meaningful way.

Dimensioning was also introduced in this chapter for the first time. It was suggested that a drawing's dimensions should be placed on a separate layer to control their visibility. The three principal options under dimensioning—Horizontal, Vertical, and Leader—were dealt with in some detail.

The **BHATCH** command eliminates all the tedious hatching work often associated with hand draughting. A library of 53 hatching patterns is supplied with AutoCAD. Hatching can only be executed in an enclosed area. The boundary hatch dialogue box is the simplest way of selecting a hatching boundary. A hatching pattern is a single entity. The **EXPLODE** command can be used to shatter the hatching pattern into many separate entities. A hatching pattern that is exploded will take on the colour of the default layer 0.

ASSIGNMENTS

Assignment 1

The drawing of the studio should be distributed over four different layers, as follows:
(*a*) the outline (walls and windows) on layer 0;
(*b*) the dimensions on a layer called DIM;
(*c*) the hatching patterns on a layer called HATCH;
(*d*) the border and text on a layer called BORDER.

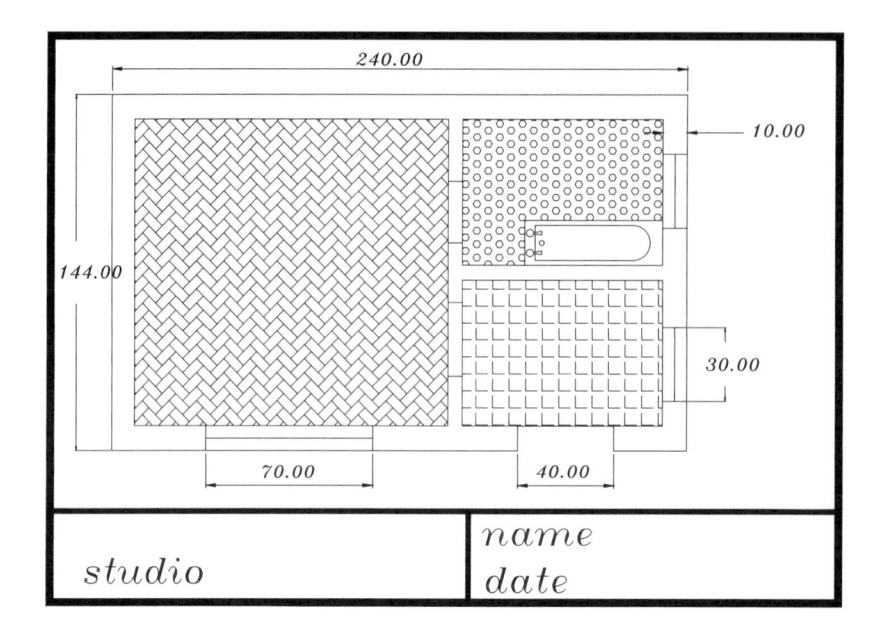

Assignment 2

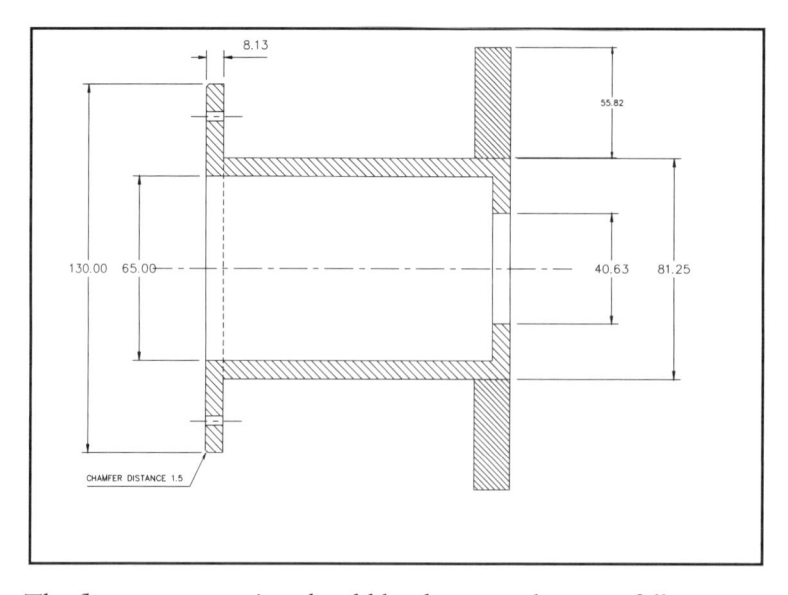

The flange cross-section should be drawn on layers as follows:
(*a*) the outline in continuous linetype on a layer named SECTION; assign it the colour white;
(*b*) the centre and hidden lines, on a layer named LTYPE and assigned the colour red;
(*c*) the hatching on a layer called SEC2 and assigned the colour blue;
(*d*) the dimensions on a layer named DIM and assigned the colour yellow;
(*e*) the border and text on a layer named BORDER and assigned the colour white.
   Note: The chamfer distance is 2.03 units.

Assignment 3

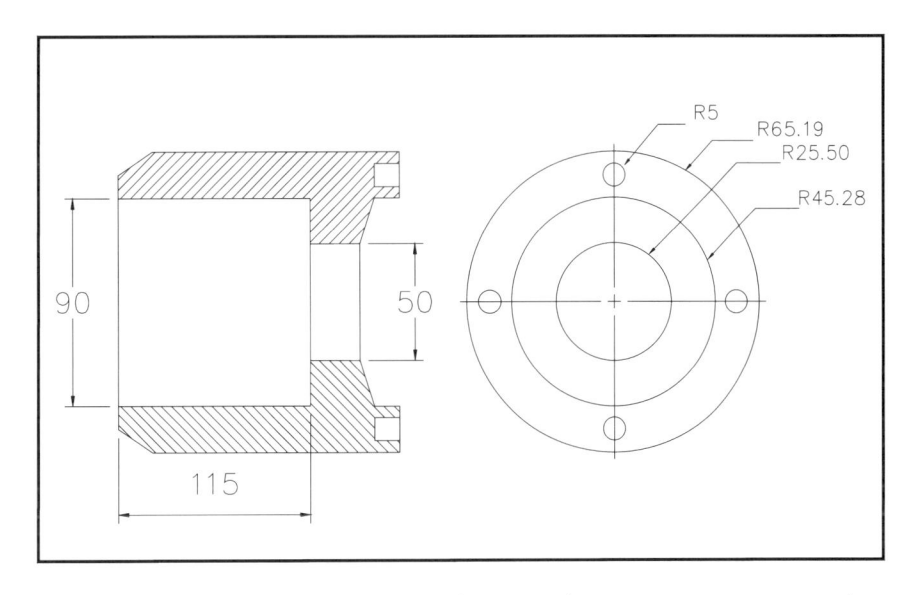

Create the drawing on four layers, each assigned an appropriate name and colour. The chamfer radius is 10 units.

Assignment 4

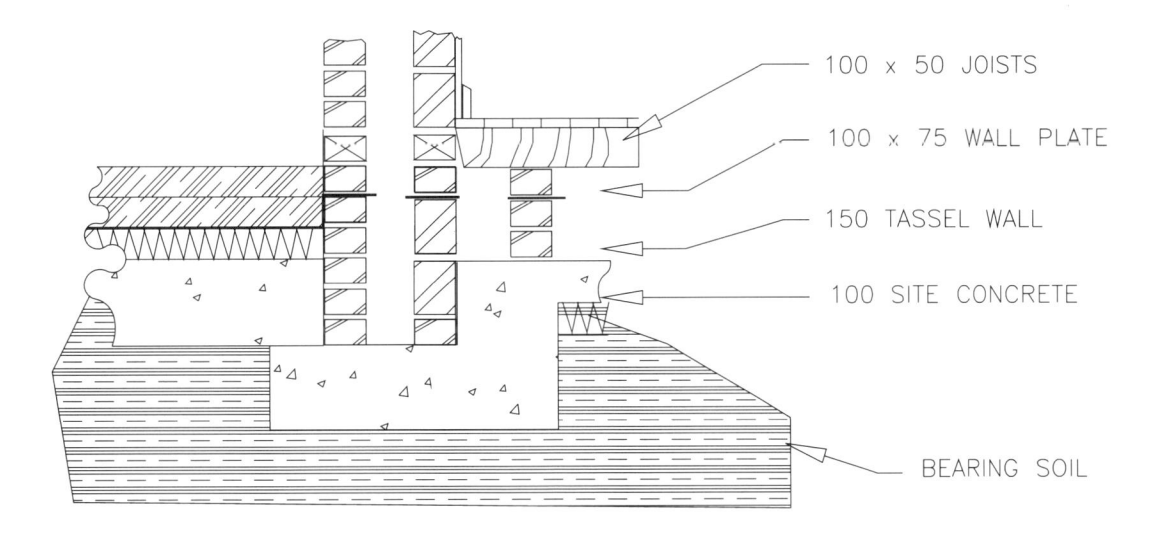

This simplified section of the foundations of a building should be constructed on several layers. The correct hatching for clay, concrete and soil must be used. The text is inserted using leader lines, found as a sub-option under DIM. The angle of the clay hatching is 25°.

Assignment 5

Target drawing

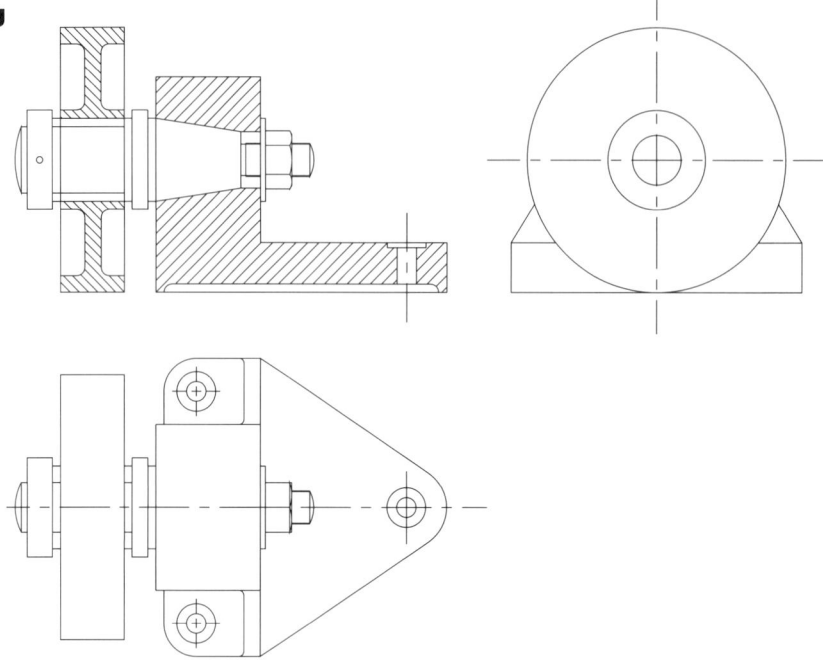

Create the drawing of the pulley mechanism on five layers. Note the different angles for the section hatching.

Drawing instructions

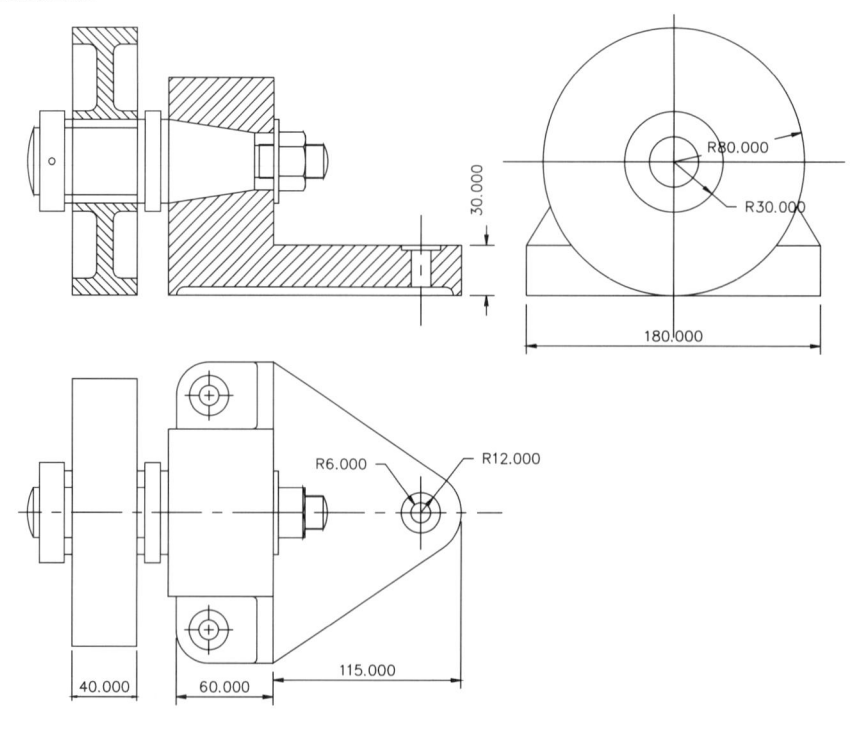

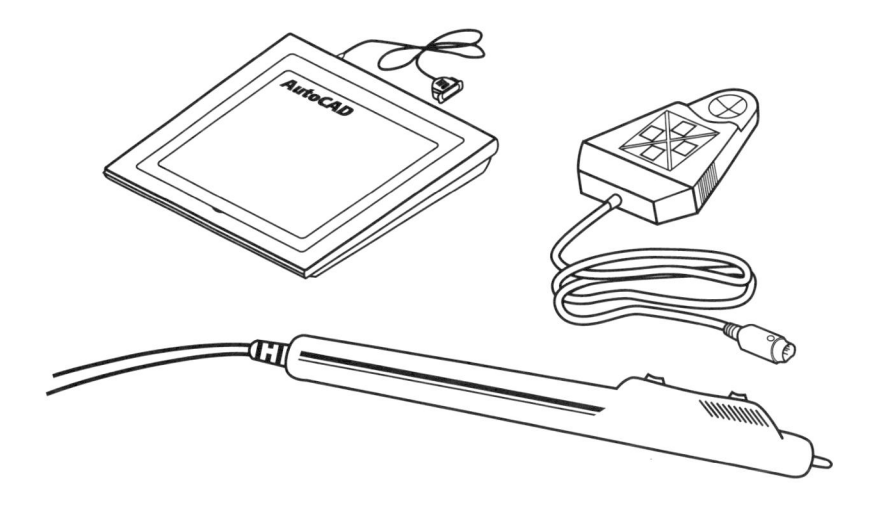

chapter 12
Multiple Prototype Drawings, Text and Style

Tutorial objectives
By the end of this chapter you should be able to
- use the SETVAR command to change some of the drawing settings
- set up multiple prototype drawings
- use the dynamic text command DTEXT
- use the quick text command QTEXT
- create a STYLE for a font

INTRODUCTION

The nature of computer-aided design work implies that the computer must supply you with specific settings for the various commands. Settings such as the size of the pickbox and the type and size of the POINT entity have been pre-defined. Some of the variables have already been changed in previous tutorials. These settings, and many others, can be changed using the **SETVAR** ('set variables') command.

The command can be executed from the command prompt, or from the screen menu under **SETTINGS** and then **'next'**.

Listing the variables

Execute the **SETVAR** command.
Command: **SETVAR**
Variable name or ?: ?
Variable(s) to list <*>:   ← Press **[enter]** to see the first page
ACADPREFIX   *"C: \R12\SUPPORT\;C: \R12\FONTS\ (read only)*
ACADVER   *"12 International" (read only)*
AFLAGS   *0*
ANGBASE   *0*
ANGDIR   *0*
APERTURE   *10*
AREA   *0.0000 (read only)*
ATTDIA   *0*
ATTMODE   *1*
ATTREQ   *1*
AUDITCTL   *0*
AUNITS   *0*
AUPREC   *0*
BACKZ   *0.0000 (read only)*
BLIPMODE   *1*
CDATE   *19930102.12335756 (read only)*
CECOLOR   *"BYLAYER"*
CELTYPE   *"BYLAYER"*
CHAMFERA   *0.0000*
CHAMFERB   *0.0000*
CIRCLERAD   *0.0000*
— *Press RETURN for more* —

Press ^C to interrupt the listing and return to the command prompt. Windows users will also need to press the F2 key.

A complete list of the variables can be found in appendix A. These variables can be categorised into two types:
(1) Those that cannot be changed by the user: these are the 'read-only' variables. They are for viewing only. For example, the variable **ACADPREFIX** displays how my copy of AutoCAD 12 is arranged on the computer's hard disk:
"C: \R12\SUPPORT\;C: \R12\FONTS\" (read only)
(2) Those that can be changed by the user.

Changing a variable

Most of these variables can be changed by entering them directly at the command prompt. They can also be changed transparently, although in many cases the change will not take effect until the command is complete. If you are unsure of the variable name you can list and change it under the **SETVAR** command.

The following variables will be explored in later assignments:
FILLETRAD
ATTREQ
ATTDIA
DIMASO
FILLMODE
SPLINETYPE
SPLFRAME
SPLINESEGS
SKPOLY

The variables that affect AutoCAD's dimensioning (the dimensioning variables) will be dealt with in chapter 15.

Prototype drawings

Before starting a drawing in the traditional draughting method of using paper and pens, you must determine a few basic set-up details. For example, you will decide what scale to work with and the size of paper to use. Other basic set-up decisions include the type of paper, the drawing units, and the type and weight of pens.

Some of these decisions also have to be made when draughting on a computer. There are some differences, of course. For example, in AutoCAD you draw in *Real World Co-ordinates:* there is no need to scale the drawing up or down. The size of the electronic page you work on is determined by the size of the drawing. You can also change the size of the drawing sheet (using the **LIMITS** command) at any time. The scale for plotting can be left until the last moment (see chapter 18 on plotting). Several copies of the drawing can be produced at different scales. Pen thicknesses can be assigned to layers as the drawing progresses and can be changed at any time.

The ACAD prototype drawing

AutoCAD comes supplied with a default drawing sheet size. This default sheet is what is presented to you when you start AutoCAD and enter the drawing editor. It is also presented when you start a new drawing.

If it is not suitable for you, it can be changed. For example, the limits and units can be modified until you have a drawing sheet with the characteristics you need. Various setvar variables can be modified to produce the exact page characteristics you want. This can then be saved as a new prototype drawing, so that AutoCAD will present it to you each time you enter the drawing editor.

Several different prototype drawings can be set up. At the time the drawing session is started you can decide which prototype drawing to use.

Tutorial 12.1

Tutorial objectives

To create two prototype drawings for two different disciplines and to call the relevant prototype when starting a drawing.

Prototype 1

The function of this prototype drawing is to contain settings that allow you to draw small electronic components. The prototype will be used in a later assignment to draw a wiring diagram for a computer joystick port.

Open a new drawing and call it **ELECTA-1**.

The prototype drawing will have the following characteristics:

UNITS in decimal to 8 decimal places
LIMITS set at 0,0, to 6,5
GRID=0.50000000
BLIPS and SNAP off.
BORDER
Customised TITLE block
LAYERS
    BORD-5-5 *border & title block*
    CASE-3-7 *case fittings*
    DIM1-2-4 *dimensions*
    TXT1-2-7 *text*
    REF1-2-7 *reference notes*
    CIR1-1-1 *electronic circuit*

Remember that our layer convention assigned the pen colour as the first digit and the pen thickness as the last digit (see chapter 11 on layers).

Assign the linetype **HIDDEN** to layer **CASE-3-7**. Remember to load the linetype before setting it in the *Layer Dialogue* box.

    FILLETRAD=0.10000000
    APERTURE=5
    PICKBOX=5
    LTSCALE=0.12500000
    DIMSCALE=0.02500000
    Switch off the UCSICON

The border and title block should be drawn with a polyline of width **0.0300000000** (see fig. 12.1 for the layout of the title block) on layer BORD-5-5. Positioning of the box and text is not critical.

Set layer **CASE-3-7** current and make layer 0 invisible.

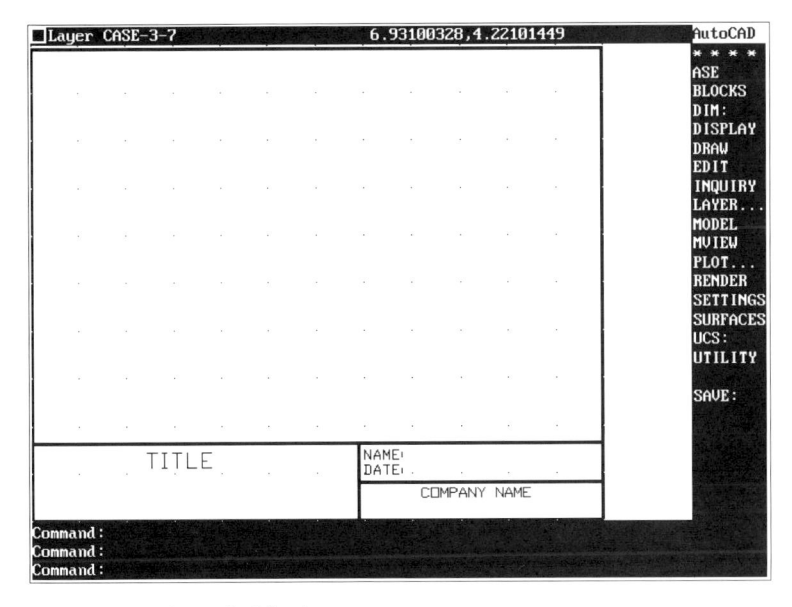

Fig. 12.1. The title block.

Save the drawing by typing **QSAVE** at the command prompt.

Using the drawing as a prototype

Select *'New'* from the *File* drop-down menu. The *'Create New Drawing'* dialogue box is displayed. After the title *'Prototype…'* is an edit box with the name **ACAD**. This is the name of the default and current prototype drawing. To use **ELECTA-1** as your prototype, delete **ACAD** from the edit box and type in **ELECTA-1**.

Click in the *'New Drawing Name…'* edit box and type in the name of the drawing you want to start (call it **PARTS**, for example). Click on **OK**. When the drawing editor is displayed, the prototype **ELECTA-1** drawing is being used; however, the name of the drawing on screen is **PARTS**.

The name of the drawing can be checked by using the system variable **DWGNAME**. Windows users will see the name above the drawing.

The command sequence is:
Command: **DWGNAME**
DWGNAME = "PARTS" (read-only)
Command:

The next time you start a drawing the **ACAD** prototype drawing will be used unless you tell it to use another prototype.

Making the drawing the default prototype

Select *New* from the *File* drop-down menu. The *'Create New Drawing'* dialogue box is displayed. After the *'Prototype...'* edit box is the name **ACAD**. Replace this with **ELECTA-1**, and then click in the box to tell AutoCAD to *'Retain as Default'*.

Click in the *'New Drawing Name...'* edit box and type in the name of the drawing you want to start.

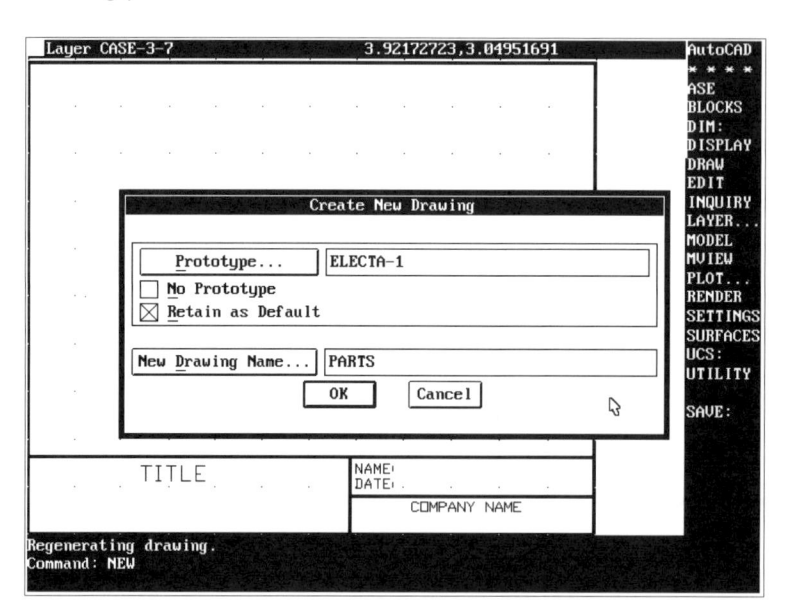

Fig. 12.2. Specifying ELECTA-1 as the new prototype drawing.

All drawings you start from now on will be supplied with the drawing **ELECTA-1** as the prototype.

An alternative way to call up a prototype drawing is to enter the name of the drawing you wish to create and put it equal to the required prototype. For example, **PARTS=ELECTA-1** entered into the *'New Drawing Name...'* dialogue box will assign the prototype **ELECTA-A** to the **PARTS** drawing.

Note: If you are using a copy of AutoCAD that is also used by other people, don't forget to reset the default prototype drawing to **ACAD**.

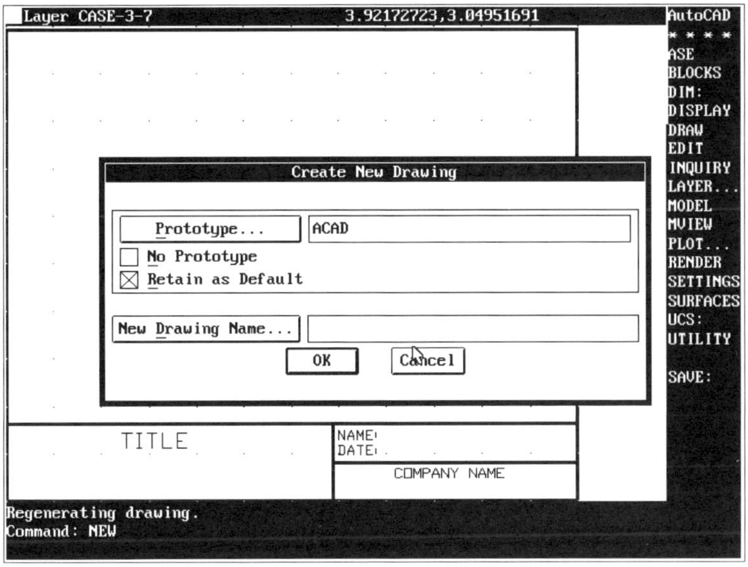

Fig. 12.3.

Prototype 2
UNITS=DECIMAL, NO DECIMAL PLACES
LIMITS=0,0 to 3000,2000
LAYERS:
DIM1 yellow
FRONT1 white
Current Layer = FRONT1

Draw your own border and title block.

Save the drawing as **ARCH14**. Call it up to test that it works properly. This simple prototype will be used in chapter 14.

Tutorial 12.2

Tutorial objectives
- some special character codes
- the DTEXT command
- the QTEXT command
- typefaces and the STYLE command

Start a new drawing using the **ARCH14** prototype and name it TUT12-2.

Some special character codes

Some special text characters, such as the degree symbol (°) and underscore, cannot be input directly from the keyboard. AutoCAD can place these special characters into text for you using the code **%%**.

For example, to toggle the 'overscore' character on and then off, use the code **%%O**. The code **%%O**this is the overscore**%%O** produced the following:

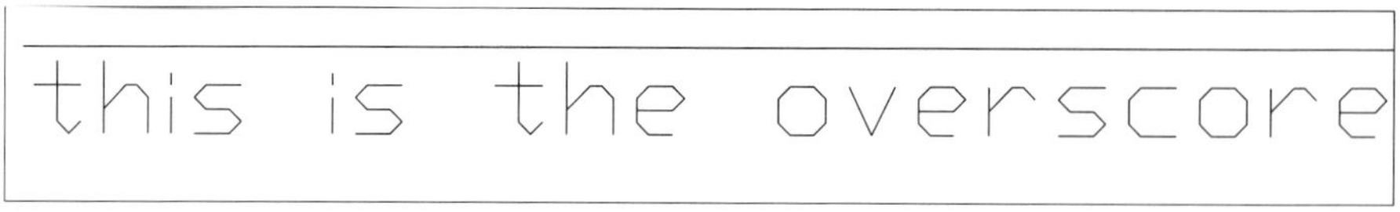

```
┌─────────────────────────────────────────┐
│  this is the overscore                   │
└─────────────────────────────────────────┘
```

Fig 12.4.

Some of the other codes are:
%%u for underlining
%%d for the degree symbol
%%p for the plus-or-minus sign
%%c for the diameter sign
%%% for the per cent sign
%%nnn will produce other special characters, where **nnn** is a whole number. Use these in your drawing. Placement of text is not critical. An example of each is illustrated in fig. 12.5.

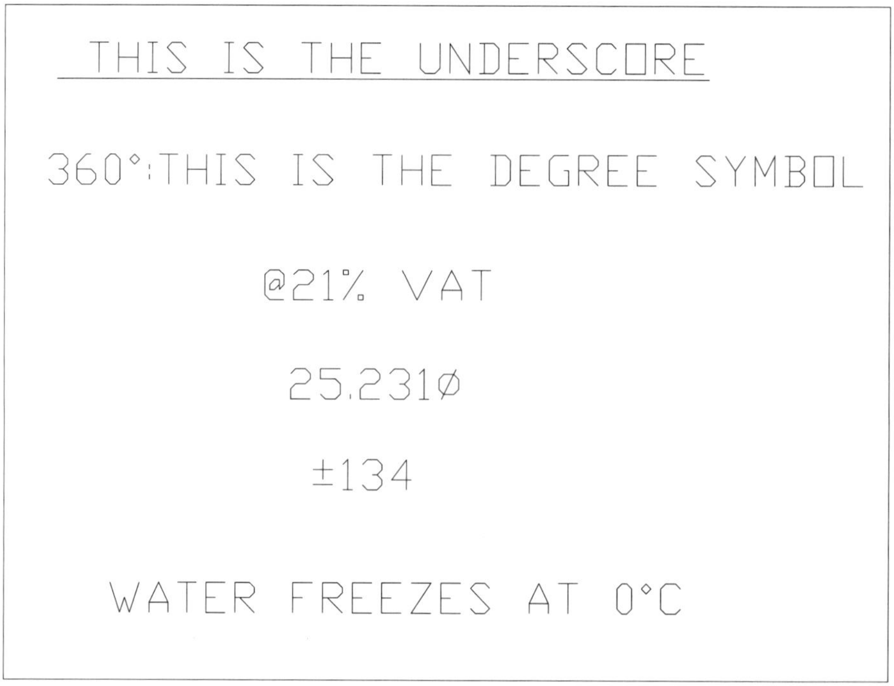

```
┌─────────────────────────────────────────┐
│      THIS IS THE UNDERSCORE              │
│                                          │
│   360°:THIS IS THE DEGREE SYMBOL         │
│                                          │
│            @21% VAT                      │
│                                          │
│             25.231⌀                      │
│                                          │
│              ±134                        │
│                                          │
│       WATER FREEZES AT 0°C               │
└─────────────────────────────────────────┘
```

Fig 12.5.

The 'dtext' command

DTEXT ('dynamic text') is very similar to the standard **TEXT** command. However, the text is displayed on the screen as you type it.

The position on the screen where the text is typed is indicated by a cursor in the shape of a box. The following points should be noted with regard to using the **DTEXT** command.

If an error is made while entering the text, you can backspace to correct it.

If several lines of text are entered, you can backspace through the text up through the lines.

The special characters discussed above can be placed in the text; however, they will not be interpreted as characters until the command is finished. In other words, a code such as **%%d** will appear as **%%d** on the screen until the **DTEXT** command is complete, then it will be displayed as the degree symbol. The command is completed by pressing **[enter]** twice.

DTEXT is a very useful version of **TEXT**, and is found under the *'Draw'*, *'Text'*, *'Dynamic'* drop-down menu and also on the screen menu. **DTEXT** can be issued at the command prompt.

Try entering the following text (height 6 units) using the dynamic mode.

An A4 sheet is 297 by 210 mm.
An A3 sheet is 420 by 297 mm.

The 'qtext' command

Text takes a considerable time to regenerate. **QTEXT** ('quick text') helps to overcome this time-consuming problem by creating a simple box in place of the text. **QTEXT** can be switched on or off. When it is on, any text in the drawing is replaced with rectangular boxes both in the screen display and in a plot.

REGEN must be executed to see the effect of the **QTEXT** command. Here is the command sequence:

Command: **QTEXT**
ON/OFF<On>: **OFF**

Issue a **REGEN** now.

The text you entered is now represented by boxes. However, it is still part of the drawing.

An interesting feature of **QTEXT** is that even if it is on (and text is replaced by boxes), any new text entered will be displayed as text (as if **QTEXT** was off). However, as soon as the drawing is regenerated (either automatically, because of the execution of some other command, or by typing **REGEN**) the new text will then be represented on the screen as a box.

Fonts and the 'style' command

AutoCAD comes supplied with several fonts. A font is a particular design applied to the characters of the alphabet. Third-party 'fonts' can be purchased and added in to the AutoCAD program for use in drawings.

The fonts supplied with AutoCAD can be viewed by selecting the drop-down menu *'Draw'*, *'Text'*, *'Set Style'*. Fig. 12.6 illustrates the first page of fonts.

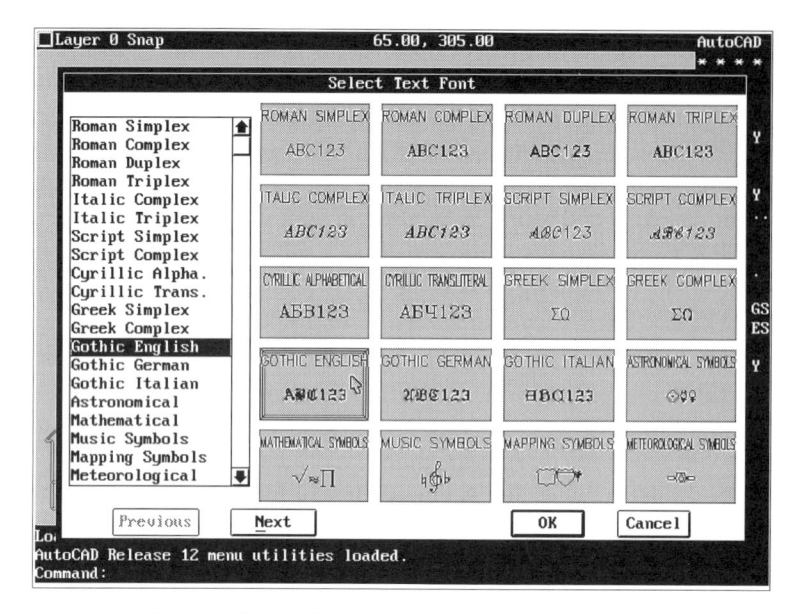

Fig. 12.6. Some of AutoCAD's typefaces.

By clicking on a font name, a selection is made. Clicking on *'Next'* will display the second page on the icon menu.

Click on *'Next'* now. The second page is displayed.

Clicking on *'previous'* will return you to the first icon page.

The various astronomical, musical and meteorological symbols can be accessed indirectly from the keyboard (see below).

Now look through the font icon menu until you find **GOTHIC ENGLISH**. Select **GOTHIC ENGLISH** by clicking in the selection box. It is selected in fig. 12.7. Click on 'OK'.

Ignore all the options and questions that AutoCAD is asking you for the moment (do this by pressing **[enter]** six times to accept the defaults, until the command prompt is presented to you).

Any text you now enter will use the typeface **GOTHIC ENGLISH** in a 'default style' called **GOTHICE**. Each AutoCAD font has a particular **STANDARD** default style associated with it.

Use the text command now.

Type in the following and press **[enter]**.

'Gothic English Gothice Style'. Your text should appear as in fig. 12.7.

> 𝕲𝖔𝖙𝖍𝖎𝖈 𝕰𝖓𝖌𝖑𝖎𝖘𝖍 𝕲𝖔𝖙𝖍𝖎𝖈𝖊 𝕾𝖙𝖞𝖑𝖊

Fig. 12.7.

Styles

The font you select can be used in different 'styles'. The style is created by you, the user, if you decide not to use AutoCAD's default **GOTHICE** (as in the above example).

To create a style for use with a font, you can either use the **STYLE** command at the command prompt or select the drop-down menu *'Draw'*, *'Text'*, *'Set Style'*.

In this example you will create a new style from the command prompt and give it the name **GOT1**. Type STYLE and press **[enter]**. The definition is created by AutoCAD from the following statements:

1. AutoCAD will ask you for the name of the style (*'Text style name'*). Type **GOT1** and press **[enter]**. As **GOT1** is a new style you are creating, AutoCAD will indicate that it recognises this by telling you *'New style'*.
2. It will then want to know the name of the font that the style you are creating is applied to. Enter **GOTHICE** or select it from the dialogue box, and press **[enter]**.
3. AutoCAD now wants to know the height of the text in your new style. If you enter a value other than 0 for this, AutoCAD will not ask you for a new text height when you use the **TEXT** command. The height you give here in defining the style will always be used. If, on the other hand, you accept the default value of 0, AutoCAD will prompt for a height for your text each time you use the **TEXT** command. Accept the default value here.
4. The *'Width factor'*. The standard style has a width factor of 1. If you enter a width factor of .5, the text will be compressed; a width factor of 1.5 will expand the font. For this exercise accept the default value of 1.
5. *Obliquing angle:* This part of the text style definition allows you to lean the letters forward or backwards. A positive angle will lean the letters forward, a negative angle leans them back. Enter a value of 60. Press **[enter]** 3 more times to accept the defaults.

Command: **STYLE**
Text style name (or ?) <GOTHICE>: **GOT1**
New style. Height <0.0000>:
Width factor <1.0000>:
Obliquing angle <0>: **60**
Backwards? <N>
Upside-down? <N>
Vertical? <N>

GOT1 is now the current text style.

Type **TEXT** to execute the text command to try the new Gothic style you have created.

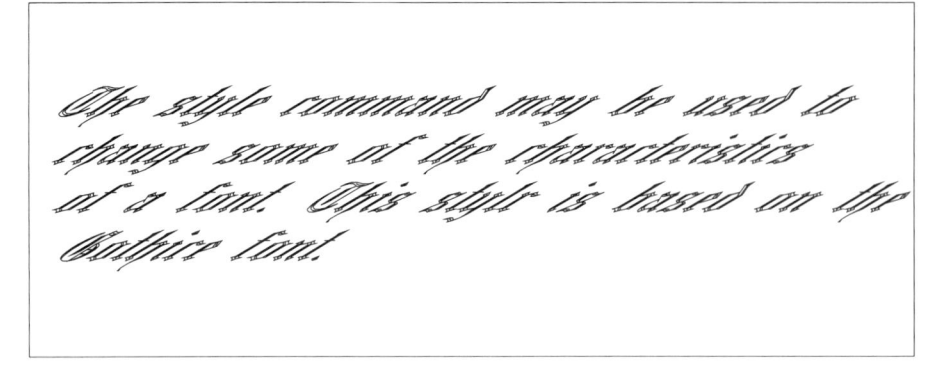

Fig. 12.8 Script.

There are two important points to bear in mind about your styles:
◆ Any style you define automatically becomes the current style.
◆ A defined style is associated with a drawing.
Try creating the text in figs 12.9 to 12.12.

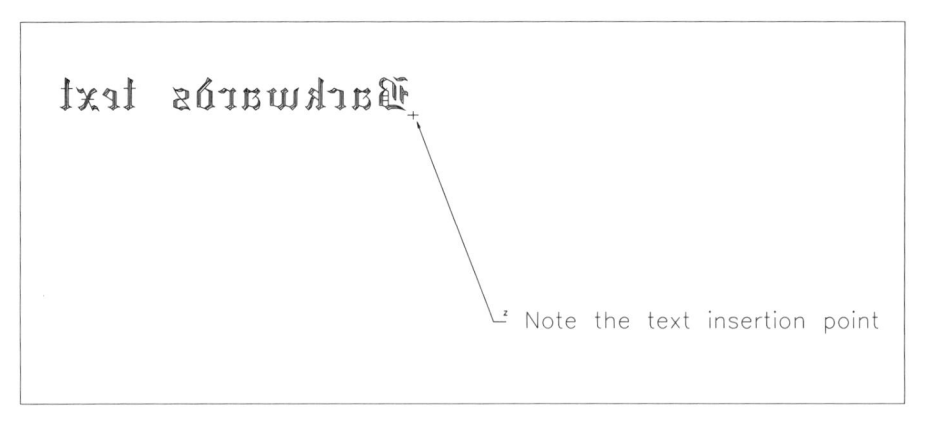

Fig. 12.9. *Backwards:* text is written backwards from the insertion point using GOT1 style.

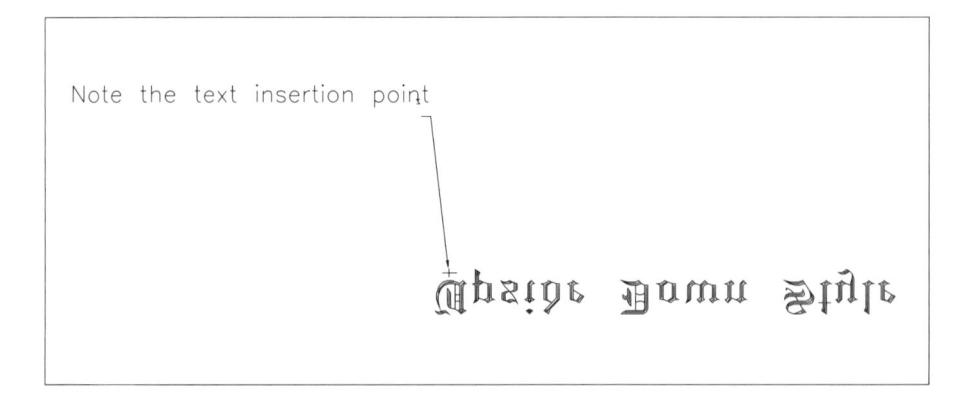

Fig. 12.10. *Upside-down:* Note the insertion point.

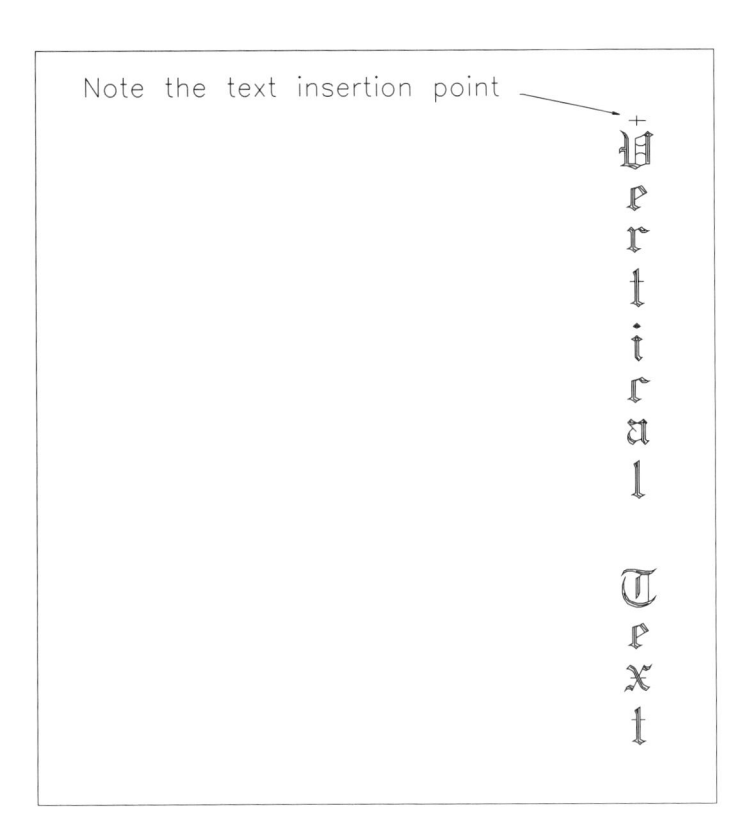

Fig. 12.11. Vertical text.

8. *Vertical:* All the typefaces supplied with AutoCAD allow the use of the vertical parameter in the style definition. However, some third-party typefaces do not. Note the location of the insertion point again.

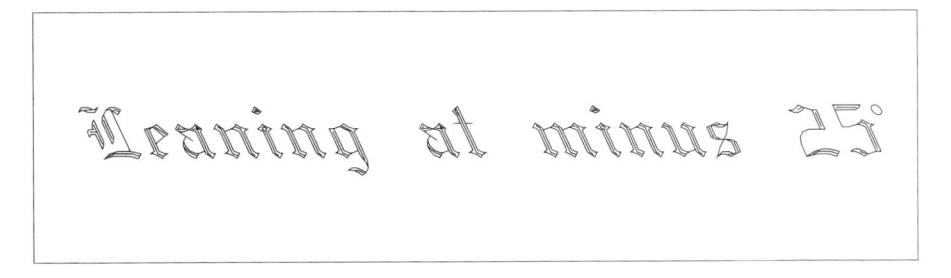

Fig. 12.12. Leaning text.

Character mapping

Some fonts can only be accessed indirectly from the keyboard. These include the mathematical, astronomical, mapping, meteorological and music symbols.

To insert these characters into the drawing editor you must first make the font the current one (see above in this tutorial).

To find which keys map the characters, refer to your AutoCAD manual. The result of mapping some of the music symbols is shown in fig. 12.13.

Fig. 12.13.

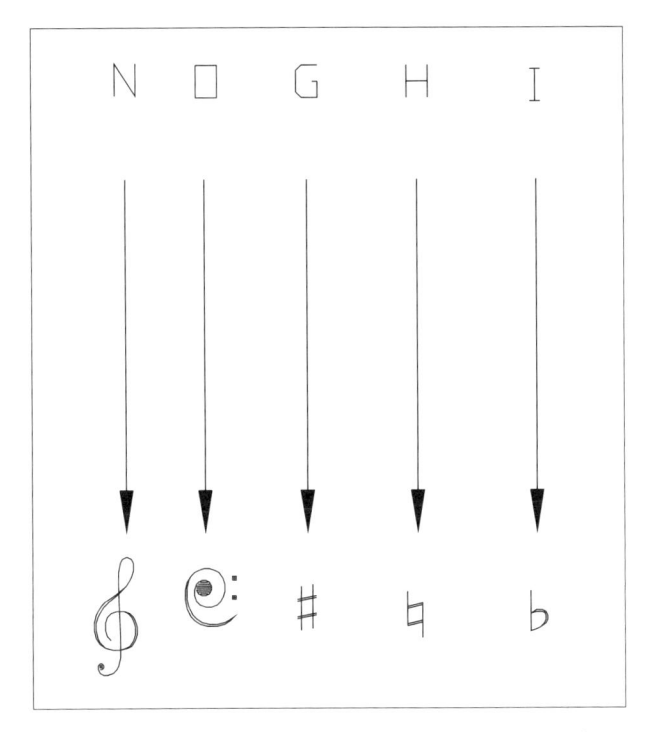

Fig. 12.14. Character mapping for the Symusic font.

Exercise

Reproduce the example shown in fig. 12.13. The font for the symbols is Music Symbols. The notes are mapped from **'F'** for the crochet and **'E'** for the minim. The other characters needed for the exercise are illustrated in fig. 12.14. The text in fig. 12.13 is in the Romantic Italic typeface.

SUMMARY

Many of the default settings of AutoCAD can be changed by modifying the system variables. These variables can be listed using the **SETVAR** command. The variables are categorised into two types: those that can be changed by the user and those that cannot be modified (termed 'read-only'). The variables control such features as the display of the dialogue boxes.

The chapter also examined the setting up and use of prototype drawings. Two prototypes were set up for use in later tutorials.

Lastly, the **DTEXT** and **QTEXT** commands were introduced in conjunction with AutoCAD's special character codes. These codes allow the insertion of underlining, the per cent sign etc. into text. Many fonts are obviously not available from the keyboard and have to be 'mapped' from the standard keys. Examples examined in the chapter were the music and mathematical symbols.

DTEXT or 'dynamic text' is very similar to the standard **TEXT** command, but the text is displayed on the screen as you type it.

Text takes a considerable time to regenerate. **QTEXT** ('quick text') helps to overcome this time-consuming problem by creating a simple box in place of the text. **QTEXT** can be switched on or off. When it is on, any text in the drawing is replaced by rectangular boxes both in the screen display and in a plot.

AutoCAD also allows the use of different fonts. These were chosen using the drop-down menu *'Draw'*. The fonts can be used with different styles. The **STYLE** command allows a font to be modified.

Assignment

Using the character mapping facility within AutoCAD, place the following on the screen, using the **TEXT** command:

$$x = \frac{-b \pm \sqrt{b^2 - 4ac}}{2a}$$

(a)

$$3\Pi R^2 h$$

(b)

(c)
$$\left(\sum_{i=1}^{n} |xi - x|\right)$$

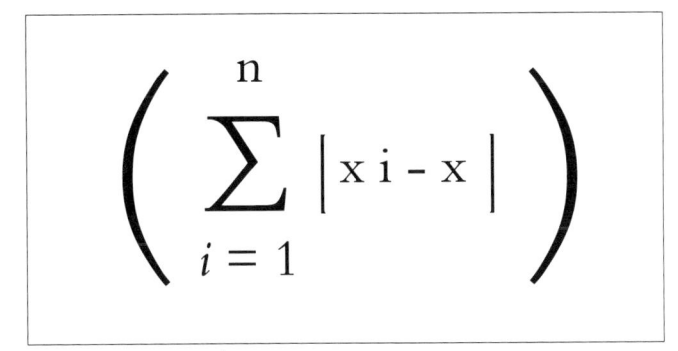

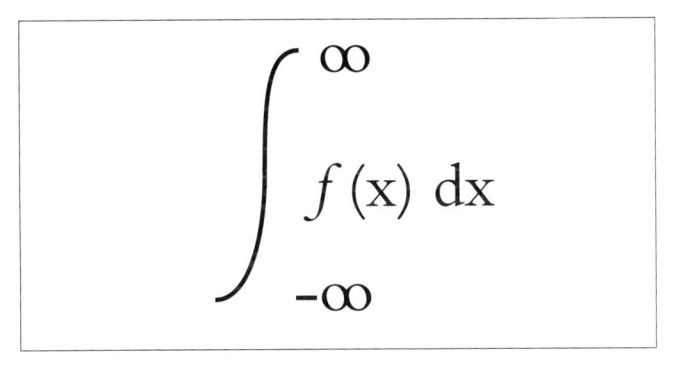

(d)
$$\int_{-\infty}^{\infty} f(x)\, dx$$

(e)
$$\sqrt{\ } x - 3\Pi$$

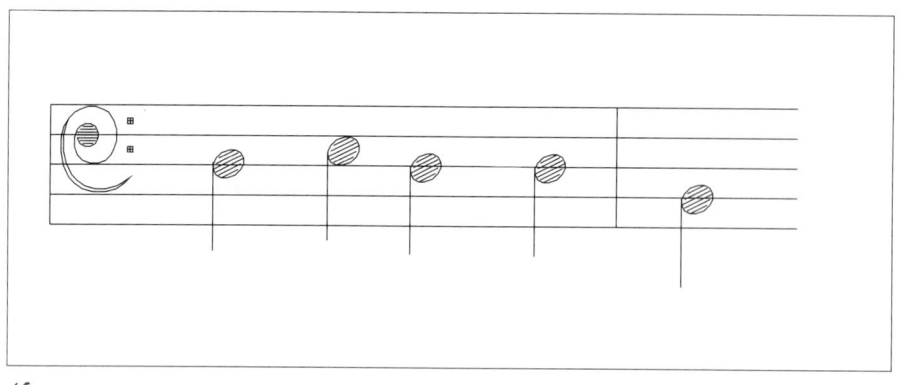

(f)

(g)

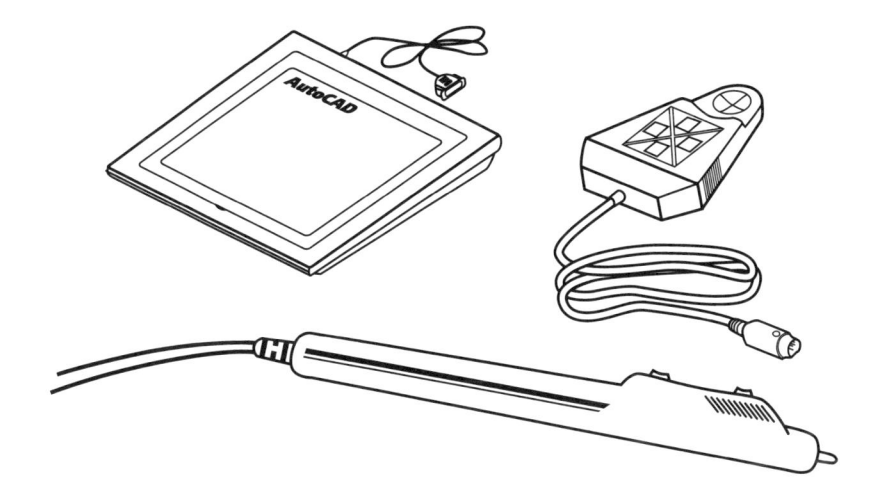

chapter 13
Working with Blocks, Divide and Measure

Tutorial objectives

By the end of this chapter you should be able to
- create BLOCK entities
- insert block entities into a drawing using the INSERT command
- use the MINSERT command to insert a block several times
- use the DIVIDE command to insert blocks in a regular manner
- use the MEASURE command
- write a block to the hard disk as a drawing using the WBLOCK command
- EXPLODE a drawing into its original component parts
- PURGE a drawing to free it from unused blocks, text styles, layers, linetypes, etc.

Target drawing

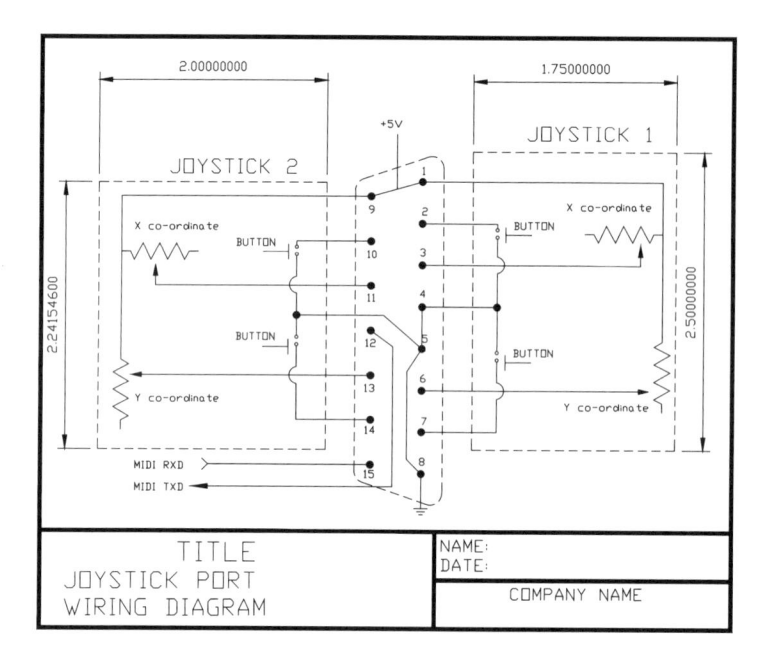

[Drawing: Joystick Port Wiring Diagram showing Joystick 2 and Joystick 1 with X co-ordinate, Y co-ordinate, and BUTTON components connected to pins 1-15, with +5V, MIDI RXD, and MIDI TXD connections. Dimensions: 2.00000000, 1.75000000, 2.24154600, 2.50000000. Title block shows "JOYSTICK PORT WIRING DIAGRAM", NAME, DATE, COMPANY NAME.]

Blocks

The **COPY** command allows entities to be copied from one position in a drawing to another. This saves the user a considerable amount of time redrawing entities that are repeated within a drawing. AutoCAD also allows the user to save a group of entities as a **BLOCK**. The **BLOCK** can then be called up and inserted into the drawing when required. Many companies develop libraries of frequently used symbols for insertion into their drawings as blocks. Fig. 13.1 illustrates some electrical symbols that could be converted into blocks.

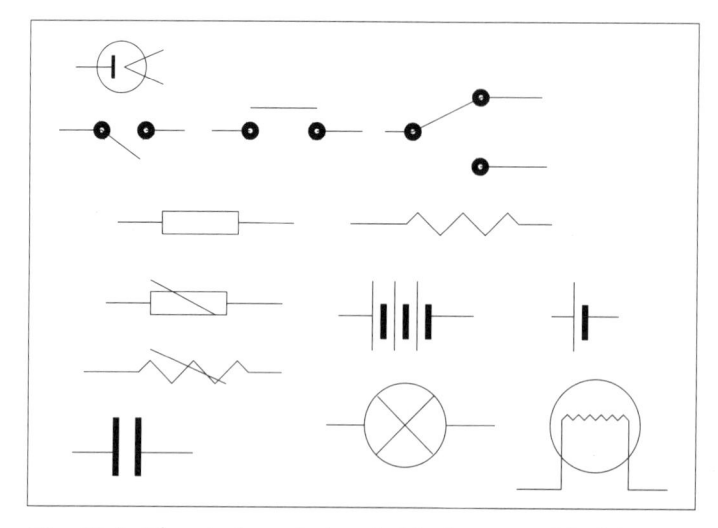

Fig. 13.1. Electrical symbols suitable for use as blocks.

A **BLOCK** must be defined by the user. The definition of the block requires the user to tell AutoCAD what group of entities to take and the insertion point or 'handle' to use to pick up the entities.

Tutorial 13.1

The target drawing shows a possible wiring arrangement for a computer joystick. The drawing has several elements suitable for treatment as blocks.

Start a new drawing called **JOYSTICK** using the **ELECTA-1** prototype drawing set up in chapter 12.

Switch on layer 0 and set it current. Create the four symbols **CON**, **RES**, **BUTTON**, and **TERMS** shown in fig. 13.2. The dimensions for the end section are also shown in fig. 13.2.

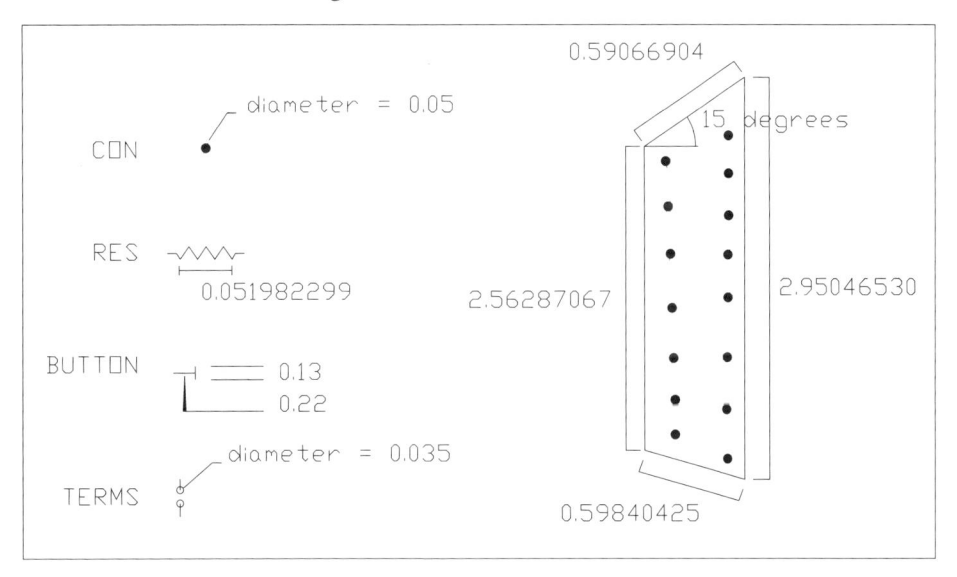

Fig. 13.2. Symbols.

The first block represents a connection point. It should be drawn using the **DONUT** command, with an internal diameter of 0.

The position of the symbols within the drawing editor is of no consequence at the moment.

How to create a block

The command **BLOCK** is used to create a block. It is found on the screen menu under *BLOCKS* and on the drop-down menu under *'Construct'*. It is also available on the tablet. The command **BLOCK** can also be typed at the command prompt.

The layer that a block is drawn on can affect its use at a later stage. In this assignment the creation of the blocks will be carried out on layer 0, the layer the symbols were drawn on.

How the command works

On execution of the command, AutoCAD will ask for a name for the block. A block name can be up to 31 characters long. Responding with a question mark will list blocks already used or created within the drawing. AutoCAD will then need to know the insertion point of the block you are going to define. The insertion point will be attached to the cross-hairs when you later go to insert the block. It is generally advantageous to select the insertion point using the object snap mode. Try to pick a useful insertion point that can be used to place the block in a drawing accurately. Lastly you will be asked to select the objects to include in the block. The selection can be made using a window or any of the usual methods used by AutoCAD.

Once the block has been successfully defined it will disappear from the display. You can recall it by typing the command **OOPS**.

Defining the connector block symbol

Zoom in on the 'doughnut'. Type **BLOCK** and press **[enter]**. Assign **CON** as the block name. The insertion base point should be the centre of the doughnut. This can be selected using the object snap mode **CEN**. The command sequence is as follows:

Command: **BLOCK**
Block name (or ?): **CON**
Insertion base point: **CEN**
of ← Pick the doughnut
Select objects: **W**
First corner: ← Pull a window around the doughnut
Other corner: 1 found
Select objects: ← Press **[enter]**
Command:

The block will disappear from the screen.

Define the rest of the symbols as blocks in the following manner:

Name the second symbol **BUTTON**, and pick the leftmost end as its insertion point.

Name the third symbol **RES**, and pick the leftmost end as its insertion point.

Name the fourth symbol **TERMS**, and pick the end of the top line as its insertion point.

Set layer **CASE-3-7** current.

Make layer 0 invisible by switching it off.

Building up the joystick drawing

Step 1
Draw the outline of the casing on layer **CASE-3-7** using the hidden linetype. See fig. 13.2 for the dimensions of the section. Fillet the corners of the section view (remember that the fillet radius was set in the prototype drawing).

Step 2
This step involves the insertion of a block. Set layer **CIR1-1-1** current.

The 'insert' command

This command can be found on the screen menu under **BLOCKS** and on the drop-down menus under *'Draw'* and *'Insert…'* It is also available on the tablet menu. If it is selected from the drop-down menus an *'Insert'* dialogue box is displayed. The command will be used here from the command prompt.

As a block is being inserted, AutoCAD gives considerable control over how it is placed in the drawing. You can scale the block by different scaling factors along the X and Y axis and rotate it into any position through 360°.

How the command works
After you type **INSERT** at the command prompt, AutoCAD requests the name of the block to be inserted. Typing a question mark will cause the listing of the blocks inserted already. After the name of the block is supplied it will appear attached to the cross-hairs at its insertion point. When an insertion point is picked on the screen, AutoCAD prompts:
'Insertion point: X scale factor <1> / Corner / XYZ:'
You have the option here of scaling the block in the X axis direction (and in the Z axis for three-dimensional blocks). The default scaling factor is 1.

After a response is given, AutoCAD asks:
'Y scale factor (default=X):'
This option allows you to scale the symbol in the Y axis direction. The default option is to allow you to keep the scale factor the same as the X axis value.

Lastly, AutoCAD wants to know if you want the symbol being inserted rotated, by asking:
'Rotation angle <0>:'

Inserting the RES Block

The command sequence is as follows:
Command: **INSERT**
Block name (or ?): **RES**
Insertion point: ← Pick a point near the bottom left of the casing—see fig. 13.3

X scale factor <1> / Corner / XYZ: ← Press **[enter]**
Y scale factor (default=X): ← Press **[enter]**
Rotation angle <0>: 90 ← Enter 90 degrees to point the symbol upwards

Command:
Note that the block took on the same colour as the layer it was inserted on. This only occurs if the block was originally created on layer 0.

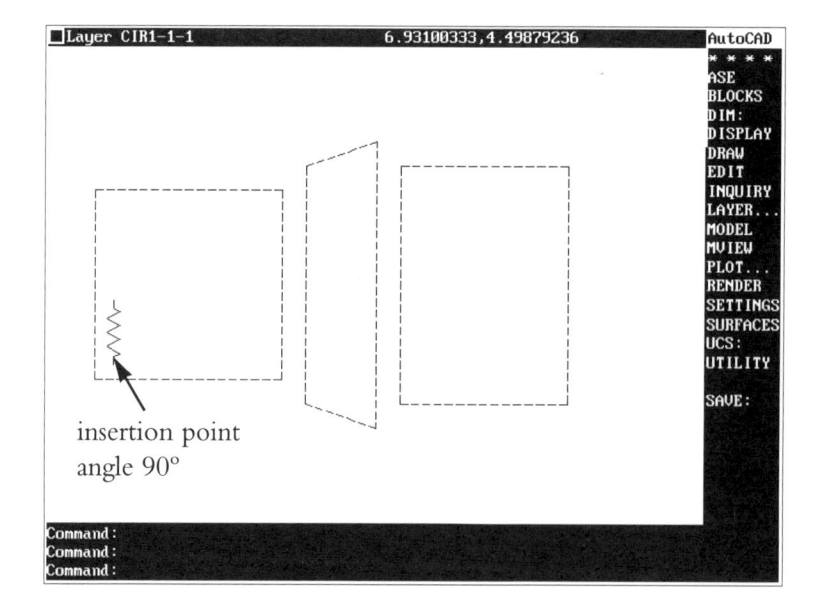

Fig. 13.3. Insertion of the RES block.

The other blocks can be inserted in a similar manner. Insert one of each of the other three blocks now into the left casing. Their position in the drawing in not critical at the moment. None of these blocks needs to be rotated or scaled. Fig. 13.4 shows the four inserted blocks.

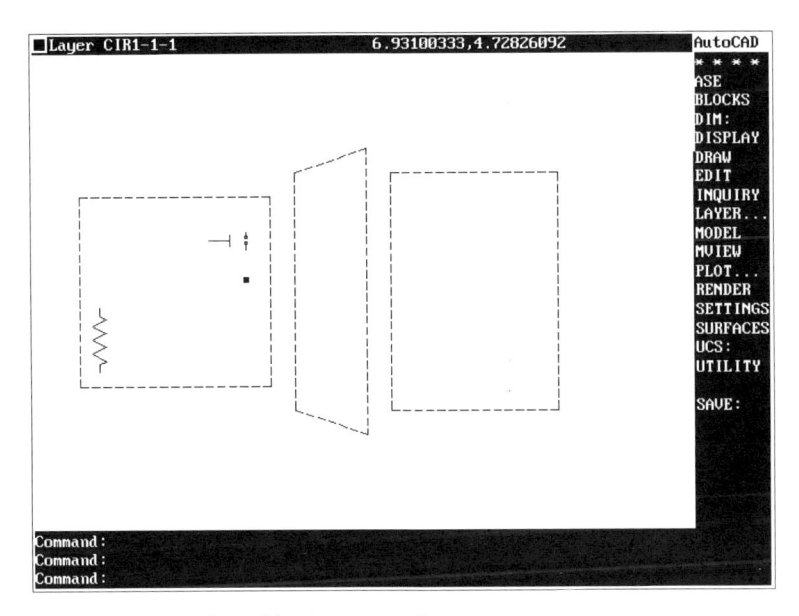

Fig. 13.4. The four blocks inserted.

Step 3
The connector symbol **CON** needs to be inserted fifteen times into the section view. It also needs to be inserted at regular intervals. This insertion can be achieved in one of two ways: using **MINSERT** or **DIVIDE**. Both methods will be used here as a means of illustration.

Using the 'minsert' command

As its name implies, this command allows the multiple insertion of a block. The command is actually a combination of the **INSERT** and **ARRAY** commands. The command can be accessed from the screen menu under **BLOCKS**. It is also found on the tablet menu, and can of course be typed in at the command prompt.

How the command works
The first part of the command is identical to the **INSERT** command: you are asked for the block name and then the scaling and rotation factors. This is followed by prompts similar to the **ARRAY** command: you are requested for the number of rows and columns and the distance between them.

Use the command now to insert eight **CON** symbols up the right side of the section. The position of the insertion point is not critical, but it should be near the bottom right of the section (see fig. 13.5). The distance between the rows is 0.35 units.

Command: **MINSERT**
Block name (or ?) <TERMS>: **CON**
Insertion point: See fig. 13.5 X scale factor <1> / Corner / XYZ:
Y scale factor (default=X):

Rotation angle <0>:
Number of rows (—) <1>: **8**
Number of columns (| | |) <1>:
Unit cell or distance between rows (—): **0.35**

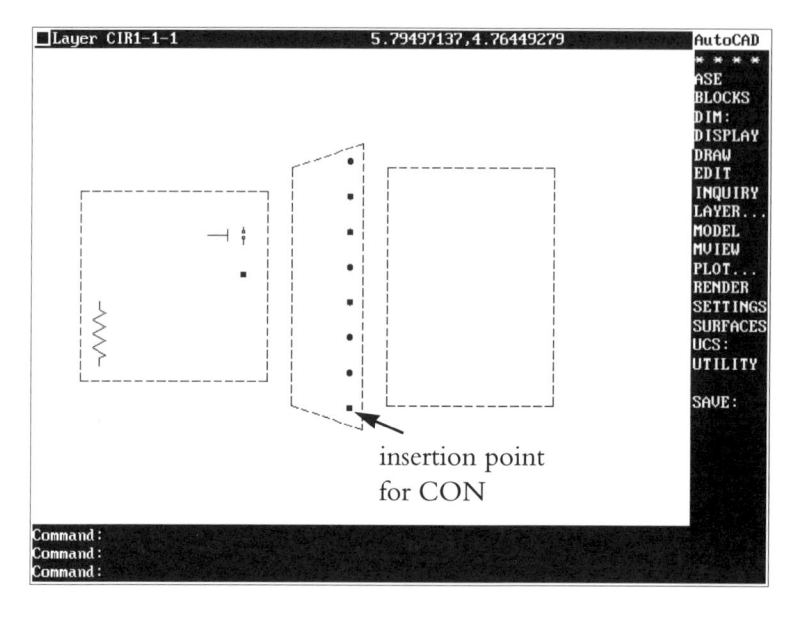

Fig. 13.5. MINSERT.

The 'divide' command

The **DIVIDE** command allows you to divide LINES, POLYLINES, ARCS and CIRCLES into an equal number of sections. The division marks on the selected entities are usually indicated by the POINT entity (see chapter 9). In this example the division marks will be indicated by the CON block instead of the POINT.

How the command works

The command is found on the screen menu under *EDIT* and on the drop-down menus under *'Construct'*. It is found under *EDIT* on the tablet menu, and can be called from the command prompt.

Before the command can be applied to the drawing section in this assignment, the left side of the section should be **OFFSET** 0.12663720 units to the right. This offset line will then be divided to place the symbols.

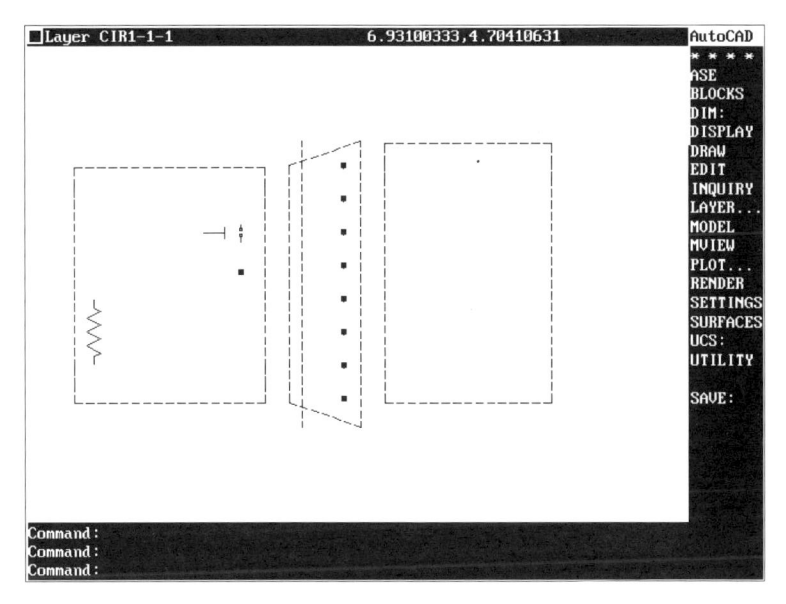

Fig. 13.6. The side of the section is OFFSET 0.12663720 units.

The command sequence is:
Command: **OFFSET**
Offset distance or Through <Through>: **0.12663720**
Select object to offset: ← Pick the right side of the section
Side to offset?   ← Pick to the left of the selected
                                              object
Select object to offset: ← **[enter]**

This line will now be divided in eight sections with seven markers. Each marker will be indicated by the **CON** block.

Here is the command sequence:
Command: **DIVIDE**
Select object to divide: ← Pick the line just offset
<Number of segments>/Block: B   ← Type **B** for block
Block name to insert: **CON**
Align block with object? <Y>
Number of segments: **8**
Command:

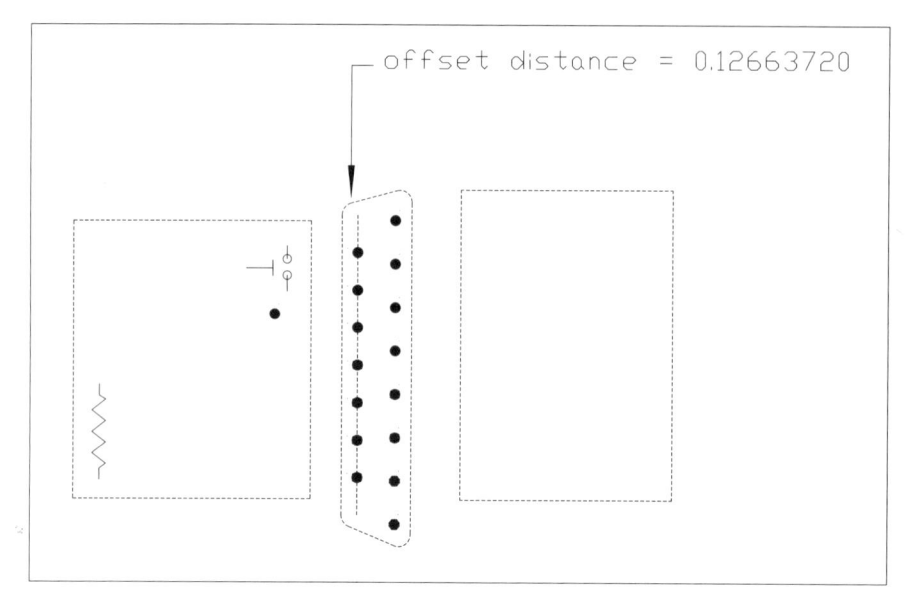

Fig. 13.7.

The original offset line can now be erased.
Note: The blocks option can only be used with blocks defined in the current drawing.

Step 4
Set the **TXT1-7-2** layer current, and number the connectors 1 to 15.

Step 5
Set the **CIR1-1-1** layer current. The rest of the instructions for this assignment refer to the wiring for joystick 2.

Draw the connection line from connector 15 to the vertical **RES** block. Draw the connection from connector 10, and join the block **TERMS** to it. Move the block **BUTTON** into place beside it.

INSERT the second **RES** block into the position marked *X co-ordinate*.

Use a polyline to draw the connection from connector 11 to the *X co-ordinate* **RES** block. The arrowhead has a starting width of 0.04 units and an ending width of 0 units.

Step 5
Draw the connection line from connector 5 to the connector in joystick 2. Fig. 13.8 shows the state of the drawing at this point.

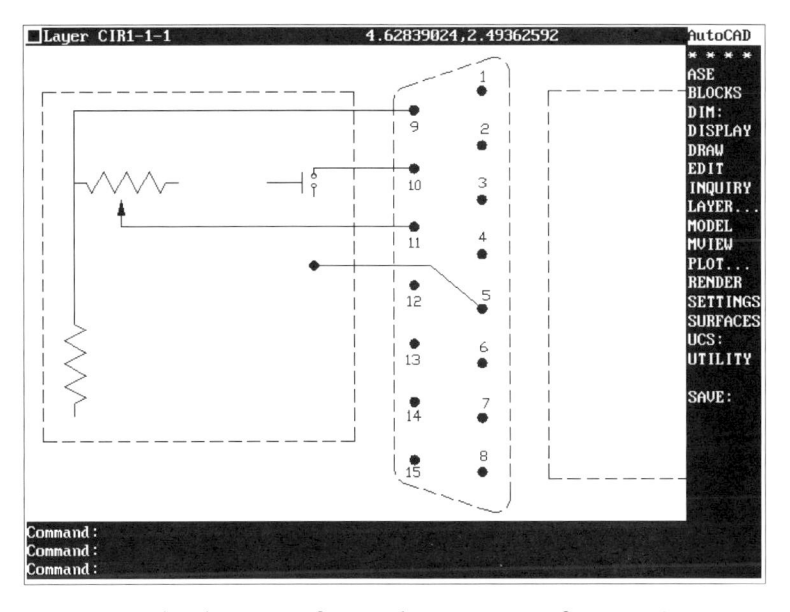

Fig. 13.8. The drawing of joystick 2 circuitry after step 5.

Step 6
The loop over the connection wire running from connector 11 to the X co-ordinate will be put in place using an **ARC**. Before the arc is put in place, extend the straight segments before and after the loop.

The 'arc' command

Make sure ORTHO is off. Select *'Start, End, Dir'* from the drop-down menu.

You should be able to finish the rest of the drawing using the commands you have covered in previous assignments.

The 'wblock' command

The blocks created in this drawing cannot be used in other drawings unless the **WBLOCK** command is used on them.

The **WBLOCK** ('write block') command writes a block or a full drawing to a disk file. The file created in this way is a new drawing file and can be inserted into any drawing using the **INSERT** command. A block must already exist before **WBLOCK** can be applied to it.

How the command works
The command is found on the screen menu under **BLOCKS**, and can be entered at the command prompt.

When executed, the **WBLOCK** command will first ask you for the **WBLOCK** file name. In other words, it requires the name you want the block to be called when it is written to disk. Secondly, it will ask you for the name of the block you want written to the disk under this new name. If the **WBLOCK** name is the same as the block name, you can enter an equals sign (=) in response to *'Block name'*. If the **WBLOCK** is of the complete drawing and the **WBLOCK** name is the same as the block name, you can enter an asterisk (*) in response to *'Block name'*.

A note on naming blocks

You can assign the actual block name as the **WBLOCK** file name. AutoCAD can distinguish between them. It is advisable to develop a standard style for naming all the **WBLOCK** files so that you can distinguish them from standard AutoCAD drawings. For example, you could place the letter B at the beginning of each block name.

The **RES** block will now be written to disk as an example.

Type **WBLOCK** and press **[enter]**. The *'Create Drawing File'* dialogue box is displayed. Type in the name you want the block to have when it is written to the disk as a drawing file: **BRES**. Click on **OK**.

AutoCAD now wants the name of the block to be written as **BRES**. Type in **RES** and press **[enter]**.

A summary of the command sequence is given below.

Command: **WBLOCK**   ← The *'Create Drawing File'* dialogue box is displayed: type in **BRES** and click on **OK**

Block name: **RES**
Command:

Exercise

WBLOCK each of the remaining blocks created in the assignment. Open a new drawing and see if they can be INSERTed into it.

ADDITIONAL INFORMATION

Some characteristics of blocks

(1) All the blocks you have created and worked with in this assignment were created on layer 0. When these blocks were inserted into the drawing they were inserted into the current layer.

(2) A block can be created from entities on different layers. The colours and linetypes associated with those layers will be retained. On insertion of such blocks, the entities will fall to their correct layers. If a block contains layers in its definition that are not in the drawing they are inserted into, AutoCAD will automatically create the new layers during the insertion.

(3) A block behaves as a single entity. This implies that any editing commands executed on the block will be performed on the block as a whole.

(4) A block can be 'shattered' into its original components using the **EXPLODE** command. This will allow more detailed editing. **EXPLODE** applies to other complex entities in AutoCAD, such as polylines, dimensions, and meshes.

If the block being defined has already been created, AutoCAD will respond with *'Block <name> already exists. Redefine it?'* At this point it is best to exit from the command and **EXPLODE** the block and then redefine it. Otherwise you are in danger of creating a block from a block.

Divide and measure

The divide and measure commands allow you to place markers on some entities. These markers can then be used with object snap to help with the construction of the drawing. **DIVIDE** divides an entity into a number of equal sections specified by the user. This was illustrated in the assignment above. **MEASURE** is similar to the **DIVIDE** command except that it allows you to measure out specified distances along the entity.

The 'measure' command

This command can be executed on lines, polylines, arcs, and circles. It is found under *EDIT* on the screen menu and under *'Construct'* on the drop-down menus. The command will ask you to specify whether to mark the units with a block (defined in the current drawing) or a **POINT** entity. The distance used to measure out the entity can be given by using the pointing device or by typing in a value. Lastly, the measurements will take place starting from the end of the entity nearest where you click in response to *'Select object to measure:'*.

AutoCAD will create a layer called **DEFPOINTS** if associative dimensioning is on. Do not **PURGE** this layer (see the purge command below).

The 'purge' command

During the creation of a drawing, a number of blocks, linetypes, layers, text styles, dimension styles and shape files that are not required can accumulate. These can be removed from the drawing using the **PURGE** command.

The command is normally issued immediately after a drawing is loaded into the drawing editor, as **PURGE** will not work if any editing or drawing takes place.

Here is an example of the **PURGE** command issued on the ACAD prototype drawing:

Command: **PURGE**
Purge unused Blocks/Dimstyles/LAyers/LTypes/SHapes/STyles/All: **A**
No unreferenced blocks found.
No unreferenced layers found.
No unreferenced linetypes found.
No unreferenced text styles found.
No unreferenced shape files found. Purge dimension style STANDARD? <N>
Command:

The *'All'* option was selected. You can choose to purge just the layer or the linetypes by responding appropriately.

SUMMARY

Blocks are composed of a group of entities that behave as a single entity. When a block is created using the command **BLOCK** it remains as part of the drawing it was created in. A block can be repeatedly inserted into a drawing to (*a*) speed up the drawing process and (*b*) maintain consistency in the drawing. The **INSERT** command allows a block to be scaled on its x and y axis. The **MINSERT** command allows for multiple insertion of a block in a manner similar to the **ARRAY** command.

The **DIVIDE** command allows you to divide lines, polylines, arcs and circles into an equal number of sections. The **MEASURE** command will set markers at a specified distance along an entity. A block can be used to mark the divisions created by both the **DIVIDE** and **MEASURE** commands.

The **WBLOCK** command writes a block to a disk as a drawing file. This allows the block to be inserted into any drawing.

Linetypes, layers, text styles, dimension styles and shape files that are not required can accumulate during the drawing process. These can be removed from the drawing using the **PURGE** command.

ASSIGNMENTS

Assignment 1

Enter the following drawing of an electrical curcuit and produce suitable blocks of three of its components. The blocks should be created on layer 0. Produce the drawing over four suitable layers. One layer must be named BLOCKS and assigned the colour red. Insert the blocks onto this layer.

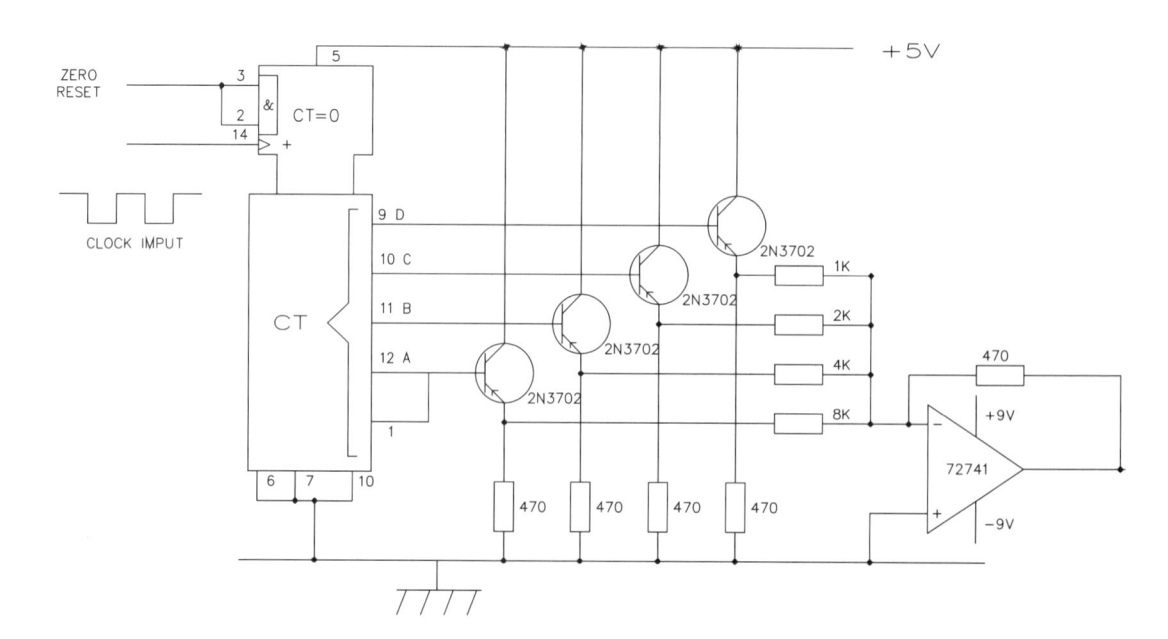

Assignment 2

The site plan shows three types of plant. Create a block for each type of plant and insert it onto the layer VEG, and assign it the colour green. None of the drawing is to be done on layer 0 (apart from the creation of the blocks).

Assignment 3

Some of the fittings in this apartment could be converted into blocks. Open a new drawing called FURN and create appropriate blocks for it. WBLOCK the blocks for use in another drawing. Open a new drawing called APART. Draw the apartment, and INSERT the blocks created in the drawing FURN.

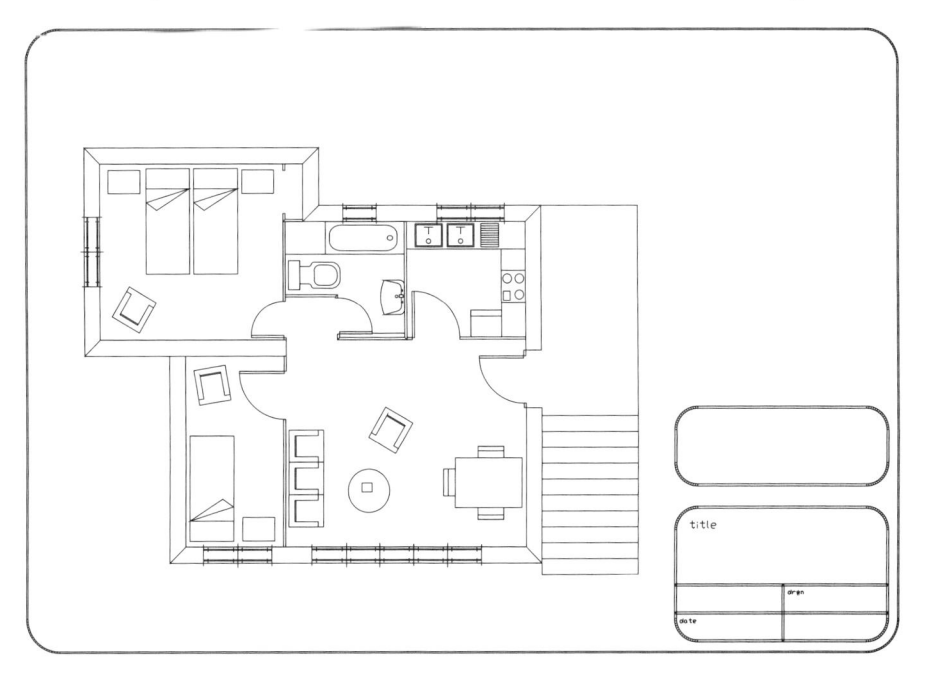

WORKING WITH BLOCKS, DIVIDE AND MEASURE

Assignment 4

Examine the façade above for the construction of blocks. Here are some suggestions to help you in its draughting:

(1) The centre window in the bay windows need only be drawn and blocked once. On insertion in the top and ground floors it can be scaled along the y axis appropriately.

(2) A block of the complete bay window may contain the block created in paragraph 1 above, i.e. one block may be nested inside another.

(3) The door should be blocked and then WBLOCKed so that it can be used in assignment 5.

(4) The ornament on the ridge tile of the roof should be created as a block and inserted using the DIVIDE or MEASURE commands.

Assignment 5

The façade can be created using blocks for the windows. The door is identical to that in assignment 4, and should be inserted if it was WBLOCKed in that assignment. The steps to the door may also be blocked.

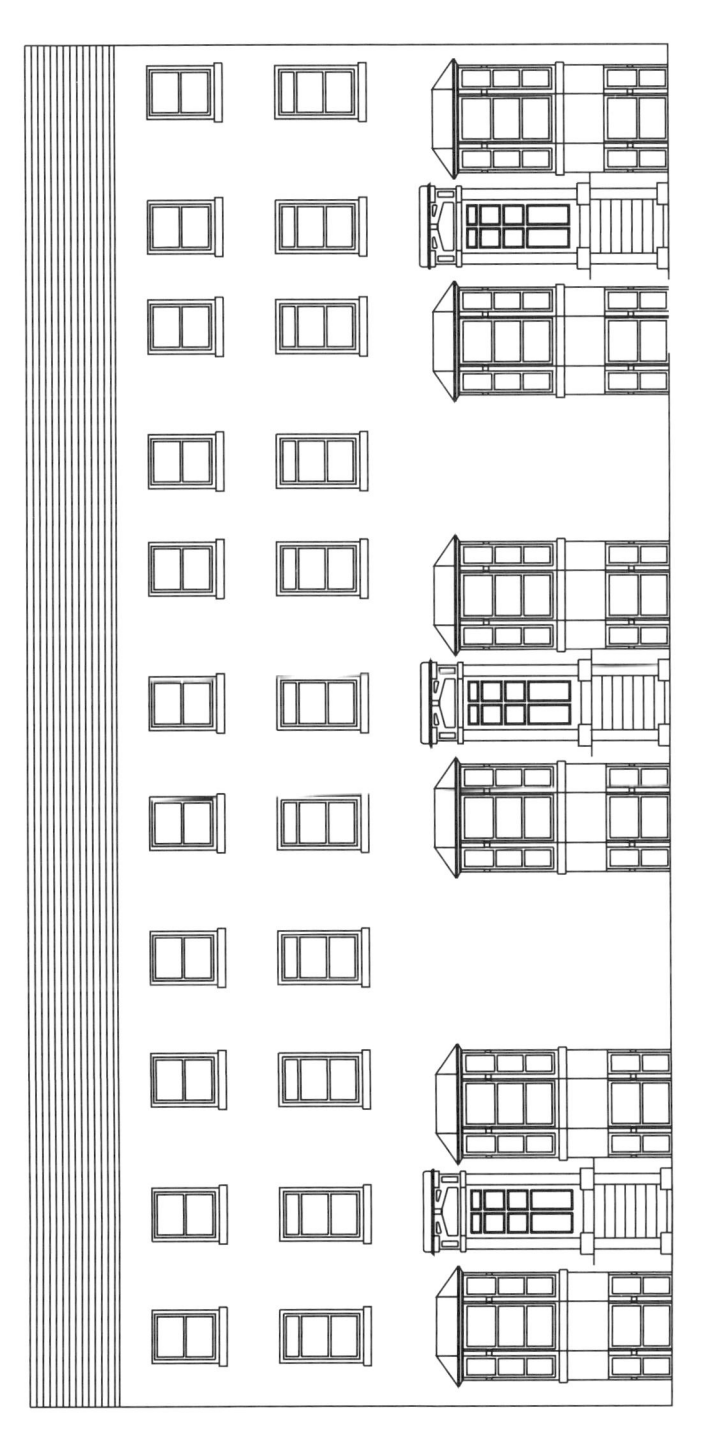

WORKING WITH BLOCKS, DIVIDE AND MEASURE

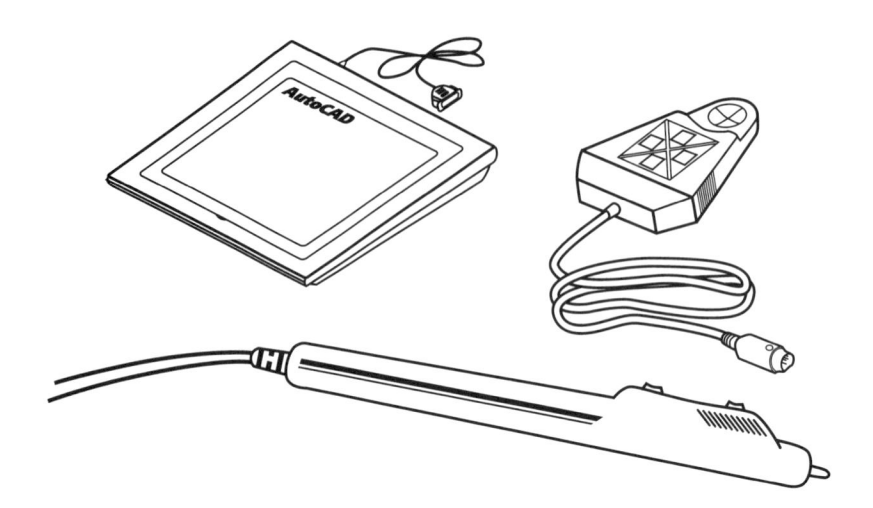

chapter 14
Attributes

Tutorial objectives

By the end of this chapter you should be able to
- explain what an attribute is
- define an attribute

What is an attribute?

The creation and insertion of blocks into a drawing speeds up the drawing process considerably and adds consistency to a drawing. Frequently it is necessary to insert text beside a block to indicate its characteristics. For example, when drawing an electric circuit the symbol for a battery might be inserted as a block, and later the voltage might need to be added as text beside it.

Instead of writing the voltage in as text beside the block each time it is inserted, AutoCAD allows you to 'attribute' the text to the block. This implies that each time the block is inserted the text is also inserted.

Using attributes can be even more advanced than that. An attribute can be defined so that AutoCAD will *ask you for the voltage* each time the block is inserted. At a later stage the voltage value can be *extracted* from the drawing and used in another program, such as a word-processor, data-base, or spreadsheet. It is this ability to extract information from a block that makes the concept of attributes so valuable.

Attributes can be defined as textual data attached to a block.

Target drawing

Drawing instructions

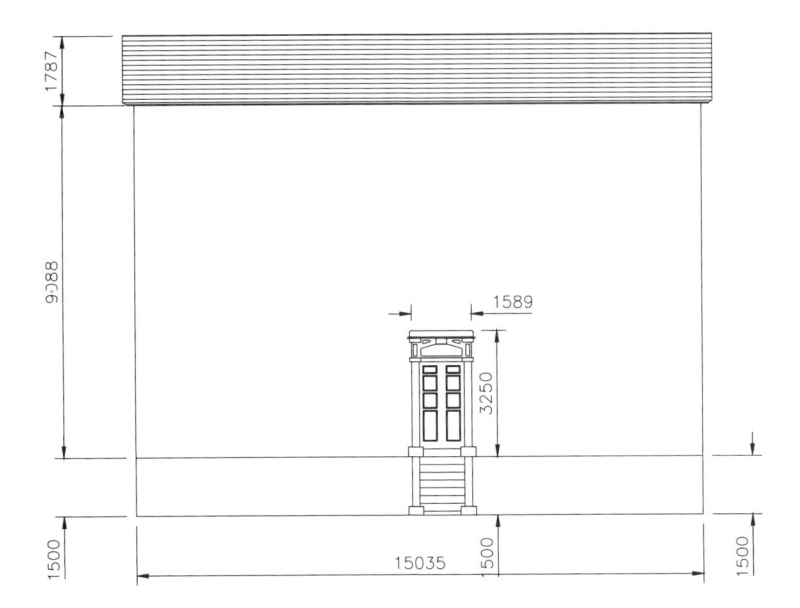

Tutorial 14.1

In this tutorial, attributes will be attached to the block of a window and inserted into the drawing.

Produce the drawing shown in the drawing instructions, and then draw a single window as illustrated in fig. 14.1. A block will be created of the window after the attributes have been defined for insertion into the drawing.

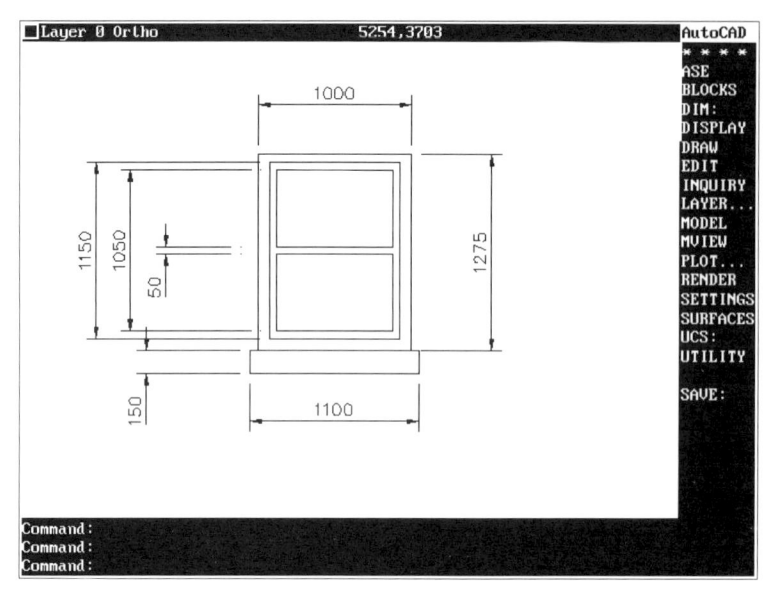

Fig. 14.1.

Creating an attribute: the 'attdef' command

Before the block is created, the attribute or attributes must be defined. This is done using the **ATTDEF** command. It is found on the screen menu under *BLOCKS* or can be typed in directly at the command prompt. When the command is executed, AutoCAD will ask you for the name of the attribute, a prompt to appear on screen when the block containing the attribute is inserted, and a default value.

How the command works
The prompts in the **ATTDEF** command ask for the following:
(1) The modes. The textual attribute can have four different modes:
- Invisible: this decides whether the attribute is initially visible on the screen when inserted.
- Constant: If an attribute is to hold the same value all the time, then set the mode to constant.
- Verify: If you answer **Y** to verify, each time you type a value into an attribute AutoCAD will ask if the value is correct.
- Preset: Answering **Y** to this mode will allow you to change a value that was defined as constant (normally a constant value is not edited).

A mode can be switched on or off by typing in its first letter (**I**, **C**, **V**, or **P**).
(2) Attribute tag. For users familiar with a data-base, a 'tag' is similar to a field. Think of a tag as a vessel into which you place a VALUE (such as the number of volts a battery carries).
(3) Attribute prompt. This is the prompt you want AutoCAD to use when asking for a value to place in the tag as the block is being inserted.
(4) Default attribute value. If a value will be entered frequently, you can tell

AutoCAD at this stage. It will then offer the value as the default as the block is being inserted.

(5) *Justify/Style/<Start point>:* This prompt and the following two are identical with the normal **TEXT** prompt, *'Height <>:'* and *'Rotation angle <0.0000>:'*.

Three attributes will first be defined and then attached to a block.

(1) The first attribute will hold information on the *TYPE* of window. The prompt will be *'WINDOW TYPE'* and the default value *'R44'*. The default attribute modes will be kept.

Use the command prompt:

Command: **ATTDEF**
Attribute modes — Invisible: N Constant: N Verify: N Preset: N Enter (ICVP) to change, RETURN when done: ← Press **[enter]** to accept the defaults
Attribute tag: **TYPE**
Attribute prompt: **WINDOW TYPE**
Default attribute value: **R44**
Justify/Style/<Start point>: ← Pick a point near the top right (see fig. 14.2)

Height <default>: **118**
Rotation angle <0.0000>: ← Press **[enter]**
Command:

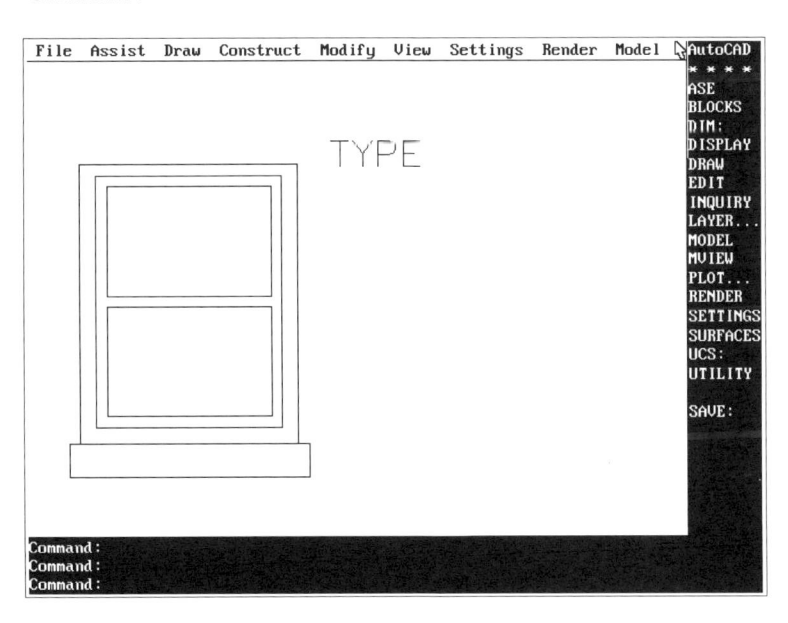

Fig. 14.2. The attribute tag TYPE in position.

(2) This second attribute will hold information on the price of a window in the tag *PRICE*. The prompt will be *'WINDOW PRICE'* and the default value '285'. The default attribute mode *'Invisible: N'* will be changed to make it visible.

Command: **ATTDEF**
Attribute modes — Invisible: N Constant: N Verify: N Preset: N Enter (ICVP) to change, RETURN when done: **I**
Attribute modes — Invisible: Y Constant: N Verify: N Preset: N Enter (ICVP) to change, RETURN when done: ← Press **[enter]**
Attribute tag: **PRICE**
Attribute prompt: **WINDOW PRICE**
Default attribute value: **285**
Justify/Style/<Start point>:   ← Press **[enter]** to place it below TYPE
Command:

(3) The third and last attribute will now be defined, using the *'Attribute Definition'* dialogue box. This dialogue box can be called up from the command prompt by typing **DDATTDEF** or from the screen menu under *'DIM'*, *'ATTDEF'*, *'AttDef dialogue'*. The attribute is to hold the name of the manufacturer of the window.

Call up the dialogue box and fill in the data shown in fig. 14.3. The same manufacturer is used for all the windows, so this value will remain constant. Click on the Constant. This will have the effect of making the prompt redundant. AutoCAD recognises this and will ghost it over. Place an X beside the 'Align below previous attribute' and pick 'OK'.

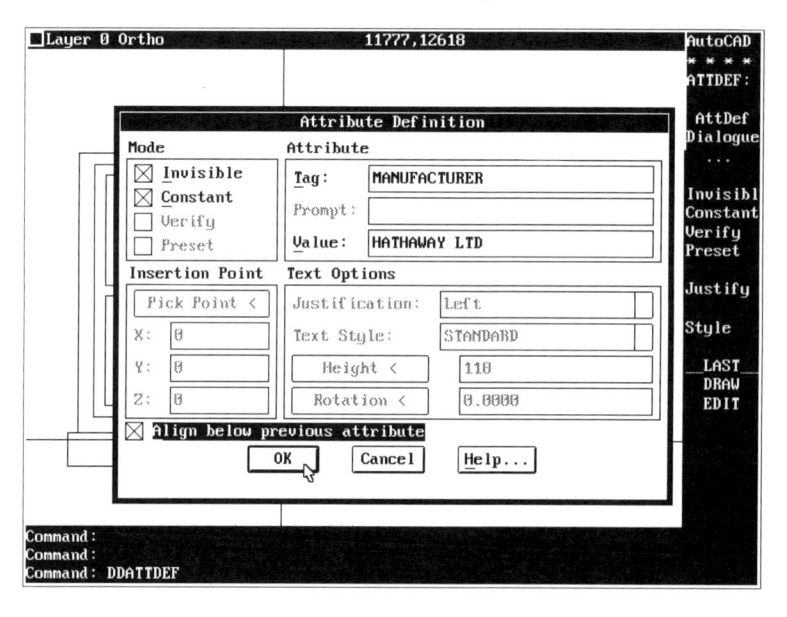

Fig. 14.3. The 'Attribute Definition' dialogue box.

These defined attributes must now be incorporated into the block by pulling a window around them during creation of the block. Name the block *WIND*, and pick the **MID** of the bottom line as the insertion point.

Command: **BLOCK**
Block name (or ?): **WIND**
Insertion base point: **MID**
of   ← The bottom line of the sill
Select objects: **W**
First corner: Other corner: 22 found
Select objects: ← **[enter]**
Command:

The block and its associated attributes will disappear from the screen.

Insertion of a block with attributes

A block with attributes is placed in a drawing with the normal **INSERT** command. Switch Snap and Grid on. Zoom all.

If the **ATTDIA** system variable is set to 1, the *'Enter Attribute'* dialogue box will be displayed when the block is INSERTed. If **ATTDIA** is set to 0, all prompts for the attributes will be displayed at the command prompt.

The **ATTREQ** system variable controls AutoCAD's acceptance of the attribute defaults. If it is set to 0, AutoCAD will insert all the variables without prompting for them. A setting of 1 will offer the defaults as options.

Set **ATTDIA** to 0 before you insert the first block, and check that **ATTREQ** is set to 1.

Command: **ATTDIA**
New value for ATTDIA <0>: **0**
Command:

Now INSERT the first block:

Command: **INSERT**
Block name (or ?): **WIND**
Insertion point: X scale factor <1> / Corner / XYZ:
Y scale factor (default=X):
Rotation angle <0.0000>:
Enter attribute values
WINDOW PRICE <285>:   ← Press **[enter]** to accept the default
WINDOW TYPE <R44>:   ← Press **[enter]** to accept the default
Command:

Note: Only the value (R44) that was placed in the tag for TYPE was displayed. This is because it was the only one you defined to be visible when the attribute modes were set.

The prompts did not ask for a value for the manufacturer, because the value was constant.

You were asked for values in the reverse order to the way they were defined.

Set **ATTDIA** to 1 and insert another block. Figure 14.4 shows the *'Enter Attribute'* dialogue box that is displayed. Change the values to R40 and 400.

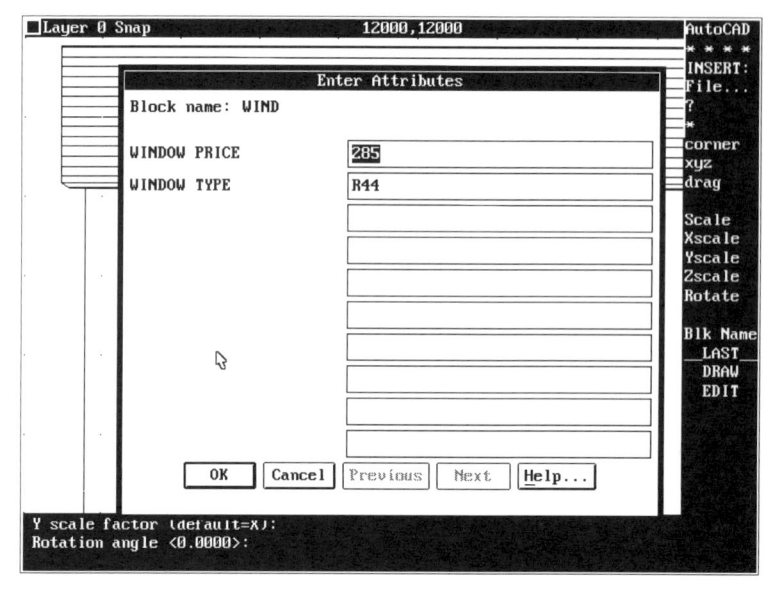

Fig. 14.4.

Insert the rest of the blocks, and vary the values as follows:
Type   Price
R40   400
R44   285
R36   114

The attribute display command: 'attdisp'

ATTDISP controls the visibility of the attributes on the screen. There are three modes: normal, on, and off.
- 'On' will display all the attributes, regardless of how they were defined.
- 'Off' will make all the attributes invisible, regardless of how they were defined.
- 'Normal' will display all the attributes as defined.

Try the three modes. The drawing will need to be regenerated to see the effect of the command. This example displays all the attributes.

Command: **ATTDISP**
Normal/ON/OFF <Normal>: **ON**
Regen queued.
Command: **REGEN**

SUMMARY

Attributes can be defined as textual data attached to a block. The ATTDEF command is used to define an attribute from the command prompt. The definition requires a name for a TAG. A tag holds the values that are attached to the block in question. The attribute definition dialogue box can be called up from the command prompt by typing **DDATTDEF**, or from the screen menu under *'DIM'*, *'ATTDEF'*, *'AttDef dialogue'*. Once the definition is completed it is attached to a block using the BLOCK command. As with any type of block, the **INSERT** command is used to place it in a drawing. If the **ATTDIA** system variable is set to 1, the *'Enter Attribute'* dialogue box will be displayed when the block is INSERTed. If **ATTDIA** is set to 0, all prompts for the attributes will be displayed at the command prompt. **ATTDISP** controls the visibility of the attributes on the screen. There are three modes: normal, on, and off.

ASSIGNMENTS

Assignment 1

Target drawing

The target drawing shows the layout of a computer training room. Create the room with a block for the computers and the chairs.

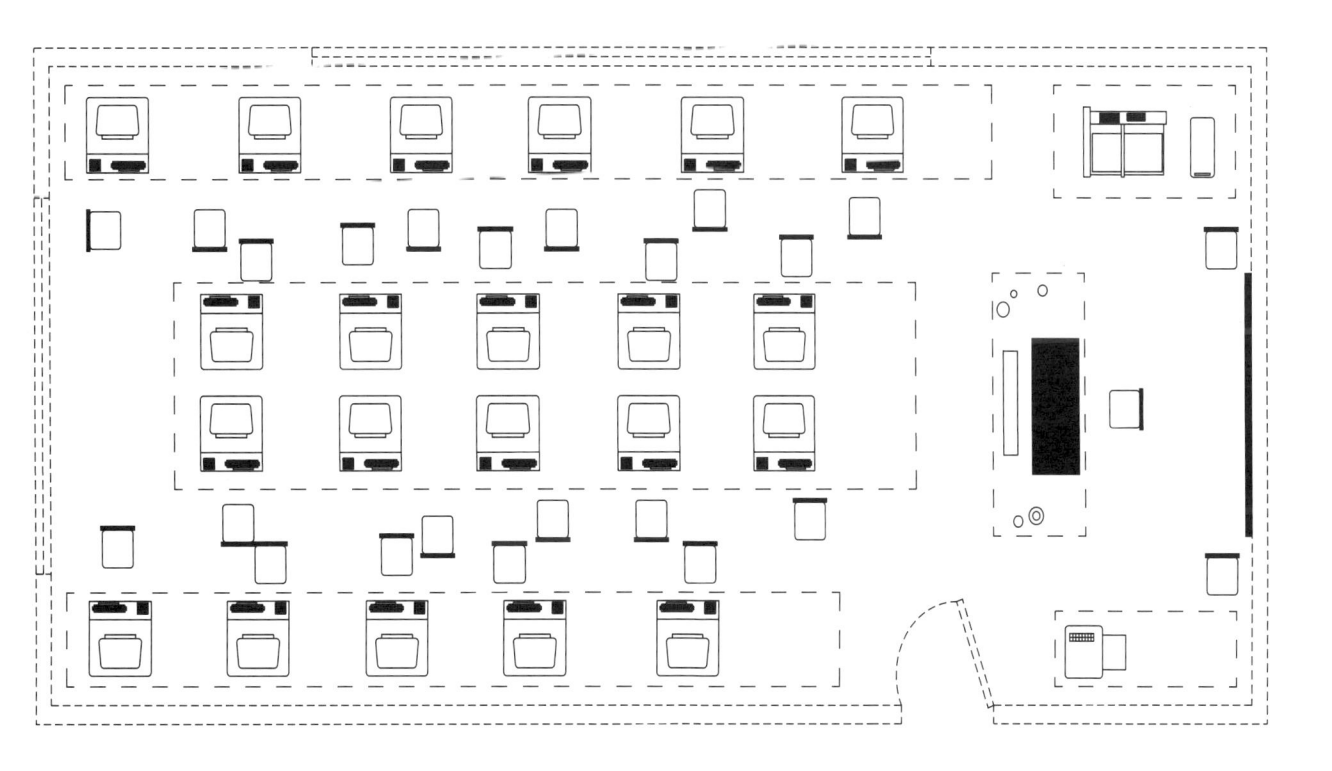

Assign the following attributes to the computer block:

	Tag	Example of values	Mode
(1)	Processor	8086 80286 80386 80486 80586	Visible
(2)	Display	EGA VGA SVGA	Visible
(3)	Roomno	230	Invisible constant
(4)	Number	1, 2, 3, 4, 5 …	Visible
(5)	Trainee	Daniel Murphy	Invisible

Assign the following tags to the chairs block:

	Tag	Value
(1)	Trainee	Daniel Murphy
(2)	Number	1, 2, 3, 4, 5 …

Assignment 2

Create the title block and insert attributes for
(*a*) company name
(*b*) title
(*c*) scale
(*d*) date.
The title should be suitable for use with an A3 sheet.

Assignment 3

Several blocks with attributes can be created for use in this drawing. Create attributes for selected blocks, to include a serial number for the component and any additional information you think is necessary.

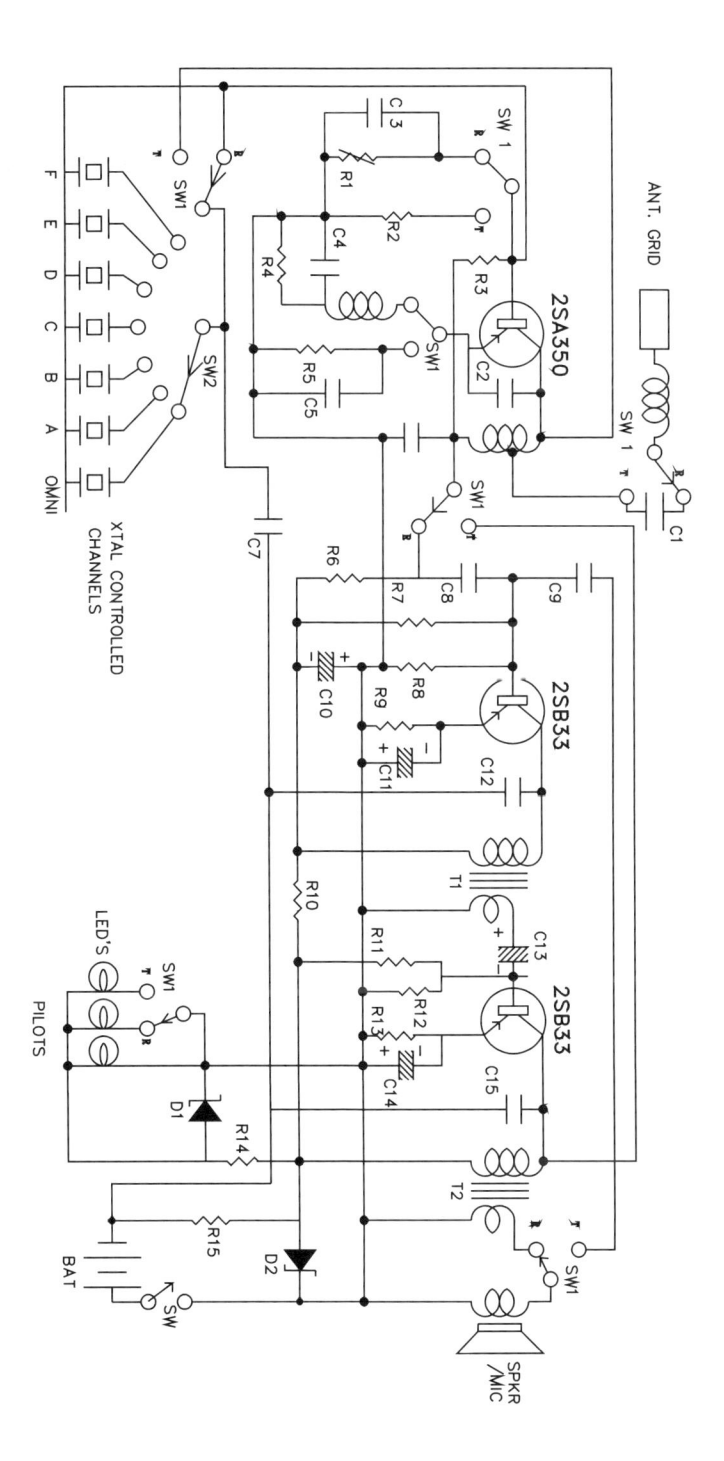

Assignment 4

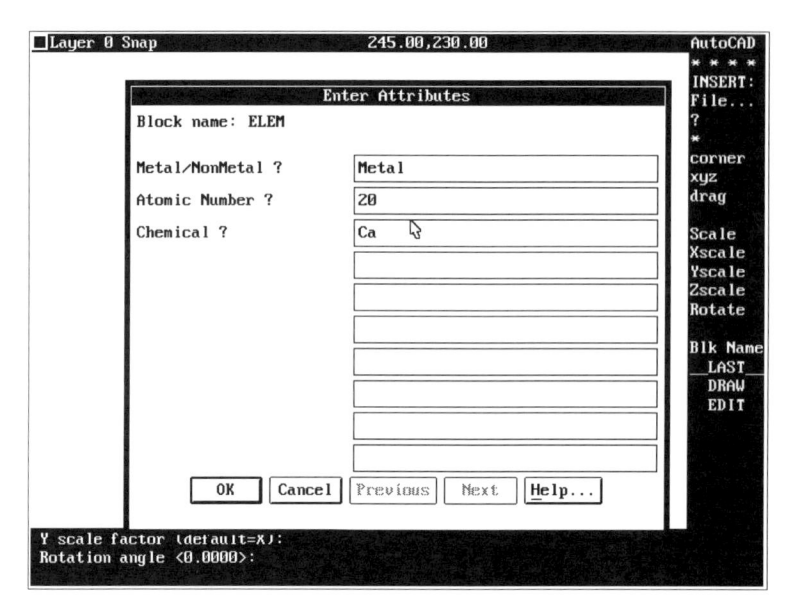

A chemist needs to insert blocks representing elements from the periodic table of the elements. The attributes she needs to work with include 'name', 'atomic number', and whether it is a metal or a nonmetal. The block and associated attributes for the element calcium is: 20

(Ca)

Metal

Create this block with attributes for the chemist. The prompt for the attribute values when she inserts the block is shown in the *'Enter Attribute'* dialogue box below.

Assignment 5

An art gallery has a large collection of paintings. The gallery cannot display all its pictures at once: some are kept in storage. At various times of the year and for special exhibitions paintings are moved to different rooms in the gallery and in and out of storage. Some paintings are only on loan to the gallery.

Design a simple block representing a picture that can be inserted into a plan view of the gallery's rooms. The attributes must be able to hold the following information:

(*a*) the artist's name;
(*b*) the title of the painting;
(*c*) the size of the painting;
(*d*) the medium it is painted in: oils, watercolour, etc.;
(*e*) the date it was hung for exhibition;
(*f*) whether it is on loan or part of the permanent collection.

chapter 15
Detailed Dimensioning

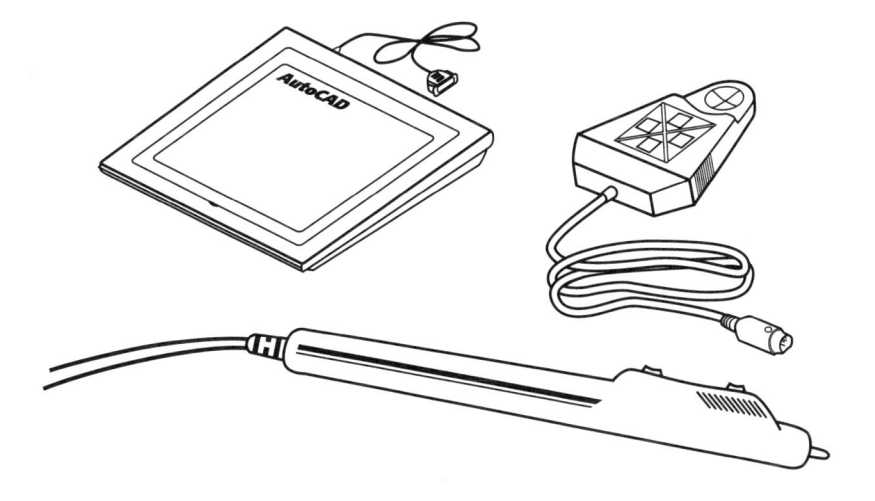

Tutorial objectives

By the end of this chapter you should be able to
- use the associative dimensioning capability
- dimension entities that are not horizontal or vertical
- place a diameter or radius on a circle, arc, or fillet
- display the co-ordinates of a point relative to the user co-ordinate system
- dimension angles
- reference several dimension lines back to a single datum point
- change the arrow on a dimension line to a dot
- change the scale of text and arrow size on a dimension block using DIMSCALE
- change the size of the text used in a dimension
- modify the size of the arrows or dots in a dimension line
- place upper and lower limits on dimension values
- place tolerances on dimension values
- use the STRETCH command
- use the SCALE command

Target drawing

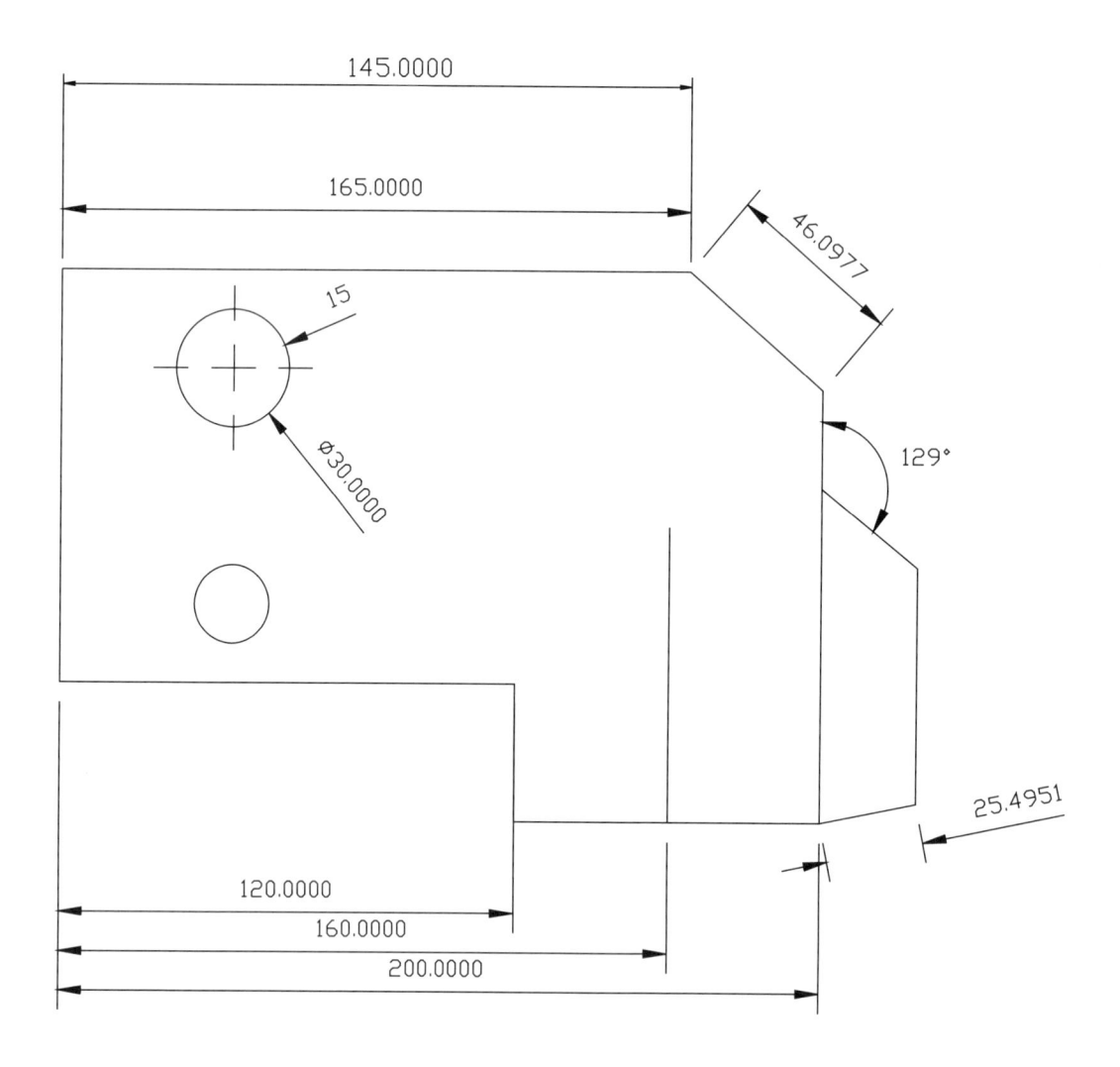

INTRODUCTION

DIM is a complex command that contains over thirty 'dimensioning variables'. These variables allow you to control features such as the size of the dimensioning text and its orientation within the drawing.

Associative dimensioning

AutoCAD allows you to place dimensions into a drawing in one of two ways:
(1) Using the associative dimensioning capability
(2) Using the non-associative dimensioning capability

In the associative dimensioning mode, the dimension text, dimension line and extension lines all behave as a single entity (similar to a block). This has the advantage of allowing the automatic updating of dimensions whenever the objects that are dimensioned are edited. For example, if the **SCALE** and **STRETCH** commands are used to change the size of an associative dimensioned line, as the size of the line entity changes the dimension values are modified to reflect the change (see below). It also means that if you later decide to update the size of the dimension text or the size of the arrowheads, the process becomes automatic: simply tell AutoCAD the size of the text or arrows and click on any part of the dimension to bring about the updating.

The associative dimensioning capability of AutoCAD is the default method. It can be switched off using the dimensioning variable **DIMASO**. Leave the value on for the moment.

The arrows at the ends of the dimension line can be replaced with ticks or any other symbol you define yourself. The symbol (other than the ticks supplied by AutoCAD) must first be defined as BLOCKS (see chapter 13 on the creation of BLOCKS).

If the dimension text is too large to be placed inside the extension lines or, in the case of a circle, inside the circle itself, AutoCAD will place it at a new location. In the case of a circle, a LEADER line is drawn from the dimension text to the entity.

Tutorial 15.1

Use the *ACAD prototype* drawing to draw the baseplate for the tutorial. Before you proceed, switch the dimension variable **DIMASO** to on. To do that, execute the following from the command prompt:

Command: **DIM [enter]**
Dim: **DIMASO [enter]**
Current value <On> New value: **ON [enter]**
Dim: **EXIT [enter]**

Draw the baseplate on layer 0. Create a layer to hold the dimensions called **DIM1-1-1** (assigned colour 1, red). Set the layer current, and select **DIM** from the screen menu.

Dimension the top horizontal line on the baseplate. This will be used later in the tutorial (see the SCALE and STRETCH commands below).

The first page of the **DIM** submenu lists the following options:
Aligned
Angular
Diameter
Horizntl
Leader
Ordinate
Radius
Rotated
Vertical
Edit
Dim Styl
Dim Vars
next
Exit
*_LAST_*
DRAW
EDIT

Tutorial 11.1 introduced dimensioning with the options Horizntl, Leader, and Vertical.

The 'aligned' option

Aligned is used when the entity being dimensioned is not vertical or horizontal. With this option, the dimension lines are placed parallel to the chosen object.

In the dimensioning in chapter 11 the endpoints of the entity being dimensioned were selected using object snap. AutoCAD also allows you to pick on the entity to be measured; the dimension is then calculated for the complete entity. This method will be used in the example below.

To dimension the top right chamfer of the baseplate, execute the following from the screen menu:

Command: _DIM
Dim: _ALIGNED
First extension line origin or RETURN to select: ← Press **[enter]**
Select line, arc, or circle: ← Pick the line
Dimension line location: ← Select a suitable position
Dimension text <46.0977>:   ← Press **[enter]** to accept
Dim:

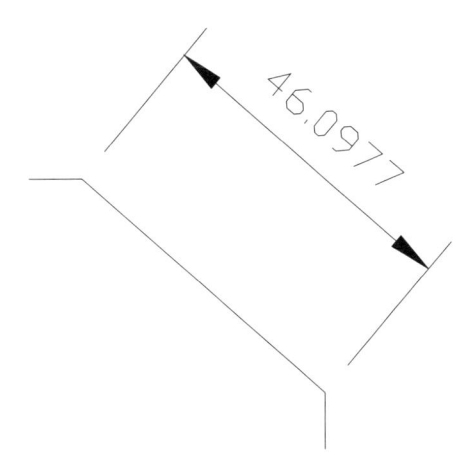

Fig. 15.1. The ALIGNED DIM option.

The 'radius' and 'diameter' options

These two options place a diameter or radius on a circle, arc, or fillet. The position of the diameter or radius on the entities will be determined by where you click on the entity with the selection aperture. The option also places a centre-line in the circle.

Zoom in on the top left circle and apply both a radius and diameter dimension to it. Zoom will automatically function transparently while in *Dim,* even if you do not use the apostrophe. If you are unhappy with where the dimension text is placed, then Undo the command and start again. Undo works from the dim prompt. Work with Snap off. The **UNITS** command has the number of decimal places set to four. All the dimensions will consequently show four decimal places. You can override the *'Dimension text <value>:'* by typing in some text yourself. For example, the circle has a radius of 10.0000 units. Try entering just 15 at the prompt instead. The command sequence below includes the transparent zoom.

Dim: **ZOOM**
>>Center/Dynamic/Left/Previous/Vmax/Window/<Scale(X/XP)>: >>>>Other corner:
Resuming DIM command.
Dim: **_RADIUS**
Select arc or circle:
Dimension text <15.0000>: **15**   ← Enter **15** and press **[enter]**
Enter leader length for text:
Dim: **_DIAMETER**
Select arc or circle:

Dimension text <30.0000>:
Enter leader length for text:
Dim:

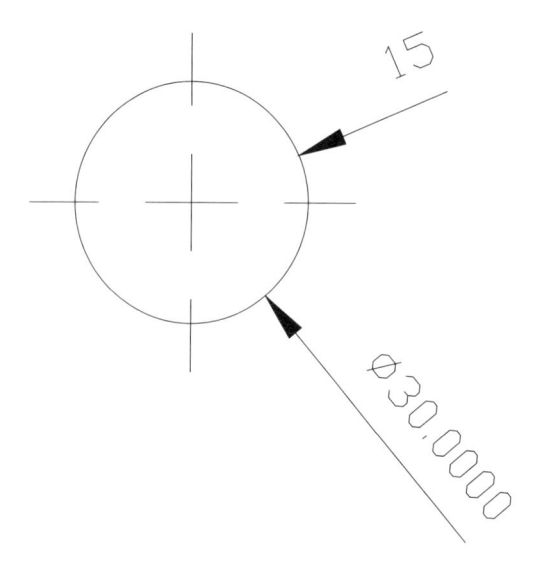

Fig. 15.2. The RADIUS and DIAMETER options.

The 'rotated' option

The rotated option is used to measure the length of lines running at specific angles. AutoCAD will ask for the angle the line is inclined at. The angle of the line can be given to AutoCAD by (*a*) typing in a value or (*b*) using the pointing device to indicate the angle.

The example used here will illustrate the method of using the pointing device.

Dimension the sloping line at the bottom right of the baseplate.

Command: _DIM
Dim: _ROTATED
Dimension line angle <0>: **END**
of ← Pick one end of the line
Second point: **END**
of ← Pick the other end of the line. From the above sequence AutoCAD has calculated the angle the line is inclined at. Next AutoCAD needs to know the entity to dimension.
First extension line origin or RETURN to select: END
of ← Pick one end of the line
Second extension line origin: END
of ← Pick the other end of the line

Dimension line location:
Dimension text <25.4951>:
Dim:

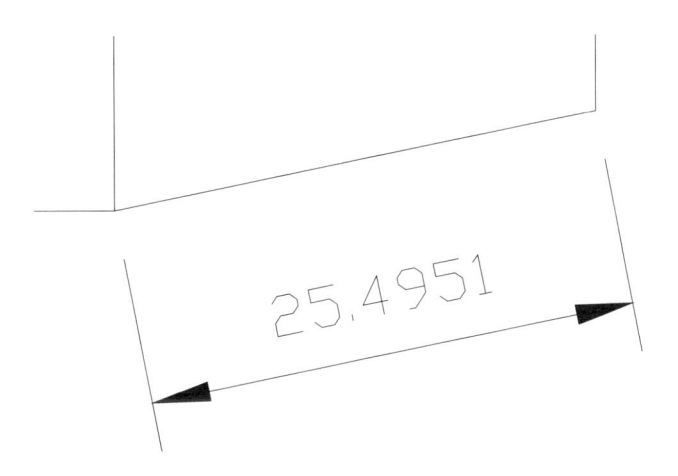

Fig. 15.3. The ROTATED option.

The 'ordinate' option

This allows you to display the co-ordinates of a point. The co-ordinates are relative to the position of the **UCS** (see chapter 16, tutorial 16.3). The **UCS** can be used to locate a datum point. Switch ORTHO on when executing this option.

The following examples will illustrate this.

Draw a circle with its centre at 170,125 and a radius of 5 units.

How the option works

When the command is issued, AutoCAD will ask you to *'Select Feature:'*. The feature can be selected in the usual ways. You will then be required to pick the *'Leader endpoint'* as the default. If ORTHO is on, your selection point will be on the x or y axis. The x and y values will be displayed at the end of the leader line. The option *'Xdatum/Ydatum:'* can be selected to override the defaults.

In the example below, the co-ordinates of the centre of the circle just drawn will be displayed with reference to the UCS with its origin at 0,0 (the default of the ACAD prototype drawing). The UCS will then be moved to the centre of the circle and the **ORDINATE** command applied to it again.

Dim: **ORDINATE**
Select Feature: **CEN**
of   ← Select the small circle

Leader endpoint (Xdatum/Ydatum):   ← Pick a point to the right of the circle
Dimension text <170.0000>:   ← Press **[enter]**
Dim: **ORDINATE**
Select Feature: **CEN**
of   ← Select the small circle
Leader endpoint (Xdatum/Ydatum):   ← Pick a point above the circle
Dimension text <125.0000>:   ← Press **[enter]**

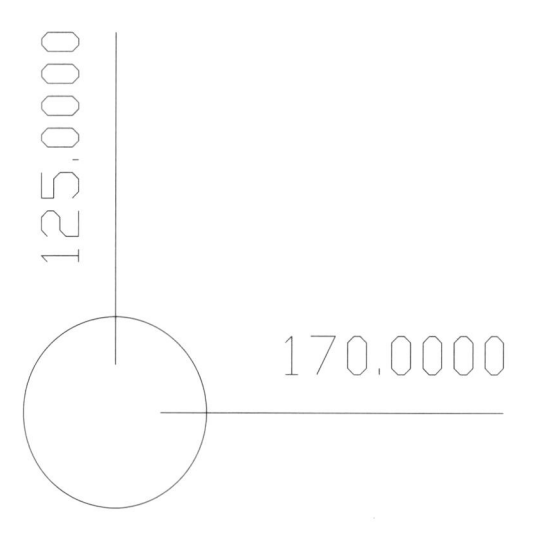

Fig. 15.4. The ORDINATE command UCS at 0,0.

Now make the centre of the circle a new datum point by moving the **UCS** to the centre of the circle.
Command: **UCS**
Origin/ZAxis/3point/Entity/View/X/Y/Z/Prev/Restore/Save/Del/?/<World>:
O
Origin point <0,0,0>: **CEN**
of   ← Pick the perimeter of the circle
Command:
    Now issue the ORDINATE option:
Dim: **ORDINATE**
Select Feature: **CEN**
of
Leader endpoint (Xdatum/Ydatum):
Dimension text <0.0000>:
Dim: **ORDINATE**
Select Feature: **CEN**
of
Leader endpoint (Xdatum/Ydatum):
Dimension text <0.0000>:

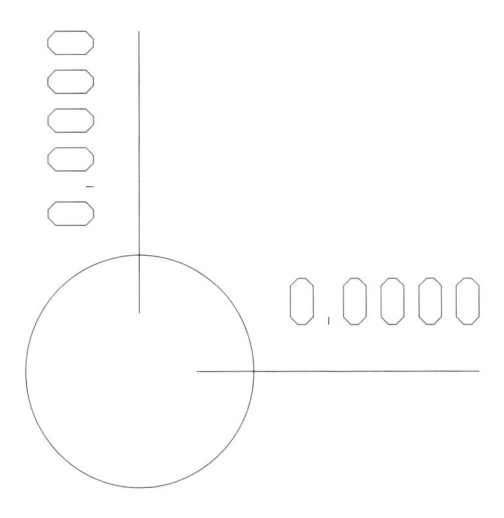

Fig. 15.5. The ORDINATE option with the UCS at the CEN of the circle.

The 'angular' option

This is used to measure angles. AutoCAD will ask you to select the entities that form the angle. An arc with the dimension text displays the angle's size. You will be asked for the position of the dimension arc and then the position of the dimension text. To dimension the angle in the target drawing, execute the following:

Command: **_DIM**
Dim: **_ANGULAR**
Select arc, circle, line, or RETURN: ← Pick one of the lines
Second line: ← Pick the other line
Dimension arc line location (Text/Angle):   ← Select an appropriate point
Dimension text <129>:   ← Press **[enter]**
Enter text location (or RETURN):   ← Press **[enter]**
Dim:

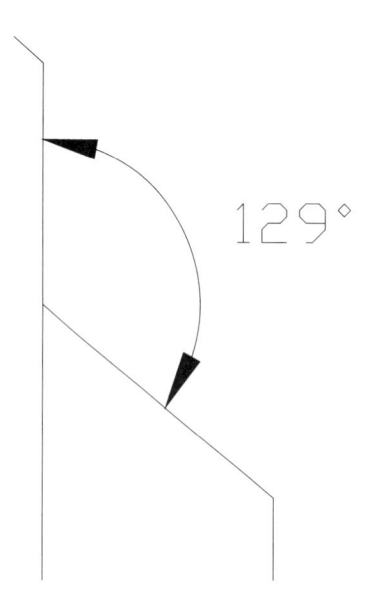

Fig. 15.6. The ANGULAR option.

The 'baseline' option

Picking *'next'* from the first menu page will open the second page:
Baseline
Continue
Centre
Status
previous

The **BASELINE** option is used for horizontal and vertical dimensioning. It allows you to reference several linear dimensions back to a single datum line. In fig. 15.7 the dimensions across the bottom of the plate are referenced back to the first extension line (this is the common datum line).

To dimension the bottom of the baseplate, execute the following:
(1) Start by executing the horizontal option in Dim.
(2) Dimension the first line of 120 units.
(3) Continue by calling up 'Baseline'.
   The command sequence is as follows:

Command: **DIM**
Dim: **HOR**
First extension line origin or RETURN to select: **END**
of   ← Pick the left end of the base line

Second extension line origin: **END**
of   ← Pick the right end of the line
Dimension line location: ← Pick a suitable location

Dimension text <120.0000>: **120**
Dim: **BASELINE**
Second extension line origin or RETURN to select: **INT**
of   ← Intersection of the vertical line and the base line
Dimension text <160.0000>: **160**
Dim: **BASELINE**
Second extension line origin or RETURN to select: **END**
of
Dimension text <200.0000>: **200**
Dim:

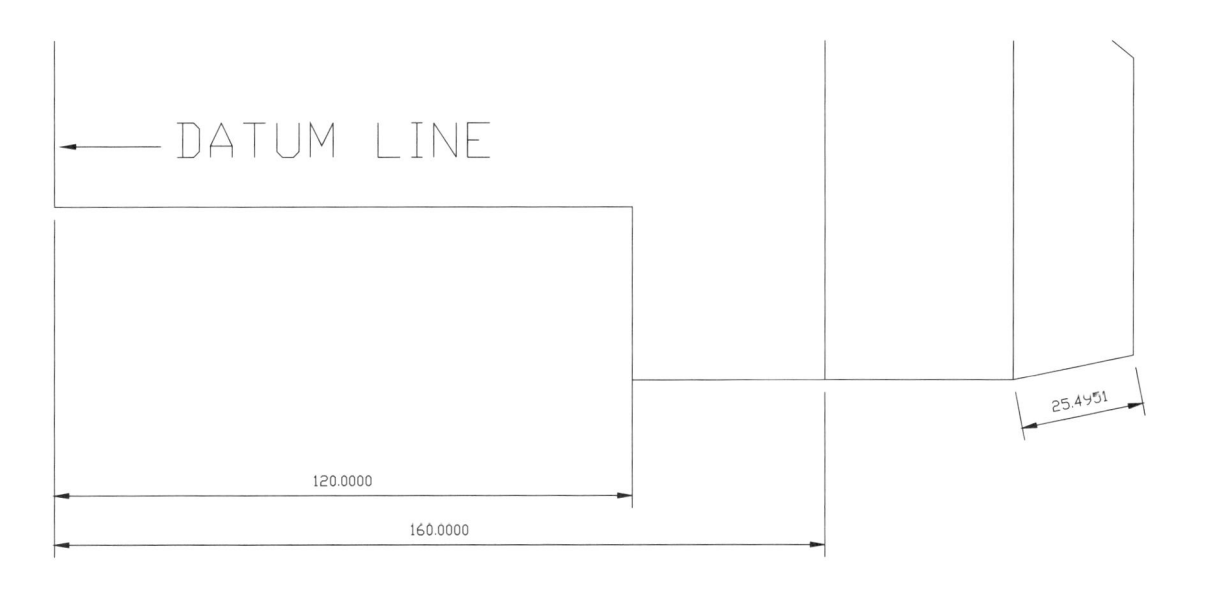

Fig. 15.7. The baseline option, showing the datum line.

Continue: allows you to continue dimensioning using the last dimension point as the first dimension point of the next dimension.

Centre: This option places a cross at the centre of the selected circle, arc, or fillet radius. The variable DIMCEN allows the cross to be replaced by a centre line.

Status: Lists the dimension variable settings.

The dimensioning variables

These variables control the characteristics of the dimension block. They allow you to change the size of the dimensioning arrows, or the placement of text inside or outside the extension lines.

Associative dimensioning can be switched on or off using them.

The settings of the variables can be viewed by either typing **STATUS** at the Dim prompt or selecting it from the screen menu. (Appendix D lists all the variables and their setting in the ACAD prototype drawing.)

Changing the arrows

AutoCAD defaults to drawing arrows at the ends of the dimension line. You can, however, create your own symbols and tell AutoCAD to place them at the ends of the dimension lines. It is also possible to place different symbols at opposite ends of the same dimension line.

Changing the arrow to a dot

As the dot is a common dimension line marker, it is supplied with AutoCAD. **ZOOM** in on the dimension **ALIGNED** at the top right of the baseplate. The arrow dimension line marker will be changed here. Follow the sequence of commands selected from the screen menu. Assuming you are on the first page of the **DIM** menu, pick *'Dim Vars'*, then *'dimblk'*. Enter **DOT** in response to *'Current value <> New value:'*.

Pick *'Dim menu'*, then *'Edit'*, and lastly *'Update'*. In response to *'Select objects'* click anywhere on the aligned dimension block. The arrows will be replaced by dots.

A summary of the command sequence is given below:

Command: **_DIM**
Dim: **_DIMBLK**
Current value <> New value: **DOT**
Dim: **_UPDATE**
Select objects: ← Pick the aligned dimension block

1 found
Select objects: ← Press **[enter]**
Dim:

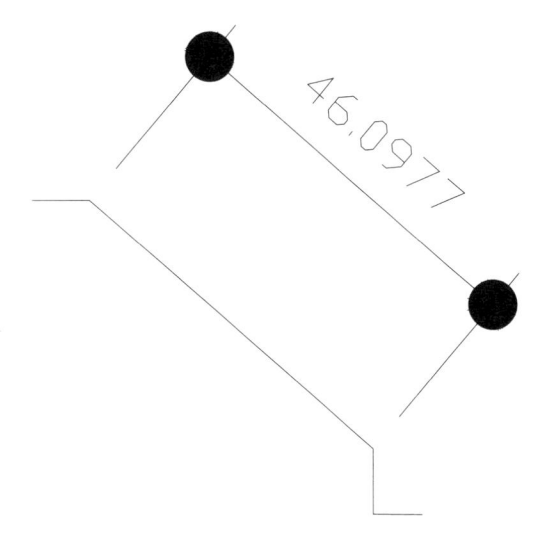

Fig. 15.8. Replacing the arrow with a dot.

Using two symbols on a single dimension line
This example will be executed from the command prompt. The dimensioning variables **DIMBLK1**, **DIMBLK2** and **DIMSAH** are used in this task.

DIMBLK1 sets the symbol to the left of the dimension line. **DIMBLK2** sets the symbol to the right end of the dimension line. **DIMSAH** must be set to *on* to allow AutoCAD to use the symbols.

Using the aligned dimension again, try the following:

Dim: **DIMSAH**
Current value <Off> New value: **ON**
Dim: **DIMBLK1**
Current value <> New value: **DOT**
Dim: **DIMBLK2**
Current value <> New value: .   ← Type a full point (.)
Dim: **UPDATE**
Select objects: ← Pick the aligned
                                         dimension block

1 found
Select objects:
Dim:

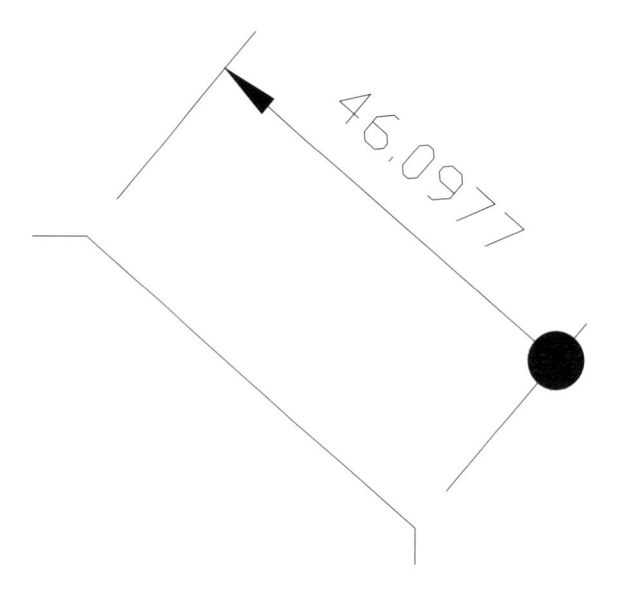

Fig. 15.9. Placing an arrow and a dot on the same dimension line.

The 'dimscale' variable

This is a variable that affects most of the other variables, including variables that control distances, sizes, and offsets. It has a default value of 1.0.

When the **ELECTA-1** prototype drawing was set up in chapter 12, the **DIMSCALE** value was placed at 0.12500000. This scaled all the elements of the dimension block down to suit the limits and units of the drawing.

The **DIMSCALE** value can be changed at any time while drawing. However, the **UPDATE** command must be applied to the dimensions you want to change in order to see the effect.

The 'dimtxt' variable

The height of the dimension text can be changed using this variable. The default value is 3.0 units. Change the value to 6 and update one of the dimensions. The effect should be to double the size of the dimension text.

The 'dimasz' variable

The size of the dimension arrows can be changed using this variable. The default value is 3.0. Change it to 6.0, and **UPDATE** to see the result.

The 'dimexe' variable

This determines the distance the extension lines project beyond the dimension line. The default value is 2.5 units. Increase it to 10 and **UPDATE** a dimension. Fig. 15.10 illustrates the **DIMEXE** distance.

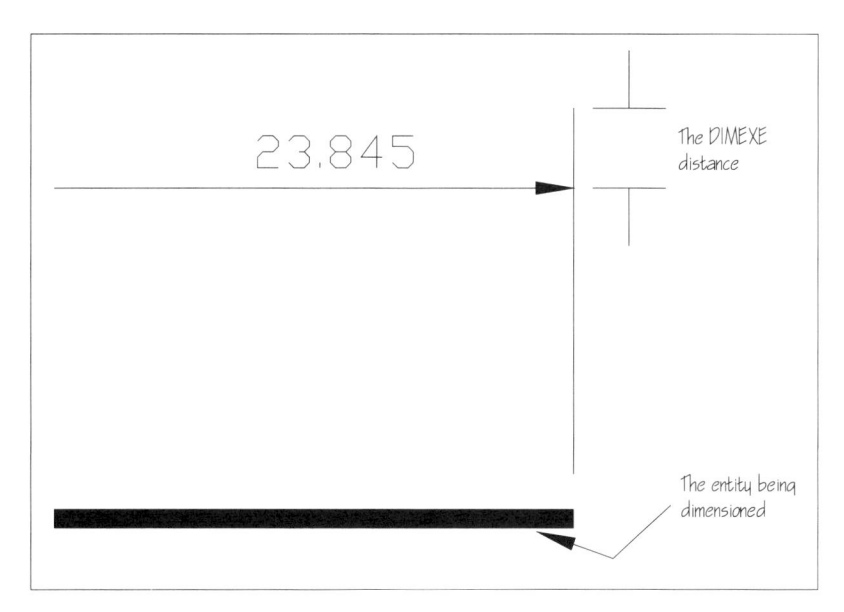

Fig. 15.10. The DIMEXE distance.

The 'dimexo' variable

DIMEXO defines the offset distance of the extension lines from the points chosen as the extension line origins. The default value is 2.5 units.

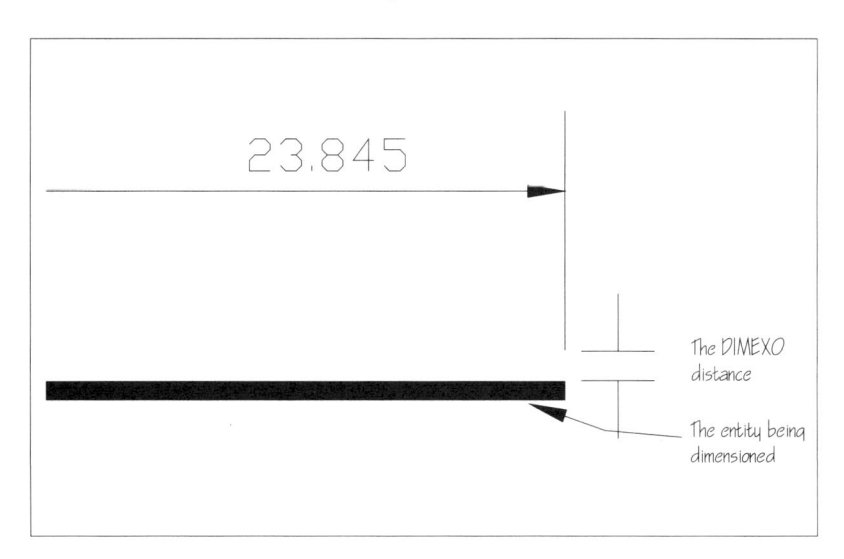

Fig. 15.11. The DIMEXO distance.

The variables 'dimlim', 'dimtol', 'dimtm', and 'dimtp'

The **DIMLIM** variable enables or disables the generation of default dimension text as upper and lower dimension limits. It is either on or off, and works in conjunction with the dimension variables **DIMTOL**, **DIMTM**, and **DIMTP**.

Try the following:

Assign the value 0.03 to **DIMTM** and 0.04 to **DIMTP**. Then set **DIMLIM** to *on*. The **DIMTM** value is subtracted from the actual dimension, and the **DIMTP** value is added.

The command sequence is:

Command: **DIM**
Dim: **DIMTM**
Current value <0.0000> New value: **0.03**
Dim: **DIMTP**
Current value <0.0000> New value: **0.04**
Dim: **DIMLIM**
Current value <Off> New value: **ON**
Dim: **UPDATE**
Select objects: 1 found
Select objects:
Dim:

Fig. 15.12 illustrates the effect of this command sequence on one of the aligned dimensions.

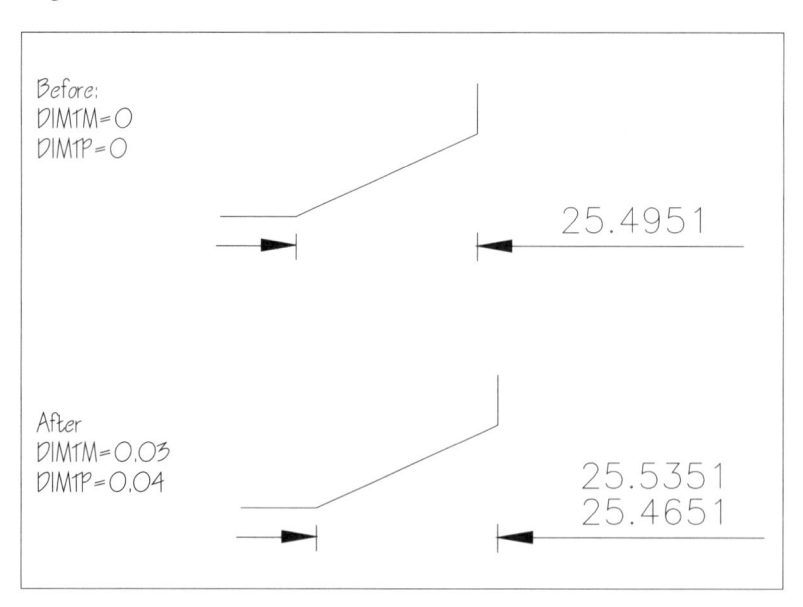

Fig. 15.12. The effect of DIMLIM, DIMTM, and DIMTP.

The tolerances variable 'dimtol'

DIMTOL is either on or off. It determines whether AutoCAD will append an upper and lower tolerance to the default dimension text. If **DIMTOL** is on, the tolerances are added to the dimension text.

When **DIMLIM** is on, **DIMTOL** is switched off. They cannot both be on at the same time. Again the tolerances are controlled by **DIMTP** and **DIMTM**. Using the settings **DIMTP = 0.04** and **DIMTM = 0.03** (they are already set from the **DIMLIM** variable above), try the following.

Command: **DIM**
Dim: **DIMTOL**
Current value <On> New value: **ON**
Dim: **UPDATE**
Select objects: ← Pick the aligned
                                                      dimension block

1 found
Select objects:
Dim:

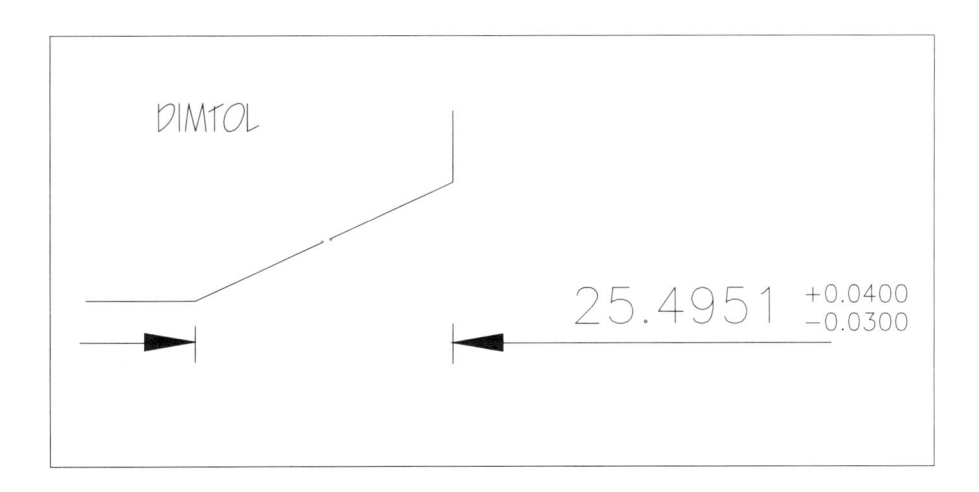

Fig. 15.13. The DIMTOL variable.

The 'dimpost' variable

This variable allows you to set a 'string' (such as 'mm' or 'in.') to follow the dimension text.

Again using the aligned dimension, try the following:

Dim: **DIMPOST**
Current value <> New value: **mm**
Dim: **UPDATE**
Select objects: 1 found
Select objects:
Dim:

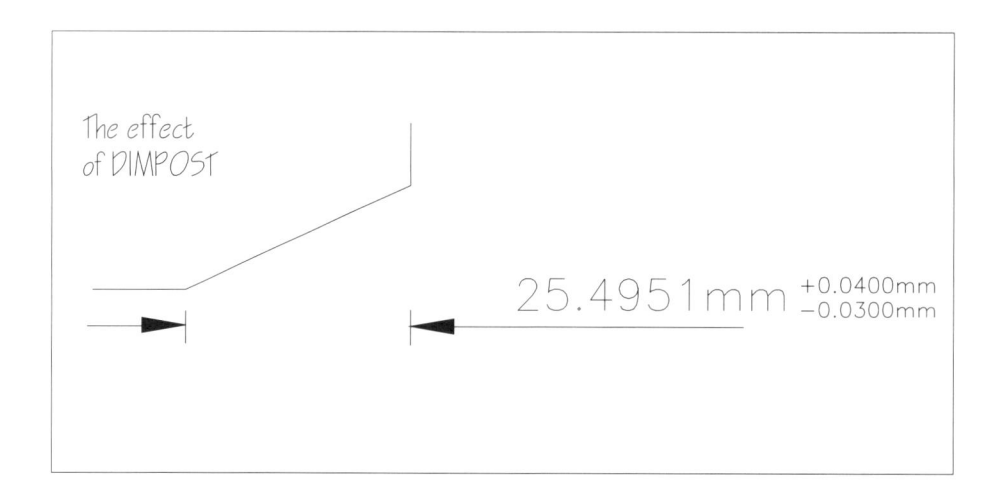

Fig. 15.14. The effect of DIMPOST.

The 'dimaso' variable

DIMASO switches the associative dimensioning on and off. All dimensioning executed while the variable was on will function associatively, even after the variable is switched off.

The top horizontal line on the baseplate is dimensioned to 145 mm. To see the effect of **DIMASO**, the **STRETCH** and **SCALE** commands will be introduced.

Switch off **DIMASO**.

Dim: **DIMASO**
Current value <On> New value: **OFF**
Dim:

Dimension the top horizontal line again, leaving the dimension block you set up at the beginning of the tutorial.

The **STRETCH** command should now adequately illustrate the value of associative dimensioning.

The 'stretch' command

This command allows entities to be moved and stretched while remaining in contact with their original entities. The command uses a method of selection called 'crossing'. Crossing is similar to the 'windows' method of selection, in that a window is used. However, parts of entities inside the window are also selected. After selection is completed you supply a *'Base point'* and a *'New point'*.

Switch ORTHO on. Use the **STRETCH** command to select the entities shown in fig. 15.15 with the crossing option.

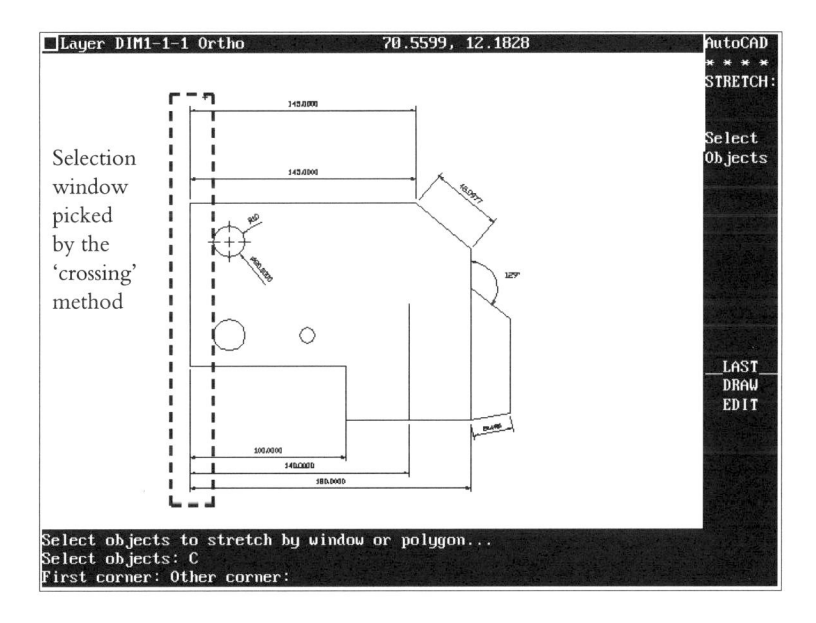

Fig. 15.15. The STRETCH command uses crossing to select entities.

Command: **STRETCH**
Select objects to stretch by window or polygon…
Select objects: **C**   ← C for 'crossing'
First corner: Other corner: 8 found
Select objects:
Base point or displacement: ← Pick a point near the vertical side

Second point of displacement: **@20<180**   ← This moves the entities 20 units to the left

Command:

DETAILED DIMENSIONING

The dimension line created at the beginning of the tutorial when **DIMASO** was on had its value updated by 20 units to 165. The dimension line created with **DIMASO** off has also been stretched, but the dimension value of 145 has remained the same.

The 'scale' command

SCALE changes the size of entities. The entities to be scaled can be selected by any of the usual AutoCAD selection methods.

Try scaling the circle that you dimensioned at the beginning of the tutorial. When the scale command asks you to *'Select objects'*, pick the circle itself and the diameter dimension.

Command: **SCALE**
Select objects: 1 found
Select objects: 1 found
Select objects:
Base point: **CEN**
of ← Pick the circle
<Scale factor>/Reference: **1.5**
Command:
The selected diameter dimension increased to 30 units.

Using the dialogue boxes

The dialogue boxes can be used to carry out most of the variable settings and modifications of the dimension text.

To modify the dimension text

Use the *'Modify'* drop-down menu to call *'Edit Dim'*. Two further menus cascade from *'Edit Dim'*.

The *'Dimension Styles and Variables'* dialogue box is opened by picking *'Settings'* from the drop-down menu and then *'Dimension Style ...'* It can also be called by typing **DDIM** at the command prompt.

The 'edit' option on the Dim: menu

The *'Edit'* option allows you to modify the associative dimensions to suit the style of the drawing. If *'Edit'* is selected from the screen menu under *Dim*, the following submenu is displayed:
DIM

Hometext
Newtext
Oblique
TRotate
Tedit
Update

Select
Objects

Undo
REDRAW

Hometext allows text to be returned to its default position after it has been changed. The **SCALE** or **STRETCH** commands (see below) may have been used to modify associative dimensions, causing a movement of the dimension text. *Hometext* will return the text to its original location. The other options listed below will allow repositioning of the text. The *Hometext* option will also allow these changes to be undone.

Newtext allows you to replace the dimension text. To change the dimension text '120' at the bottom of the baseplate, select *'Newtext'*. AutoCAD will ask *'Enter new dimension text:'*. Enter **120 mm** and select the dimension text you want replaced.

The command sequence is:

Command: **_DIM**
Dim: **_NEWTEXT**
Enter new dimension text: **120 mm**
Select objects: 1 found
Select objects:
Dim:

The *Newtext* option also allows you to append text to the existing dimension text by typing **<>** followed by the appended text. For example, to append **'in all cases'** to **120 mm**, execute the following:

Command: **_DIM**
Dim: **_NEWTEXT**
Enter new dimension text: <>in all cases
Select objects: 1 found
Select objects:
Dim:

Note that the dimension text reverted to its original setting of four decimal places set by the UNITS command.

Oblique allows the existing dimension extension lines to be altered to an angle other than the default 90°. When the command is issued, you select the dimension to alter, and AutoCAD will ask for the *'obliquing angle'*.

TRotate: Dimension text can be placed at an angle other than that used by the dimension settings. The *TRotate* ('text rotate') option allows you to rotate the text any way you wish. When the option is selected, AutoCAD will ask you to *'Enter text angle:'*. Lastly, you will again select the associated dimension text to be rotated. The dimension text line will be broken to accommodate the rotated text.

The following command sequence was used to rotate the text **'120 mm'** 45°.

Dim: **_TROTATE**
Enter text angle: **45**
Select objects: 1 found
Select objects:
Dim:

Tedit allows the dimension text to be moved or justified. The default option is to move the text to a new location. This can be done using the cursor.

The command sequence to move text is given below.

Dim: **_TEDIT**
Select dimension:
Enter text location (Left/Right/Home/Angle):
Dim:

The *'Left/Right/Home/Angle'* options work as follows:

Left: aligns text to the left of the dimension line.
Right: aligns text to the right of the dimension line.
Home: moves the text back to its default position.
Angle: allows the text to be positioned at an angle.
Update: allows you to apply any new settings of the dimension variable to associative dimensioning. When the command is entered, you need to select the objects to update.
Select objects:
ALL
Last
Previous
Crossing
Fence
CPolygon
WPolygon
Window
Add
Remove
Undo

SUMMARY

DIM is a complex command that contains over thirty dimensioning variables. These variables allow you to control features such as the size of the dimensioning text and its orientation within the drawing. In the associative dimensioning mode, the dimension text, dimension line and extension lines all behave as a single entity (similar to a block). The variable DIMASO switches the associative dimensioning mode on and off.

The *aligned* option is used when the entity being dimensioned is not vertical or horizontal. The radius and diameter options dimension a circle, arc, or fillet radius. The rotated option is used to measure the length of lines running at specific angles. The ORDINATE option allows you to display the co-ordinates of a point. The co-ordinates are relative to the position of the UCS. The angular option is used to measure angles. The **BASELINE** option is used for horizontal and vertical dimensioning. It allows you to reference several linear dimensions back to a single datum line.

The dimensioning variables **DIMBLK1**, **DIMBLK2** and **DIMSAH** are used to change the arrow on the dimension line to a tick or any other predefined block. **DIMBLK1** sets the symbol to the left of the dimension line. **DIMBLK2** sets the symbol to the right end of the dimension line. **DIMSAH** must be set to on to allow AutoCAD to use the symbols.

The DIMSCALE variable affects most of the other dimensioning variables, including variables that control distances, sizes, and offsets. It has a default value of 1.0. The **DIMLIM** variable enables or disables the generation of default dimension text as upper and lower dimension limits. It is either on or off, and works in conjunction with the dimension variables **DIMTOL**, **DIMTM**, and **DIMTP**.

The STRETCH command allows entities to be moved and stretched while remaining in contact with their original entities. The command uses a method of selection called 'crossing'. The SCALE command changes the size of entities. The entities to be scaled can be selected by any of the usual AutoCAD selection methods.

ASSIGNMENTS
Assignment 1

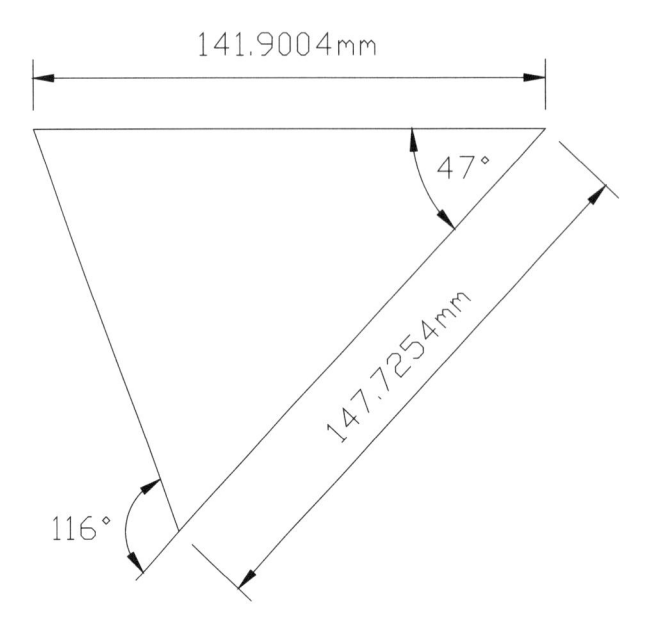

Assignment 2

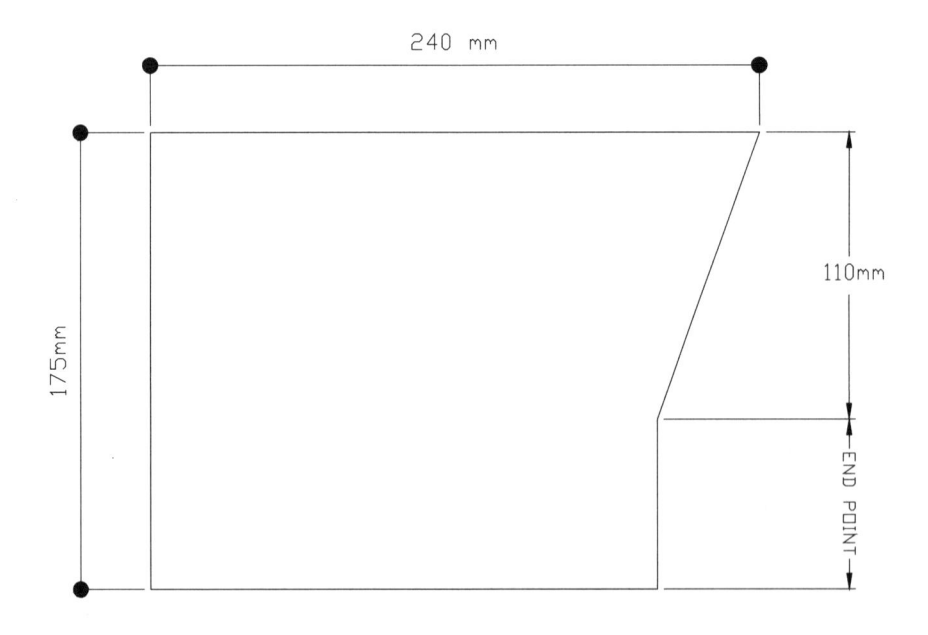

Assignment 3

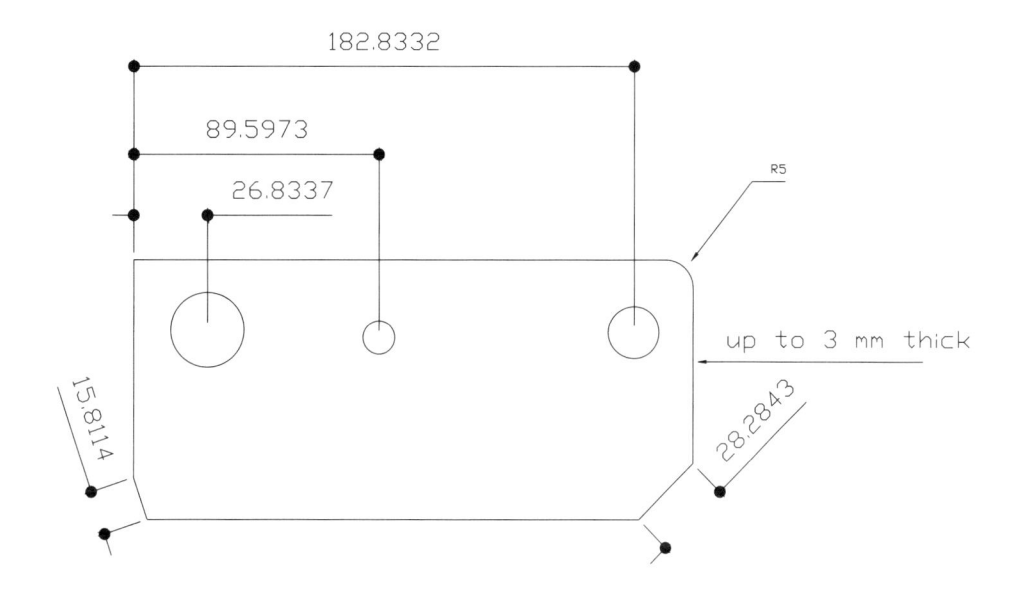

Assignment 4

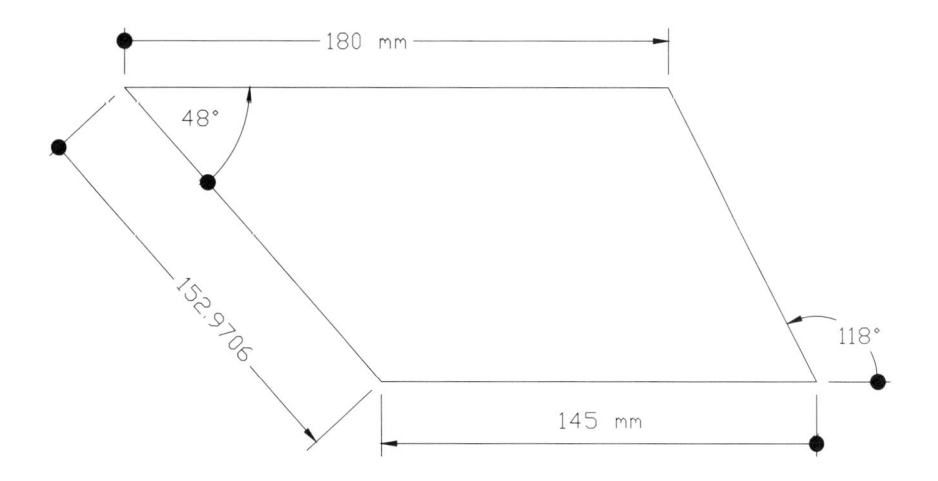

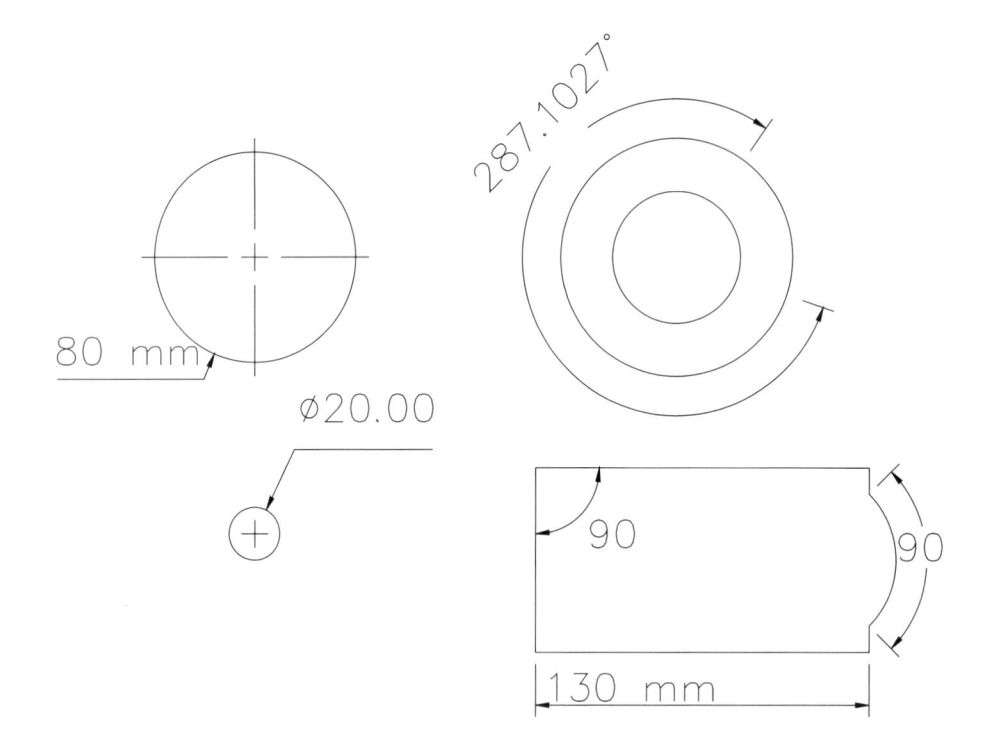

Assignment 5

chapter 16

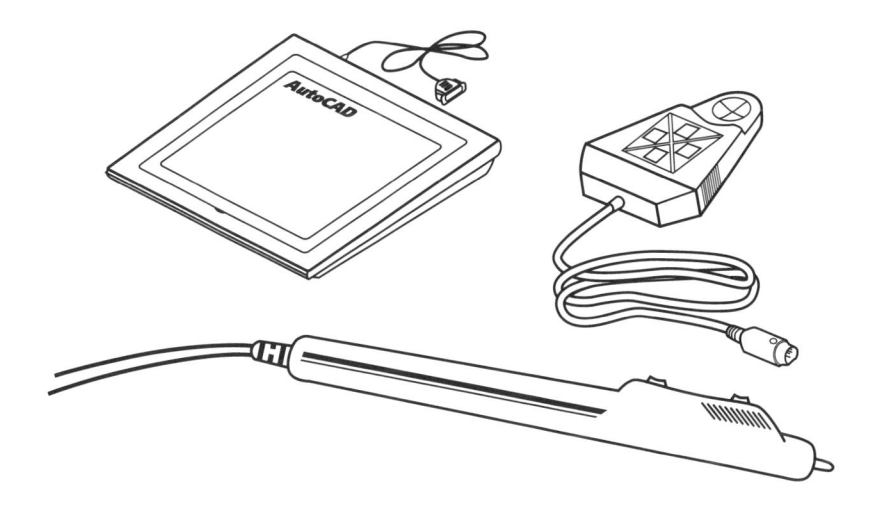

Isometric Drawing and Sketching, UCS

Tutorial objectives

By the end of this chapter you should be able to
- produce simple isometric drawings
- use the ISOPLANE command
- use the SKETCH command
- use the user co-ordinate system (UCS)

Tutorial 16.1

Target drawing

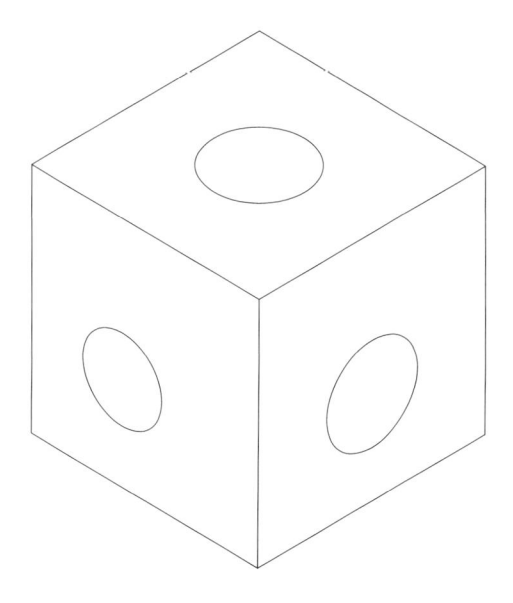

INTRODUCTION

AutoCAD allows you to produce two-dimensional isometric drawings (30/60) with great ease.

Isometric drawing does not put you in three-dimensional mode: you cannot view an isometric drawing from different views. The image you produce is strictly on a two-dimensional plane, as it would be if it were draughted by hand.

Setting up the isometric mode

To execute a drawing in the isometric mode, you must
- set the ISOMETRIC style in the SNAP command, and then
- select the ISOPLANE that you will work on.

The screen in fig. 16.1 is set up to produce an isometric drawing. The faces LEFT, RIGHT and TOP of a cube are referenced in AutoCAD by the command ISOPLANE.

The cross-hairs in the illustration are aligned for the top face.

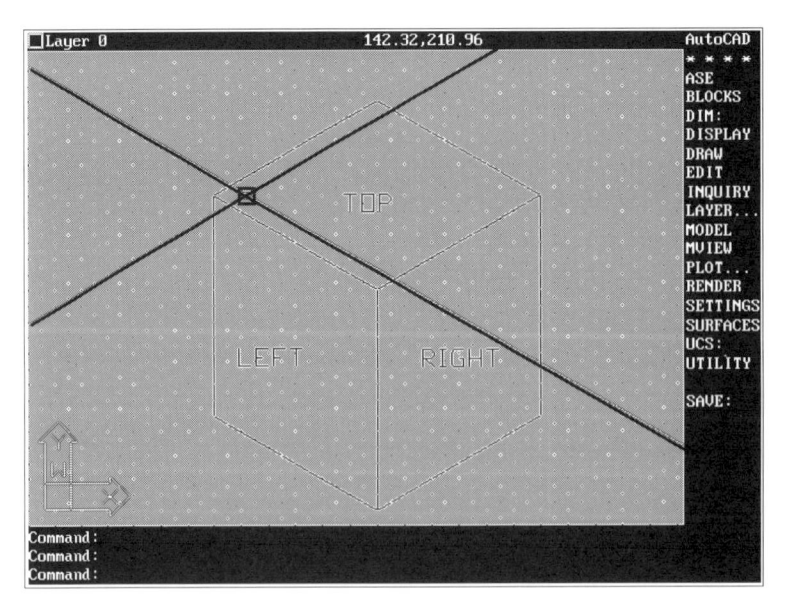

Fig 16.1. AutoCAD in isometric mode.

Start a new drawing and name it **ISO21**. Set the **LIMITS** to 0,0 and 80,60 in decimal **UNITS** and **Zoom All**.

The *'Drawing Aids'* dialogue box can be used to place you in isometric mode and to set the isoplane, grid, and snap. The dialogue box can be accessed from the sub-option *'Drawing Aids...'* in the *'Settings'* option on the drop-down menu or by typing **DDRMODES** at the command prompt.

Using the *'Drawing Aids'* dialogue box, assign the following settings:
- Set the SNAP and GRID to on.
- Set Isometric to on.

- Set the GRID and SNAP Y spacing to 2.
- Set the isoplane to LEFT.
- Click on OK to **[enter]** to the drawing editor.

You are now placed in isometric mode. The cross-hairs are aligned for the left face. AutoCAD always defaults to the LEFT plane when the isometric mode is selected.

Try drawing the left face of the cube now.

The 'isoplane' command

To draw the right-hand face you must make the right-hand isoplane current. To do this use the **ISOPLANE** command or open the *'Drawing Aids'* dialogue box and click on *'Right'*.

The **ISOPLANE** command issued at the command prompt calls up the four options. Typing **L**, **T** or **R** selects the appropriate face. **^E** will also toggle you to the next face in the cycle *Left Top Right*. The command can be issued transparently ('ISOPLANE).

The command sequence to move to the right isoplane is:

Command: **ISOPLANE**
Left/Top/Right/<Toggle>: **R**
Current Isometric plane is: Right
Command:

Pressing **[enter]** without typing anything will toggle you to the next face. The key combination **^E** will also toggle you from one face to the next. Note the change in the orientation of the cross-hairs.

Now draw the right face of the cube. Change the isoplane to top face (try using **^E**), and draw that side of the cube.

It's easy to check which face is current by aligning the cross-hairs on each side until they run parallel to the edges. Finish the cube by drawing the top.

Drawing circles in isometric mode

To draw a circle in isometric mode, the **ELLIPSE** command is used.

Call up the Ellipse command on the Screen menu. The options presented to you on the right of the screen are:

Center
Rotation
Iso
Diameter

Click on *'Iso'*. AutoCAD now realises you want to draw a circle in isometric mode. You can see this from the prompt:

Center of circle:

Select a point on the top face of the cube (it is still current). Use the cross-hairs to draw the circle.

Draw a circle on each of the faces (be sure you make each face current as you work around the cube).

Using viewports with isometric drawings

By setting up three viewports with a different isoplane active in each port, isometric drawings can be constructed rapidly.

Fig. 16.2 shows a possible viewport configuration for the cube drawing. The top port has the top isoplane active; the left and right ports have the left and right isoplane active.

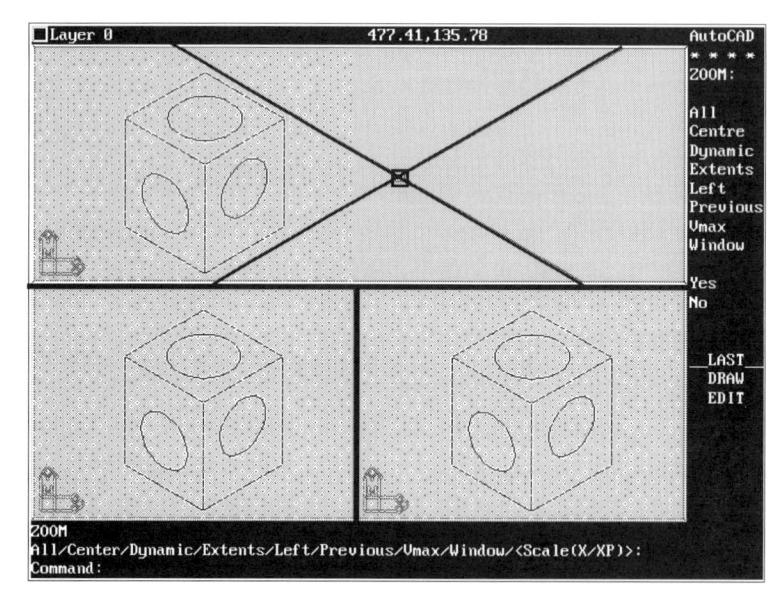

Fig. 16.2.

Tutorial 16.2

Start a new drawing and name it **TUT16**.

The 'sketch' command

The **SKETCH** command tries to emulate freehand movements of a pen in the drawing editor. It takes you out of the realm of CAD. Object snap and co-ordinate input, the normal elements to ensure accuracy in CAD, cannot be used with the command. **SKETCH** should only be used when there is no other suitable AutoCAD command.

The cross-hairs represent the pen. Moving the cross-hairs draws the **SKETCH** lines. The pen can be UP or DOWN. In the down position it will draw a sketch line.

The command can be called up from the command prompt, the Screen menu, or the tablet. The command prompt shows:
Command: **SKETCH** *Record increment <1.00>:*

A **SKETCH** line is composed of many small LINES or POLYLINES.

The increment that AutoCAD is asking you for is the length of these lines and polyline. Type in a value of 0.1 and press **[enter]**.

The prompt line now displays:
Command: **SKETCH** *Record increment <1.00>: 0.1*
Sketch. Pen eXit Quit Record Erase Connect .

AutoCAD is now almost ready to sketch a line. If you move the cross-hairs over the drawing editor, nothing will happen, because the pen is **'up'**.

The pick button is used to move the pen down and up.

Try SKETCHING a line similar to that in fig. 16.3.

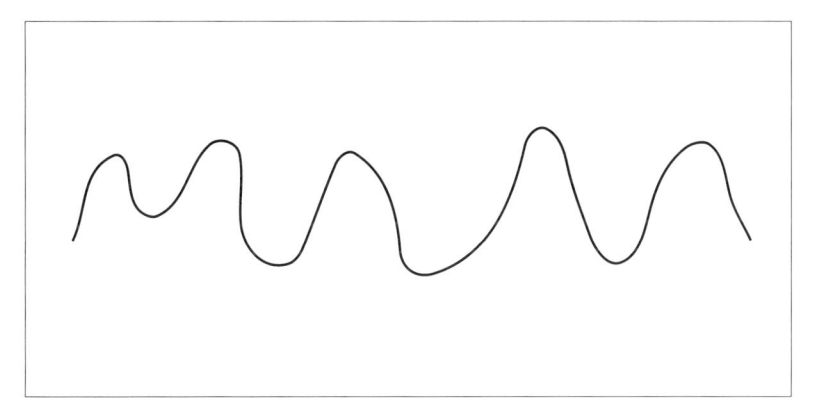

Fig. 16.3.

Start by positioning the cross-hairs to the top left of the screen, and click on the pick button. Sketch a rough sine wave across the screen, and press the pick button to lift the pen up.

This line is not yet recorded by AutoCAD as part of the drawing: to record the line, click the cursor on *'Record'* or type **R** at the command prompt. AutoCAD's response will be:
Command:
Record increment <1.00>: 0.1
Sketch. Pen eXit Quit Record Erase Connect . (Pen down)
(Pen up)
1 polyline with 112 edges recorded.

The click of the pick button is reflected by *(Pen down) (Pen up)*. The sketch has 122 polyline edges (yours may be different). This is a considerable number of edges for such a simple sketch line.

The **SKETCH** command can very quickly use up the computer's RAM. While SKETCHing you may suddenly hear the computer bleeping; this is to warn you that the memory is low, and you should record the sketch before you go any further.

The smaller the increment (remember that we chose 0.1), the greater the number of edges recorded.

Draw a circular scribble on the left of the screen similar to that illustrated in fig. 16.4, until the computer bleeps. Once it bleeps, press **P** for 'pen up'.

Click on *'Record'*.

Fig. 16.4.

The 'exit' and 'quit' options

eXit will record any unrecorded lines and exit from the **SKETCH** command. Pressing **X** will accomplish the same thing.

Quit will remove unrecorded lines, and leave the **SKETCH** command.

The 'erase' and 'connect' options

Erase will allow you to erase an unrecorded line. Sketch another sine wave across the screen, and raise the pen. Click on **ERASE**; AutoCAD will respond with:

Erase: Select end of delete.

Move the cross-hairs back over part of the line you have just sketched; it will be deleted (do not delete it all). Click the pick button when you have erased whatever you wanted to. Click on *'Connect'*. AutoCAD responds with:

Connect: Move to endpoint of line.

Move the cross-hairs to the end of the line. AutoCAD will find the last endpoint and pick it up for you.

You can continue to sketch the line.

Record the sketch.

The 'dot' option

The dot option is found at the end of the list of options:
Sketch. Pen eXit Quit Record Erase Connect .

It allows you to draw a straight line from the end of the last SKETCH line to the position your pen is now at.

Use **SKETCH** to draw part of a sine wave, then click the pick button to *Pen up* at the end of it. Now move the cross-hairs some distance from the sketch.

Press the full point (.) on the keyboard. A straight line is drawn to the new cursor position from the end of the SKETCHed line.

Error messages and the 'sketch' command

The following messages may be returned by AutoCAD to you:

Erase aborted
If you decide not to erase a line after selecting 'Erase', you can press the pick button or any subcommand other than P. Erase will be cancelled and the message 'Erase aborted' returned.

Connect command meaningless when pen down
Connect can only occur when the pen is up. An attempt to connect with the pen down produces the message
Connect command meaningless when pen down

No last point known
You will receive this message if you try to use 'Connect' when there is no line to conncct to.

Connect aborted
You will receive this message if you decide not to connect the lines after 'Connect' is selected. Connect can be abandoned by typing any of the command keys, Erase, Record, Quit, Exit.

Please raise pen!
When the computer's memory is nearly full you will be requested to lift the pen (by pressing **P**). The SKETCH will then be saved to disk and you can continue. Once that is complete, the following message appears:
Thank you. Lower pen and continue.

Tutorial 16.3

Tutorial objectives

The user co-ordinate system
This tutorial is not a continuation of the above tutorial on isometric drawing. UCS is a separate concept. Its function lies mainly in the area of three-dimensional drawing.

The world co-ordinate system

All the work you have carried out up to now has been executed on AutoCAD's 'world co-ordinate system'. This consists of three axes at an angle of 90° to each other. The origin is at 0,0,0.

AutoCAD presents the world co-ordinate system as if you were looking directly down the Z axis. The plane you execute your two-dimensional drawing on is essentially an X-Y Cartesian plane.

The UCS

AutoCAD allows you to define your own co-ordinate system, referred to as a user co-ordinate system or UCS. This co-ordinate system can be set up anywhere within the three-dimensional X, Y and Z axes. In this tutorial a UCS will be created on the two-dimensional X-Y plane.

A UCS can be set up from the command prompt by using the command **UCS** or from the drop-down menu *'Settings'*.

Open a new drawing using the AutoCAD prototype drawing, and draw a circle with a radius of 25 units with its centre at co-ordinates 200,160.
Zoom-All. This circle will be used to illustrate how a UCS can be created.

Setting up a UCS

To set up a UCS with the centre of the circle as the origin of the new co-ordinate system, open the drop-down menu *'Settings'*, then *'UCS'*, *'Origin'*. AutoCAD will ask for the position of the new origin. Use the object snap mode CEN and pick on the perimeter of the circle.

This circle now has its centre at 0,0,0.

Note that the **UCSICON** has lost the **'W'**, implying that the world co-ordinate system is not in use and that a UCS has been defined.

Two simple exercises will demonstrate the location of the new origin:
(1) **Use the LIST command.** This command will provide data on an entity. When the command is entered you will be asked to select an entity. AutoCAD will then proceed to display a list of the entity's co-ordinates (the insertion point in the case of blocks or text), the colour assigned to it, the layer it is on, and the linetype. The command is found on the drop-down menu under *'Assist'*, *'Inquiry'*. On the screen menu it is found under *'INQUIRY'*, or **LIST** can be typed at the command prompt.

Execute the command now and pick the circle. Here is the data you should obtain:

CIRCLE *Layer: 0*
Space: Model space
center point, X= 0.00 Y= 0.00 Z= 0.00 radius 25.00
circumference 157.08
area 1963.50

The centre point of the circle is listed as being at 0,0.

(2) **Draw two lines (100 units long) from the centre of the circle**, one horizontally to the right and one vertically. Use absolute and polar co-ordinates. Here are the readings:

Command: **LINE**
From point: **0,0**
To point: **@100<0**
To point:
Command:
LINE From point: **0,0**
To point: **@100<90**
To point:
Command:

Note how the first co-ordinates, 0,0, pick up from the centre of the circle.

Saving a UCS for use later

When the command **UCS** is entered at the command prompt, fourteen options are presented. One of these allows you to **SAVE** the **UCS** set-up. Issue the command now and Save the UCS as **FIRST**. The command sequence is:

Command: **UCS**
Origin/ZAxis/3point/Entity/View/X/Y/Z/Prev/Restore/Save/Del/?/<World>: **S**
?/Desired UCS name: **FIRST**
Command:

Restoring the world co-ordinate system and a UCS

To restore the world co-ordinate system, enter the *UCS* command and respond with **W** (for 'world'). Note how the *'W'* has returned to the icon. Test the position of the origin by drawing two lines from the new origin.

To return to the UCS named as **FIRST**, respond with **R** (for 'restore'), and answer the prompt *'?/Name of UCS to restore:'* with FIRST.

Rotating the X-Y plane around the Z axis

In the creation of the UCS in the above example, the *X* and *Y* axes remained parallel to the original *X* and *Y* axes. Only the origin was moved. The position of the *X* and *Y* axes can be changed by rotating them around the *Z* axis. The UCS icon will reflect the change.

To rotate the *X-Y* plane 45° around *Z* in a positive direction, enter the following command and responses:

Command: **UCS**
Origin/ZAxis/3point/Entity/View/X/Y/Z/Prev/Restore/Save/Del/?/<World>: **Z**
Rotation angle about Z axis <0.0000>: **45**

Note how the cross-hairs responded by remaining parallel to the *X* and *Y* axes. Save this UCS as SECOND45.

You can return to the previous UCS by responding with **P**.

AutoCAD will allow you to create any number of user co-ordinate systems.

A summary of the UCS options

Origin allows you to set the origin of the new UCS.
ZAxis allows you to define the direction of the *z* axis.
3point allows the UCS to be defined by selecting three points in the display. One point defines the origin and the other two the direction of the *x* and *y* axes.
Entity can be used as the basis for the definition of the UCS. This is useful if you want to develop some detail in the entity, particularly in three-dimensional work.
View is used mainly in three-dimensional drawing. It allows you to align a UCS parallel to a VIEW.
X/Y/Z/ allows a UCS to be rotated around the selected axis.
Prev allows you to return to the previous UCS.
Restore is used to restore a saved UCS.
Save allows a UCS to be saved.
Del allows a UCS to be deleted.
? provides a listing of the saved user co-ordinate systems.
World returns you to the default world co-ordinate system.

SUMMARY

To create an isometric drawing you must work in isometric mode. The isometric mode can be set from the *'Drawing Aids'* dialogue box. The isometric mode consists of three isoplanes, termed LEFT, RIGHT, and TOP. An isoplane must be made current before you can draw on it. The isoplane can be toggled by using the ^E option. Viewports can be used to help speed up the drawing process. Three viewports, with a different isoplane set in each port, are recommended.

The **SKETCH** command emulates freehand drawing. Sketch lines are composed of **LINE** and POLYLINE entities. To draw using **SKETCH** you must give AutoCAD a drawing increment. The increment is the length of these **LINES** and **POLYLINES** that make up a **SKETCH** line. AutoCAD allows you to set up your own user co-ordinate system. Any number of user-defined co-ordinate systems can be set up. They are particularly useful in three-dimensional drawing. You can return to the standard world co-ordinate system whenever you like.

ASSIGNMENTS

Assignment 1

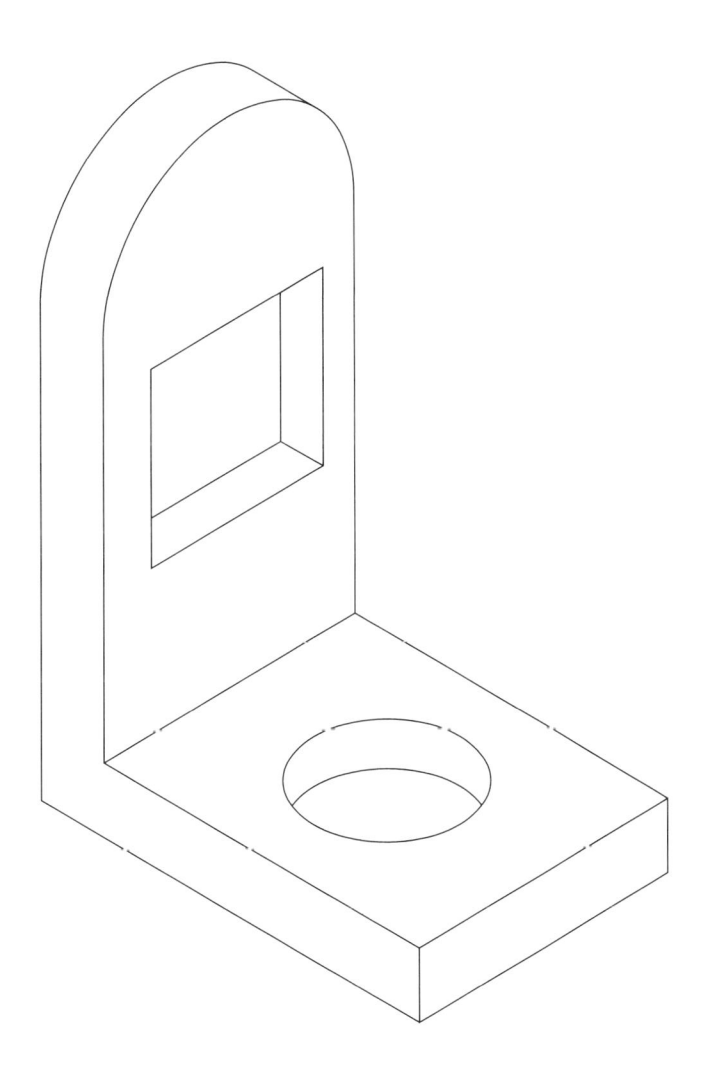

Produce the isometric drawing.

Assignment 2

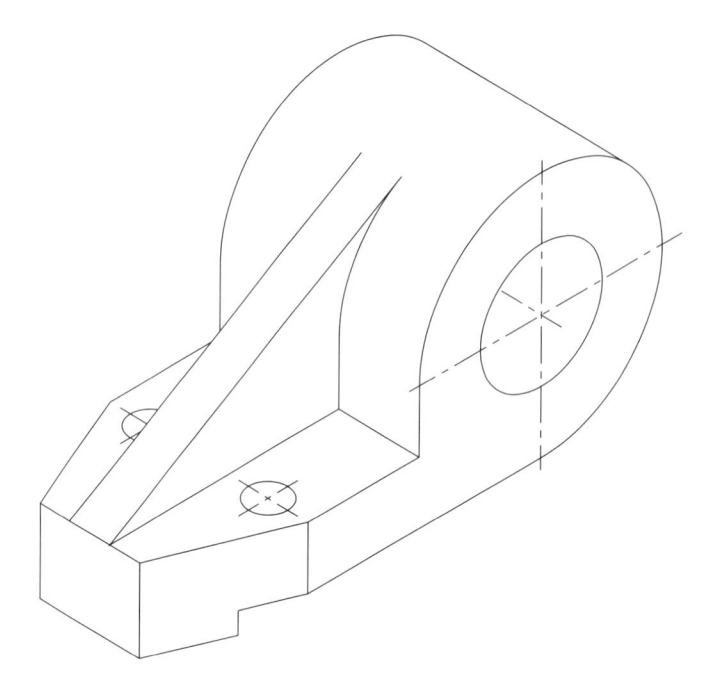

Produce the isometric drawing. Place the centre-lines on a separate layer.

Assignment 3

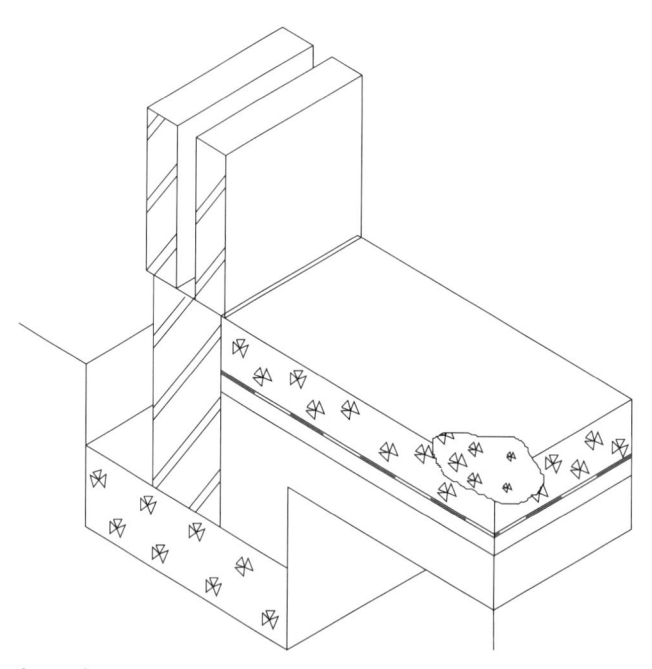

Produce the isometric view of a foundation. Use the sketch command where suitable.

Assignment 4

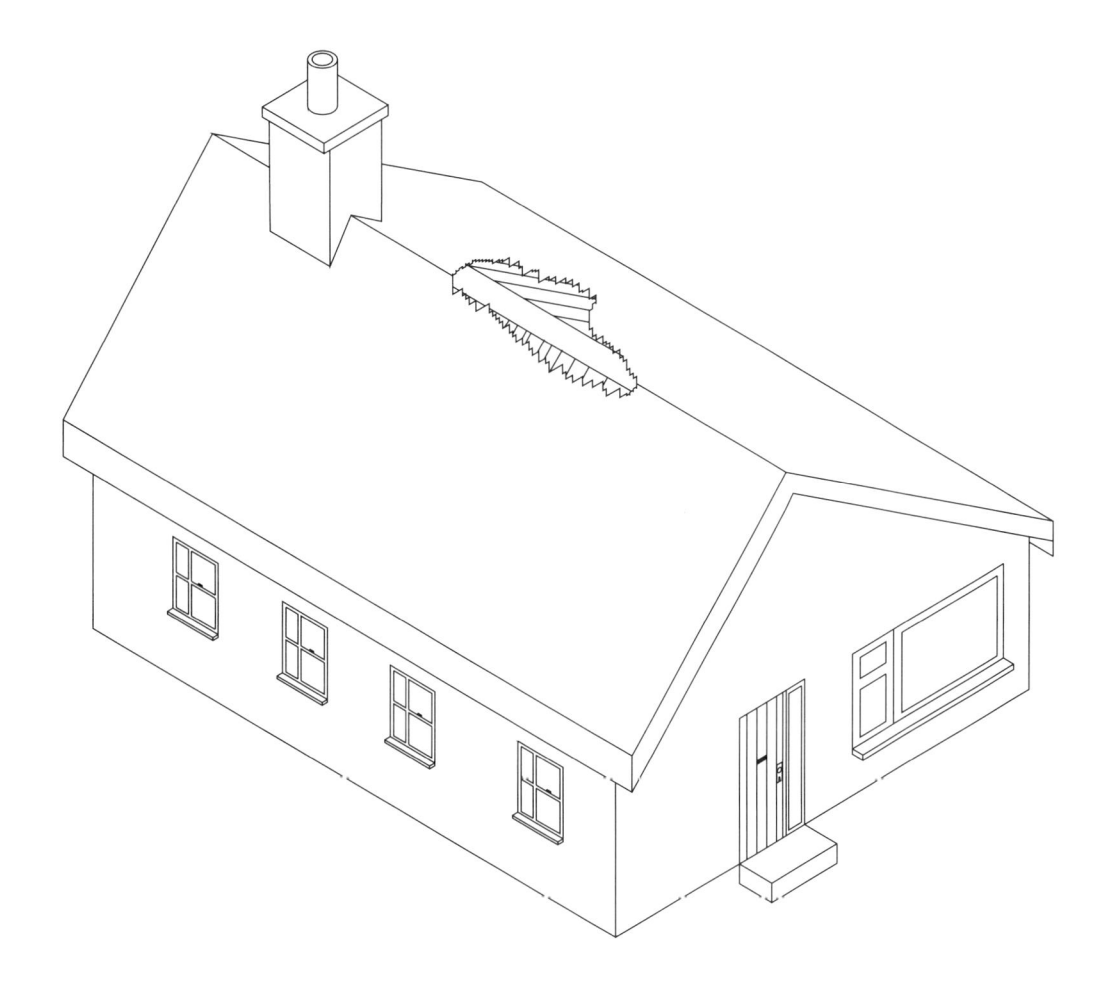

Produce the isometric view of the house. Use separate layers for roof, windows, doors, and walls. Use the sketch command to show the cut-away of the rafters.

Assignment 5

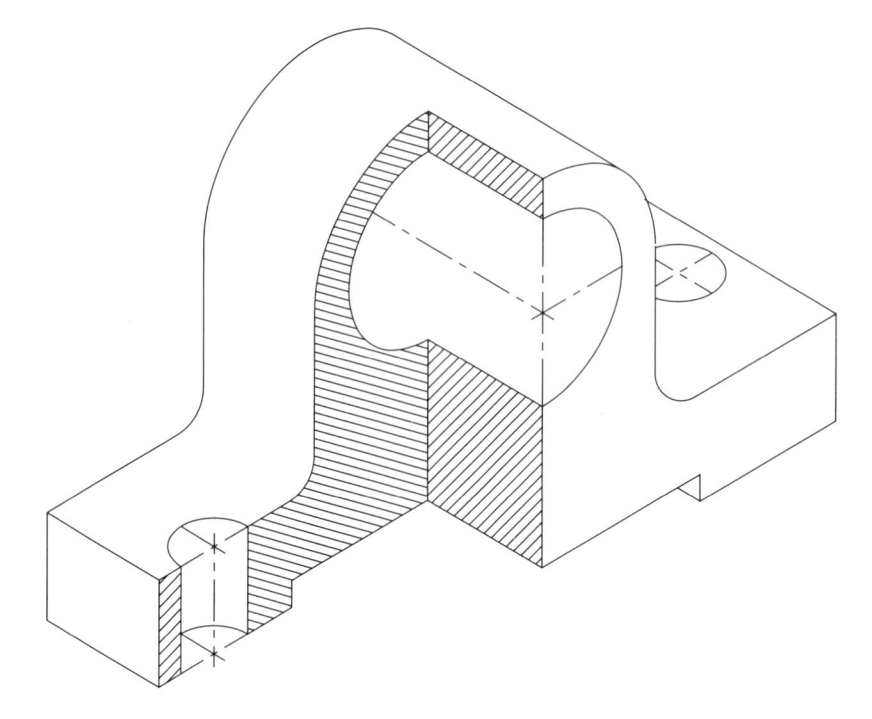

Produce the isometric drawing.

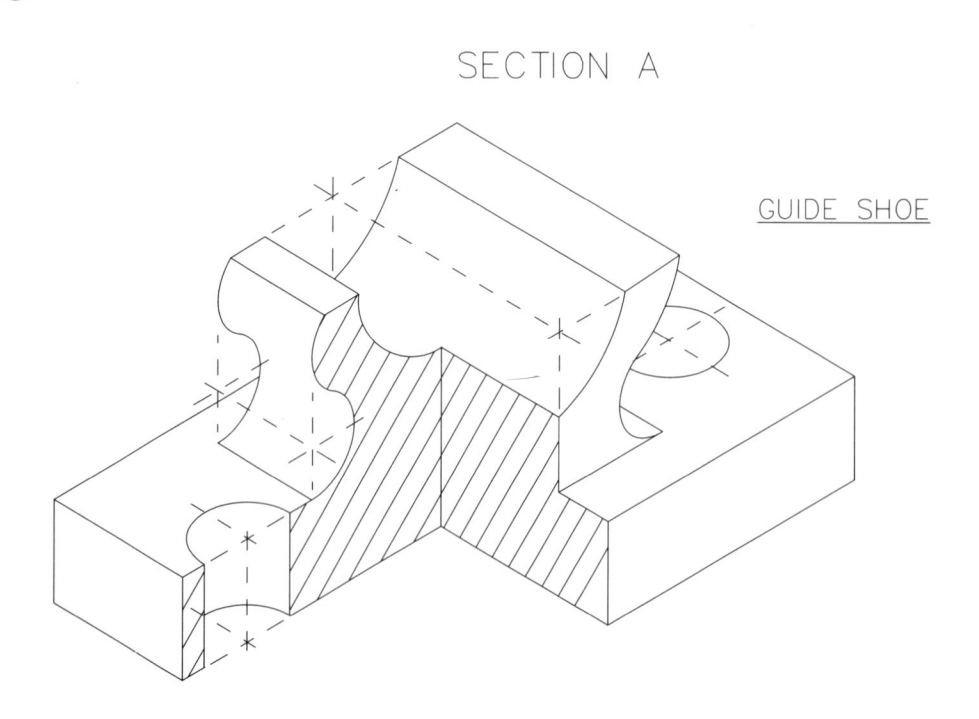

Assignment 6

SECTION A

GUIDE SHOE

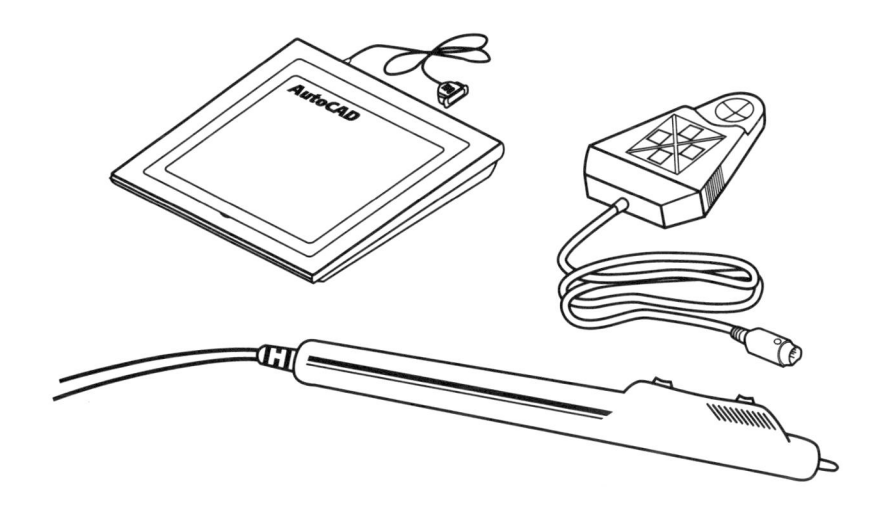

chapter 17
Editing Polylines

Tutorial objectives
By the end of this chapter you should be able to
- use the PEDIT command to edit polylines
- convert existing LINES to PLINES
- join several PLINES to form one polyline
- edit vertices
- fit curves to polylines
- convert PLINES to SPLINES
- explain the function of the system variable SPLINETYPE
- explain the function of the system variable SPLFRAME
- explain the function of the system variable SPLINESEGS

Tutorial 17.1
Introduction

The **PEDIT** command is used to edit polylines. It is found on the drop-down menu under *'Modify'* and *'Poly Edit'* and on the screen menu under *'EDIT'* (second page).

Start a **NEW** drawing and name it **PED1**. Set the **LIMITS** at 0,0 to 2400,1800

Draw the entities illustrated in fig. 17.1 using the instructions on page 276 and label them A to F.

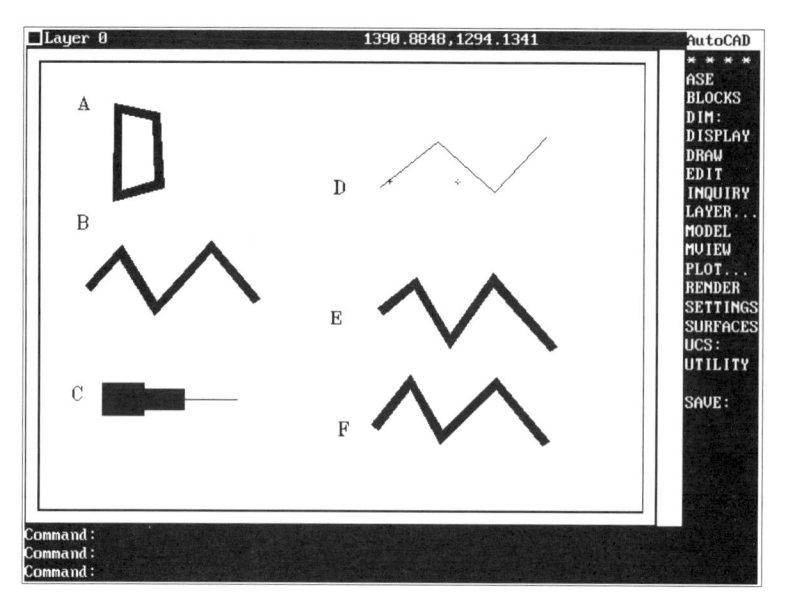

Fig. 17.1. Polylines for editing.

A is a CLOSED polyline. Draw three polylines with a width of 30 units, and use 'C' to close. The starting co-ordinates are 350,1240.
B is a sequence of four joined polylines (width 30 units). Do not use the CLOSE option to complete it. The starting co-ordinates are 240,890.
C is a sequence of two joined polylines of widths 120 and 80 and a single LINE entity. The starting co-ordinates are 295,470.
D is a sequence of three LINE entities. The starting co-ordinates are 1358,1276 to 1576,1449.5 to 1788.5,1258 to 1980.7,1468.
E is a sequence of joined polylines (width 30 units). The starting co-ordinates are 1358,807.
F is a sequence of joined polylines (width 30 units). The starting co-ordinates are 1338.5,369.

A *vertex* marks the beginning and end of one polyline segment and the beginning of another. Polyline E, for example, has five vertices.

The PEDIT command

When you enter the **PEDIT** command you are asked to select an entity, and then ten options are presented:
Open/Join/Width/Edit vertex/Fit curve/Spline curve/Decurve/Ltype gen/Undo/eXit <X>:

Each of these will be examined in this assignment. **Undo** will simply undo the last polyline edit command. **X** will exit from the options back to the command prompt.

Exercise 1: Open and closed polylines
Enter the **PEDIT** command and select the entities at **A**.
Command: **PEDIT**
Select polyline: ← Click on **A**
Open/Join/Width/Edit vertex/Fit curve/Spline curve/Decurve/Ltype gen/Undo/eXit <X>:

The first option is *'Open'*, because you selected a closed polyline. If the polyline had been an open one, AutoCAD would have given you this first option as *'Close'*.

Type **O** to make it an open polyline. Press **[enter]** to end the command.

Exercise 2: Polyline conversion and the 'join' option
Some entities that are not polylines can be converted to polylines by using **PEDIT**.

To see this in action, type **PEDIT** and select the beginning of the entities labelled **D**. **D** consists of three lines. AutoCAD will then announce that the entity is not a polyline, but *'Do you want to turn it into one? <Y>'*. Answering **Y** will convert the first line segment to a polyline. Lastly, AutoCAD will present all its **PEDIT** options again. Selecting **J** for join will allow you to join the other LINEs to the first to produce a *joined polyline* (join will also allow you to add arcs to polylines).

The command sequence is given below.
Command: **PEDIT**
Select polyline: ← Pick the beginning of D
Entity selected is not a polyline
Do you want to turn it into one? <Y>   ← **[enter]** to accept the default
Close/Join/Width/Edit vertex/Fit curve/Spline curve/Decurve/Ltype genUndo/eXit <X>: **J**
Select objects: 1 selected, 1 found.   ← Pick each of the entities
Select objects: 1 selected, 1 found.
Select objects: 1 selected, 1 found.
Select objects: 2 segments added to polyline
Close/Join/Width/Edit vertex/Fit curve/Spline curve/Decurve/Undo/eXit <X>: X

X will exit from the command.

The width option

This option allows you to change the width of existing polylines. **C** consists of three polylines of different widths. Select the leftmost spline, and assign it a width of 1.
Command: **PEDIT**
Select polyline: ← Pick the first segment of C
Close/Join/Width/Edit vertex/Fit curve/Spline curve/Decurve/Ltype gen/Undo/eXit <X>: **W**
Enter new width for all segments: **1**

Close/Join/Width/Edit vertex/Fit curve/Spline curve/Decurve/Ltype gen/Undo/eXit <X>: **X**

Width can be shown to AutoCAD by using the pointing device.

The 'fit curve' and 'decurve' options

The 'fit curve' command will fit a smooth curve to a polyline.
Command: **PEDIT**
Select polyline: ← Select polyline **B**
Close/Join/Width/Edit vertex/Fit curve/Spline curve/Decurve/Ltype gen/Undo/eXit <X>: **F**

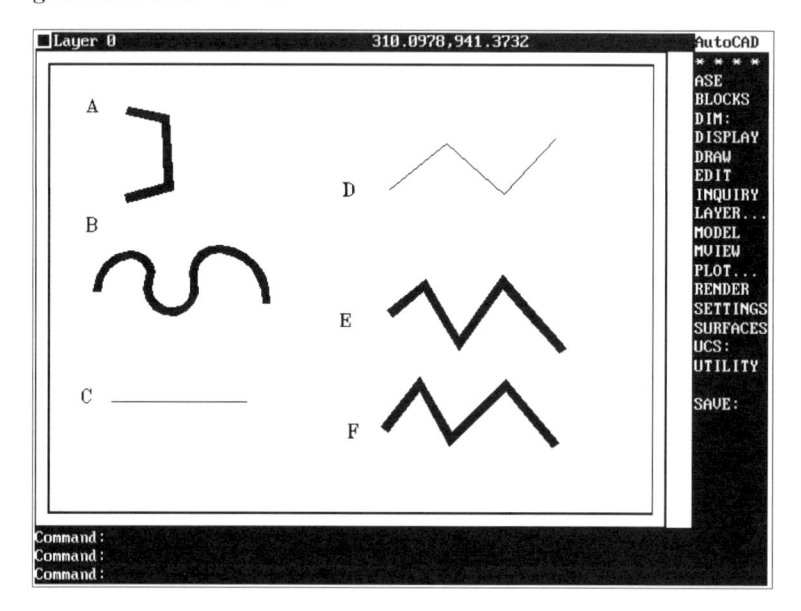

Fig. 17.2. Edited polylines.

The curve is really a series of arcs, which AutoCAD maps through the vertices of the polyline. Sometimes AutoCAD will add new vertices to the original polyline to make a better curve. Selecting **D** will 'decurve' the polyline and return it to its original state.

The 'spline curve'

Like the 'fit curve' option, this will produce a smooth curve from the original polyline. There is an important difference, however: a spline will only pass through the beginning and end vertices of the original polyline (if it is open). The intermediate vertices will act to pull the curve towards themselves.

The original polyline is termed the *FRAME*. AutoCAD remembers the structure of the frame, so that you can decurve the spline back to its original polyline. Fig. 17.3 shows the polyline **E** edited to a spline.

Note the original polyline (frame) and the fact that the spline only passes through the first and last vertices.

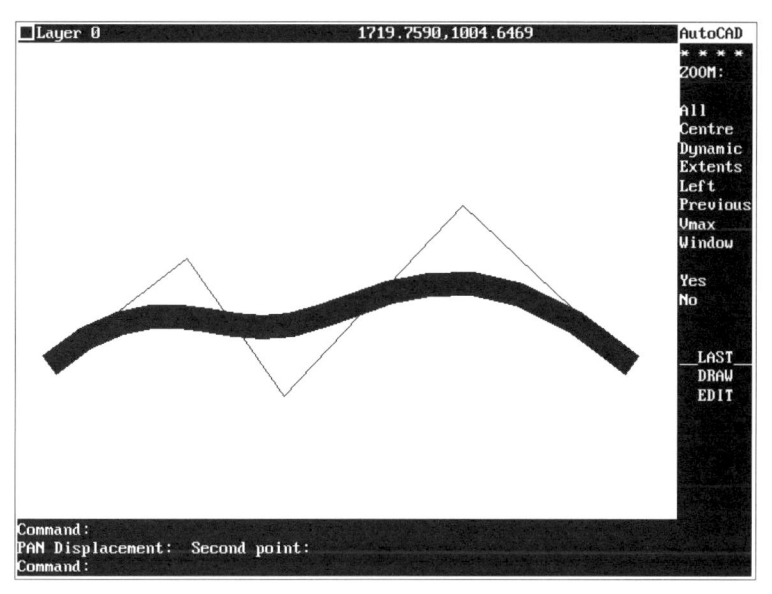

Fig. 17.3. Polyline E edited to a spline.

The frame of a spline can be viewed by changing the value of the variable **SPLFRAME** from 0 to 1 and REGENerating the drawing. Try the following on polyline **E**:

Command: **PEDIT**
Select polyline: ← Pick E
Close/Join/Width/Edit vertex/Fit curve/Spline curve/Decurve/Ltype gen/Undo/eXit <X>: **S**
Close/Join/Width/Edit vertex/Fit curve/Spline curve/Decurve/Ltype gen/Undo/eXit <X>: **X**
Command: **SETVAR**
Variable name or ? <SPLFRAME>: **SPLFRAME**
New value for SPLFRAME <0>: **1**
Command: **REGEN**
Regenerating drawing.

The 'splinetype' variable

The system variable **SPLINETYPE** determines whether the spline is quadratic or cubic. A value of 5 is a quadratic spline; a value of 6 is a cubic spline. Both of these are shown in fig. 17.4.

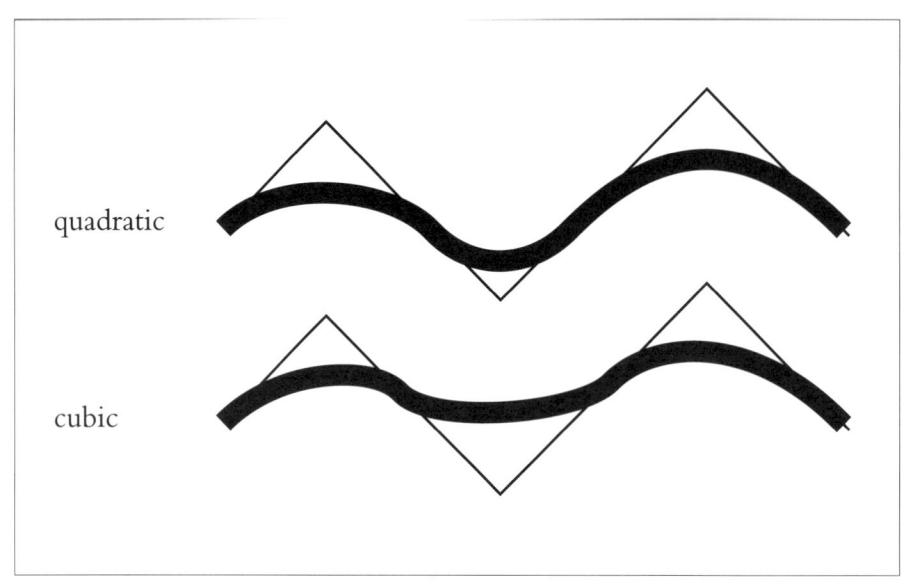

Fig. 17.4. The effect of the SPLINETYPE variable on a spline.

The 'splinesegs' variable

The smoothness of a spline is determined by the number of line segments used for its construction. The number is controlled by the system variable **SPLINESEGS**. Its default value is 8.

Here are some important points regarding splines:
(1) If there is an arc as part of the original polyline, it will be smoothed out.
(2) If the original polyline has varying widths, the spline will taper the width from the first vertex to the last.
(3) The frame of splines and 'fit curves' is unavailable if you use the edit commands **TRIM**, **EXPLODE**, or **BREAK**.

The 'edit vertex' option

This option allows the detailed editing of the vertices that make up a polyline. It allows you to insert or remove vertices, for example.

When the option is selected, AutoCAD marks the first vertex of the selected polyline with an **X** and then presents you with a new prompt:
Command: **PEDIT**
Select polyline: ← Pick D
Close/Join/Width/Edit vertex/Fit curve/Spline curve/Decurve/Ltype gen/Undo/eXit <X>: **E**
Next/Previous/Break/Insert/Move/Regen/Straighten/Tangent/Width/eXit <N>:

The **X** marking the editable vertex can be moved to the next or previous vertex with 'N' and 'P'.

Insert allows you to insert a vertex after the position of the marked vertex. For example, to place a new vertex after the second one on the polyline

marked **D**, execute the following:
Command: **PEDIT**
Select polyline:
Close/Join/Width/Edit vertex/Fit curve/Spline curve/Decurve/Ltype gen/Undo/eXit <X>: **E**
Next/Previous/Break/Insert/Move/Regen/Straighten/Tangent/Width/eXit <N>: **N**
Next/Previous/Break/Insert/Move/Regen/Straighten/Tangent/Width/eXit <N>: **I**

Enter the location of the new vertex: 1650,1300 (this is about half way down the second segment). The 'location of new vertex' can be selected by any of AutoCAD's usual selection methods.

The *Move* option allows you to move the current vertex to a new location. To move the first vertex, for example, make it current using Next or Previous, then select Move, and respond with the co-ordinates 1400,1450.
Command: **PEDIT**
Select polyline: ← Pick **D**
Close/Join/Width/Edit vertex/Fit curve/Spline curve/Decurve/Ltype gen/Undo/eXit <X>: E
Next/Previous/Break/Insert/Move/Regen/Straighten/Tangent/Width/eXit <N>: M
Enter the new location: 1400,1450.

Regen will simply regenerate the drawing.

Removing a vertex

The *'Straighten'* option allows you to remove any number of vertices between two specified vertices. Before you select *Straighten,* move to the first vertex you wish to specify. Then select **S**. This option produces a new prompt:
Next/Previous/Go/eXit <N>:

The Next and Previous options work in the usual way. Use them to select the second vertex. Go will then execute the edit, while X will exit the submenu without executing the edit.

The 'break' option

This option will allow you to remove a polyline segment, or to break a polyline into two separate entities. It is very similar to the normal break command. Like the 'Straighten' option, it produces the submenu *'Next/Previous/Go/eXit <N>:'* when it is called.

To remove a segment of the polyline, first move the vertex marker to the beginning of the segment you want to remove (*PEDIT, Edit vertex, Next,* or *Previous*). Then invoke the *Break* option and use Next or Previous to mark the second vertex. Select *Go* to remove the segment.

The 'ltype gen' option

When this option is set to *on*, the linetype will be drawn uniformly through the vertices of the polyline. When set to *off*, the linetype will start and end with a dash at each vertex.

The 'width' option

This option allows you to change the width of the polyline or a segment of it. In the following example you will change the thickness of the first segment of the polyline **D** from 0 to 25.

Command: **PEDIT**
Select polyline:
Close/Join/Width/Edit vertex/Fit curve/Spline curve/Decurve/Ltype gen/Undo/eXit <X>: **E**
Next/Previous/Break/Insert/Move/Regen/Straighten/Tangent/Width/eXit <N>:
Next/Previous/Break/Insert/Move/Regen/Straighten/Tangent/Width/eXit <N>: **W**
Enter starting width <0.0000>: **25**
Enter ending width <25.0000>:
Next/Previous/Break/Insert/Move/Regen/Straighten/Tangent/Width/eXit <N>: **X**
Close/Join/Width/Edit vertex/Fit curve/Spline curve/Decurve/Ltype gen/Undo/eXit <X>: **X**
Command:

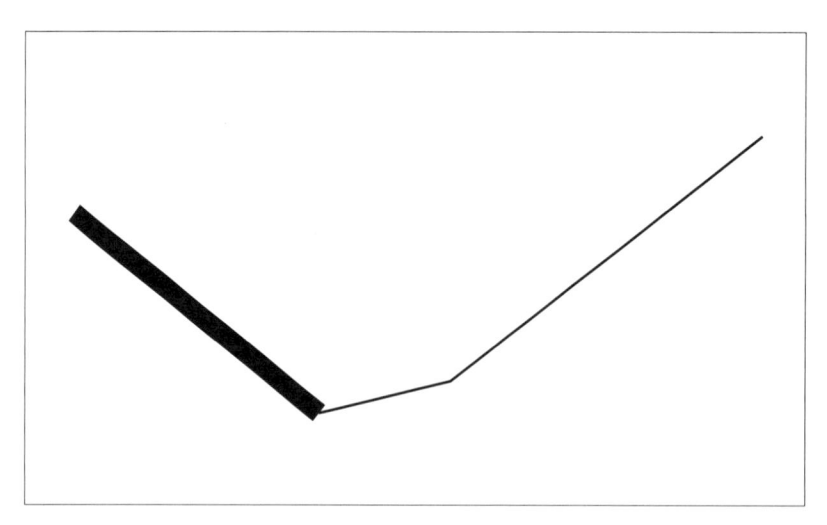

Fig. 17.5. The effect of the width option.

The 'tangent' option

When AutoCAD is fitting a curve to a polyline, it uses arcs to fit the curve. The arcs are constructed using the polyline's tangent information. The direction of the tangents used in the curve fit can be changed to user-specified ones using the tangent option. This will then influence the direction of the fitted curve.

The direction of the tangent can be specified using the cross-hairs. It is marked at a vertex by a small arrow.

SUMMARY

This chapter examined the editing of polylines in detail. The **PEDIT** command was used to convert the standard line entity to a polyline. It also allowed you to join several separate polylines to form a single polyline entity. Polylines were then converted to curves using the Fit and Spline options. The smoothness of a curve was set using the **SPLINESEGS** variable. Lastly, the spline curves were defined as being cubic or quadratic, using the system variable **SPLINESEGS**.

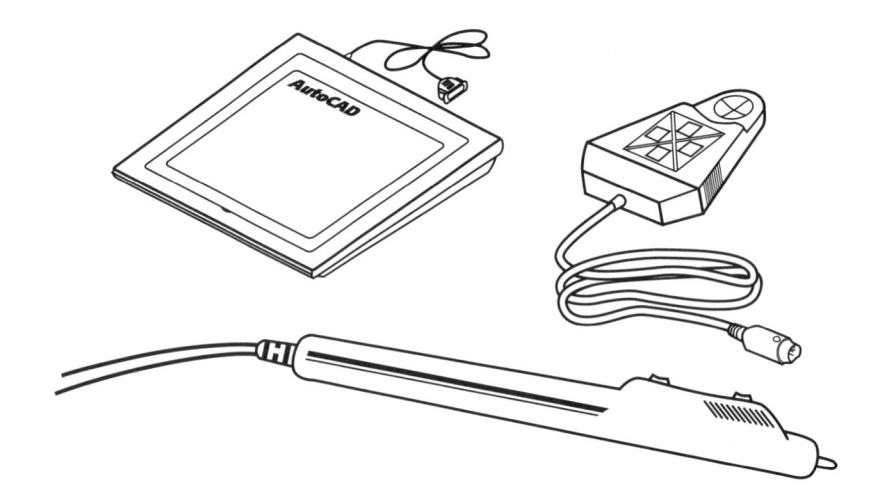

chapter 18
Plotting

Tutorial objectives
By the end of this chapter you should be able to
- produce a quick plot of any of the drawings completed in the assignments
- gain a more detailed understanding of the PLOT command
- produce a plot to a file instead of to paper

INTRODUCTION

The command **PLOT** allows you to produce a printed copy of a drawing. The copy can be produced either on a printer or on a plotter. AutoCAD, however, refers to both as a 'plotter'.

AutoCAD must be 'configured' for a printer or a plotter before a plot can be produced. If you are unsure whether this has been done, select the *'Configure'* option of the *'File'* drop-down menu. The AutoCAD configuration set-up will be listed. Press **[enter]** to display the *'Configuration Menu'*. If a plotter or printer has been configured for use, select option **0** from this menu and return to the AutoCAD drawing editor. If you need to configure for a plotting device, go to option 4 (detailed in chapter 19).

Eight steps to producing a plot quickly

This section will help you to produce a printed copy of your drawing with very little explanation of the procedure or terms involved.

Step 1: To ensure that the *'Plot Configuration'* dialogue box will be displayed, check that the system variable **CMDDIA** is set to 1 when you load the drawing you want to plot.

Step 2: ZOOM-All.

Step 3: Enter the command **PLOT** at the command prompt. The *'Plot Configuration'* dialogue box is displayed.

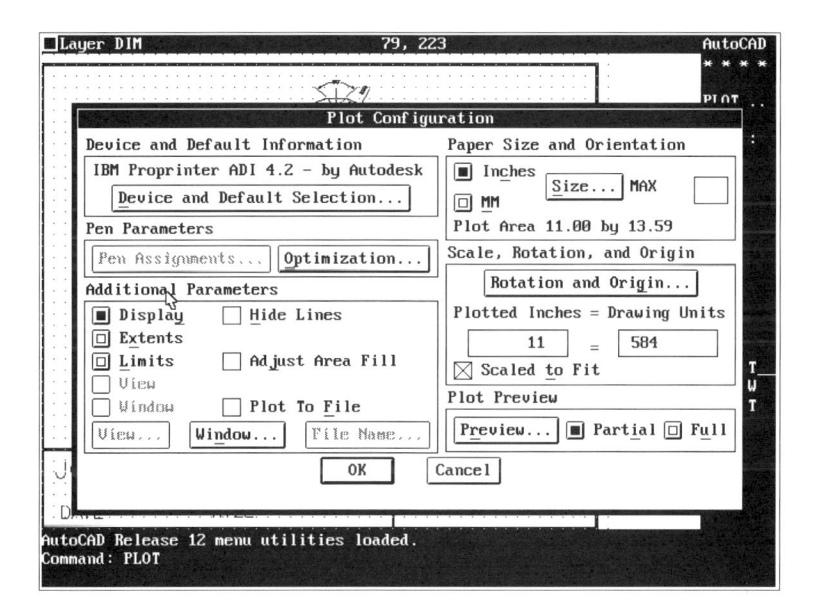

Fig. 18.1. The 'Plot Configuration' dialogue box.

Step 4: Check that the button 'Display' in the *'Additional Parameters'* box is highlighted.

Step 5: Check that the *'Paper Size and Orientation'* box is set for a *Plot Area* that your plotter can cope with. If the size of the plot area is too big, click on the box *'Size...'* and select a paper size to suit the plotter. Click on **OK** to return to the *'Plot Configuration'* dialogue box.

Step 6: Place an **X** in the *'Scaled to Fit'* box in the *'Scale, Rotation and Origin'* box. This will force the drawing to fit on the paper in the plotter and prevents you from having control over the scale the drawing is plotted at.

Step 7: Check how the drawing will appear on the paper by highlighting the *'Full'* button in the *'Preview...'* subdialogue box. The outer black line represents the size of the paper in the plotter. Click on *'End Preview'*.

Step 8: Click on 'OK' to send the drawing to the plotter.

Step 9: Respond to the prompt *'Press RETURN to continue or S to stop for hardware set-up'*. Check that the plotter is ready for the drawing.

Possible plotting problems

If the plotter fails to respond, the **PLOT** command can normally be interrupted by **^C**. If you fail to obtain a plot, check the following:
(1) Check that the printer or plotter is On Line or in Ready mode.
(2) The plotter may not be connected to the correct port. Normally the printer connects to the LPT1 port and the plotter connects to COM1 or COM2.
(3) AutoCAD may not be configured for the printer you are using. If your printer is not on the AutoCAD list of plotters, check the printer/plotter manual to see which printer it emulates or is compatible with.
(4) Many plotters have a 'pause' button. Make sure it is set to *off*.

A more detailed look at 'Plot Configuration'

Device and default information

The first item of information displayed in the '*Plot configuration*' dialogue box is the type of plotter AutoCAD has been configured for. If more than one plotter was selected during configuration, the current plotter is the only one displayed. To use one of the other plotters, click on '*Device and Default Selection...*' A subdialogue box listing the available plotters is displayed.

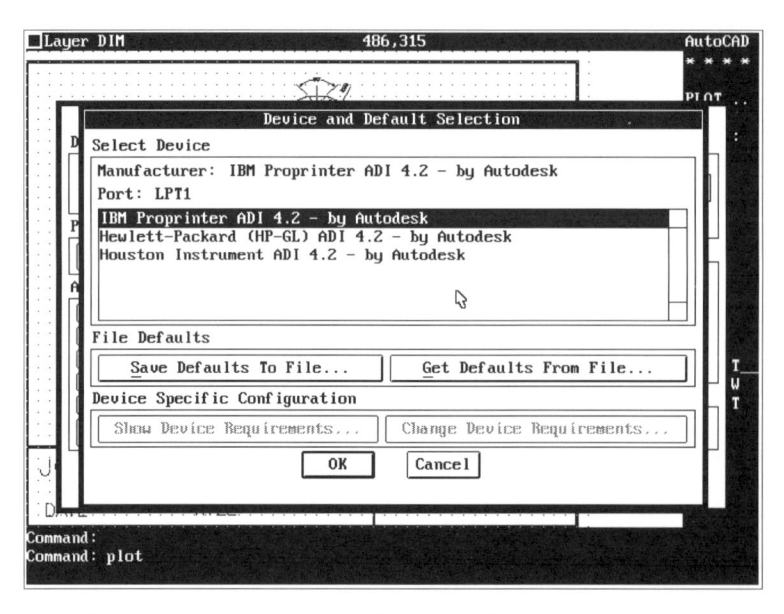

Fig. 18.2. Device and default selection sub-dialogue box

To select a different plotter, make a selection by highlighting the plotter you want and clicking on '*OK*'. The '*Save Defaults To File...*' and '*Get Defaults From File...*' options allow you to save and retrieve more detailed information, such as the port the plotter is attached to and the pen parameters of a specific plotter.

Click on **OK** to return to the '*Plot Configuration*' dialogue box.

Pen parameters

Two subdialogue boxes may be called from this section. The *'Pen Assignment...'* box will be ghosted (indicating that it is not available) if the current plotter (a printer, for example) has only one pen or no pens available. If *'Pen Assignment...'* is available it will open to a subdialogue box that allows control of the colour, speed, linetype and pen speed of a plotter.

The *'Optimisation...'* subdialogue box controls the efficiency of the plotter output.

Additional parameters

Display refers to what is displayed on the screen at the time the **PLOT** command is entered.

Extents refers to the extents of your drawing.

Limits refers to the limits of the drawing.

View refers to a named view you may already have saved. If you reply with **V** (for 'view'), AutoCAD will ask:

View name:

Give the name and proceed.

Window refers to a window of the display, as in the **ZOOM** command. You cannot use the window option to plot a perspective view.

All the above options apart from *View* will use the current viewport.

Hide refers to hidden lines created in three-dimensional drawings.

Adjust Area Fill allows control over the accuracy with which filled polylines, traces and solids in a drawing are drawn.

Plot to File allows a plot to be sent to a file on the hard disk or a diskette instead of directly to the plotter. A plot file has the extension PLT. (See chapter 20 and appendix C on file names and extensions. See also 'Additional information' at the end of this chapter for an explanation of plotting to a file.)

Paper size and orientation

The 'radio buttons' allow you to change between inches and millimetres. *'Size...'* allows the selection of pre-defined paper sizes that suit your plotting device. You can also assign a size yourself. The 'Max' size depends on the plotter you are using.

Scale, rotation, and origin

The *'Scaled to Fit'* option guarantees that the drawing will fit on whatever paper size you have set in *'Paper size and orientation'*. If you wish to plot at a particular scale, remove the X from the *'Scaled to Fit'* box and enter values in the *'Plotted Inches/MM = Drawing Units'* boxes. For example, **1=1** will plot the drawing at real size.

Plot preview

When the *Partial* button is selected, a small sheet is displayed in two colours. The red shows the size of the drawing on the paper the plot is being sent to, and the blue shows the effective plotting area on the paper.

Plotting in 'text' mode

If the **CMDDIA** variable is set to 0, or if you are using the Windows version of AutoCAD, the **PLOT** command will be executed in text mode. A quick plot in the text mode is outlined below.

Step 1: Load the drawing you wish to plot into AutoCAD.
Step 2: ZOOM-All.
Step 3: Enter the command PLOT at the command prompt.

Command: **PLOT**
What to plot — Display, Extents, Limits, View or Window <D>: **D**
A list similar to that shown below will be displayed:
Plot device is IBM Proprinter ADI 4.2—by Autodesk
Plot will NOT be written to a selected file
Sizes are in Inches and the style is landscape
Plot origin is at (0.00,0.00)
Plotting area is 10.50 wide by 8.00 high (A size)
Plot is NOT rotated
Hidden lines will NOT be removed
Plot will be scaled to fit available area

Step 4: If you are in agreement with the above list, answer **N** to the next question.

Do you want to change anything? (No/Yes/File/Save) <N>: **N**

AutoCAD will then attempt to plot the drawing. Answering **Y** for yes will lead to several other questions about the plot device, the paper size, etc. (See the section 'A more detailed look at Plot Configuration, above.)

ADDITIONAL INFORMATION

Assigning pen widths instead of colours

If a drawing is distributed over different layers with different colours assigned to the layers, different pen widths can be placed in the plotter to give control over the weight of lines in the drawing.

For example, to mimic the traditional monochrome output of a hand-draughted drawing the pen colours in the plotter can be replaced with pens of differing widths. Pen 1 (red) could be assigned a pen with of 0.25 mm, pen 2 (yellow) to a width of 0.35 mm, etc.

Plotting to a file

The *'plot to a file'* option allows the instructions that move the pen in a plotter or that move the print head on a printer to be stored in a file for later use. This facility is particularly useful if there is only one plotter available or if it is not economical to keep a computer tied up while sending the plot data to the plotter. A plot file is created very quickly compared with a printed copy.

Many computer programs that involve the use of graphics, such as word-processor and page make-up programs, allow plot files to be used in them to create the graphics if the file was produced using HPGL (Hewlett-Packard Graphics Language). Files can be produced in HPGL even if you do not have a Hewlett-Packard printer or plotter: simply select a Hewlett-Packard plotter (for example the HP 7475 plotter) when configuring AutoCAD and answer **Y** when plotting to send the plot to a file. This file can then be imported into the word-processor or page make-up program. The files created in this way have the extension PLT or LST.

SUMMARY

AutoCAD produces printed copies using the **PLOT** command. This command calls up the *'Plot Configuration'* dialogue box if the **CMDDIA** system variable is set to 1. If **CMDDIA** is set to 0, AutoCAD will interact with you in text mode. Either method allows detailed control over the production of the printed copy or the plot file. The scale, orientation of paper, speed of pens, rotation of the drawing on the paper etc. can all be controlled.

The dialogue box in particular allows great control over the plotting parameters, and several plot configurations can be stored in a plot configuration file.

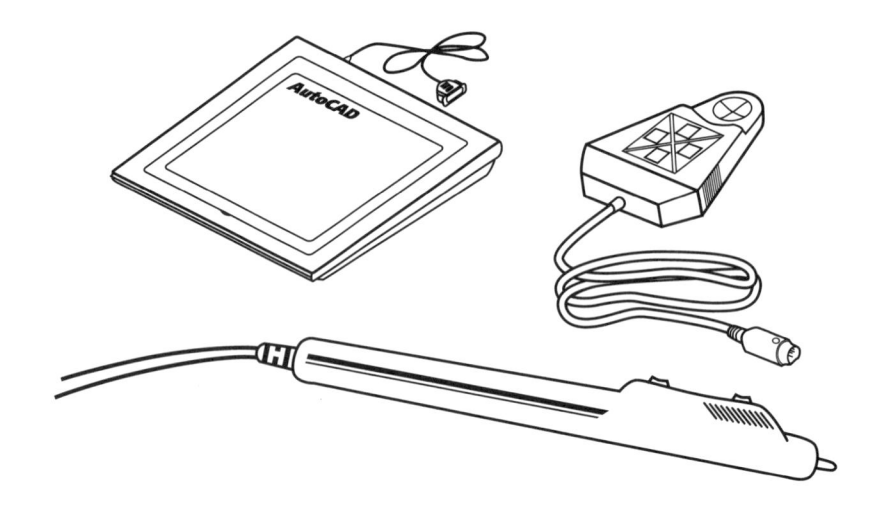

chapter 19
Installing and Configuring AutoCAD

Tutorial objectives

By the end of this chapter you should be able to
- install AutoCAD for the first time
- reconfigure AutoCAD
- configure AutoCAD to work with a digitiser
- calibrate the digitiser for digitising (tracing) a drawing
- load a menu using the MENU command
- explain what ADI drivers are

Tutorial 19.1

Preparing to install AutoCAD

This tutorial refers to the DOS version of AutoCAD release 12. Windows users use Program Manager's 'File', 'Run' option and then type **A:setup**. Follow the screen prompts after that.

The **INSTALL** procedure of AutoCAD involves copying the program from the diskettes onto the computer's hard disk. This is done using an **INSTALL** program, which is found on the disk labelled *'Executable 1'*.

Before you proceed with the installation it is essential that a back-up copy of all the original disks is made. The **INSTALL** program can then be run from the back-up copy.

How to make a back-up copy

Make the original AutoCAD disks 'write-protected' before you proceed.
(1) If you have a single diskette drive designated A, type the following:
C:\>DISKCOPY A: A:
and press **[enter]**. The computer will respond with:
Insert SOURCE diskette in drive A:
Press any key to continue . . .
The source diskette is the original AutoCAD disk. Place it into drive A and press **[enter]**. The computer will respond with:
Copying 80 tracks
18 sectors per track, 2 side(s)

When the computer has copied part of the first disk into memory you will be asked to insert the 'target diskette'. This is the blank diskette you are backing up onto. Insert the diskette and press **[enter]**.
Insert TARGET diskette in drive A:
Press any key to continue . . .

MSDOS 6.2 will copy a disk with only one change. Label the disks exactly as the originals. Put the original disks in a safe place and use the back-up copy for the next stage.
(2) If you have two diskette drives designated A and B, back up the disks as follows:
C:\>DISKCOPY A: B:
and press **[enter]**. Follow the instructions on the screen.

Switch off the computer and place the hardware lock device into the parallel port. Switch the computer on. At the C: prompt enter the DOS command **CHKDSK**. This will list the available space on the hard disk. You must have more than 12 Mb free to install the complete copy of AutoCAD 12.

Installing AutoCAD for the first time

Place the disk labelled *Executable 1* in drive A. Log on to drive A by typing **A:**. The prompt will change to
A:\>
Type **INSTALL**, and follow the instructions that appear on the screen. The INSTALL program will create the subdirectories on the hard disk for the storage of AutoCAD. Accept the default unless you are sure you know what you are doing.

Near the end of the installation procedure you will be asked if you want to make changes to the CONFIG.SYS and AUTOEXEC.BAT files. Answer **Y** unless you are clear about how the computer is set up.

Lastly the INSTALL program will ask you if it should write a batch file to the C drive to allow you to run AutoCAD. Respond with **Y** again. The installation program will then write a batch file called ACADR12.BAT to the root directory of drive C and terminate. AutoCAD will have been copied to your hard disk.

To start the AutoCAD program, type the name of the batch file while in the root directory of C—i.e. the prompt should be

C:\>

AutoCAD will attempt to run. However, because the program does not know what kind of monitor or pointing device is being used, it will display the message *'AutoCAD not configured',* and show a list of display devices. The prompt below will take you through all the steps involved in setting up AutoCAD to run on a computer with a standard VGA graphics card, a Microsoft or compatible mouse, and an IBM Proprinter dot-matrix printer. If you are using a digitising tablet instead of a mouse, read tutorial 19.2 first.

A U T O C A D (R)
Copyright (c) 1982-92 Autodesk, Inc. All Rights Reserved. Release 12 International (7/1/92) 386 DOS Extender
Serial Number: XXX-XXXXXXXX — Licensed to: ,
Obtained from:
Available video displays:
1. Null display
2. 8514/A ADI 4.2 Display and Rendering - By Panacea for Autodesk
3. ADI display v4.0
4. ADI display v4.1
5. Compaq Portable III Plasma Display <obsolete>
6. Hercules Graphics Card <obsolete>
7. IBM Enhanced Graphics Adapter <obsolete>
8. IBM Video Graphics Array ADI 4.2 - by Autodesk
9. SVADI Super VGA ADI 4.2 - by Autodesk
10. Targa+ ADI v4.2 Display and Rendering - by Autodesk
11. VESA Super VGA ADI v4.2 Display and Rendering - by Autodesk
12. XGA ADI 4.2 Display and Rendering - By Panacea for Autodesk
Select device number or ? to repeat list <1>: 8
Do you want to do detailed configuration of IBM VGA's display features? <N>
If you have previously measured the height and width of a "square" on your graphics screen, you may use these measurements to correct the aspect ratio.
Would you like to do so? <N>
Do you want a status line? <Y>
Do you want a command prompt area? <Y>
Do you want a screen menu area? <Y>

Available digitisers:
1. None
2. ADI digitiser (Real Mode)
3. Calcomp 2500 and 9100 Series ADI 4.2 - by Autodesk
4. GTCO Digi-Pad (Types 5 & 5A) <obsolete> ADI 4.2 - by Autodesk
5. Hitachi HICOMSCAN HDG Series ADI 4.2 - by Autodesk
6. Kurta IS/1, Series I <obsolete> ADI 4.2 - by Autodesk
7. Kurta XLC, Series II and III <obsolete>, IS/3 ADI 4.2 - by Autodesk 8.

Logitech Logimouse ADI 4.2 - by Autodesk
9. Microsoft Mouse Driver ADI 4.2 - by Autodesk
10. Numonics 2200 <obsolete> ADI 4.2 - by Autodesk 11. Summagraphics MM Series v2.0, ADI 4.2 - by Autodesk
12. Summagraphics MicroGrid v1.0 (Series II or later) ADI 4.2 - by Autodesk
Select device number or ? to repeat list <1>: 9
Supported model:
1. Microsoft Mouse
One choice, selection is automatic.
Do you want to change the mouse scaling parameters? <N>

Available plotters:
1. None
2. ADI plotter or printer (installed - pre v4.1) - by Autodesk
3. AutoCAD file output formats (pre 4.1) - by Autodesk
4. CalComp ColorMaster Plotters ADI 4.2 - by Autodesk 5. CalComp DrawingMaster Plotters ADI 4.2 - by Autodesk 6. CalComp Electrostatic Plotters ADI 4.2 - by Autodesk 7. CalComp Pen Plotters ADI 4.2 - by Autodesk
8. Canon Laser Printer ADI 4.2 - by Autodesk
9. Epson printers ADI 4.2 - by Autodesk
10. Hewlett-Packard (HP-GL) ADI 4.2 - by Autodesk 11. Hewlett-Packard (HP-GL/2) ADI 4.2 - by Autodesk
12. Hewlett-Packard (PCL) LaserJet ADI 4.2 - by Autodesk
13. Hewlett-Packard (PCL) PaintJet XL ADI 4.2 - by Autodesk
14. Houston Instrument ADI 4.2 - by Autodesk
15. IBM 7300 Series ADI 4.2 - by Autodesk
16. IBM Graphics Printer <obsolete> ADI 4.2 - by Autodesk
17. IBM Proprinter ADI 4.2 - by Autodesk
18. JDL 750 & 750E <obsolete> ADI 4.2 - by Autodesk
19. NEC Pinwriter P5/P5XL/P9XL <obsolete> ADI 4.2 - by Autodesk 20. PostScript device ADI 4.2 - by Autodesk
— Press RETURN for more —
21. Raster file export ADI 4.2 - by Autodesk
Select device number or ? to repeat list <1>: 17
Supported models:
1. Proprinter
2. Proprinter II
3. Proprinter XL
4. Proprinter XL24
Enter selection, 1 to 4 <1>: 2
Connects to Parallel Printer port.
Standard ports are:
    LPT1
Enter port name, or address in hexadecimal <LPT1>:
Plot will NOT be written to a selected file Sizes are in Inches and the style is landscape Plot origin is at (0.00,0.00)

Plotting area is 8.00 wide by 11.00 high (MAX size) Plot is NOT rotated
Hidden lines will NOT be removed
Plot will be scaled to fit available area
Do you want to change anything? (No/Yes/File) <N>:
Enter a description of this plotter: BUBBLEJET
Login Name:
Enter default login name < , >:
Do you wish to enable file-locking? <Y>: **N** ← See 'additional information' below

This screen lists the present configuration.
Current AutoCAD configuration
Video display: SVADI Super VGA ADI 4.2 - by Autodesk
SVADI v1.8d (21jun92). Universal Super VGA ADI (Display/Render) DOS Protected Mode ADI 4.2 Driver for AutoCAD.
Config file is C:\ACAD\DRV\SVADI.CFG
Configured for: IBM Video Graphics Array. Text font: 8x16. Display - 640x480 in 16 colours on Black background.
Rendering - 320x200 in 256 colours.
 Version: A.1.18
 Digitiser: *Microsoft Mouse Driver ADI 4.2 - by Autodesk*
      Microsoft Mouse
 Version: A.1.18
 Plotter: *IBM Proprinter ADI 4.2 - by Autodesk*
     Proprinter II
 Port: Parallel Printer LPT1 at address 378 (hex)
 Version: A.1.18
Press RETURN to continue
Configuration menu
 0. Exit to drawing editor
 1. Show current configuration
 2. Allow detailed configuration
 3. Configure video display
 4. Configure digitiser
 5. Configure plotter
 6. Configure system console
 7. Configure operating parameters
Enter selection <0>:
If you answer N to the following question, all configuration changes you have just made will be discarded.
Keep configuration changes? <Y>
The drawing editor is displayed.

 Use *'Configure'* from the *'File'* drop-down menu if you have a problem or want to change the configuration just set up.

Tutorial 19.2

Configuring the digitiser

Tablet configuration

There are two steps involved in configuring the tablet to work with your computer.
(1) After connecting up the hardware you must tell AutoCAD the name of the tablet connected to it. This is done using *'Configure'* from the *'File'* drop-down menu and then selecting option 4, *'Configure digitiser'*, from the *Configuration* menu.
(2) When AutoCAD knows which tablet is connected to it, it will then need to be told where the menu areas and screen area are on the tablet. This second stage involves using the command **TABLET** at the command prompt in the drawing editor.

Telling AutoCAD what tablet is connected to it

When a tablet is physically connected to the computer, AutoCAD will need to know its name so that it can load a suitable 'device driver'. This is a small program that will enable AutoCAD to send and receive messages from the tablet. The tablet device drivers supplied with AutoCAD have the file extension DRV.

In the following exercise it will be assumed that you have a Calcomp 2500 digitising tablet and that you have connected it to the computer through the serial port, COM2.

If you wish to configure for a different digitising tablet it should be easy to select the correct options as you read through the selections.

Step 1

Select *'Configure'* from the *'File'* drop-down menu. The current AutoCAD configuration is displayed in text mode.
Current AutoCAD configuration
Video display: IBM Video Graphics Array ADI 4.2 - by Autodesk
IBM VGA v1.8e (14jul92). Universal Super VGA ADI (Display/Render) DOS Protected Mode ADI 4.2 Driver for AutoCAD.
Config file is C:\R12\DRV\SVADI.CFG
Configured for: IBM Video Graphics Array. Text font: 8x16. Display - 640x480 in 16 colours on Light background.
Rendering - 320x200 in 256 colours.
  Version: A.C.04
  Digitiser: Microsoft Mouse Driver ADI 4.2 - by Autodesk
                      Microsoft Mouse
  Version: A.C.04
  Plotter: IBM Proprinter ADI 4.2 - by Autodesk
                      Proprinter XL
  Port: Parallel Printer LPT1 at address 378 (hex)

Version: A.C.04

— Press RETURN for more —

The following screen is displayed with the configuration menu:

A U T O C A D (R)

Copyright (c) 1982-92 Autodesk, Inc. All Rights Reserved. Release 12_c1 International (8/26/92) 386 DOS Extender Serial Number: xxx-xxxxxxxx

Licensed to: xxxxxxxx,xxxxxxx,xxxxxx

Obtained from: xxxxxxx,xxxxxxx

Configuration menu

    0. Exit to drawing editor
    1. Show current configuration
    2. Allow detailed configuration
    3. Configure video display
    4. Configure digitiser
    5. Configure plotter
    6. Configure system console
    7. Configure operating parameters

Enter selection <0>:

To configure the tablet, select option 4, *'Configure digitiser'*. The following is displayed:

Your current digitiser is: Microsoft Mouse Driver ADI 4.2 - by Autodesk Do you want to select a different one? <N>

Answer **Y** for yes and press **[enter]**. A screen listing the available digitisers is displayed:

A U T O C A D (R)

Copyright (c) 1982-92 Autodesk, Inc. All Rights Reserved.

Release 12_c1 International (8/26/92) 386 DOS Extender Serial Number: xxx-xxxxxxxx

Licensed to: xxxxxxxx,xxxxxxx,xxxxxx

Obtained from: xxxxxxx,xxxxxxx

Available digitisers:

    1. None
    2. ADI digitiser (Real Mode)
    3. Calcomp 2500 and 9100 Series ADI 4.2 - by Autodesk
    4. GTCO Digi-Pad (Types 5 & 5A) <obsolete> ADI 4.2 - by Autodesk
    5. Hitachi HICOMSCAN HDG Series ADI 4.2 - by Autodesk
    6. Kurta IS/1, Series I <obsolete> ADI 4.2 - by Autodesk
    7. Kurta XLC, Series II and III <obsolete>, IS/3 ADI 4.2 - by Autodesk
    8. Logitech Logimouse ADI 4.2 - by Autodesk
    9. Microsoft Mouse Driver ADI 4.2 - by Autodesk
    10. Numonics 2200 <obsolete> ADI 4.2 - by Autodesk
    11. Summagraphics MM Series v2.0, ADI 4.2 - by Autodesk
    12. Summagraphics MicroGrid v1.0 (Series II or later) ADI 4.2 - by Autodesk

Select device number or ? to repeat list <9>:

Enter **3** for the Calcomp 2500 digitiser. The various Calcomp models are listed; select model 25120.

Supported models:
1. *2500 Series, Model 25120*
2. *2500 Series, Model 25180*
3. *9100 Series, Model 9136*
4. *9100 Series, Model 9148*
5. *9100 Series, Model 9160*

The digitiser can have the following types of cursor:
1 button
4 buttons
16 buttons

Select the four-button option.

Now AutoCAD will need to know which communications port the digitiser is connected to. Select COM2 by typing **COM2** at the prompt.
Connects to Asynchronous Communications Adapter port.
Standard ports are:
COM1
COM2

You are returned to the configuration menu.

By accepting the default you can return to the drawing editor, and the new configuration is changed.

If you have selected the incorrect configuration it may be that you will have lost control over the cross-hairs when the drawing editor is displayed. To re-enter the configuration menu type **CONFIG** at the command prompt, or use the *'File'* drop-down menu.

At this stage AutoCAD is aware of the type of tablet connected to the computer. You should have some control over the cross-hairs in the drawing editor if you have made the correct choice. To configure the tablet itself so that AutoCAD understands how you want to use it, you must use the **TABLET** command at the command prompt.

Step 2

It is now time to configure the tablet itself. Make sure the tablet is powered up before you proceed. Start up a drawing, and follow the procedure outlined below.

When you first enter the drawing editor you will have very little control over the movement of the cross-hairs.

The standard AutoCAD template is divided into four menu areas and a screen area. These are shown in fig. 19.1. A similar representation of the tablet is found in your AutoCAD reference manual. Place the AutoCAD template on the digitiser and secure it so that it cannot slip. By using the command **TABLET** you can tell AutoCAD where the menu areas and screen area are. The menu areas are defined by rows and columns; these rows and columns are used during the configuration.

- Menu area 1 consists of 25 columns and 9 rows
- Menu area 2 is 11 columns by 9 rows
- Menu area 3 is 9 columns by 13 rows

♦ Menu area 4 is 25 columns by 7 rows

The labelling 'UPPER LEFT' and 'LOWER RIGHT' of each menu area will be used in the following configuration.

After typing **TABLET** at the command prompt, select **CFG** (for 'configuration').

Command: **TABLET**
Option (ON/OFF/CAL/CFG): **CFG**
Enter number of tablet menus desired (0-4) : **4**
Do you want to realign tablet menu areas? **Y**

After you respond with yes, AutoCAD will ask you to define each of the menu areas. When, for example, you are asked for the 'upper left corner of menu area 1,' click with the puck or pen on the black dot that marks this point.

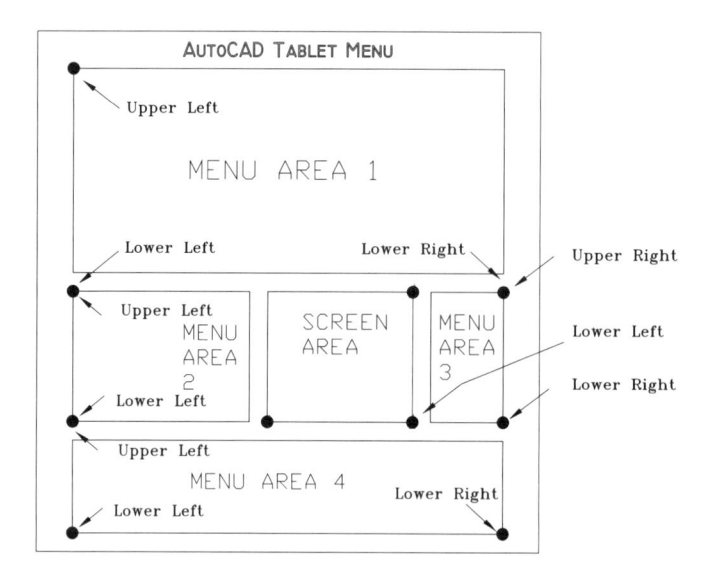

Fig. 19.1. The areas of the standard AutoCAD template.

Digitize upper left corner of menu area 1: ← Click with the pointer
Digitize lower left corner of menu area 1: ← Click with the pointer
Digitize lower right corner of menu area 1: ← Click with the pointer
Enter the number of columns for menu area 1: **25**
Enter the number of rows for menu area 1: **9**
Digitize upper left corner of menu area 2: ← Click with the pointer
Digitize lower left corner of menu area 2: ← Click with the pointer
Digitize lower right corner of menu area 2: ← Click with the pointer
Enter the number of columns for menu area 2: **11**
Enter the number of rows for menu area 2: **9**
Digitize upper left corner of menu area 3: ← Click with the pointer
Digitize lower left corner of menu area 3: ← Click with the pointer
Digitize lower right corner of menu area 3: ← Click with the pointer

Enter the number of columns for menu area 3: **9**
Enter the number of rows for menu area 3: **13**
Digitize upper left corner of menu area 4:   ← Click with the pointer
Digitize lower left corner of menu area 4:   ← Click with the pointer
Digitize lower right corner of menu area 4:   ← Click with the pointer
Enter the number of columns for menu area 4: **25**
Enter the number of rows for menu area 4: **7**
Do you want to respecify the screen pointing area? **Y**
Digitize lower left corner of screen pointing area: ← Click with the pointer
Digitize upper right corner of screen pointing area: ← Click with the pointer
Command:

Configuration is complete. The motion of the cross-hairs in the display should accurately reflect the motion of the puck or pen on the digitising tablet.

Test the commands by selecting Line or Circle.

Tutorial 19.3

Tutorial objectives

- Digitising drawings
- Calibration of the digitiser
- Digitising a drawing

The tablet can be used to 'digitise' a drawing. The drawing is placed over the tablet and traced with the puck or pen. Before this can be done, however, the tablet must be calibrated to match the co-ordinate system of the drawing. This is done using the command **TABLET**.

At the end of the book you will find a simple drawing to digitise: it is named DIG2. To calibrate a tablet to the drawing's co-ordinates you need at least two co-ordinates from the drawing. In this case the co-ordinates you know are 200,160 and 320,130.

The calibration process

Place the drawing to be digitised (DIG2) on the tablet. It can be placed anywhere within the active area of the tablet and at any orientation (just make sure it will not move).

Because the drawing is larger than the screen pointing area on the tablet, you must first redefine the screen pointing area to include the drawing. Type **TABLET** at the command prompt and respond with **0** for the number of menu areas. Answer **Yes** to respecify the screen pointing area and pick the bottom left and top right of the areas of the drawing you wish to digitise.

Here is the command sequence:

Command: **TABLET**
Option (ON/OFF/CAL/CFG): **CFG**
Enter number of tablet menus desired (0-4) <<0>>:
Do you want to respecify the screen pointing area? <<N>>: **Y**

Digitise lower left corner of screen pointing area: ← Pick with the pointing device
Digitise upper right corner of screen pointing area: ← Pick with the pointing device
Command:

Next calibrate the drawing. Type **TABLET** at the command prompt and select **CAL** from the options offered. In response, AutoCAD will ask for the two known points on the drawing. Click on the known points with the puck or pen and type in the co-ordinate of each.

Command: **TABLET**
Option (ON/OFF/CAL/CFG): **CAL**
Calibrate tablet for use…
Digitize first known point:
Enter co-ordinates for first point: **200,160**
Digitize second known point:
Enter co-ordinates for second point: **320,130**

You can now proceed to digitise the complete drawing. For example, to digitise it as a polyline, execute the **PLINE** command and in response to *'From point'* etc. pick the points off the drawing. All AutoCAD's editing and drawing commands will function while you are digitising. The object snap modes are particularly useful.

ADDITIONAL INFORMATION

Using a different menu

The AutoCAD drop-down, tablet and screen menus are stored in a file named ACAD.MNU. Each time the ACAD prototype drawing is used the ACAD.MNU file is loaded into the drawing editor with it. It is possible for advanced users to modify the menu to suit the draughting requirements of a company. Specialised menus can be written, particularly for the tablet, to help speed up the efficiency of drawing electronic circuits or machine parts. All menu files must have the extension MNU (see chapter 20 on MSDOS).

To load a new menu into AutoCAD, use the command **'MENU'** at the command prompt. A *'Select Menu File'* dialogue box is displayed (if the **Filedia** variable is set to 1) with a list of available menus. Click on the menu required, and click on *'OK'*. As the menu is loaded it is compiled to allow it to run faster.

If the **Filedia** is set to 0, AutoCAD will respond at the command prompt with:
Command: MENU
Menu filename or . for none<acad>:

AutoCAD release 12 has a menu called TUTOR.MNU in the Tutorial subdirectory (see chapter 20 on subdirectories). This can be loaded by responding with C:\ACAD\TUTORIAL\TUTOR if your AutoCAD is set up in the standard way with the tutorial option loaded.

If you do not have a different menu to load, try entering the full point (.) to see the effect of no menu in the drawing editor.

Note: Even with no menu, all the AutoCAD commands are still available from the command prompt. If you save a drawing with a menu (or no menu), the menu is also saved with the drawing. The next time the drawing is opened AutoCAD will look for that particular menu.

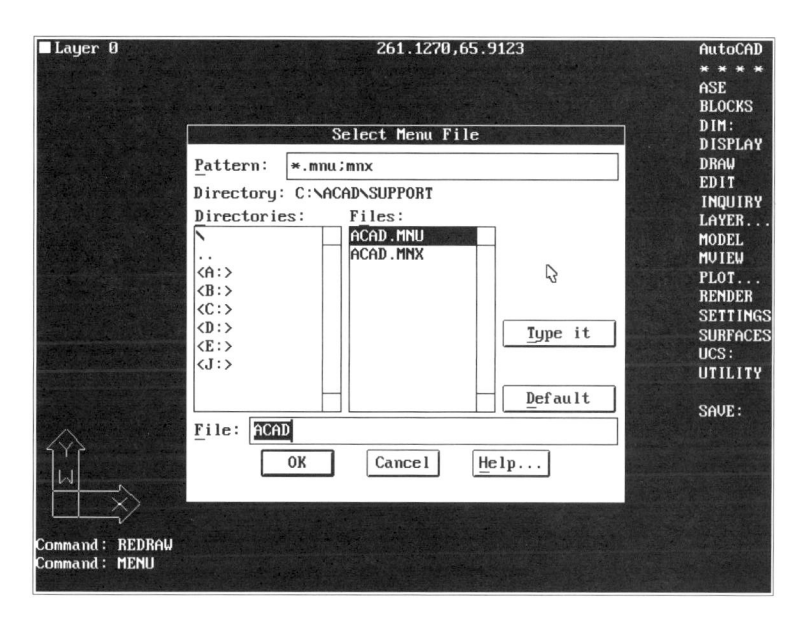

Fig. 19.2. The 'Select Menu File' dialogue box.

Device drivers

Small programs called 'drivers' are needed by AutoCAD to enable it to communicate with peripheral devices. During the configuration procedure detailed above, AutoCAD needed to know the type of hardware the computer was using for this reason. Once the configuration is complete, AutoCAD will then load the required drivers for the peripherals each time it is run.

The drivers supplied with AutoCAD are called ADI (Autodesk device interface) drivers. For example, the graphic card selected was an SVADI SVGA ADI. These ADI drivers can be divided into two types: (*a*) real-mode drivers and (*b*) protected-mode drivers.

The real-mode drivers

These drivers are normally used if you buy a peripheral device that is not in the AutoCAD list. For example, if you have a digitiser such as a Huston Instruments Hipad, you will have to use the device driver supplied with the digitiser, because it is not found in the AutoCAD listing.

Real-mode drivers have to be loaded into memory before AutoCAD each time the program is run. They load into the 640 kb area of MSDOS memory. AutoCAD must then be told to look for the real-mode driver in memory. This is done (in the case of the digitiser) by selecting option 2, *'ADI digitiser (Real Mode)'*.

If there are problems in running a non-listed peripheral, they are often caused by the incorrect installation of the supplied device driver.

Protected-mode drivers

These are supplied with AutoCAD and load into memory above 640 kb. Protected-mode drivers do not need to be loaded into memory before starting AutoCAD.

File locking

A file that is locked is unavailable to the user. When AutoCAD is running on a network of computers it is possible for two or more people to access a file (particularly a drawing file) at the same time. This would invariably lead to corruption of the file and to the data it contains being lost. In situations like this it is advisable to set the file locking mode to *on* by answering **Yes** to the question *Do you wish to enable file-locking? <Y>:* when configuring AutoCAD. To unlock a file use the **FILE** command described in chapter 20.

It is advisable to answer **No** to this question if you are running AutoCAD on a 'stand-alone' (non-networked) computer.

SUMMARY

It is essential to make a back-up copy of AutoCAD before it is installed. The DISKCOPY command will produce identical copies of the original disks. The source disk is the original AutoCAD program disk, the target disk is the blank formatted disk you are backing up to. Install AutoCAD from the copies you have made. During installation follow the prompts that appear on screen. Before you proceed to configure AutoCAD be clear about the hardware that you have, in particular the type of graphics card on the computer and the type of pointing device you are using.

To configure AutoCAD to work with a digitising tablet, (*a*) tell AutoCAD the type of digitiser you have connected to the computer and (*b*) the position of the menu areas on the template you are using.

The digitising tablet can be used to input a drawing by digitising it. This is done by using the CAL option from the TABLET command. Before a drawing can be digitised you must know the co-ordinates of at least two points on the drawing. Once these are entered you can proceed with the digitising.

AutoCAD allows you to use different menus with a drawing. The MENU command will load a menu into the current drawing editor. The full point (.) will load no menu. If you have installed the TUTORIAL option, a menu named TUTOR will be found in the subdirectory Tutorial.

Peripherals need drivers to allow them to function with AutoCAD. Autodesk supplies ADI (Autodesk device interface) drivers. These consist of real-mode and protected-mode drivers.

Drawings to Digitise

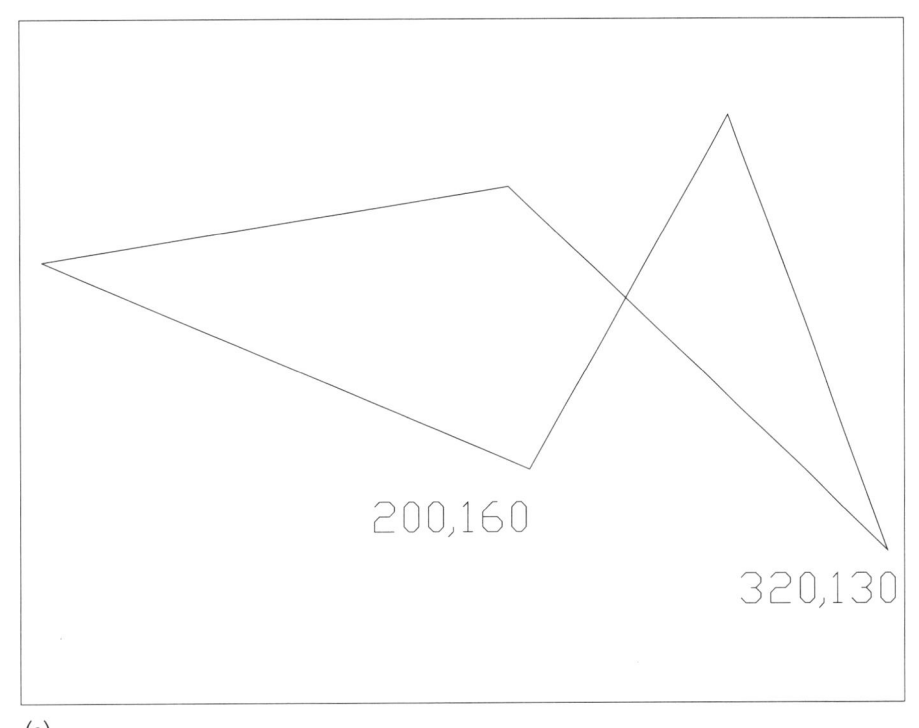

(a)

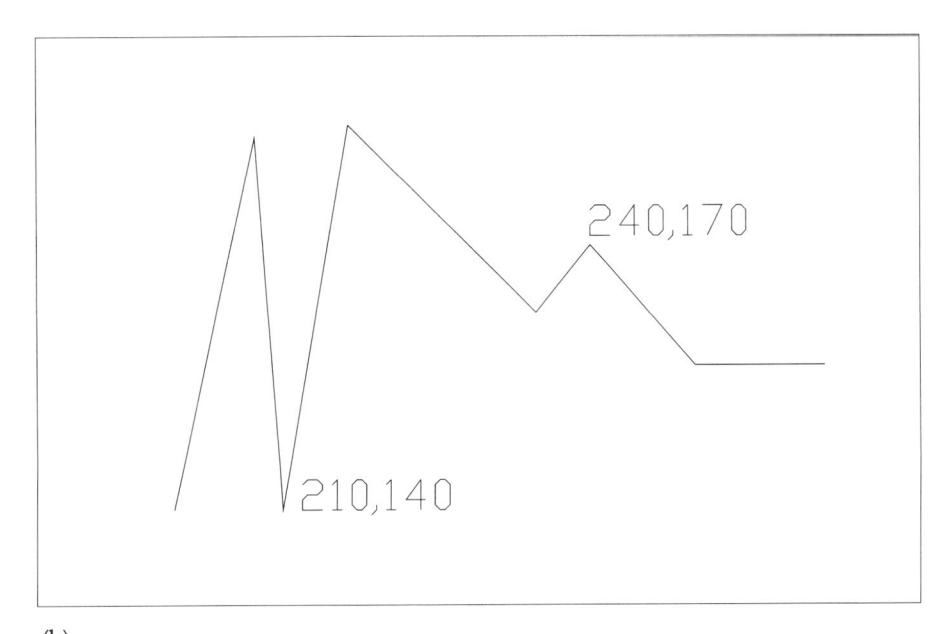

(b)

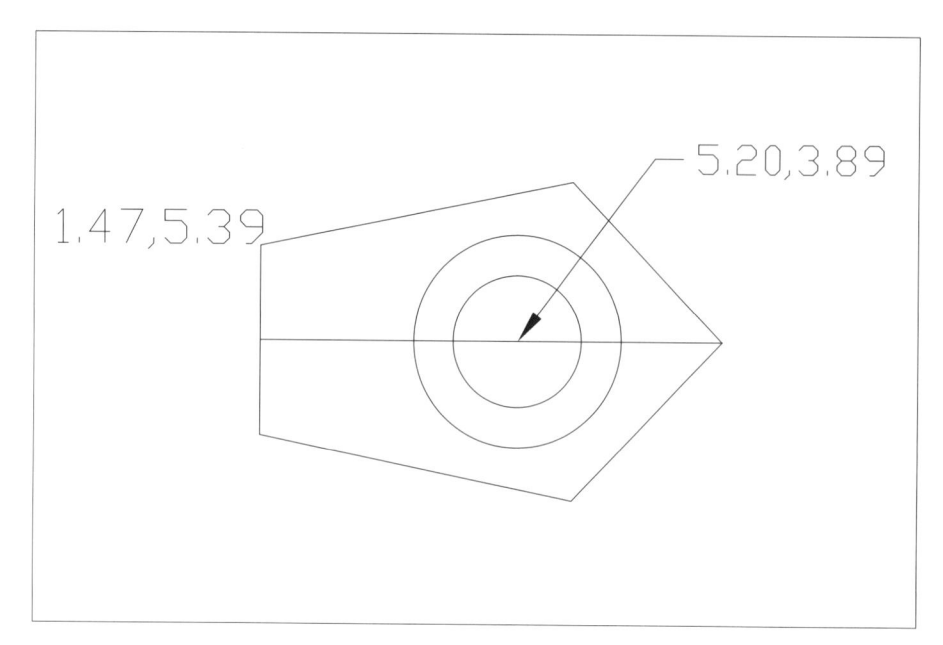

(c)

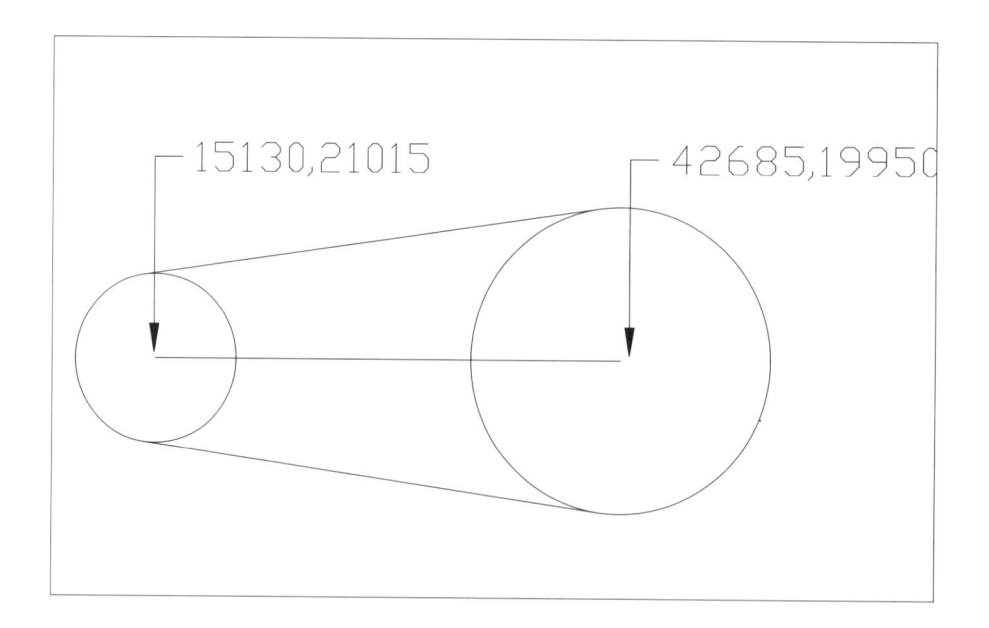

1.47,5.39

5.20,3.89

(d)

15130,21015

42685,19950

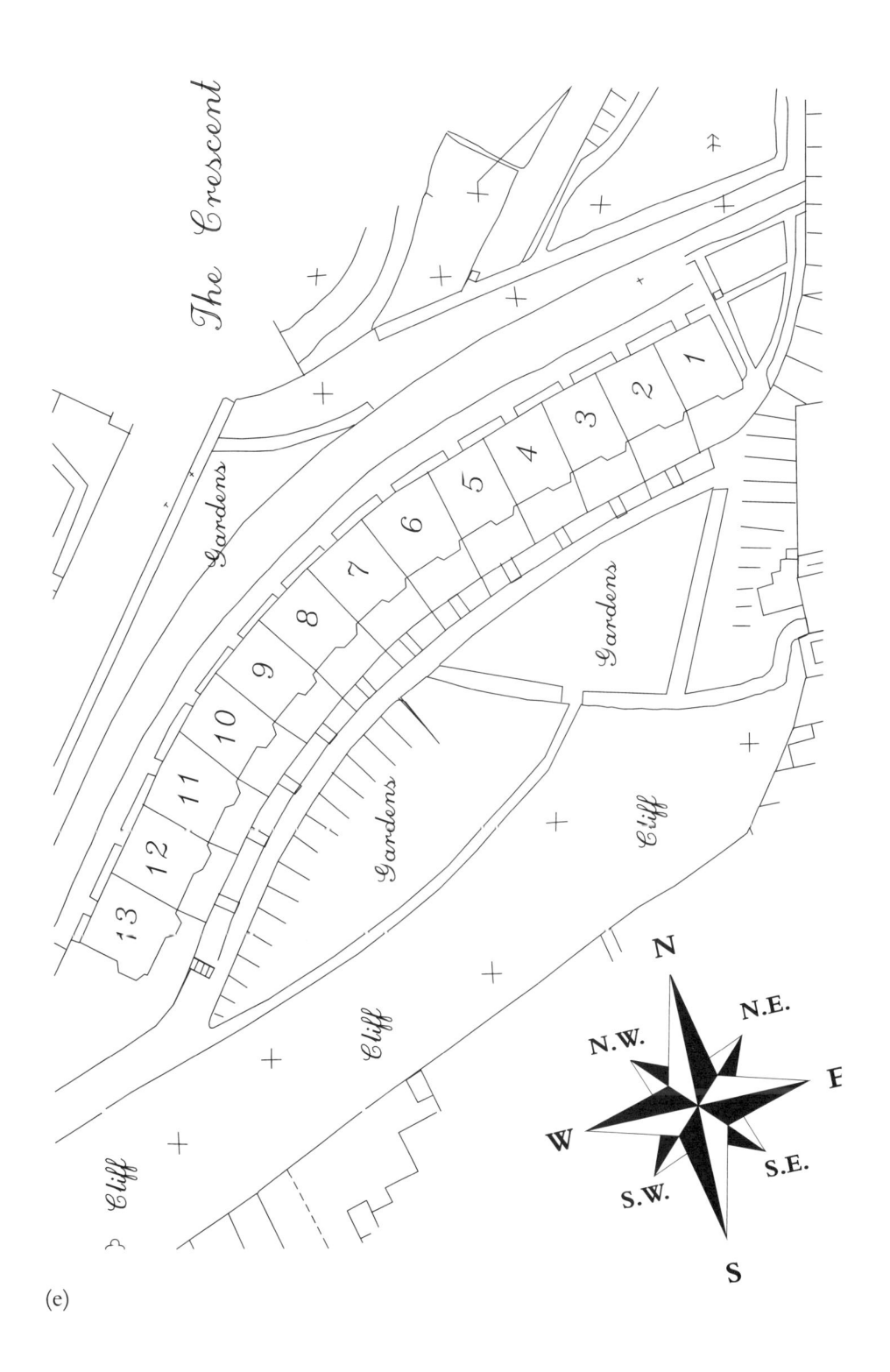

(e)

INSTALLING AND CONFIGURING AUTOCAD **305**

chapter 20
DOS for AutoCAD users

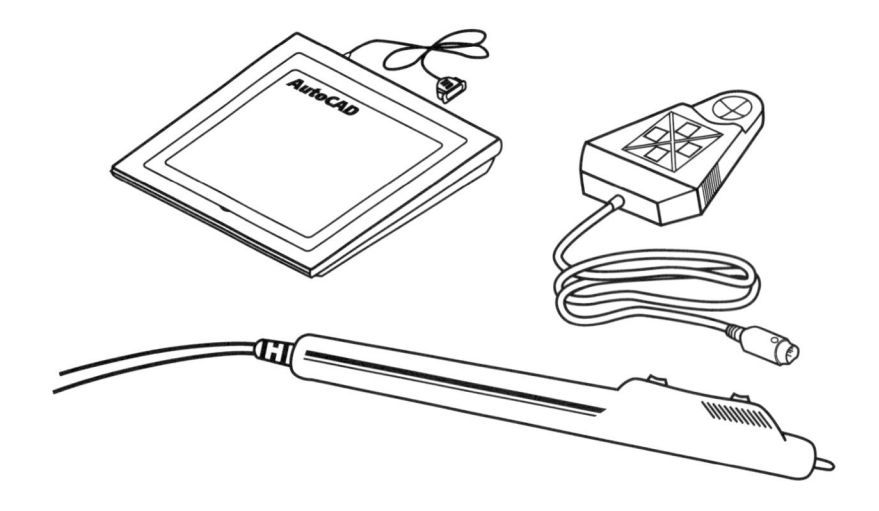

Tutorial 20.1

Tutorial objectives

By the end of this chapter you should be able to
- use the following DOS commands:
  BACKUP
  COPY
  DEL
  ERASE
  FORMAT
  MD
  RD
- use the File Utility Menu within AutoCAD

Before you proceed with this tutorial you must have a blank diskette. All the commands in this section refer to an 80386SX (or higher) DOS computer, as AutoCAD release 12 will not run on a computer with a lower specification.

Starting the computer

When a computer is switched on it goes through the 'boot-up' routine, checking its memory and the peripherals attached to it. It then proceeds to look for the DOS files in drive A (the light indicating disk drive activity flashes for that reason). If the DOS files are not present it will look for them on the hard disk. Once the DOS files are found it will complete the boot-up procedure and display the system prompt:

C:\>

During boot-up the computer will read two important files, CONFIG.SYS and AUTOEXEC.BAT, if they are present. Both are normally present on hard disk systems: they will have been put there by the supplier. Your supplier of the AutoCAD program may also have modified these two files to help the program run more efficiently.

File names

DOS file names consist of two parts, separated by a full point. The three letters after the point are the 'file extension': they normally give you some indication of the type of data the file stores. For example, the CONFIG.SYS file is used to configure the system.

Typical extensions in AutoCAD are DWG for a drawing file and SLD for a slide. (Appendix C contains a list of AutoCAD file extensions.)

The actual name of the file precedes the full point. File names cannot be any longer than eight characters and must not contain certain characters (see your DOS manual for other restrictions on file names).

Preparing a diskette for use on the computer

A new diskette must be 'formatted' before it can be used on the computer. The formatting process is carried out by the computer's operating system. During the formatting process the diskette is marked magnetically so that DOS understands how to store files on it. This is similar to ruling a sheet of paper to hold the letters or numbers you place on it.

The FORMAT command

The format command must be used with extreme care. The most basic form of the command is **FORMAT A:**. This will format a disk in drive A.

All data on a disk is destroyed when it is formatted. Be careful not to format the hard disk on the computer. This will destroy the AutoCAD program and any other files on it.

To format a disk in drive B the basic syntax **FORMAT B:** is used.

How the command works

Type the following at the C prompt:

FORMAT A:/U

and press **[enter]**. DOS will respond with:

Insert new diskette for drive A:
and press ENTER when ready...

Place your blank disk in drive A (and close the latch on the drive door if it is a 5.25 in. disk). Press **[enter]**. The formatting of the disk will begin, and a message similar to this will be displayed:

Formatting 1.44M
x percent completed.

If you are formatting a 5.25 in. disk the response will refer to a 1.2 Mb disk. (See chapter 1 on disk types.)

Once the formatting is complete, the message

Volume label (11 characters, ENTER for none)?

will appear. Type in a name such as **MYDISK** and press **[enter]**. DOS will now display some statistics about the formatted disk:

1457664 bytes total disk space
1457664 bytes available on disk
512 bytes in each allocation unit.
2847 allocation units available on disk.
Volume Serial Number is 2F3D-11D1
Format another (Y/N)?

If the response is **Y** then the format command is repeated. Answering **N** will return you to the C prompt. The disk can now be used to store program or data files such as drawings.

The oblique stroke (/) in the command is referred to as a 'switch'. The switch U deletes all the data on the disk and prevents you using another DOS command, UNFORMAT. If you leave out the U switch and type

FORMAT A:, DOS will respond with

Checking existing disk format.
Saving UNFORMAT information.
Verifying 1.44M

Possible formatting problems

If DOS is unable to format your disk check the following:

- that the write-protect tab is closed, allowing the format data to be written to the disk;
- that you are using a high-density (HD) disk; if you want to format a double-density (DD) disk on an 80386 computer or higher, the F switch must be used;
- that the disk is not physically damaged: grit particles on the magnetic surface of the disk will prevent formatting.

Using the F switch

(1) To format a double-density 3.5 in. disk, use the following switch:
FORMAT A:/U/F:720
(2) To format a double-density 5.25 in. disk use the following switch:
FORMAT A:/U/F:360
Note that you can use more than one switch with a command.

The COPY command

The COPY command allows you to make copies of files on the disk. This is an important command. It can be used to copy drawing files from the hard disk to a diskette. *The copy command will leave the original file on the hard disk: only a copy will be made of it.*

When using the COPY command it is important to state where the file is being copied from (the 'source') and where it is being copied to (the 'destination').

To copy the CONFIG.SYS file from the hard disk to the diskette in drive A, enter the following:
C:\> **COPY C:\CONFIG.SYS A:\CONFIG.SYS**
Once the file is copied, DOS will respond:
1 file(s) copied

- The *C:\>* is referred to as the C prompt.
- COPY is the DOS command followed by a space.
- C:\ is the source: the file is going to be copied from the C disk drive.
- CONFIG.SYS is the name of the file and its extension.
- A:\ is the destination: the file will be copied to the A drive.
- CONFIG.SYS is the name assigned to the file when it arrives on the disk in drive A.

The insertion of spaces is very important in all DOS commands. The COPY command can be used both to copy a file and give it a new name. For example, the CONFIG.SYS file could have been copied as follows:
C:\> **COPY   C:\CONFIG.SYS   A:\JOHN.DOC**
In this case the CONFIG.SYS file was copied to the disk in drive A and assigned the name JOHN.DOC. Do this now.

Logging on to a disk drive

The prompt on the screen will tell you which disk drive you are logged on to. At the moment the C:\> indicates that the hard disk, C, is current. To log on to the disk in drive A, type **A:** at the C prompt. Before you log on to a drive make sure there is a disk in it. If the log-on is successful, the prompt will show it by responding with *A:\>*.

Possible problems

If there is no disk in drive A or if the disk is faulty, DOS may respond with:
Not ready reading drive A
Abort, Retry, Fail?
You respond by typing **A**, **R**, or **F**. There is no need to press **[enter]** after typing one of the letters.

'Abort' will stop DOS trying to execute the command to log on. 'Retry' will cause DOS to make another attempt at logging on. Select this option if you have inserted or changed the disk since trying to log on. 'Fail' will accept that it cannot log on to the drive in question. DOS will issue the prompt *Current drive no longer valid>*; respond by typing in the name of the drive you wish to log on to. Normally after a failed attempt at A you would enter **C:** to return to drive C.

Looking for files on your disk

A listing of files on a disk is called a 'directory'. To see a disk's directory type **DIR** and **[enter]**.

*A:\> **DIR***
Volume in drive A is MYDISK
Volume Serial Number is 1505-11E7
Directory of A:
CONFIG   SYS   247   04/02/93   12:53
JOHN   DOC   247   04/02/93   12:53
2 file(s)   583 bytes
1407488 bytes free
A:\>

The **DIR** command displays the disk's name (MYDISK) and the two files, each with its name and extension. The number following the extension is the size of the file in bytes (1,024 bytes constitute a kilobyte). Following this is the date and time the file was created or last altered.

Organising the files on a disk

Because of the large number of files that can accumulate on the hard disk of a computer, the operating system has been designed to allow files to be stored in groups by organising them into subdirectories. The two files listed above are on the disk's 'root directory'. The root directory is indicated by the reverse stroke (\). The prompt *A:\>* is interpreted as the root directory of A.

Subdirectories can be placed on the root directory, and groups of files can be placed in them. Each subdirectory must have a name (but no extension).

How to make a subdirectory

The DOS command **MD** will make a subdirectory. To make a subdirectory called ACCOUNT on the root directory of A, enter the following command:

A:\> **MD\ACCOUNT**

This instruction is interpreted as 'Make a subdirectory called ACCOUNT on the root directory (\) of the disk in drive A.'

Try that now. If the subdirectory was made successfully, the A prompt will be displayed again.

List the directory of the disk in drive A now.

A:\> **DIR**

Volume in drive A is MYDISK
Volume Serial Number is 1505-11E7
Directory of A:
ACCOUNT <DIR>   05/02/93   21:22
CONFIG SYS 247   04/02/93   12:53
JOHN DOC 247   4/02/93   12:53
*   3 file(s)   494 bytes*
1456128 bytes free
A:\>

The subdirectory you created is listed with *<DIR>* after it.

Looking inside a subdirectory

There are two ways to look at the contents of a subdirectory.

(1) Open the subdirectory (this is referred to as making the subdirectory 'current'). Then enter the command **DIR**. To make the subdirectory current use the command **CD** (for 'change directory'). Try this:

A:\> **CD\ACCOUNT**

A:\ACCOUNT> **DIR**

Volume in drive A is MYDISK
Volume Serial Number is 1505-11E7
Directory of A:\ACCOUNT
.   <DIR>   05/02/93   21:22
..   <DIR>   05/02/93   21:22
*   2 file(s)   0 bytes*
*   1456128 bytes free*
A:\ACCOUNT>

Note the following:

◆ The command **CD\ACCOUNT** is read as 'Change to the subdirectory ACCOUNT, which sits in the root directory of A.' The subdirectory is now open.

◆ Two files are already in the subdirectory. They are known as hidden files and are placed there by DOS for its own administrative purposes. A subdirectory in this state is said to be empty.

- The prompt has changed to *A:\ACCOUNT>* to remind you that the ACCOUNT subdirectory is current.
- The **DIR** command only listed the contents of the subdirectory that was current: the files in the root directory were not displayed.

To return to the root directory of A type **CD** ('Change to the root directory'). The prompt will show the root as the current directory with *A:\>*

(2) The **DIR** command can be used to look into a subdirectory without making it current. From the root of A, enter the following:

A:\> **DIR A:\ACCOUNT**
Volume in drive A is MYDISK
Volume Serial Number is 1505-11E7
Directory of A:\ACCOUNT
.   <DIR>   05/02/93   21:22
..   <DIR>   05/02/93   21:22
*   2 file(s)   0 bytes*
*   1456128 bytes free*
A:\>

In this case the **DIR** command was entered followed by the 'path' (**A:\ACCOUNT**) to where MSDOS was to look for the files.

The 'tree' command

The TREE command will present you with a graphical representation of the layout of subdirectories on a disk.

Type **TREE** at the prompt and press **[enter]**.

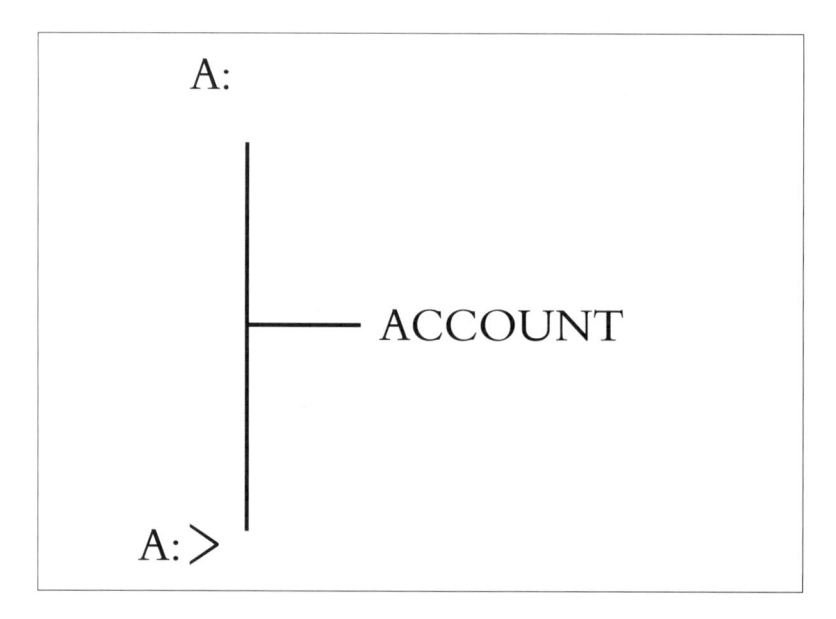

```
A:
|
|
|
|------ ACCOUNT
|
|
|
A:>
```

The subdirectory ACCOUNT is shown as branching off the root directory.

The command can be ENTERED with the switch **F** to show the files that are in the subdirectories. For example, **TREE/F** will display:

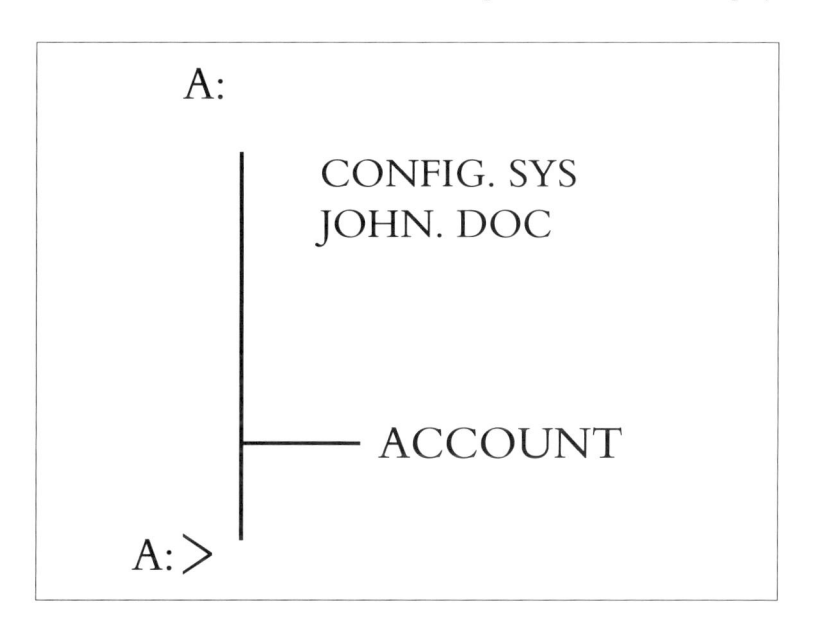

```
A:
    │       CONFIG. SYS
    │       JOHN. DOC
    │
    │
    │
    ├────── ACCOUNT

A:>
```

The files CONFIG.SYS and JOHN.DOC are shown in the root directory.

A subdirectory can have another subdirectory branching from it. To create a subdirectory called JAN to hold the files related to your JANUARY accounts, enter the following:

A:\> **MD\ACCOUNT\JAN**

This command is interpreted as 'Make a subdirectory JAN, to branch from the existing subdirectory ACCOUNT, which branches from the root directory of drive A.'

The **TREE** command shows this arrangement graphically:

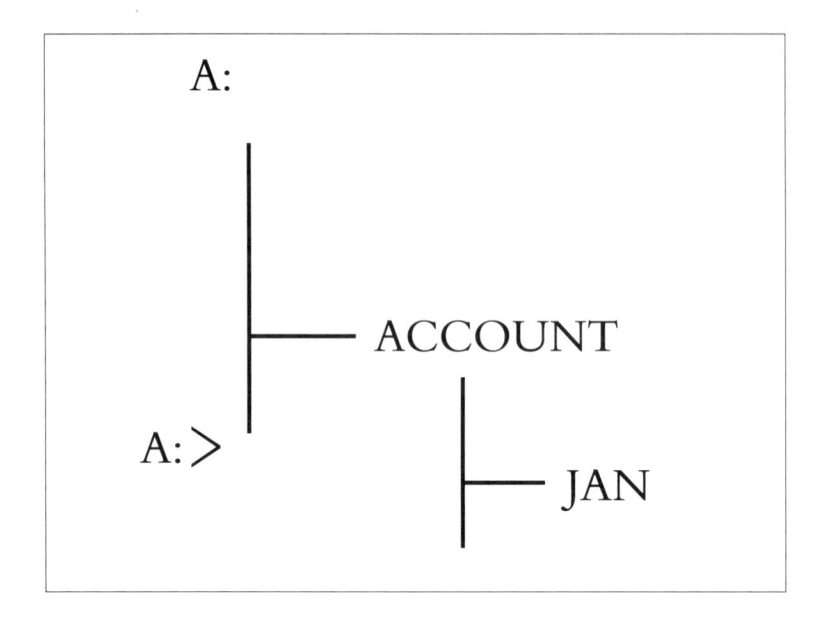

```
              A:
              │
              │
              ├──── ACCOUNT
              │       │
  A:>                 │
                      └── JAN
```

Using the 'copy' command with subdirectories

When files are being copied between subdirectories on a disk, you should indicate clearly the path that the command is expected to be executed across: that is, state the source and destination of the files. To copy the files from the root directory of A to the subdirectory ACCOUNT, enter the following:

A:\> **COPY   A:\CONFIG.SYS   A:\ACCOUNT\CONFIG.SYS**
    1 file(s) copied
A:\> **COPY   A:\JOHN.DOC   A:\ACCOUNT\JOHN.DOC**
    1 file(s) copied

Exercise 20.1
Use the **MD** command to create the following subdirectory structure:

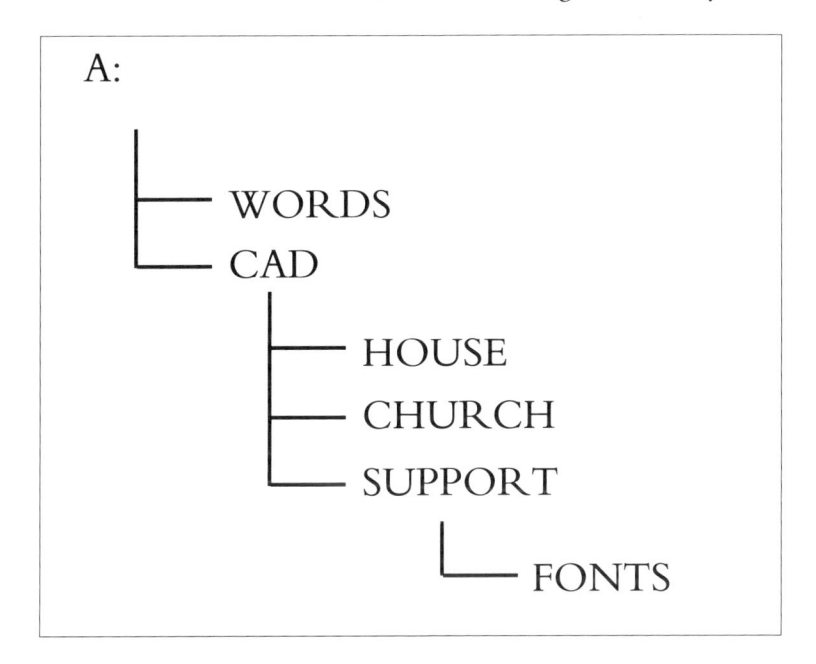

```
A:
├── WORDS
└── CAD
     ├── HOUSE
     ├── CHURCH
     └── SUPPORT
          └── FONTS
```

Global replacement characters

The asterisk (*) can be used as a substitute for a file name or extension. This is called a global replacement character or 'wild card'. For example, to copy the two files from the root directory of A to the subdirectory JAN, the following command could be entered:

A:\> **COPY   A:*.*   A:\ACCOUNT\JAN**

This command is interpreted as 'Copy all the file names and all file extensions from the root directory of drive A to the subdirectory JAN, which branches from the subdirectory ACCOUNT, which branches from the root directory of drive A.'

Note that both files were copied with a single command, and that they were not given a name in the destination subdirectory. In a situation like this the files keep the name they had in the source directory.

When the files are copied, DOS responds with:
A:\CONFIG.SYS
A:\JOHN.DOC
   2 file(s) copied

Exercise 20.2
Copy the files from the root directory of drive A to the subdirectory CHURCH.

Exercise 20.3
Copy the two files from the subdirectory JAN to the subdirectory FONTS and the subdirectory WORDS.

More on global characters

Global replacement characters or 'wild cards' can be used with other MSDOS commands, such as **DIR** and **DEL**.

Variations on the 'dir' command

The **DIR** command can be followed by the switches **P** and **W**. For example, **DIR/W** displays the directory across the screen. Not as much information is given about the files as when **DIR** without the switch is executed. The advantage of the **/W** is that a large number of files is displayed on the screen at once. When the command is used with **/P**, the files return to scrolling directly down the screen, but only one 'page' (screen) at a time.

The asterisk (*) can be used in place of a file name or extension. For example, **DIR *.SYS** will list all files with the extension SYS. Similarly, **DIR *.DOC** will list only the files with the extension DOC.

Removing files

Files can be removed from the disk using the command
ERASE [filename].[extension]
or
DEL [filename].[extension]
There is no functional difference between the two commands.

To erase the JOHN.DOC file in the root directory, type
DEL A:\JOHN.DOC

Removing a directory

A directory has to be empty (apart from the system files, . and ..) before it can be removed from the disk. To remove the directory WORDS on your work disk, carry out the following procedure:
♦ Open the directory with **CD\WORDS**
♦ Erase all its files with the command **DEL *.*** and answer **Y** to the DOS prompt
♦ Return to the root directory with **CD** and type **RD\WORDS**.
♦ Check that the directory has been removed by listing the contents of the disk or by using the **TREE** command.

Backing up your drawing files

It is essential to back up your drawing files regularly. While in the drawing editor you should save your work at regular intervals, especially after a major editing session.

Here are some ways of backing up your work:
- To a tape back-up system
- To a removable hard disk
- To an optical disk
- To a diskette
- To a separate subdirectory

Tape back-up systems are expensive and a little slow for major back-up jobs. They are easy to use. At the end of each day, or perhaps at the end of an editing session, a single drawing can be copied to the tape. The tape should then be stored in a separate area from the computer.

Removable hard disks provide a very fast method of storing drawings. Again the disk should be stored in a different place from the computer.

Optical disks are fast and are essential if your drawing files are large (5 to 10 Mb).

Smaller drawings can be saved or copied to a diskette. If the drawing has a greater capacity than the disk, the DOS command **BACKUP** or **RESTORE** will have to be used, as this will allow you to spread the file over two or more disks (see below). As a last resort you could open a separate directory and copy the files to it.

Regardless of the technique you use, it is essential that drawings are backed up and kept up to date.

The 'backup' and 'restore' commands

A simple example of the command is:
C:\> **BACKUP C:\ACAD*.DWG A:**
All the drawing files in the ACAD directory will be backed up on the disk in drive A.

Note: Any files on drive A will be erased.

The backed-up files on disk A cannot be read by the normal MSDOS commands. For example, they cannot be restored to the hard disk using the **COPY** command: instead the command **RESTORE** must be used. To return the drawing files on drive A to the hard disk in this case, use
RESTORE A: C:\ACAD

Your DOS manual will have further examples of the **BACKUP** and **RESTORE** commands.

The AutoCAD file utility menu

Some MSDOS commands can be executed by using the *File Utility* menu from within AutoCAD. Select *File* and then *Utility* from the drop-down menu. If the **FILEDIA** system variable is set to 0, the text mode version of the menu is displayed. If **FILEDIA** is set to 1, the dialogue box version is displayed.

The text mode version of the menu is shown below.

0. Exit File Utility Menu
1. List Drawing files
2. List user specified files
3. Delete files
4. Rename files
5. Copy file
6. Unlock file

Enter selection (0 to 6)<0>:

The options

0. Exit File Utility Menu
This option returns you to AutoCAD.

1. List Drawing files
This option lists drawing files in the current subdirectory. You can enter the path to a subdirectory if you like, e.g. **C:\ACAD\CHURCH**. In the dialogue box option, the two full points (..) will step you down a subdirectory (similar to **CD..** in DOS). The letter A, B, C etc. refers to other disk drives on your computer. Clicking on one of these will list the drawing files found there.

2. List user-specified files
This option allows you to specify the files you want listed. For example, all files with the back-up drawing files can be listed by responding with the DOS symbols ***.BAK**.

3. Delete files
Enter the name of the file or the extension (such as ***.BAK**) that you want deleted. In the dialogue box the *Select All* option allows you to select a complete list of files in a subdirectory. The *Clear All* option allows you to deselect all the files.

4. Rename files
This option allows you to rename a file. It is particularly useful if you accidentally delete a drawing file and want to call up its BAK version. The BAK version will not load into the drawing editor until it has the extension DWG. The rename option allows you to assign the DWG extension to the file. In both the dialogue box and text modes options you will be asked for the old name and the new name of the file. You must give the extension.

5. Copy file
This option copies files from a source to a destination. Give the extension of the file when naming it.

6. Unlock file

If the *Lock File* option was selected during configuration (see chapter 19) it is possible that some files may become locked, even though you are not working on a network. To unlock a file, the filename and extension must be given. If, for example, AutoCAD responds with *ACAD.MNU file locked* when you try to load a drawing, you must unlock the file ACAD.MNU and not just the file ACAD.

Note: Never delete the files that end with the extensions .$AC, .$A or .AC$ while AutoCAD is running. These are AutoCAD's temporary files. If you delete them you will lose the drawing you are working on.

See appendix C for a list of the file extensions found in AutoCAD.

SUMMARY

The 'boot-up' procedure on a DOS computer will look for the operating system in drive A. If it is not there it will look in drive C. Once it is found it will load it into memory. DOS will then attempt to read two files, CONFIG.SYS and AUTOEXEC.BAT, if they are present. These files hold information on settings that you want to have on the computer each time it is switched on.

The **FORMAT** command is used to format a new disk. Any data on a disk that is formatted is lost. The **COPY** command is used to copy files to and from the hard disk and diskettes. Files can be copied across subdirectories. The **DIR** command can help you to find files, especially when used with the global character or 'wild card' option. **DIR** will list the contents of the current directory unless a path is specified.

Subdirectories can be made with the command **MD** for holding files. This helps to keep the disk tidy. Similar files or files related to a specific program are normally placed in a single subdirectory. A subdirectory is made current by using the command **CD** followed by the 'path' to the subdirectory. A subdirectory can be removed from the disk only if it is empty and is not current. Files are deleted using the **DEL** or **ERASE** commands. The **TREE** command will display the directory structure of a disk in graphical form.

Lastly the *File Utility* menu can be used to carry out some of the above MSDOS commands using prompts and menus from within AutoCAD.

SOLUTIONS

Solution to exercise 20.1
A:\> **MD\WORDS**
A:\> **MD\CAD**
A:\> **MD\CAD\HOUSE**
A:\> **MD\CAD\CHURCH**
A:\> **MD\CAD\SUPPORT**
A:\> **MD\CAD\SUPPORT\FONTS**

Solution to exercise 20.2
A:\> **COPY A:*.* A:\CAD\CHURCH**
A:\CONFIG.SYS
A:\JOHN.DOC
2 file(s) copied

Solution to exercise 20.3
A:\> **COPY A:\ACCOUNT\JAN*.* A:\CAD\SUPPORT\FONTS**
A:\ACCOUNT\JAN\CONFIG.SYS A:\ACCOUNT\JAN\JOHN.DOC
2 file(s) copied
A:\> **COPY A:\ACCOUNT\JAN*.* A:\WORDS**

AutoCAD release 12 directory structure layout

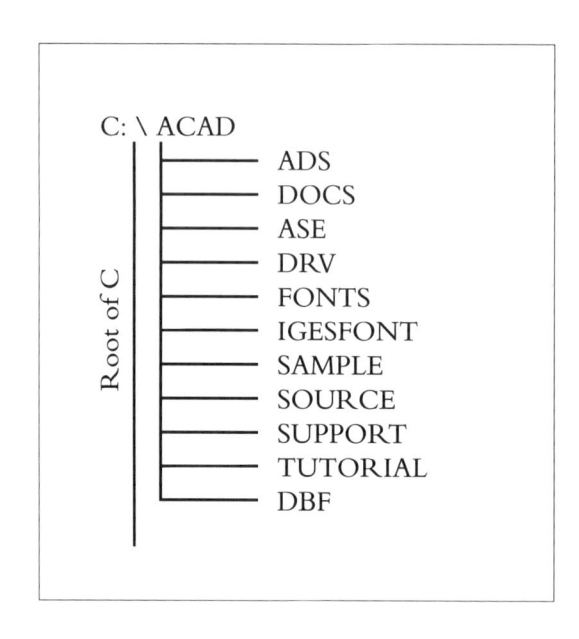

```
C:\ ACAD
Root of C
         ├── ADS
         ├── DOCS
         ├── ASE
         ├── DRV
         ├── FONTS
         ├── IGESFONT
         ├── SAMPLE
         ├── SOURCE
         ├── SUPPORT
         ├── TUTORIAL
         └── DBF
```

Appendix A

AutoCAD System Variables

These variables are listed when the command SETVAR - ? is entered at the command prompt.

ACADPREFIX   "C:\R12\SUPPORT\;C:\R12\FONTS\;C:\R12\ADS\"   (read only)
ACADVER	"12 International"	(read only)
AFLAGS	0	
ANGBASE	0	
ANGDIR	0	
APERTURE	10	
AREA	0.0000	(read only)
ATTDIA	0	
ATTMODE	1	
ATTREQ	1	
AUDITCTL	0	
AUNITS	0	
AUPREC	0	
BACKZ	0.0000	(read only)
BLIPMODE	1	
CDATE	19930102.12335756	(read only)
CECOLOR	"BYLAYER"	
CELTYPE	"BYLAYER"	
CHAMFERA	0.0000	
CHAMFERB	0.0000	
CIRCLERAD	0.0000	
CLAYER	"0"	
CMDACTIVE	1	(read only)
CMDDIA	1	
CMDECHO	1	
CMDNAMES	"SETVAR"	(read only)
COORDS	1	
CVPORT	2	
DATE	2448990.52461343	(read only)
DBMOD	0	(read only)
DIASTAT	1	(read only)
DIMALT	0	
DIMALTD	2	
DIMALTF	0.0390	
DIMAPOST	""	
DIMASO	1	
DIMASZ	3.0000	

DIMBLK	""	(read only)
DIMBLK1	""	(read only)
DIMBLK2	""	(read only)
DIMCEN	−3.0000	
DIMCLRD	0	
DIMCLRE	0	
DIMCLRT	0	
DIMDLE	1.2500	
DIMDLI	10.0000	
DIMEXE	2.5000	
DIMEXO	2.5000	
DIMGAP	1.5000	
DIMLFAC	1.0000	
DIMLIM	0	
DIMPOST	""	
DIMRND	0.0000	
DIMSAH	0	
DIMSCALE	1.0000	
DIMSE1	0	
DIMSE2	0	
DIMSHO	0	
DIMSOXD	0	
DIMSTYLE	"STANDARD"	(read only)
DIMTAD	0	
DIMTFAC	0.7500	
DIMTIH	0	
DIMTIX	0	
DIMTM	0.0000	
DIMTOFL	0	
DIMTOH	0	
DIMTOL	0	
DIMTP	0.0000	
DIMTSZ	0.0000	
DIMTVP	1.5000	
DIMTXT	3.0000	
DIMZIN	0	
DISTANCE	0.0000	(read only)
DONUTID	0.5000	
DONUTOD	1.0000	
DRAGMODE	2	
DRAGP1	10	
DRAGP2	25	
DWGCODEPAGE	"dos850"	
DWGNAME	"UNNAMED"	(read only)
DWGPREFIX	"C:\R12\BOOK\"	(read only)
DWGTITLED	0	(read only)

DWGWRITE	1	
ELEVATION	0.0000	
EXPERT	0	
EXTMAX	-1.0000E+20,-1.0000E+20,-1.0000E+20	(read only)
EXTMIN	1.0000E+20,1.0000E+20,1.0000E+20	(read only)
FILEDIA	1	
FILLETRAD	0.0000	
FILLMODE	1	
FRONTZ	0.0000	(read only)
GRIDMODE	0	
GRIDUNIT	10.0000,10.0000	
GRIPBLOCK	0	
GRIPCOLOR	5	
GRIPHOT	1	
GRIPS	1	
GRIPSIZE	3	
HANDLES	0	(read only)
HIGHLIGHT	1	
HPANG	0	
HPDOUBLE	0	
HPNAME	""	
HPSCALE	1.0000	
HPSPACE	1.0000	
INSBASE	0.0000,0.0000,0.0000	
INSNAME	""	
LASTANGLE	0	(read only)
LASTPOINT	0.0000,0.0000,0.0000	
LENSLENGTH	50.0000	(read only)
LIMCHECK	0	
LIMMAX	420.0000,297.0000	
LIMMIN	0.0000,0.0000	
LOGINNAME	"??"	(read only)
LTSCALE	1.0000	
LUNITS	2	
LUPREC	4	
MAXACTVP	16	
MAXSORT	200	
MENUCTL	1	
MENUECHO	0	
MENUNAME	"acad"	(read only)
MIRRTEXT	1	
MODEMACRO	""	
OFFSETDIST	-1.0000	
ORTHOMODE	0	
OSMODE	0	
PDMODE	0	

PDSIZE	0.0000	
PERIMETER	0.0000	(read only)
PFACEVMAX	4	(read only)
PICKADD	1	
PICKAUTO	1	
PICKBOX	3	
PICKDRAG	0	
PICKFIRST	1	
PLATFORM	"386 DOS Extender"	(read only)
PLINEGEN	0	
PLINEWID	0.0000	
PLOTID	""	
PLOTTER	2	
POLYSIDES	4	
POPUPS	1	(read only)
PSLTSCALE	1	
PSPROLOG	""	
PSQUALITY	75	
QTEXTMODE	0	
REGENMODE	1	
SAVEFILE	"AUTO.SV$"	(read only)
SAVENAME	""	(read only)
SAVETIME	120	
SCREENBOXES	26	(read only)
SCREENMODE	0	(read only)
SCREENSIZE	574.0000,414.0000	(read only)
SHADEDGE	3	
SHADEDIF	70	
SHPNAME	""	
SKETCHINC	1.0000	
SKPOLY	0	
SNAPANG	0	
SNAPBASE	0.0000,0.0000	
SNAPISOPAIR	0	
SNAPMODE	0	
SNAPSTYL	0	
SNAPUNIT	5.0000,5.0000	
SORTENTS	96	
SPLFRAME	0	
SPLINESEGS	6	
SPLINETYPE	6	
SURFTAB1	18	
SURFTAB2	18	
SURFTYPE	6	
SURFU	18	
SURFV	18	

SYSCODEPAGE	"dos850"	(read only)
TABMODE	0	
TARGET	0.0000,0.0000,0.0000	(read only)
TDCREATE	2448990.51998033	(read only)
TDINDWG	0.00648808	(read only)
TDUPDATE	2448990.51998033	(read only)
TDUSRTIMER	0.00648877	(read only)
TEMPPREFIX	""	(read only)
TEXTEVAL	0	
TEXTSIZE	3.0000	
TEXTSTYLE	"STANDARD"	
THICKNESS	0.0000	
TILEMODE	1	
TRACEWID	0.0500	
TREEDEPTH	3020	
TREEMAX	10000000	
UCSFOLLOW	0	
UCSICON	1	
UCSNAME	""	(read only)
UCSORG	0.0000,0.0000,0.0000	(read only)
UCSXDIR	1.0000,0.0000,0.0000	(read only)
UCSYDIR	0.0000,1.0000,0.0000	(read only)
UNDOCTL	5	(read only)
UNDOMARKS	0	(read only)
UNITMODE	0	
VIEWCTR	221.3987,159.5771,0.0000	(read only)
VIEWDIR	0.0000,0.0000,1.0000	(read only)
VIEWMODE	0	(read only)
VIEWSIZE	319.1542	(read only)
VIEWTWIST	0	(read only)
VISRETAIN	0	
VSMAX	1328.3923,957.4625,0.0000	(read only)
VSMIN	−885.5948,−638.3083,0.0000	(read only)
WORLDUCS	1	(read only)
WORLDVIEW	1	
XREFCTL	0	

Appendix B
Character Mapping

Character mapping for symbol typefaces.

Appendix C

AutoCAD File Extensions

As you will see if you list your AutoCAD files with the **DIR** command, there is a large number and variety of file types. Below is an alphabetical list of the file extensions of all the files that AutoCAD either uses or creates.

While working with AutoCAD at the draughting or design level you will rarely need to refer to the file extensions directly.

.ADS	ADS applications file
.ADT	Audit report file; the locked version is .ADK
.BAK	Backed-up drawing file; the locked version is .BKK
.BDF	VESA font file for a specialised video card
.BKn	Emergency back-up file, where n is a number increased sequentially
.CFG	AutoCAD configuration file; the locked version is .CFK
.DCC	Dialogue box colour control file (in MSDOS versions only)
.DCE	Dialogue control box error report file
.DCL	Dialogue control language description file
.DFS	Default file settings file
.DWG	AutoCAD drawing file; the locked version is .DWK
.DXB	Drawing binary interchange file; the locked version is .DBK
.DXF	Drawing interchange file; the locked version is .DFK
.DXX	Attribute extract file in DXF format; the locked version is .DXK
.EPS	Encapsulated Postscript file
.ERR	Report error file, created or appended when AutoCAD crashes
.EXP	ADS executable file
.FLM	Autoshade film-roll file; the locked version is .FLK
.HDX	AutoCAD help index file
.HLP	AutoCAD help file
.IGS	IGES interchange file; the locked version is .IGK
.LIN	Linetype library file; the locked version is .LIK
.LSP	Auto LISP file
.LST	Printer plot file; the locked version is .LSK
.MAT	AME materials file

.MNL	Auto LISP functions related to a menu file
.MNU	Menu file; the locked version is .MNK
.MNX	Compiled menu file; the locked version is .MXK
.MSG	Message file displayed when AutoCAD is loaded
.OLD	Original version of a drawing file; the locked version is .OLK
.PAT	Hatching pattern library file: holds the AutoCAD hatching patterns
.PCP	Plot configuration parameters file; the locked version is .PCK
.PFB	Postscript font file
.PGP	Program parameter file
.PLT	Plot file; the locked version is .PLK
.PS	Postscript file
.PSF	Postscript support file
.PWD	AutoCAD log-in file; the locked version is .PWK
.SCR	Script file
.SHP	Shape or font file
.SHX	Compiled shape or font file; the locked version is .SHK
.SLB	Slide library file
.SLD	Slide; the locked version is .SDK
.TXT	Text file—attribute extract and template files; the locked version is .TXK
.UNT	Units file
.XLG	External references log file; the locked version is .XLK
.XMX	External message file

The following extensions are found on AutoCAD release 10 and 11 files.

.BAK	Backed-up file
.CFG	AutoCAD configuration file
.DOC	Text document; the README.DOC supplied on the AutoCAD disks can be loaded into a word-processor for viewing
.DRV	Driver (special program to enable AutoCAD to interface with your peripheral devices, such as digitising tablets, graphics cards, etc.)
.DVP	Driver initialisation file for peripherals
.DWG	Drawing files
.DXB	Binary files used for exchanging drawings between CAD systems
.DXF	Text file listing all the elements in a drawing
.ERR	AutoCAD error file: stores errors encountered in running AutoCAD
.EXE	Executable file
.FLM	Autoshade file
.HDX	Help index file: keeps track of data in the AutoCAD help file
.HLP	AutoCAD help file; this is the file that is accessed when you type **HELP** while in AutoCAD

.IGS	File created to enable drawings to be exchanged between different CAD packages; the **IGESIN** (Initial Graphics Exchange Specification *in*) and **IGESOUT** commands create and read files with this extension
.LIN:	File that holds the definitions of different AutoCAD linetypes
.LSP	Auto LISP file (AutoCAD can be programmed using Auto LISP, a variation of the computer language LISP)
.LST	Printer plot drawing
.MID	Master identification file
.MND	Menu definition file
.MNU	User menu file
.MNX	Compiled menu file
.MSG	AutoCAD sign-on message; this can be modified and your own message placed on the screen instead
.OVL	Overlay file; some overlay files are created when AutoCAD is configured
.PAP	File created by device interface programs for output to a plotter
.PAT	Hatching pattern file (normally ACAD.PAT)
.PGP	Program processor file (file that allows you to use some non-AutoCAD files from within AutoCAD)
.PLT	File created when a drawing is plotted to a file
.SCR	File containing a collection of AutoCAD commands that are executed sequentially when the file is executed
.SHP	Shape file (a shape is a symbol that can be inserted into an AutoCAD drawing)
.SHX	Compiled shape file (all shape files must be compiled before they can be inserted into a drawing)
.SLB	Library of slides
.SLD	AutoCAD slide created with the command **MSLIDE**
.TXT	Data extracted from a drawing using the **ATTEXT** ('attribute extract) command

Appendix D

Dimensioning System Variables

The settings are those found in the ACAD prototype drawing.

DIMALT Off	Alternative units selected
DIMALTD 2	Alternative unit decimal places
DIMALTF 0.0390	Alternative unit scale factor
DIMAPOST	Suffix for alternative text
DIMASO On	Create associative dimensions
DIMASZ 3.0000	Arrow size
DIMBLK	Arrow block name
DIMBLK1	First arrow block name
DIMBLK2	Second arrow block name
DIMCEN −3.0000	Centre mark size
DIMCLRD BYBLOCK	Dimension line colour
DIMCLRE BYBLOCK	Extension line and leader colour
DIMCLRT BYBLOCK	Dimension text colour
DIMDLE 1.2500	Dimension line extension
DIMDLI 10.0000	Dimension line increment for continuation
DIMEXE 2.5000	Extension above dimension line
DIMEXO 2.5000	Extension line origin offset
DIMGAP 1.5000	Gap from dimension line to text
DIMLFAC 1.0000	Linear unit scale factor
DIMLIM Off	Generate dimension limits
DIMPOST	Default suffix for dimension text
DIMRND 0.0000	Rounding value
DIMSAH Off	Separate arrow blocks
DIMSCALE 1.0000	Overall scale factor
DIMSE1 Off	Suppress the first extension line
DIMSE2 Off	Suppress the second extension line
DIMSHO Off	Update dimensions while dragging
DIMSOXD Off	Suppress outside extension dimension
DIMSTYLE STANDARD	Current dimension style (read-only)
DIMTAD Off	Place text above the dimension line

DIMTFAC 0.7500	Tolerance text height scaling factor
DIMTIH Off	Text inside extensions is horizontal
DIMTIX Off	Place text inside extensions
DIMTM 0.0000	Minus tolerance
DIMTOFL Off	Force line inside extension lines
DIMTOH Off	Text outside extensions is horizontal
DIMTOL Off	Generate dimension tolerances
DIMTP 0.0000	Plus tolerance
DIMTSZ 0.0000	Tick size
DIMTVP 1.5000	Text vertical position
DIMTXT 3.0000	Text height
DIMZIN 0	Zero suppression

Practical Assignments

Assignment 1

The tutor should provide the student with the basic components of a computer system, with the operating system installed. The object of the assignment is to see if the candidate is capable of setting up the hardware, booting the operating system, configuring AutoCAD, setting up a prototype drawing, configuring and calibrating the digitiser, and using the character mapping facilities within AutoCAD.

Candidates' instructions

There is no time limit for this assignment.

1. Connect together the hardware provided. The system should power up in the root directory.
2. Run the AutoCAD program, and configure it for use with the hardware listed below [the tutor should place his/her own hardware specifications here]:
Screen:
Digitiser:
Plotter:
3. Create a new drawing called PROTOPA, using the ACAD prototype drawing. Set the drawing limits to 300,400. Set up a layer called MAIN, and make it the current layer. Save the drawing, and end AutoCAD.
4. Start AutoCAD again and configure it to use PROTOPA as the default prototype drawing.
5. Start a new drawing called SAMP1A, using your new default prototype drawing (PROTOPA).
6. Digitise the 6 line segments drawing shown in diagram A by attaching it to the digitising tablet. The digitising is to be done using the polyline entity. The co-ordinates given are to allow for calibration of the digitiser.
7. Edit the digitised drawing by fitting a spline to it.
8. With the tutor present, enter the dimension shown in diagram B. The dimension line must have a dot at one end and an arrow at the other.
9. Create a text style for the mathematical symbols shown in diagram B, and enter the symbols exactly as seen.
10. Create a title block, as shown in diagram B, and place your name in it.
11. Save the drawing as SAMP1A.
12. Produce drawing N in diagram C with the name SAMP1B. The outline must be drawn with the line entity.
13. With the tutor present, write your name twice on the drawing in ROMANC style, and then edit one entry of your name to COMPLEXC style. Save the drawing.

14. Start a new drawing called SAMP1C. Load a new menu (ACADUK, for example). Configure the digitising tablet for use with the standard AutoCAD template with four menu areas.

15. Draw the base plate in diagram C. Set up a UCS with its origin at the centre of the large circle. Align the X and Y axes parallel to the bottom and left-side of the drawing respectively.

16. Using the following co-ordinates, draw a polyline shape, and use the 'fit' option of the **PEDIT** command to fit a curve to the polyline.

225, 204
185, 184
165, 144
215,114
255,124
265,174
C for close

17. Demonstrate the use of the **Zoom Dynamic** command to the tutor.

18. Set up two viewports, and place a view of each of the drawings in each port. Save the viewport configuration and then return to a single view. Demonstrate to the tutor how you can restore the saved viewport arrangement.

19. Save the drawing, and then produce a plot of the drawings, SAMP1A, SAMP1B and SAMP1C on A4 paper.

Assignment 2

Candidates' instructions

1. The time allotted for the assignment is two hours. You have an additional ten minutes to read the assignment before starting and to query your tutor on any points you do not understand. Drawing must not begin within this period.

2. Start a new drawing called SAMPA2, using the default ACAD prototype drawing.

3. Set the drawing limits to 420,297.

4. Create layers called TBLOCK and MAIN.

5. Produce the drawing in Diagram D. The border and title block with your name and date are to be placed on the layer named TBLOCK. The rest of the drawing should be placed on the layer MAIN.

6. Plot the drawing to fit on an A4 page.

7. Copy the drawing to a diskette and hand it to the tutor.

Assignment 3

Tutor's instructions

The drawing SAMP3A should be prepared by the tutor and given to the students without the dimensions on a diskette. The drawing on the diskette should be named SAMP3B. Tutors may allow the candidates to prepare

SAMP3A before the assignment is taken. However, the candidates' drawings should be checked by the tutor to ensure that they have reached the standard required.

Candidates' instructions

The assignment must be completed within two-and-a-half hours. You have ten minutes to read the assignment before the two-and-a-half hours begins, in order to query the tutor on any points you do not understand. You must not start the assignment during this ten-minute period.

1. Copy the drawing SAMP3B from your diskette to the relevant subdirectory, and start the AutoCAD program. Load SAMP3B into the drawing editor.
2. Edit the drawing so that it appears as in SAMP3C.
3. Enter your name in the title block and save it with the name SAMP3C.
4. Plot the edited drawing to fit on an A4 page.
5. Create a plot file to the hard disk with the name SAMP3C.
6. Copy both the drawing and the plot file to your diskette.
7. Reload the drawing SAMP3C and save it with the name SAMP3D. Add 5 dimensions shown in SAMP3A.
8. Save this drawing and produce a printed copy on an A4 sheet. The files SAMP3C and SAMP3D and all plot files should be copied to the diskette provided.
9. Create the plan of the garden shown in diagram F. Text height and position need only be similar to that in the diagram. Create the two blocks of plants shown. Each block must have three attributes. These must be defined as follows, and written to the hard disk.

Block Name: PLANT1
Attribute 1:
Draw as a circle of diameter 5 units
Tag: Name
Mode: Constant, Visible
Attribute Value: ROSE
Insertion point: Centre of the circle
Attribute 2:
Tag: Soiltype
Mode: Not constant, invisible
Default attribute type: ACID
Attribute 3:
Tag: Light
Mode: Constant, invisible
Block Name: PLANT2
Attribute 1:
Draw as an ellipse
Tag: Name
Mode: Constant, visible
Attribute value: LAVENDER

Insertion point: Centre of the circle
Attribute 2:
Tag: Soiltype
Mode: Not constant, invisible
Default Attribute type: NEUTRAL
Attribute 3:
Tag: Light
Mode: Not constant, invisible
Default Attribute value: SUN

10. Insert the blocks to produce the drawing diagram F. Save the drawing as GARDEN1.

11. Demonstrate to the tutor the effect of switching the attribute display *on* and *off*. Save the drawing.

12. Copy the following files to the diskette provided:
GARDEN1
PLANT1
PLANT2

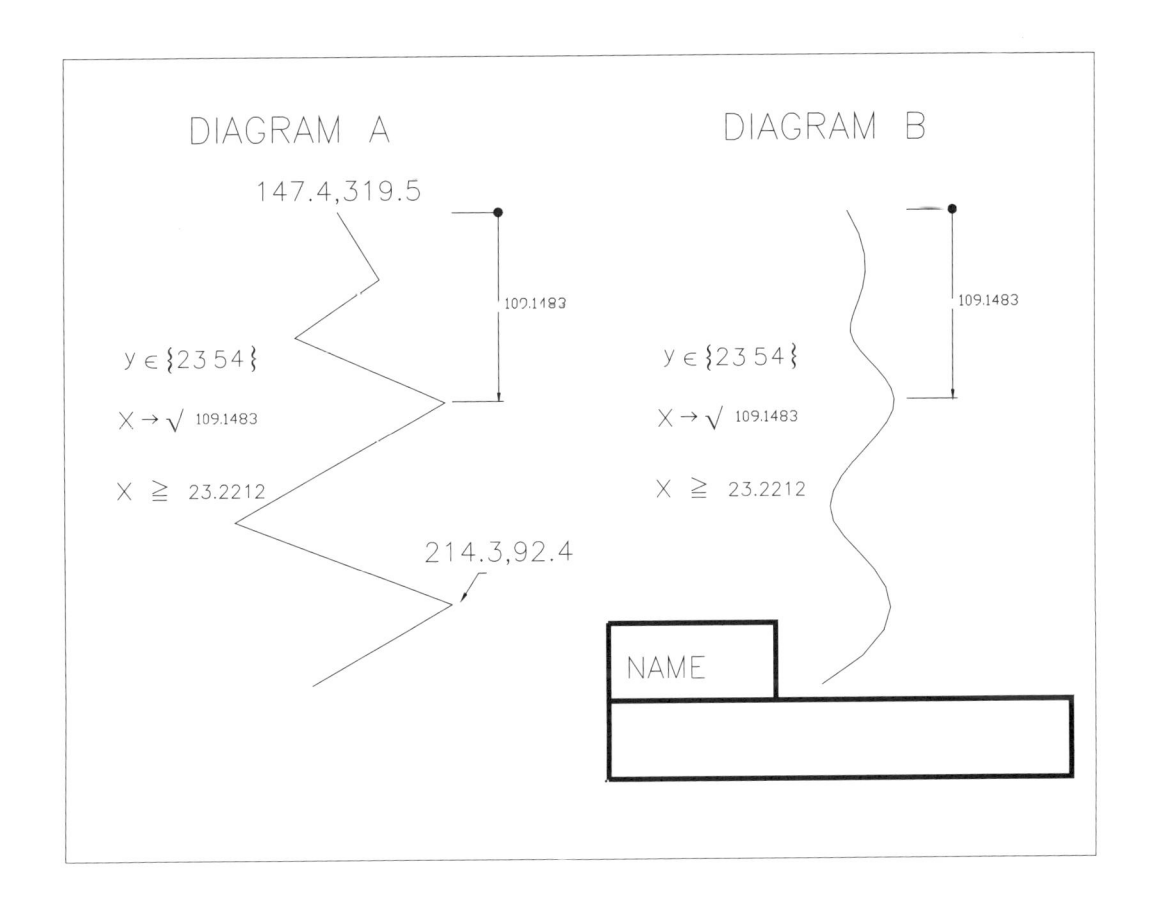

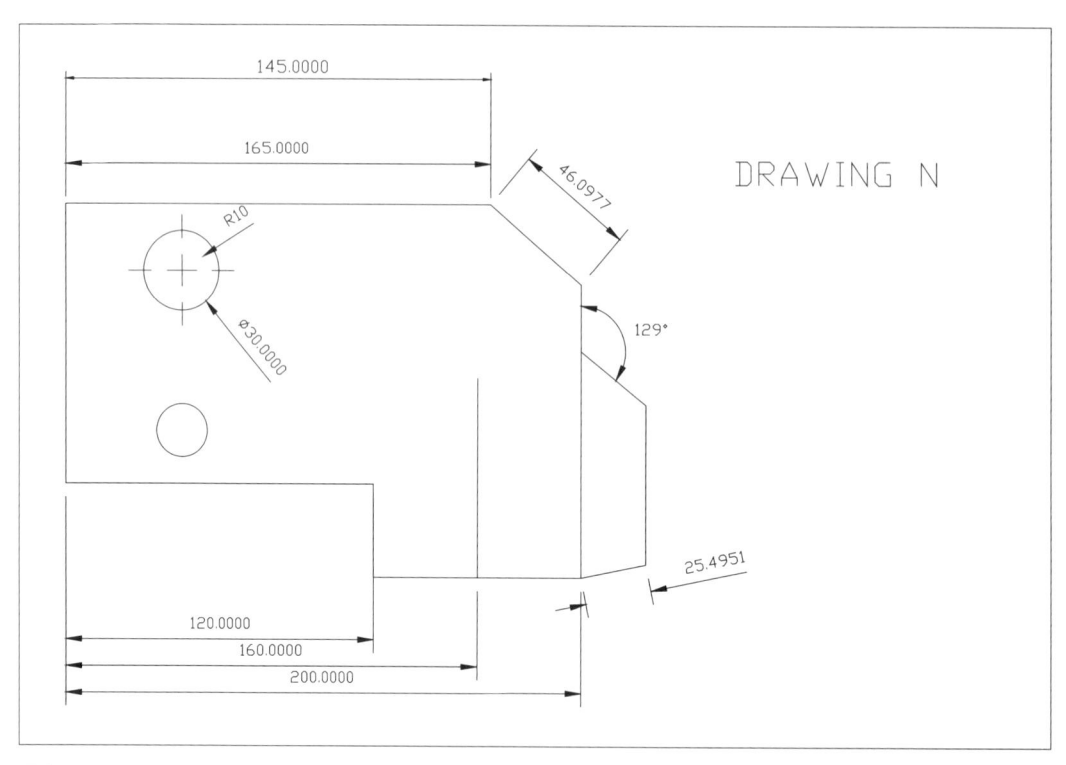

Diagram C

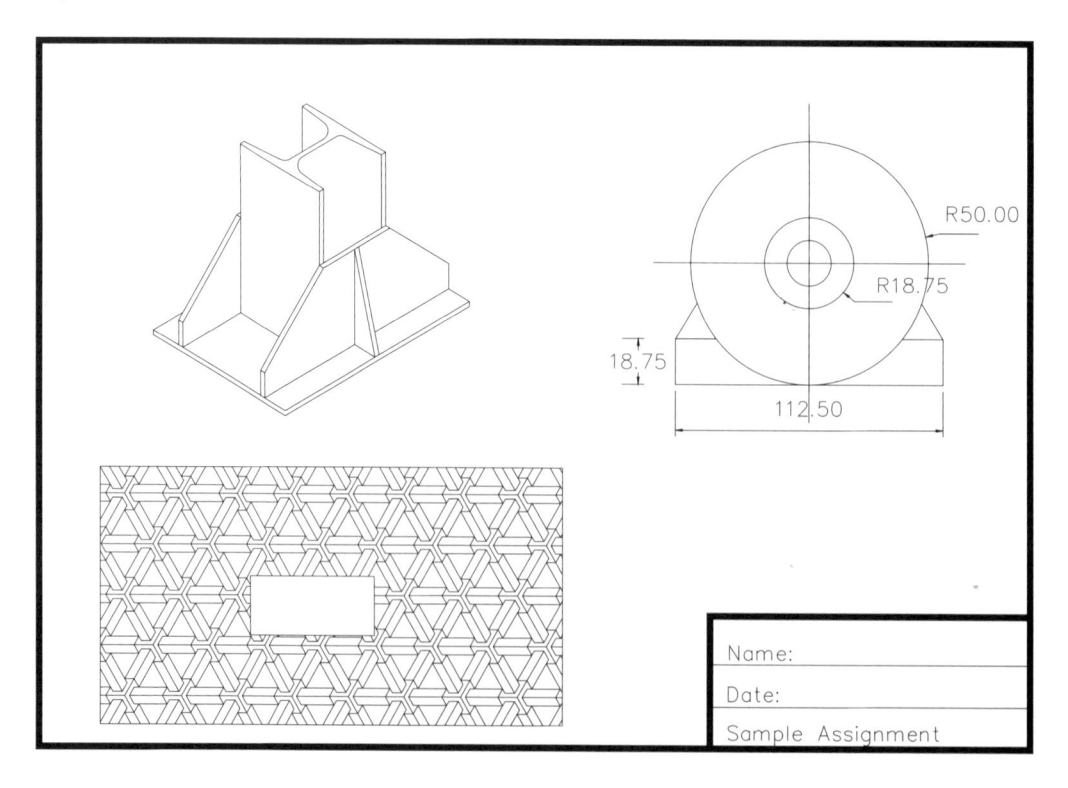

Diagram D

336 AUTOCAD ASSIGNMENTS

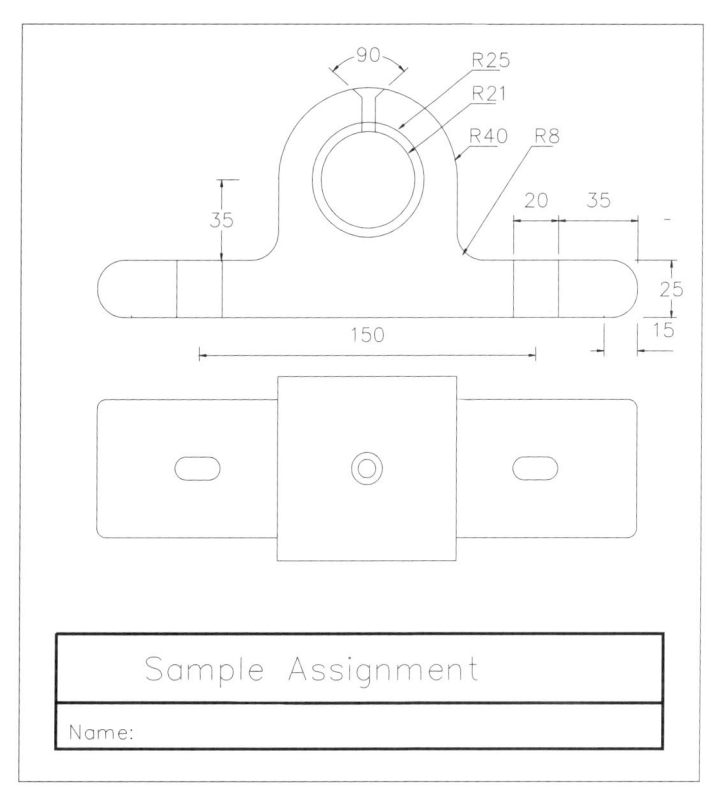

Diagram E

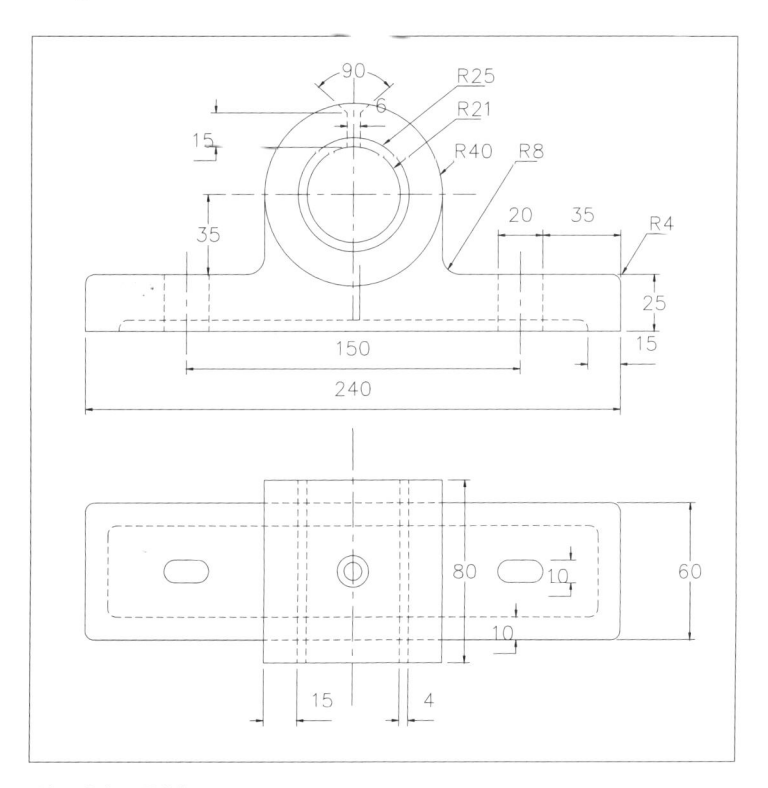

Fig. SAMP3A

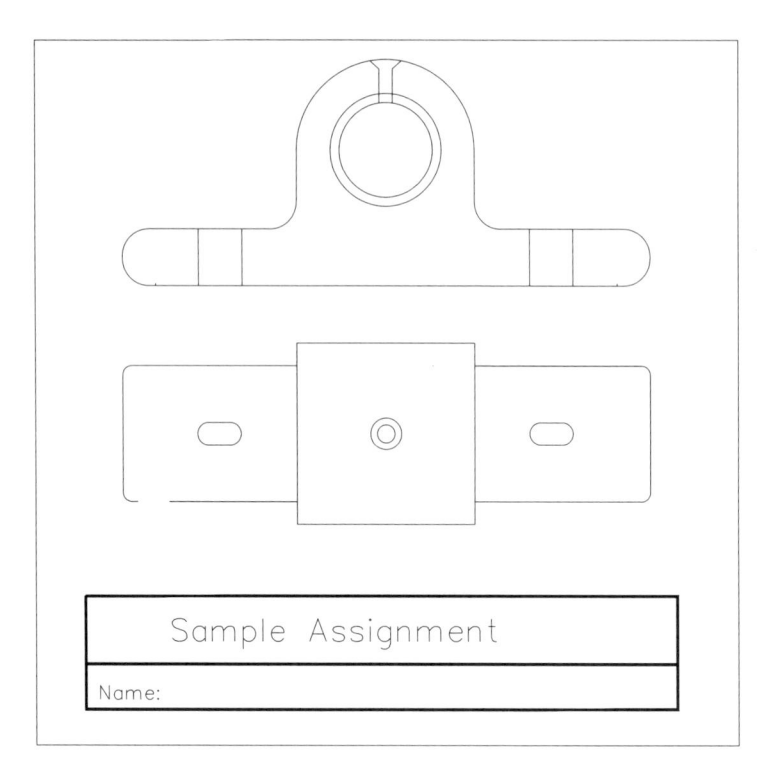

Fig. SAMP3C

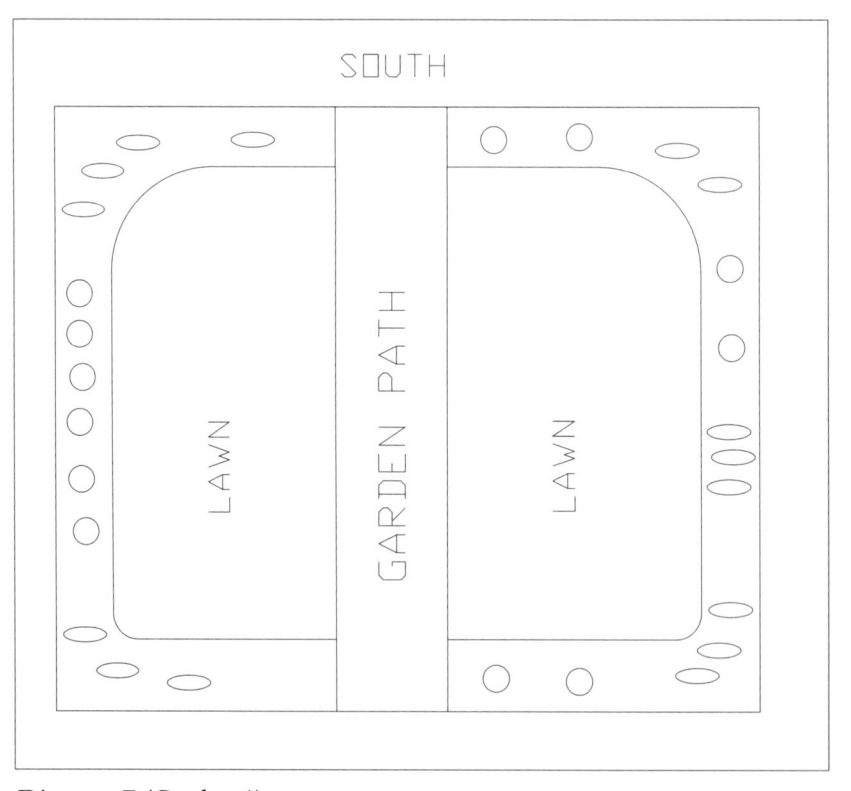

Diagram F (Garden 1)

Multiple-choice Questions

Candidates' instructions

This test consists of 34 multiple-choice questions. In order to pass you must answer a minimum of 28 of them correctly. You have one hour to complete the test. Your answers must be made on the written test answer sheet.

Question 1
The suitability of a puck for digitising a drawing is due to the fact that—
(a) the position of the puck on the tablet reflects the position of the cross-hairs on the screen
(b) the position of the puck on the tablet is sometimes relative to its position on the screen
(c) the motion of the puck on the tablet is slower than the speed of the cross-hairs on the screen
(d) the puck is much more accurate than a mouse

Question 2
Which one of the following is the minimum RAM requirement for AutoCAD release 10 and Auto LISP?
(a) 512 kb
(b) 640 kb and 1 Mb of extended memory
(c) 512 kb and 2 Mb of expanded memory
(d) 640 kb

Question 3
Which DOS command allows you to create a subdirectory on the root directory?
(a) CD
(b) RD
(c) MD
(d) DIR

Question 4
To look for a drawing file in a subdirectory, which of the following commands is the most suitable?
(a) LIST DWG
(b) DIR DWG
(c) DIR *.DWG
(d) DIR DWG.*

Question 5
Which one of the following files contains the standard AutoCAD linetypes?
(a) SHP
(b) SHX
(c) PAT
(d) LIN

Question 6
The HELP index file has the extension
(a) HDX
(b) HAX
(c) HLP
(d) SHX

Question 7
If the digitiser you wish to use with AutoCAD is not listed in the drivers, you will have to call up a special driver called—
(a) AVP
(b) ADI
(c) AID
(d) SHP

Question 8
Which one of the following statements most closely defines the function of a prototype drawing?
(a) It allows you to compare your completed drawings.
(b) It allows you to select units for a drawing.
(c) It allows you to use pre-set settings for a drawing.
(d) It allows you to back up a drawing quickly.

Question 9
Polar co-ordinates are input as—
(a) @56.66,13
(b) 56.66,13
(c) @56.66<13
(d) 56.66<13@

Question 10
The UCS can best be defined as—
(a) an icon
(b) a co-ordinate system for defining 'trapped' entities
(c) a co-ordinate system defined anywhere in a drawing
(d) a co-ordinate system to aid isometric drawing

Question 11
An unused layer can be removed from a drawing using the command—
(*a*) DELETE
(*b*) REMOVE
(*c*) PURGE
(*d*) CHANGE

Question 12
The SETVAR command cannot be used when—
(*a*) you are in the DIM mode
(*b*) you are at the command prompt
(*c*) a UCS is in use
(*d*) you are at the *Configuration* menu

Question 13
A layer is said to be current if—
(*a*) you are working on it
(*b*) it is switched *on*
(*c*) it contains the main part of your drawing
(*d*) it is 'frozen'

Question 14
When drawing a design for a watch, the measurements should be input at a scale of—
(*a*) 1:100
(*b*) 100:1
(*c*) 1:20
(*d*) 1:1

Question 15
The UNDO command allows you to—
(*a*) undo editing commands only
(*b*) undo drawing commands only
(*c*) undo all editing and drawing commands
(*d*) undo all AutoCAD commands

Question 16
Which of the following commands is best suited for speeding up your work on a complex multi-layered drawing?
(*a*) FREEZE
(*b*) REGEN
(*c*) REDRAW
(*d*) EDIT

Question 17
The REDRAW command affects AutoCAD in the following way:
(a) it refreshes the screen display
(b) it recalculates the complete drawing data-base
(c) it recalculates the position of drawing entities
(d) it rescales all the drawing entities

Question 18
Which of the following statements about BLOCKS is true?
(a) A block must contain a minimum of three entities.
(b) A block cannot be loaded from a diskette.
(c) A complete drawing can be treated as a block.
(d) A block cannot be composed of two different linetypes.

Question 19
To find the co-ordinates of a line entity, the following command should be used:
(a) LIST
(b) ID
(c) UTILITY
(d) STATUS

Question 20
Which of the following closely resembles a description of 'pickbox'?
(a) a system variable
(b) a DIM subcommand
(c) an editing variable
(d) a station variable

Question 21
An attribute can be described as—
(a) textual information attached to a block
(b) an exploded block
(c) a description of a mirrored block
(d) a block created from two blocks

Question 22
Attributes are defined using the command—
(a) ATTDIF
(b) ATTDEF
(c) ATTDEFT
(d) DEFATT

Question 23
The dialogue box for attributes is controlled by the system variable—
(*a*) ATDIA
(*b*) ATTDIA
(*c*) ATTREQ
(*d*) ATTDIM

Question 24
The system variable DIMASO controls—
(*a*) the size of the dimension arrowhead
(*b*) the size of the centre mark
(*c*) associative dimensioning
(*d*) leader dimensioning

Question 25
The SKETCH command is most suitable for—
(*a*) detailed work after using ZOOM Dynamic
(*b*) freehand drawing
(*c*) outlining the structure of mechanical parts
(*d*) creating non-standard typefaces

Question 26
Which of the following variables is set to 1 to show the spline frame?
(*a*) SPLFRAME
(*b*) SPLINETYPE
(*c*) SPLINESEGS
(*d*) SPLCURVE

Question 27
The QTEXT command is most useful because—
(*a*) it displays text on the screen exactly as it will plot
(*b*) it can be edited quickly
(*c*) it quickly deletes text from a specified layer
(*d*) it replaces text with a box showing its position

Question 28
The UPDATE command is most useful for—
(*a*) updating a complete drawing
(*b*) updating specified dimensions
(*c*) updating the drawing data-base before plotting
(*d*) updating attributes

Question 29
Dimensioning variables can be used to—
(a) apply specified tolerances to dimensions
(b) dimension circles outside the drawing limits
(c) specify whether a dimensioned FILL is on or off
(d) close a dimensioned polyline

Question 30
The WBLOCK command allows you to—
(a) insert a block written to a disk
(b) write a block to a disk
(c) insert a block with attributes only
(d) insert a block that is automatically exploded

Question 31
Before a block can be edited it must be—
(a) WBLOCKed
(b) PURGEd
(c) EXPLODed
(d) MIRRORed

Question 32
Entities can be moved from one layer to another using the command—
(a) MOVE
(b) EDIT
(c) CHANGE
(d) LAYER

Question 33
Before an active digitising tablet can be used to digitise a drawing, the tablet must first be—
(a) CONFIGURED
(b) CALIBRATED
(c) INITIALISED
(d) PICKed
to read the drawing.

Question 34
A back-up drawing is created by using the command—
(a) BACKUP
(b) SAVE
(c) QUIT
(d) END

Index

%% 195
★ 174
★★★★ 85
... 16
/ 44
> 16
@ 183
\ 44
^C 21, 37, 38, 178
absolute co-ordinates 66
ACAD prototype 191
ACADR12 21
ACADR12.BAT 291
aperture variable 114
ARC 115
AREA 74
ARRAY 26, 81, 89, 90, 94
aspect ratio 50
associative dimensioning 237
ATTDEF 226
ATTDIA 229
ATTDISP 230
ATTREQ 229
attribute, definition 224, 228
AutoCAD 10 4
AutoCAD 11 2, 5
AutoCAD 11-286 5
AutoCAD 12 9

backup 317
BHATCH 180
blips 17, 25, 53, 85
BLOCK 210
block 36
blocks 208, 218
boundary hatch 181
BREAK 154, 158
BS304 140
bytes 5

calibration, tablet 299
cancel 40
cd, change directory 311
CEN 25, 92
central processing unit 2
CHAMFER 69, 72
chamfer distances 73
CHANGE 134, 136, 175
character codes 195
character mapping 202
chkdsk 291
CHPROP 175
CIRCLE 25, 38, 51, 56

CMDDIA 285, 288
co-ordinate system icon 19
com port 7, 4, 42
command prompt 44
configure 13
construction lines 81
COORDS 54
copy 309, 314
COPY 81, 92, 93, 96
cpu 2
cubic spline 279

DDATTDEF 228
DDLMODES 184
DDRMODES 262
default option 52
del 316
device drivers 301
dialogue box 16, 18
digitising a drawing 42, 299
digitising tablet 2, 8, 42, 43
DIM, ALIGNED 238
DIM, ANGULAR 243
DIM, BASELINE 244, 245
DIM, DIMBLK 246
DIM, NEWTEXT 255
DIM, ORDINATE 241
DIM, RADIUS 239
DIM, ROTATED 240
DIM, TEDIT 256
DIM, TROTATE 256
DIM, UPDATE 246
DIM 177, 236
dim dialogue boxes 254
DIM1 184
DIMASO 237
DIMASO 252
DIMASZ 248
DIMBLK1 247
DIMBLK2 247
dimensioning 176, 178, 179
dimensioning terms 177
dimensioning variables 246
DIMEXE 248
DIMLIM 250
DIMPOST 252
DIMSAH 247
DIMSCALE 248
DIMTM 250
DIMTOL 250
DIMTP 250
DIMTXT 248
dir 310

diskcopy 291
disks 5, 6
displacement 96
DIST 161
DIVIDE 214
dongle 4
DONUT 105, 209
dos 9
drawing aids 18, 23, 81
drawing names 44
DTEXT 196
dwg 40
DWGNAME 193

edit box 25
edit vertex 280
electronic page size 49
electronic pen 42
ELLIPSE 116
END 5, 41
entities 36
ERASE 38
EXIT 178
EXTEND 134, 135, 159

F1 14
F7 19
F7 53
F8 38
F9 15
file locking 302
file names 307
file utility menu 317
filedia 300, 317
FILL 98, 117
FILLET 30, 31, 67, 72, 137
fillmode variable 120
filter 185
fonts 197
format 307
function keys 7

graphic cards 3
graphics screen 14
GRAPHSCR 15
GRID 19, 49, 56

hard disks 5, 6
hardware 1, 2
hardware lock 4
hardware requirements 10
HATCH 184
hatch options 181

hatching 180
HELP 74

ID 161
input devices 6
INSERT 211
instaling AutoCAD 290
Intel 2
INTersec 86
isometric style 262
ISOPLANE 262, 263

kb 5
keyboard 2, 7
kilobyte 5

LAYER 170, 174
layer - current 173
layer 0 170
layers 15, 25, 169
layers - naming 176
layers - properties 170
leader 180
LIMITS 22, 36, 48
LINE 17, 28
LINETYPE 132, 133
LIST 268
lpt1 4
LTSCALE 134

maths co-processor 2, 10
Mb 5
md, make directory 313
MEASURE 219
memory 5
menu 300
MINSERT 213
MIRROR 31, 138
mirrtext variable 141
modes, attribute 226
monitor 2
Motorola 2
mouse 7, 43, 44
msdos 10

naming a drawing 37
naming of layers 176
NEW 37

object snap 32, 85, 114
OFFSET 81, 83 oops 40
operating system 9
ORTHO 36
output devices 6, 9

PAN 113
paper size 35, 36
parallel port 4
path 44
pcdos 10

pdmode variable 140
pdsize variable 140
PEDIT 275, 276
PEDIT 53
pick button 7
pickbox 38, 85
pickbox variable 114
pixels 3
PLINE 26, 53, 82, 92
PLOT 284
plot configuration 286
plotter 9
plotting to a file 288
POINT 129, 130
pointers 8
pointing device 42
points style box 131
polar co-ordinates 50
POLYGON 118, 119, 160
POLYLINE 53
printer 9
protected-mode drivers 302
prototype drawing 37, 48, 191, 193
puck 42
PURGE 219

QSAVE 40
QTEXT 197
quadratic spline 279
QUIT 19, 41

ram 5
rd, removing directory 316
real world 22
real world co-ordinates 35
real-mode drivers 301
REDRAW 53, 97
REDRAWALL 97
REGEN 97, 197
REGENALL 97
REGENAUTO 97
relative co-ordinates 66
restore 317
root directory 310
ROTATE 29, 109

SAVE 5, 40
SAVEAS 5, 41
SCALE 104, 254
scale 35
scanner 8
screen menu 14, 15
select colour dialogue 26
serial port 4
SETVAR 141, 189, 190
SKETCH 264-267
snap 15, 23
software 1, 9
SOLID 117

special character codes 195
splframe 279
spline 278
splinesegs 280
splinetype 279
starting AutoCAD 21
status line 14, 15
STRETCH 253
style 197, 199
subdirectory 311
symusic font 203
system unit 2, 3, 4
system variable 54

tablet, calibration 299
TABLET 297, 299
tablet configuration 295
template 8, 42
template areas 298
TEXT 106
TEXT 52
TEXT options 57
text screen 14
TEXTSCR 15
toggle 22
TRACE 98
transparent 4
transparent commands 97
tree 312, 313
TRIM 129
TTR 51

UCS 268
ucs icon 14
UCSICON 19, 268
UNDO 73, 98
UNITS 24, 48
units 35, 36

variables - changing 190
VIEW 158
viewports 97, 264
VIEWRES 88, 89, 150, 151
visibility, attributes 230
VPORTS 148, 149

WBLOCK 217, 218
wildcard 174, 315
world co-ordinate system 268

ZOOM, drop-down options 49
ZOOM options 55
ZOOM-All 23, 50
ZOOM-Dynamic 111, 112
ZOOM-Extents 32, 110
ZOOM-Window 68